D1106003

We Have

A

Problem

A PARENT'S SOURCEBOOK

We Have
A
Problem

A PARENT'S SOURCEBOOK

Jane Marks

Collected from columns
originally published in
Parents Magazine

American Psychiatric Press, Inc.

Washington, DC
London, England

Note: The authors have worked to ensure that all information in this book concerning drug dosages, schedules, and routes of administration is accurate as of the time of publication and consistent with standards set by the U.S. Food and Drug Administration and the general medical community. As medical research and practice advance, however, therapeutic standards may change. For this reason and because human and mechanical errors sometimes occur, we recommend that readers follow the advice of a physician who is directly involved in their care or the care of a member of their family.

Books published by the American Psychiatric Press, Inc., represent the views and opinions of the individual authors and do not necessarily represent the policies and opinions of the Press or the American Psychiatric Association.

Collected from columns originally published in *Parents Magazine* between 1987 and 1991. Reprinted by permission of Gruner + Jahr USA Publishing.

American Psychiatric Press, Inc.
1400 K Street, N.W., Washington, DC   20005

Library of Congress Cataloging-in-Publication Data
Marks, Jane.
    We have a problem : a parent's sourcebook / Jane Marks. — 1st ed.
        p.   cm.
    Includes index.
    ISBN 0-88048-504-3
    1. Emotional problems of children—Case studies.   2. Child
rearing—Case studies.   I. Title.
BF723.E598M37   1992
649′.1—dc20   92-7391
                                                                                        CIP

British Library Cataloguing in Publication Data
A CIP record is available from the British Library.

Contents

Bill and I knew that adopting a nine-year-old would be a challenge. But we felt sure we had enough love and "people skills" to carry it off. How could we have been so wrong?

Isabel liked me a lot . . . until I married her dad and got pregnant. Now she hates me—and Neal blames me for upsetting her! Could a little girl's jealousy wreck our marriage?

John lets his son act up—and my daughters resent it terribly. How can the five of us ever blend into a real family . . . so long as John thinks that rules are fine for my kids, but not for his?

Livia was the perfect mother-in-law . . . until she came to stay. Now we're forced to choose between her comfort—and our sanity.

Introduction

This book is full of problems—problems that even the best families face or could face at any time. That's why all the parents here are good, with no bad guys or villains. Just smart, sensitive, caring people, trying to do the right thing in situations where the standard remedy or logical solution simply doesn't work.

Some of the stories are about kids' inappropriate, puzzling, annoying, or scary behavior, such as

- A little girl's incessant tantrums
- A compulsive eater . . . and a frail, skinny boy of three, who won't eat unless his parents cater to his every whim
- A sweet girl, suddenly turned mean and belligerent
- A child who allows herself to be dominated by a sneaky, trouble-making friend
- A baby who won't respond to his parents
- A happy boy's sudden and persistent refusal to go to school
- A good, middle-class 14-year-old, hooked on drugs
- A child's sudden inability to walk, for no medical reason
- A little boy who's shy and has no friends
- A teenager's frightening cry for help
- A girl who insists, "My teacher hates me" (Could it be true?)
- A young boy's depression that looks like a learning disability
- A kindergarten child who suddenly can't or won't talk

- A thirteen-year-old diabetic girl who rebels against her mother—and her own crucial self-care
- A charming little girl's new—and cruelly aggressive—imaginary playmate
- A seven-year-old's persistent bed-wetting
- A toddler's terror of falling asleep
- A little girl who's selfish and rude—and friendless
- A perfectionist who's never satisfied with her grades or herself (despite her parents' reassurance)
- A young daredevil who's begun to court real danger
- A little boy who's never pleased
- A child suffering from chronic, painful constipation (Is he holding back on purpose?)
- A pleasant six-year-old who's become outrageously rude
- A boy who is out of control at school and at home
- An honest ten-year-old involved in several recent stealing incidents

Other stories have to do with altogether unexpected problems within the family, such as

- Remarriage . . . and problems!
- Blending families . . . and problems!
- Adopting a nine-year-old—a lot harder than it looked
- A mother's distress when her young kids avoid instead of embrace their dying father
- A beloved grandmother who moves in—causing chaos and guilt
- A mother's mid-life crisis and alcohol problems
- A child with a minor disability who tyrannizes the whole family
- A mother's excessive fear of letting go that relates to her own troubled history
- An alcoholic father who stops drinking, but the tension at home is worse than ever
- Sexual abuse in the family
- A father's unemployment and shame, and a child's misconceptions
- A child's recovery from cancer—but the relieved family seems to be falling apart
- Divorce—is it on or off?

- A sensitive and dedicated single mother's burnout
- A warm father's puzzling—and all too obvious—dislike for one of his children
- Two brothers who suddenly can't get along

Still other stories have to do with shocking, tragic events (and their aftermaths) that even the most loving, careful parents cannot foresee or prevent. These include

- A young boy's secret victimization
- Infant death—and a four-year-old sister's puzzling reaction
- The rape of a twelve-year-old
- A father's depression and resulting suicide
- Living with a shocking birth deformity
- A little girl's reaction to her uncle's death from AIDS
- A boy's self-blame following his brother's accidental death
- One family's good fortune resulting from another's tragedy

Each story is told in two voices: first, it's a parent's voice describing the problem as it gathers steam and eludes common sense. It may seem to get solved or nearly solved . . . only to prove, moments or days later, to be totally out of control. That's when the second voice comes in: the counselor.

The counselor might be a psychiatrist, a psychologist, a social worker, or a teacher. Many are specialists in the particular kind of problem they are asked to help solve. All are eminently human and approachable and smart and compassionate—and effective.

Why stories? Why didn't we just write a how-to book? We chose this format because we believe that reading about other families' problems can give enormous insights into solving our own, even if the details are different.

We believe that when the chips are down, families are resilient and can work things out. It's our hope that reading these stories of problems and solutions will deepen your understanding, enhance your own coping strategies, and give you assurance that even the most difficult situations can lead to good change, healing, and growth.

J.M.

Acknowledgments

Because all the stories in this book appeared originally in the "We Have a Problem" column in *Parents Magazine*, I especially want to thank Elizabeth Crow, former editor-in-chief of *Parents Magazine*, and President of Gruner + Jahr USA Publishing, who liked my idea for the column, gave it a name, and hired me to write it every month, beginning in February 1987. I am also very grateful to Ann Pleshette Murphy, who, as editor-in-chief of *Parents Magazine*, makes sure that the column stays relevant and lively. I also thank Cliff Gardiner for the wonderful illustrations each month, and Sara Evans for her years of gentle and respectful editing.

Needless to say, the column could never have existed without the massive contributions of the very gifted psychiatrists, psychologists, social workers, and other therapists, whose expertise, warmth, and clarity made the research so much fun. I'm talking about the late Sandra S. Fox, A.C.S.W., Ph.D., who directed the Good Grief Program at the Judge Baker Children's Center in Boston, Janice I. Cohn, D.S.W., Jeannette Lofas, Ph.D., Marjorie A. Slavin, A.C.S.W., C.S.W., Elliot M. Kranzler, M.D., Elizabeth B. Weller, M.D., Stanley Greenspan, M.D., Jan Drucker, Ph.D., Stanley Turecki, M.D., Stella Chess, M.D., L. Eugene Arnold, M.D., Russell A. Barkley, Ph.D., E. Gerald Dabbs, M.D., and Ellyn M. Satter, C.S.W., registered dietitian and psychotherapist. Also Cynthia R. Pfeffer, M.D., Gregory K. Fritz, M.D., Cece Carsky, R.D., Esther Rosenthal, M.S.W.,

B.C.D., A.C.S.W., Barrie Sanford Greiff, M.D., Betty B. Osman, Ph.D., Marilyn Reed Lucia, M.D., Alex Weintrob, M.D., Alan Trager, A.C.S.W., Philip Diaz, M.S.W., Ph.D., Richard Ferber, M.D., Martin B. Scharf, Ph.D., Robert L. Selman, Ph.D., Ronald J. Prinz, Ph.D., Marion E. Breland, M.S.W., C.S.W., B.C.D., and Ann S. Kliman, M.A.; and The Hospice of Northern Virginia at Arlington's team consisting of home care nurse and primary contact Sister Catherine Higley, Gretchen Lane, M.S.W., and art therapist Anita K. Epstein.

I want to thank another group of experts: the people at American Psychiatric Press, for their absolute professionalism. Tim Clancy, who believed in the project and said so before he left; Carol Nadelson, M.D., editor-in-chief; Ronald E. McMillen, General Manager; Claire Reinburg, Editorial Director; Pamela Harley, Managing Editor, Books; Jane H. Davenport, Electronic Prepress Director; Julie Glass, former Marketing Manager; and Cary Wyman, Sales and Promotions Manager. They have all been a joy to work with.

A special thank you to Angela Miller, president of the Miller Agency. (I don't know how I could have managed this without you.) And finally, I want to thank the three people I love most in the world: my husband, Robert Marks, and our sons, Joshua and Chris, who were there for me in every possible way, with ideas and suggestions, inspiration, good criticism, patience, humor, and love.

J.M.

ADOPTION
AND
BLENDED
FAMILIES

> *Bill and I knew that adopting a nine-year-old would be a challenge. But we felt sure we had enough love and "people skills" to carry it off. How could we have been so wrong?*

Erica's Story

"Friends said we were crazy to take an older child," said Erica Mitchell, 32. "They said, 'You can form an infant the way you want, but you can't undo damage that's already been done.'

"But Bill and I both came from large families and we felt we could really relate to kids and their problems. Besides, we knew people were clamoring to adopt the few available *babies,* but what about the older kids nobody wanted? If we could nurture a child like that, then we should do it.

" 'You guys trying to save the world?' Bill's brother, Duncan, teased us when he heard our plan. But we didn't feel like do-gooders! In fact, I was afraid we sounded picky, telling the adoption agency that we hoped 'our' child would be in good health and of at least average intelligence. 'I understand,' the social worker, Pat Calder, assured us. Now all we had to do was wait.

" 'Don't say yes if you're not sure,' Pat cautioned us the day she finally called us in to see the photograph of Tammy, an almost-pretty blond, blue-eyed nine-year-old with wildly frizzy hair. The story was that Tammy's mom—who'd never married—died four years ago, leaving Tammy with an aunt who had six children of her own and a drinking problem. After neighbors had reported seeing Tammy wandering naked and filthy, Tammy, then six, was placed in a foster home. But at this foster home they complained that she was too greedy, and so at seven, she was placed in a group home, with eight older children and a constantly changing staff of workers.

" 'But she's really a wonderful child,' Pat said, 'especially when you think of all she's been through. For a long time, she's been asking for a family all her own. And I know that she'd blossom with reassurance and affection.' Hopeful and excited, I glanced at Bill. 'I think we could help her settle down and feel good about herself,' he said. And I felt like cheering.

"We wanted to bring her home right away, but there was an established procedure. First, we were to drive to the group home and take Tammy out for a picnic. How nervous we were—and how quiet, polite, and shy she was! But after a few awkward moments, we laughed together at a man in a chicken suit advertising fast food. Later, as Tammy talked about a pal 'who got adopted and unadopted,' she seemed much older than nine. But when she saw the sandwiches and lemonade and chocolate cake we'd brought, she said, 'Oh—a party!' with such little-kid delight, I was touched.

" 'We're in love with her!' I told Pat. The next weekend, we brought Tammy to our house for a two-night visit, and we hated to have to take her back on Sunday. In the week that followed, we begged Pat to hasten the paperwork, and we painted the guest room—Tammy's room.

"When we drove up to get her the following Saturday, we were floating on air. Tammy was happy, too, and asked if she could call us Mom and Dad. When Pat called on Monday to ask how things were going, I said, 'Tammy's a joy.' And she was! She seemed to want so much to please us—she even picked us a good-morning bouquet from my little garden.

" 'I thought this was supposed to be hard,' I told Bill happily, 'but it's a snap.' He kissed me and said, 'That's because you're such a great mom.'

"The only pang I felt that week was in having to get rid of Caesar, the Persian cat we'd had for all nine years of our marriage. Tammy was allergic. And how she apologized! But I played down the loss and said we could always go visit the cat, what we really wanted was to be a family. Tammy gave me a baleful look. 'Honey,' I told her, 'I'm not sad at all.'

"I knew she needed megadoses of reassurance! Instead of going out to play, she kept begging me for chores, like neatening closets. 'Honey, you don't have to,' I'd tell her. But she insisted. Once or twice, I thought she'd taken some of my loose change. But Bill said, 'Forget it. What's a dollar or two? She's never had anything she's needed. When she feels more certain of her place here, she won't need to do it anymore.'

"If only everyone else were that understanding! Tammy's teacher, Mrs. Dranow, had complained that Tammy was disruptive, calling out and keeping the other children from doing their work. I begged her to be patient. 'She'll settle down soon,' I promised. 'I'm sure of it!'

"And maybe she would have—if I hadn't had to go away for two weeks. My father had a stroke, and I had to take the next plane to Chicago. 'I'll be back before you know I'm gone,' I promised. Bill said, 'Don't worry, we'll be fine.' But when I returned, I could see a change. Tammy stiffened when I tried to hug her. 'I didn't miss you at all,' she said, pulling away. 'Not even a little.'

"Poor Tammy! Clearly, my absence awakened old fears of desertion. 'Well, I missed you,' I said. 'A lot!' That night, Tammy refused to go to bed. She argued and cried, and finally, she sneaked downstairs and ate some ice cream. 'You need your sleep,' I said gently, taking her back to bed.

"Then, at four in the morning, we heard her crying her heart out. She couldn't explain what was wrong. We sat with her, murmuring reassurance. I held her hand, and gradually the sobbing subsided. 'Don't worry, Tammy,' Bill said. 'It just takes time to learn to live in a new family.'

"The next day, when Tammy was at school, I saw the cat sculpture I had made and given her, broken in pieces on the rug. 'It was an accident,' she said later. But I saw the little smirk on her face. And just before suppertime, I looked out the kitchen window and saw her in the garden, pulling up and breaking peonies.

"When we sat down to eat, I watched her help herself to enormous portions of everything—far more than she could manage to eat. Bill and I kept still until she started eating Jell-O right from the serving bowl. I said, 'Tammy, please *serve* yourself some,' and she exploded: 'Damn you! My mother never made me do that. *She* let me eat whatever I wanted. *She* loved me. And you know what? I think this is a stupid place to live.' She left the table and went to her room. I started to get up, but Bill shook his head. 'Let her be,' he said.

"The next afternoon, I had a call from Mrs. Dranow. Tammy was pushing other children, talking back to the teacher, and writing four-letter words on her workbook. 'We're not prepared to deal with this kind of troubled child,' she said sourly.

" 'Well, I'm sorry she's causing you problems, but I know what she *doesn't* need, and that's more rejection,' I said. 'She's testing, and she needs to know that we won't throw her out, no matter how she behaves.' 'How far will she go, Mrs. Mitchell?' 'I don't know,' I replied. 'But we'll handle this ourselves.' At that moment, I felt lonelier and more upset than I'd ever felt in my life.

" 'What are we doing wrong?' I whispered to Bill late that night. 'Why can't we make her feel secure?' 'God, Erica,' Bill said. 'You always want things to happen right away. This takes work.'

"The next day Pat Calder, from the agency, called. 'And how are things going?' she wanted to know. 'School's still acting stuffy,' I told her. 'They think Tammy needs counseling, but we're trying to help her our own way. She must feel different *enough* . . . I mean, maybe we're all a little tired,' I said, forcing a lighthearted laugh.

" 'It *isn't* easy,' Pat said.

" 'Oh, but we're going to make it!' I insisted. 'We're very optimistic.' But then why was I shouting? Because I believed it or because I didn't?

"In the next four weeks, Tammy bounced back and forth between defiance and clinging. She still hoarded food on her plate, even though I said that she could have as much as she wanted, but why not take a little at a time? I'd feel a mixture of anger and despair when I felt sure that she'd taken change from my pocketbook. But then, when she'd see me sketching and sit down beside me and say, 'Mom, will I still be your daughter when I'm sixteen?' I would smooth her hair and kiss her and tell her, 'Yes, of course! Forever.' And I meant it with all my heart.

" 'See?' Bill said at one of those tender moments. 'I told you everything would work out.' But the very next day, I got a call from our local supermarket. Tammy had been caught red-handed, stealing candy and little toys. When I got there, she was arguing unconvincingly that the items had come from home.

"I was mortified, apologetic to the store, and terribly upset. 'We can take a lot of things in this family, but not a kid who steals from stores,' I said to Bill that evening.

" 'Well, if I'm not good enough, send me back,' Tammy shouted from behind our closed door. She bolted for her room. The next morning, Bill called Pat. 'We're having a rough time,' he said. 'I guess we'll make it, but we've tried to give Tammy everything, and it just hasn't been enough.'

" 'Some kids have been through experiences that leave them very needy,' Pat said. 'I know how hard you've been trying, but you've reached a point where it would be constructive to get some help for Tammy so that we can understand her needs better, and so that she can begin to work on what's getting her into trouble.' At this point, we'll try anything!"

The Counselor Replies

Sandra S. Fox, A.C.S.W., Ph.D. (deceased), was director of The Good Grief Program at the Judge Baker Children's Center in Boston. Fox is survived by her two children, who were adopted at the ages of four and seven.

"I could see right away that the Mitchells were good people with a lot to give Tammy. But they didn't realize that it would take more than love to heal the hurts and losses and upheavals she had experienced—as well as the fears she must have for the future.

"I asked to see Tammy alone for two appointments, and then to meet with Bill and Erica again to make recommendations.

"When Tammy came in the first time, she was very reserved. But as soon as she started playing with a dog puppet 'who had to store a year's supply of bones because he always got hungry,' I could see that this little girl was deeply afraid that the world would not meet her needs. At the end of the session, she begged for reassurance: 'How do I know you'll be here next time?' she asked, and 'Should I have my mom call you?'—questions most kids wouldn't need to ask.

"When I met with Bill and Erica again, I strongly recommended counseling for Tammy, to help her with that issue of trust *and* to help with the normal and predictable issues surrounding her adoption and adjustment to the family.

" 'What does her need for outside help say about us as parents?' Bill asked unhappily. 'Tammy's behavior is not a result of your failure as adoptive parents,' I assured them. 'But allowing her to be in treatment says you're trying to be good parents and you care about your child, and it's okay to need some help along the way.'

" 'I don't think I'll be staying with the Mitchells very long,' Tammy told me when we next got together. 'My mom says it's forever, but it never was before . . . and I *know* she thinks I'm a hassle,' Tammy said. I said, 'Let's give it time.' I told her that by getting together and talking—mostly about feelings—we could get some things sorted out so that she wouldn't keep finding herself in trouble.

"For several months, I saw Tammy regularly. One week, she told me how she'd come from school and found Erica packing summer clothes in a carton. Tammy had panicked. Was Erica just making room for winter things—or would Tammy be moving again? That night, she had taken three dollars from her father's wallet and hidden it under her mattress.

"A few sessions later, Tammy's play with the dolls and puppets showed me that she wasn't sure her parents had 'any love in their hearts.' 'They didn't cry when they had to get rid of their *cat*,' she said. 'Tammy, it's not that they didn't care about the cat,' I explained. 'They just cared much, much *more* about you.' Tammy frowned. I could almost see her thinking, 'Could this be true?'

"The next week, Tammy came in with an embarrassed expression and handed me a ballpoint pen, which I recognized as mine. 'My dad made me bring it back,' Tammy mumbled. I thanked her and then I said, 'Tammy, is it easier for you to have something of mine to hold on to between appointments?' 'Yes,' she said feelingly. I quickly found something she *could* have: a little calendar, in which she could write down all her appointments *and* my office phone number.

"The stealing then stopped. But Tammy still had a long way to go in terms of getting along at school and at home. 'There are so many rules,' she complained. We talked about how hard it can be when you're moved from one environment to another. In the group home, Tammy probably had had to grab for what she needed.

" 'Maybe grabbing was the only way you could be sure of getting all the food and attention you needed, so it was a good survival tactic. But that was then.' Now, I suggested, she would actually do better and get more of the love, approval, and security she craved, if she didn't grab.

"We worked a lot on the give-and-take of getting along in a family: how it's better to ask for what you need instead of assuming you aren't going to get it and then angrily sneaking it or 'getting even' by destroying something you love, like the cat sculpture or the flowers in the garden.

"It was a slow process, but Tammy was bright, and soon her 'testing' was not the provocative 'How far can I go before you throw me out?' but a beginning of trust. When I'm fair to Jean and Megan, they're fair to me,' she told me one day in amazement, speaking of classmates. And as Tammy learned to settle down and raise her hand instead of shouting, she found more acceptance from everyone. Even Mrs. Dranow gave Tammy a major role in the class play, and Tammy did well.

"Eight months after we started, I felt that things had stabilized enough so that Tammy didn't need to come in anymore. Tammy and her parents also agreed. They understood that troublesome issues might come up again, and if so, they could always call me. Adolescence, in particular, would likely be a time when Tammy would have reemerging questions about her identity, and that—combined with the challenges of the teenage years—might be very stressful. But for now, at least, the worst of the storm was over.

"The Mitchells were very grateful, but I told them that they had done the most important work. 'Your loving Tammy was the meat and potatoes,' I said. 'The therapy is medicine, and Tammy needed both.' Fortunately, when the going got tough, the Mitchells were flexible enough to seek help. And every day, Tammy feels a little more like Tammy Mitchell and a little less like the little girl that nobody could love."

Isabel liked me a lot . . . until I married her dad and got pregnant. Now she hates me—and Neal blames me for upsetting her! Could a little girl's jealousy wreck our marriage?

Jody's Story

"Neal was crazy about Isabel," said Jody Spencer, 24. "Not every man who's been divorced for five years even *sees* his kids. But Neal kept his Sundays for Isabel, who was seven when we met, no matter what else might have come along to tempt him. 'I think that's a very attractive quality in you,' I told him—and he invited me to join them on a trip to the zoo, which was one of Isabel's favorite expeditions.

"That Sunday morning, I must have put on—and discarded— four different outfits. Maybe it was silly, worrying about making the right impression on this little girl. But I'd heard stories from friends about romances breaking up just because some little tyrant said, 'No, Daddy, I don't *like* that lady.'

"But Isabel was natural, friendly, and fun. She told me two really funny jokes. And by the time we got to the zoo, she'd given me a total rundown on all her friends, her cat, and the way her toe looked one time when a horse had stepped on it. 'I want to sit next to Jody,' she announced when we stopped for lunch. Neal smiled. I felt very elite.

"Over the next months, the three of us spent a lot of Sundays

10

together. I was glad that Isabel treated me as an extra friend she could have in addition to her dad, *not* as someone who was taking her dad away.

"That was why I never slept over at Neal's when she was there. And if the three of us went anywhere overnight, like skiing, we divided ourselves very chastely: me and Isabel in one room, Neal by himself in the other.

"Neal was touched by my concern for Isabel's feelings. 'I don't think her mother's ever been shy about flaunting *her* sex life,' Neal commented. 'But you,' he said, 'you really seem to know what she needs.' Neal's words made me glow! Isabel and I had just had a hilarious time making a mess of Neal's kitchen as we tried to frost a cake that kept crumbling. 'Isabel's a trouper,' I told Neal. 'She won't give up.' 'Jody's great,' Isabel giggled. 'She just said the word that Mom gets mad at whenever *I* say it!'

"We laughed, but late that night in bed—*after* we'd taken Isabel home—Neal said, 'Jody, you're so special, I didn't think I'd want to get married again. But . . . what I mean is, I love you. And Isabel loves you. Would you . . . that is, will you marry me—and maybe even have some more kids?' 'Oh, YES!' I answered. It was all I wanted in the world!

"The next day, we told Isabel. 'Oh, goody!' she squealed, and started dancing around. 'Does that mean I get to be a bridesmaid and have a special dress and walk down the aisle and stay up late?' Yes, we assured her. All of the above.

"'I'm so lucky, getting a husband *and* a great kid,' I told everyone. We were going to have such a wonderful life!

"We went to Europe on our honeymoon—three glorious weeks—and as soon as we got back, we wanted Isabel to come for the night. 'But where's *your* bed?' she asked when I'd made up the sofa bed in the living room for her.

"'In there, with your dad,' I said. Isabel frowned. 'In *there?*' she repeated in evident amazement. 'But why?' 'Because we're married now,' I answered. 'But it was so nice *before*,' she said. 'Why does it have to be different?'

"I was trying to think how to answer when the oven timer rang. I said, 'Quick! come help me get dinner on the table, okay?' Isabel nodded. 'Okay,' she said with a sigh. During supper, she kept put-

11

ting her head on Neal's shoulder.

"Afterward, I suggested a variety of games for the three of us to play, but Isabel wrinkled her nose at each suggestion. 'I just want to play checkers—with my *dad*,' she said. Neal glanced at me and shrugged. 'Okay, a quick one,' he said. But it was nine-fifteen before they were done with all their rematches and 'championships.' Trying to be a good sport, I offered to play the 'ultimate world champion,' who just happened to be Isabel, but she said, 'I guess not.'

"I said, 'Lovey, are you mad at me?' But she shook her head, 'I'm just tired,' she said with an exaggerated yawn. 'Okay, then. Come on!' Neal picked her up and put her on his shoulder, fireman-style. 'I'll read you a quick story,' he told her. But I'd showered and read 100 pages of *my* book before he tiptoed quietly into the bedroom.

" 'What did you read her, *War and Peace?*' I asked.

" 'Come on, Jody. You're the sensitive one. You should understand that this is new for her, our being married.'

" 'I guess you're right,' I murmured, putting down my book and snuggling into his arms. Soon we were making love.

" 'Hey, Jody!' *Isabel was walking into our room!* 'I have a joke.' There was a long pause. 'Isabel, can you . . . uh . . . save it until morning?'

" 'Oh, never mind!' She turned dejectedly and padded back down the hall. 'JUST NEVER MIND!'

"With a deep sigh, Neal sat up and put his robe on. 'I'll go,' he said, and left the room, closing the door behind him. He was gone a long time, and I fell asleep.

"The next morning, we were all tired and grumpy. Isabel looked at me accusingly and said she'd had a nightmare. 'Come on,' Neal interceded, giving his daughter a playful swat. 'Finish up your breakfast so we can try out your new dirt bike.' But the banana pancakes and Canadian bacon she'd asked me for were sitting untouched on her plate, growing cold. 'This is all yucky,' she said, giving it a poke with her fork. 'Daddy, do I *have* to eat it?'

" 'How did *I* get on her neon enemy list?' I asked Neal that night. 'Beats me,' he said. Then, 'Well . . . now that you mention it, you might try to be a little *friendlier . . .* ' I wanted to say, 'I already *am*, for crying out loud,' but I forced a smile and said, 'Yes, okay. I will.' And I did!

"But no matter how often I tried to cater to Isabel, to sit down with her, to tell her jokes, and no matter how often I offered to take her places, nothing really helped, and she didn't let down her guard. In fact, as the weeks passed, I thought she seemed more antagonistic than ever.

"When the three of us were together, she was Daddy's girl and I was the intruder. When it was just Isabel and me, she watched TV. And she wouldn't even admit to me how angry she really was.

" 'Maybe she's upset because her mother's involved with some guy,' Neal suggested. I knew that Isabel *had* taken to phoning when her mom went out and asking Neal to come over to see her.

" 'Honey, I understand,' I told Neal warmly the first time he went, and the second. But then I started wondering how he could be so insensitive—to me.

"One Friday night, I was getting dressed to meet Neal for dinner at our favorite spaghetti and seafood place, when Isabel called. 'I'm lonesome and I need my dad,' she said.

" 'Are you all *alone?*' I asked, shocked. 'No, I've got a babysitter,' she admitted. 'But I need my dad.'

" 'This time Dad can't come, Isabel,' I told her. 'I'm afraid we have plans.' (This was to be *our* evening.)

"But Neal disagreed. 'We *could* have brought her,' he said. 'When my daughter needs me, please don't ever interfere.'

"But our real crisis came two weeks later—when I went to my gynecologist and learned for sure that I was pregnant. 'Neal,' I said excitedly that evening, 'isn't this *great!*' 'Well, I guess so,' he said cautiously.

" 'But you don't sound happy.'

"Neal patted my cheek. 'I just hope that Isabel won't be too upset.' So that was how it was: Neal wouldn't welcome our baby unless he had *Isabel's* permission! But my anger that night barely compared with Isabel's the next day.

" 'Just don't expect me to come and visit anymore,' she said. 'This whole place is going to smell of *barf!*' She wrinkled up her nose, as if it smelled already. 'Anyway, Daddy lied. He said that I could be his only child forever.'

" 'I didn't say that,' Neal protested. 'I just said nobody could ever replace you, Isabel. That's different.' Later, in private, he said to me,

13

'I don't think it's what was *said* that's the problem. It's what's *done*. And maybe this really wasn't the greatest time for you to go and get pregnant.'

"That made me furious! Neal had no joy or hope for our baby, nor any for me. What does he want me to do, have an abortion? Well, I won't! If necessary, I'll go off and have this baby by myself. I thought we'd be such a happy family. I wish I knew what to do."

The Counselor Replies

Janice I. Cohn, D.S.W., chief of consultation and education in the Department of Psychiatry, Newark–Beth Israel Medical Center, in New Jersey, is in private practice in New York City and Montclair, New Jersey.

"Neal and Jody Spencer came in—obviously caring very much for each other, but both feeling very guilty, angry, and rejected. Still in their first six months of marriage, they were torn by a loyalty conflict involving two children—one eight years old and one not even born yet.

" 'I feel like a third wheel in my own marriage,' Jody sighed. 'It's the two of them against me—but what did I *do?*'

"Neal turned to me and said, 'I suppose you're going to tell me I'm a terrible husband, and I haven't been supportive and loving enough.'

"I said, 'Is that what you think?'

" 'Hell, no!' he said, shaking his head. 'I've been trying—honestly. But Jody doesn't understand.'

" 'Tell me,' I said.

"Neal took a deep breath. 'My little girl, who has been the most important—the *only* important—person in the world to me for eight years, is in so much pain. She feels unloved, she's lost her trust in me. She's depressed, and she never used to react this way.'

" 'But you *wanted* more children,' Jody cried.

" 'Yes, I did . . . at least I thought I did. Well, yes, I do! But not now for God's sake! Isabel needs more time to adjust. You should have thought about that. You should have used your diaphragm.'

" 'You never said I should!' Jody was flushed.

14

" 'Well, how did I know you'd be so . . . quick? It took Andrea three years to get pregnant with Isabel.'

" 'Neal,' I said. 'You have a daughter and a pregnant wife. You're upset and you're angry. But I'm having trouble understanding what you *want*.'

" 'I don't know,' Neal said. 'It's a terrible choice . . . '

" 'Why does it have to be a choice?' I asked. 'Maybe you're afraid that you don't have enough love for Isabel and Jody *and* the new baby. But chances are you have *more* than enough for them all.'

" 'Just because Isabel's upset now, don't assume that she will always be,' I continued. 'Right now, she just has a lot to handle.' We talked about Isabel's predicament: not only was she experiencing some inevitable jealousy and wondering if the baby *would* replace her in her father's love, but there was much more.

"First, there's always going to be some distress when a parent remarries, as it makes the divorce—a shadowy but still painful fact of the child's life—truly irrevocable.

"In addition, I told them, 'No child finds it easy to have to face her parents' sexuality.' Unlike Andrea, Isabel's mother, Neal and Jody *had* been appropriately tactful and discreet in keeping their premarital intimacy strictly private. But once they were married, it shocked Isabel to realize that Jody, her pal and sometime roommate, was now to share a bed (and a sex life) with Neal. 'On a certain level,' I explained, 'Isabel *must* feel that Jody betrayed her.'

" 'I wondered why she seemed so angry at Jody,' Neal said. 'But being a superdoting father hasn't helped.'

"Perhaps, I suggested, Neal could try a different strategy: instead of turning himself (and his marriage) inside out to reassure his daughter that he wasn't deserting her, he could help Isabel *more* if he gave in *less* to her manipulation. 'Good kids like Isabel feel guilty when they're allowed to get away with being bratty,' I said.

" 'Besides, too much catering and preferential treatment isn't helping Isabel accept the reality: that you *are* a couple with a private life that doesn't always include a child.' I urged Neal to look at Jody as an ally for a change, instead of a problem-maker. 'Jody needs your support . . . and Isabel needs to see you two as a united front,' I said.

"I explained that it was normal for Isabel to test—to see if she could drive a wedge between Jody and Neal. 'But try to settle your differences in private,' I said. 'Then Isabel will see Jody as a valued grown-up she can respect and depend on, and definitely not some extraneous person she can just decide to get rid of.'

"This, I said, would help to cool the tensions, especially once Isabel was given some clear-cut rules such as 'Please knock before coming into our bedroom.'

" 'Well, fine,' Neal said at last. 'But I don't think Isabel will ever be thrilled about the baby.'

" 'She might not—and she doesn't have to,' I said. 'You can take some pressure off if you let Isabel know that it's okay if she doesn't like the idea of the baby, that maybe she'll change her mind sometime, but that's *her* business.'

"When Neal did have this talk with Isabel, she balked at first mention of the baby, then listened, and finally looked relieved. Neal felt better, too. 'I still think our timing was lousy,' he said the next time we got together.

" 'I'm not sure there's ever a perfect time to have a baby,' I said. But as we talked about the joy, as well as the inconvenience and upset, babies cause, Neal began to smile. 'I *am* excited,' he said, squeezing Jody's hand.

"As Neal's whole sense of anguish and guilt began to subside, he found that he was less likely to 'rush over and rescue Isabel' when she phoned and said she was lonesome. 'I can't come now, but we can talk on the phone,' he suggested on one occasion. When Isabel saw that her father *was* friendly but wasn't going to drop everything (including Jody), the come-get-me game was no longer interesting.

"Six months later, Colin Jeremiah Spencer was born, creating the usual chaos and turmoil that babies bring. But to Neal's and Jody's relief, it was no *more* difficult. 'He's cute,' Isabel admitted. 'I like how he grabs onto my finger.'

"Jody is glad to have Isabel's company and tells her so. They are friends again—now that Neal has leaned how to keep the 'specialness' with Isabel, while at the same time letting Jody in and making it less of an exclusive club.

"Changes and additions in a family, even very positive and much desired ones, can still create stresses that seem insurmountable at times. In therapy, the Spencers were able to resolve their own conflicts, enabling them in turn to respond more helpfully to Isabel's. And in this way, Isabel—who never received any therapy directly—was able to benefit fully from Neal's and Jody's work.

"I'm sure the Spencers *will* have adjustments to make, especially as Colin grows out of babyhood, but they'll do fine because they've learned that it was facing and solving problems—not avoiding them—that finally made them all feel like a real family."

*John lets his son act up—and
my daughters resent it terribly.
How can the five of us ever blend
into a real family . . . so long as
John thinks that rules are fine for
my kids, but not for his?*

Susan's Story

"We couldn't have been a more comfortable fit," said Susan Wellyn, 35. "I was a divorcee with eight-year-old twins, and John was a widower with an eleven-year-old son. We met on the subway of all places, on the way to work—and eight months later we were married.

" 'Will there be problems with the children?' my mother wondered. But I said, 'No way.' We all got on so well. My daughters, Julia and Amy, thought John was 'totally rad,' and I looked at John's son, Scott, as the son I'd never had and always wanted.

"But when we got back from the honeymoon and all started living together, our basic differences really started to surface.

"Scott left his dirty socks and empty soda cans in the living room—and John said nothing about it. I also didn't like having to chase down all the things Scott borrowed.

" 'He *is* a little scattered,' John admitted. 'But that's because he's been without a mom for so long.' John touched my cheek. 'Please try to be patient with him, will you?'

"But the more time passed, the more chaotic Scott seemed.

18

I couldn't count on him. He'd say, 'Sure!' very agreeably if I asked him not to put his sopping towels in the hamper, but he went ahead and did it anyway.

"And then there was the food thing. Scott wouldn't have a snack after school. But twenty minutes before dinner he'd get ravenous and raid the potato chips and cookies. Then he'd blame his not eating supper on whatever I'd made.

"If I asked him to join us at the table anyway, he'd sit there, kicking his chair leg and jabbing his fork through his place mat until John gave him permission to go and watch TV. Then I'd hear him later foraging for ice cream. But as usual, John didn't scold him, so what could I do?

"The girls were enraged about the double standard. 'How come Scott's such a privileged character?' Julia demanded. Scott didn't have to go to bed early on school nights or mop the bathroom if he got it wet, and he hardly had to do anything to get his allowance.

" 'Some of it's because he's older, and he's a boy,' I began uncomfortably. That sounded sexist and inadequate, even to me, but how could I explain that I had no choice but to follow John's be-gentle-with-Scott prescription?

"But the girls were even more upset about Scott's unfriendliness. 'He won't even let us in his room,' Julia said. 'We try to come in, and he pushes us out and calls us "Buttbrains" and "Dipstick." '

"One chronic irritant for me was the TV and homework controversy. The twins knew that TV could be turned on after homework, not during. But lately, if I got home from work a little late, I'd find three kids with books and notebooks spread out on the floor and all eyes on *Three's Company.*

" 'You girls go to your room and just forget TV for a week!' I snapped when it happened for the third time in a week. Angrily, they both picked up their notebooks.

"Scott reached over and turned up the volume. Furious and helpless, I looked at John, but he just shrugged. I said, 'You're really undermining me! I can't get the girls to obey me when they see you letting Scott do anything he wants. They've even given up saying "please" and "thank you." I think we've got to come to an agreement.'

" 'Don't be so rigid,' John said.

" '*Rigid?* Have you taken a look at Scott's grades?'

" 'Well, grades aren't everything,' John said, stretching out on the couch. 'Do what you want with *your* kids, but it's good we'll have one kid who isn't repressed!'

"Later, John apologized, but the tension didn't go away. The girls teased and taunted Scott—who ignored them—but they also took their anger out on John by turning their backs on him.

"In return, John began ignoring them. In the evenings, he would play some game with Scott while I would try to entertain the girls. There was little time for John and me to talk, and I couldn't remember the last time we'd made love.

"I had to face the fact that we were two separate families living under one roof, and I didn't know whether to be mad at Scott (and John) or at myself for not knowing know to do a better blending job.

"At least Christmas was coming soon—a happy time that might help our own lions and lambs to be more peaceful together. We'd spent Thanksgiving with John's folks, and now we were going to Florida to see my mother.

"The girls were excited. They hadn't been down there in two years, but they still remembered our hotel and the boats in the canal and the incongruous fun of making a sand castle on Christmas Day. We were all excited as we headed for the airport—almost as if we were a *real* family—and I felt hopeful.

"The good mood continued right into the next day, until it was time to change out of beach clothes and meet my mother for Christmas dinner. Julia and Amy were ready and looking beautiful in their new flowered dresses. But Scott was lying on his bed, reading a comic book. I could see sand in his hair, and he was wearing old gym shorts and a T-shirt with a stain on the front. I said, 'Scotty, it's time to get ready.'

" 'I am,' he said.

" 'But you can't go that way! Your grandma would die. Come on,' I said gently. 'I packed your blazer and your good pants.'

" 'I didn't even want to come,' he grumbled when he'd finally put on a clean T-shirt and a pair of surfer shorts. 'Why can't I stay in the room and have a hamburger?'

"At the restaurant, Scott's manners were even worse than usual.

'Please, Scott, there's a knife for putting butter on your roll,' I whispered. When he reached across the table to stab a potato with his fork, I saw my mother's lips tighten.

"By the end of Christmas dinner, I was seething—but John was even angrier. 'You're ruining this holiday with all your demands,' he said.

" 'Oh?' I replied. 'You thought he was acting fine? Fiddling and jiggling, ignoring my mother, and eating cake with his mouth wide open?'

"John didn't answer—or speak to me directly for the rest of the evening. I tried to talk to him, but he refused. He didn't even say good night to me, just snored loudly while I tossed and turned.

"I feel like such a failure—and so disappointed. One night last week, Julia said, 'I wish it was just the three of us again.' Is this the way it will always have to be?"

The Counselor Replies

Jeannette Lofas, Ph.D., is president and founder of the Stepfamily Foundation, a counseling and information center in New York City. Lofas (who is a stepchild and a stepparent) is the author of several books on the subject, including Stepparenting *(Zebra).*

"Susan and John were very discouraged. 'I just wanted us to be a good family,' Susan said. 'But there's just resentment. It started with the kids, but now it's even ruining our marriage.'

" 'I thought Sue was so loving, but she can't stand Scott because he isn't perfect,' John retorted. 'And her kids have absolutely no use for me. We had a lot of potential, but we've sure made a mess of things.'

" 'No, you haven't,' I said firmly. 'You are a classic stepfamily with classic problems. The conflicts and resentments you've described occur naturally in stepfamilies; the problems you're having are not because you've failed but because of the basic situation; two separate family systems, each with years of doing it "my way," can't feel like it would if you two had met and married and had years of private couple time.'

" 'So, you mean it's absolutely hopeless?' John asked.

" 'No,' I said, 'not at all. It's just that you'll never be the so-called real family you imagined; you'll be a stepfamily—always. But that doesn't mean you can't be happy. However, it will take some effort and change and real collaboration.'

"We spent the first session talking about John's and Susan's different backgrounds and ideas of how a family should run. 'It's important to respect one another's outlook, even if you don't agree with it,' I said.

"After we'd done some work together, John concluded that he *was* unusually permissive. 'I came from a rigid background and decided that I'd rather be a nice dad than a drill sergeant,' he said. 'I guess I really stopped making any kind of demands on Scott when he was six, after Kitty, my first wife, died. I felt guilty about all the mothering Scott had lost, and I hated to make his life any harder.'

"Susan took John's hand and squeezed it. 'You never told me that before,' she said. 'I guess I was the opposite. My parents were very strict but loving, and that's the combination that I've tried to give my girls. I admit I can get a little compulsive. Especially when I get home from work and find the living room is a total mess.'

" 'I see what you mean about different family systems,' John said. 'It's as though we're coming from different planets! I'm not really crazy about mess and chaos either, but how can we get such differently raised kids to start obeying the same rules?'

" 'You are a new household, and you can establish house rules,' I said. 'You can make up a manual and post it on the refrigerator. Once kids see that the game has rules, they will play by the rules. Kids want predictability in their lives.'

"I suggested that the Wellyns be positive and start with an upbeat 'We get up in the morning, we make our beds and brush our teeth, and we hang our wet towels on the rack.'

" 'You make it all sound so easy,' Susan laughed. But by the end of that session, she and John had agreed on a policy limiting snacking to before 5:00 P.M. and making dinner a family ritual at least four times a week.

"It was also decided that everyone could keep their bedrooms the way they liked as long as the living room was always neat.

"As we went on hashing out specifics, we tackled the complex issue of fairness: It was decided that all things didn't have to be uniform. (Fairness is a matter of recognizing differences, I explained.)

"The Wellyns both agreed that Scott, as an older kid, deserved some older-kid privileges, such as a later bedtime. He also deserved more allowance than the girls and a much bigger share of responsibilities.

"As for doing homework with the TV on, John thought it over and agreed with Susan that it *is* hard to focus with all that distraction. The new rule said, 'You can have a radio or stereo on in your room, but no TV until homework's finished.' 'It sounds good,' Susan said. 'But how am I supposed to enforce the rules with Scott when John isn't around? Scott's made the point often enough that I'm not his mother—in fact, once he said to me, "You're nothing!" '

" 'You're not his mother,' I agreed. 'But you certainly aren't nothing! You are the female head of the household, and John is the male head of the household; that gives you both the authority to make and enforce rules as a couple and see that they're followed. The kids will respect that idea when they see that you two agree on it and support each other.'

"John sighed. 'That makes sense,' he said. 'But we also have a major problem with dislike between the kids. And I don't see how any house rules can force those kids to become close.'

" 'True,' I agreed. 'You can't legislate friendly feelings in the household, but you can insist that everyone be treated respectfully. After all, you wouldn't tolerate an employee who's sloppy and sullen, loses your things, and talks with his mouth full—so why accept it in your child?'

"I told the Wellyns that when terrible manners are tolerated, it shows that the kids are dominating. 'Table manners, eye contact, hellos, good-byes, please, and thank-yous are what's expected of them outside the home, so it's not good to let them get away with bad manners at home.'

"Susan and John agreed whole-heartedly and added a clause: 'We call each other by name, not "Buttbrains" or "Dipstick," especially not when the adults can hear.'

"The 'Respectful Treatment' section also covered borrowing: 'We always ask permission before we borrow, and then we return the item promptly and in good condition, or we clean, repair, or replace it.'

"There was also a privacy clause, stating, 'When anybody's bedroom door is open, you ask permission to come in; when a door is ajar, you knock, announce yourself, and ask permission to come in; but if the door is closed tight, you go away unless it's a major emergency.'

"After six sessions of formulating the new rules, refining them, and even discussing them with the children, the process began in earnest. The kids tested, of course, but discovered that John and Susan were serious. There was a real change in the atmosphere as each person began to feel a little less shortchanged.

"Even dinner improved: Scott was there, eating with acceptable if not wonderful manners. And the conversation got off the old, tedious 'You're getting gravy all over your mat' and the 'I'm tired of hearing you complain about my cooking' tracks and shifted to interesting topics.

"During the third week of the new regime, Susan walked into the kitchen one afternoon and saw Scott showing the list of rules on the refrigerator to a friend. 'Maybe you guys should try it at your house,' Scott suggested to his friend. Susan thought to herself, 'I really think we will make it after all!'

"The Wellyns will never be the seamlessly fitting family that Susan was hoping for, because that involves blood relationships. But Susan and John are feeling pretty solid and together these days, and so are the kids. And they're all glad that no one decided to call it quits."

> *Livia was the perfect mother-in-law . . . until she came to stay. Now we're forced to choose between her comfort—and our sanity.*

Nancy's Story

"Jake's mother always had a horror of imposing on anyone,' said Nancy Barnes, 43. "Even after a stroke, she wanted to go on living alone. But last year, she fell in her shower and fractured her hip. She was 80 and she could have died. 'That settles it,' I said to Jake. 'Now she's *got* to come and live with us.'

"Was I trying to please my husband? Well, naturally—and he was pleased! But there was more—I truly empathized with her. Orphaned at nine, I had spent eight months in an orphanage before an aunt took me in, and I sympathized fully with Livia's 'I'd-rather-they-kill-me' dread of any institutional care. Besides, how could we *not* want to take in this warm and funny woman who had gone to work mopping floors when her husband died so that Jake could go to college?

"Our daughters, Kim, ten, and Hilary, seven, were thrilled that their only Granny was coming to stay. They associated her with holiday visits—lots of fun, good food, good smells, and marathon snowball fights. The girls didn't even fuss about the fact that they'd have to double up in one room.

" 'You people are the best and I promise not to be a burden for one single minute,' Livia said, hugging and kissing each of us the night we met her plane. I saw her blink back tears when she walked in and saw the big, splashy 'WE LOVE YOU GRANNY!' poster the girls had made.

"In Livia's honor, Jake had brought home a beautiful lemon meringue pie from the bakery in town. 'Oh, store-bought!' Livia chortled. 'From now on, I'll make you real pies—from scratch.' 'These girls don't even know what home-baked means,' I laughed. 'Oh, Livia, you came just in time.'

"Late that night, I was awakened by the sound of water running. The shower—at four in the morning? It was Livia! I grabbed my robe—I couldn't let her risk another fall.

" 'I don't want to trouble you, Nancy, I just felt like freshening up a bit,' she said. 'No problem!' I lied. I knew I'd be exhausted for work in the morning, but so what? Livia was accepting this enormous upheaval in her life without a single complaint.

" 'Oh, poor you!' my friend Jean, at the next desk at work, commiserated. 'I wouldn't have my mother-in-law for a million bucks.' 'You don't understand,' I told her. 'Livia's a *joy.*'

"But as the weeks passed, I became concerned. Livia had no complaints and said she was happy, but she continued to wake up at night and stay up, sitting quietly or watching TV. And I noticed she was hardly eating anything. I coaxed her, I even used her recipes, but she was all skin and bones. Jake said, 'Relax.' I said, 'But look how her clothes hang on her.' He shrugged and said, 'It's really annoying to hear you nag her.'

"But whether I nagged or not, dinner—which had once been our happy family time—was tense. She didn't eat and she didn't seem to relate to anything we talked about. She just sat there in silence and didn't tune in at all to what was going on. It was hard for me to sit there and let her be ignored. One evening I went to get the coffee, and when I came back, I caught Hilary dumping Livia's chicken, broccoli, and rice into the garbage. 'Why are you wasting good food?' I demanded. 'And don't you know you're hurting Granny by doing that!' Hilary's eyes filled with tears. 'I was just clearing the table and helping like you always say I should,' she gulped.

"Poor Hilly—of course she'd side with Granny! She knew how it felt to be badgered by Mom, so she'd taken Granny's plate and dumped it. 'I love you, Hill,' I whispered. But I felt like kicking myself.

"Kim had already left the table. Lately she was never there when I wanted to talk to her. Was she just beginning to be an elusive teenager—or was it more?

"Actually, I was finding it hard to find the time to talk to anyone. For example, I'd get home from work and as soon as I had one foot in the door, both Hilary and Livia would start talking a mile a minute. Whom do I listen to first? Out of respect, the youngster should wait her turn . . . but on the other hand, the older one ought to have the grace to let the kid say hello. 'MOM, YOU NEVER LISTEN!' Hilary shouted one day in frustration. That night, I had to grit my teeth when I heard Livia tell Jake, 'Those girls need more discipline.'

"Well, they were at their worst—sulking, squabbling. It irritated Livia—who never suspected that she was the cause. But when I wondered if I'd made a mistake in urging Livia to come to us, I felt so selfish. 'After all, isn't this what families are for?' I remembered my aunt's words when she picked me up at the orphanage. Now I vowed to try harder. But the more I tried to make Livia feel included, the worse things got. One evening I insisted we take her with us to a lecture—and she fell asleep, snoring loudly. I've never seen Jake look so embarrassed. I told him I was sorry, since it had been my idea.

" 'Damn it, can't you stop apologizing?' he exploded later that night. He had always been gentle and calm before, and now was so impatient and quick to push me away.

"Well, of course he was tense. Our usual ways of relaxing—getting away for a weekend in the country with the children or having friends in for dinner—were no longer possible. Leaving Livia alone overnight was out of the question. And the last time we'd had guests, poor Livia—cooped up by herself all day—had monopolized the conversation, keeping everyone at the table while her food sat untouched.

"And there was another problem: at first, I'd gotten angry when Hilary and Kim had complained about an odor in the house. But then I started smelling it, and my heart sank. Yes, Livia must be having accidents; but I couldn't mention it to such a proud and fastidious woman. I bought some pine-scented room fresheners, but the problem didn't really go away.

"I was feeling pressed and lonesome. Jake had taken to watching

27

TV all evening. When I mentioned how rarely we made love these days, he said, 'Well you fall asleep too early.' But I had to grab what sleep I could! Jake slept soundly, but Livia's nocturnal showers got me up like a shot.

"She wanted so much to feel independent. I had to admire her spirit. She even wanted to pay us rent. Naturally, Jake said, 'No way!'

"But Livia managed to find a way! She said, 'I'm going to air-condition this house for you.' I said, 'What a lovely, generous idea,' but Jake hit the roof. 'I don't *want* it,' he yelled. 'But she's old and needs air-conditioning, and summer is almost here . . . '

" 'Sure, *she* needs,' he interrupted. 'But what about me? It's bad enough that I have to put up with it at work—that's why I always have a cold in the summer. You let her install it, and I swear I'll get my own place.' With that, Jake slammed out of the house and didn't come home until three in the morning.

"We didn't speak to each other for three excruciating days. On the third day, I came home from work to find Hilary hugging a matted gray cat with one eye missing. 'Mom,' she cried, 'isn't he cute? He was homeless, but now he can make Granny happy—*and you and Dad, too.*'

" 'Oh, Hill!' It broke my heart to tell her that Granny was violently allergic to cats. Even now, I could hear her sneezing. 'If I have to give this cat away, then I *hate* Granny,' Hilary shouted. 'And I wish she were dead.'

"I felt like slapping her, but then I realized no, she's only telling the truth. Livia had turned this family into a bunch of angry strangers. I had thought we had more than enough to give, but I was wrong. What now? Do we wait until our lives become unbearable? Or do we put the woman out—like that poor one-eyed cat?"

The Counselor Replies

Marjorie A. Slavin, A.C.S.W., C.S.W., is a family therapist in Riverdale, New York. She is also a coauthor of What to Do When Your Son or Daughter Divorces *(Bantam Books).*

"I was happy that Nancy called on me, as the situation—from all she told me—was a difficult one.

"The Barnes family had welcomed Granny with the rosiest expectations. But all those years of brief—and festive—visits had not prepared them for what it would be like to have Livia there all the time—lonesome, dependent, and intrusive. Inevitably those roses turned into wilted flowers, and the Barneses were struggling with a sense of defeat.

"I told them they had taken on a very big commitment—and one that would probably get harder over time; nevertheless, there was much they could do to ease the pressures *right now,* so that everyone could feel much, much better.

"Number one was to contact an agency for someone to stay with Livia now and then so that the rest of the family—or, perhaps more urgently, just Jake and Nancy—could get away together—something they clearly needed to do. Because Nancy had spent time in an orphanage and then grown up with a single aunt, she idealized what a family should and could be. And because she had felt left out during certain times of her childhood, she felt she needed to include her mother-in-law in every aspect of their family life, so Livia wouldn't feel left out. I stressed, however, that they needed to do more things without Livia and to try to encourage Livia to form a life of her own.

"At first Livia grumbled about 'a roomful of old biddies,' but when Nancy took her one Saturday to the attractive senior citizen center in the local library, she agreed to try it. To Livia's own amazement—and the family's delight—she found she liked the people at the center enormously, which made her feel less isolated and less dependent on her family.

"I stressed the need for everyone in the family to talk to one another. If they were finding this hard, they could come to me, and I could provide a safe place for them to discuss difficult and explosive feelings.

"In this process, a lot of important feelings came out. Kim, for example, had been feeling pushed out. Kim said, 'I *do* love Granny a lot, but since she's come here, I can't ever be in the living room with my friends without her sitting around. And Mom, I can't even *laugh out loud* anymore because you say, "Granny's napping now, so keep it quiet." '

"Jake revealed for the first time, that he had been feeling like a fatherless adolescent again, with 'Mother constantly on my case.' This had made him feel defensive, grouchy, and unavailable to Nancy, who saw his moodiness as a criticism that she wasn't doing enough for Livia. Actually, he was already feeling badly and resented Nancy for being so much more attentive to Livia (who was *his* mother) than he was!

"Hilary, meanwhile, had experienced the tension at home as anger and punishment directed at *her* for secretly not thinking Granny was fun anymore. And sensing the chilling distance between her parents, she was frightened that they'd get a divorce unless she did something dramatic—like presenting them with the one-eyed orphan cat.

"All this talking provided a wonderful and necessary safety valve for each of them. At this time, too, I urged Jake and Nancy to bring Livia into a session so that she, too, could participate as an equal family member. They did, and learned that she felt like a parasite *and* that she couldn't sleep because she was sweltering in her room. Together they worked out a solution: she could air-condition her own room—and perhaps the kitchen if Jake didn't mind—but not the rest of the house. Livia also made it clear that it was important to her to contribute financially and to share in the household chores so that she could feel useful and responsible.

"As the family did more talking and less suffering in silence, they got to know Livia in a new way—not as the old TV commercial–perfect Granny who put on Christmas feasts and threw snowballs with the kids, and *not* as the elderly burden-in-residence, but as a person—with some physical impairment, *but* with her own ideas and feelings that mattered.

"When the issue of Livia's not eating enough came up—something that was still distressing Nancy—I said, 'Let her eat what she wants, and if you're afraid she's going to die, take her to the doctor and let him talk to her.' I pointed out that the stress of leaving her own home and moving in with her son's family could still be affecting Livia's appetite, and if so, the problem would pass.

"When Livia said she would prefer to eat earlier and make her own small sandwich for supper, Nancy reluctantly let her. Nancy said that it *was* great to get back to those delightful and relaxed family dinners they had had before Livia came, but that she still felt guilty because Livia *should* be part of the family.

" 'Livia *is* part of your family,' I assured her, 'but with a life of her own, too.' Nancy had thought that inviting Livia to stay meant *totally* absorbing her into the family routine and that anything less spelled failure, but this was not correct. In fact, Livia—who had been living alone and loving it before—actually welcomed the new routine, and her appetite improved.

"To help Livia feel more independent, Nancy and Jake bought special equipment—handrails and a chair—for the shower. Now Livia could even wash her hair by herself.

"Another issue we explored was setting limits so that the family doesn't have to make any more sacrifices than necessary for the comfort of one member. I told Jake and Nancy that their tact with Livia had been excessive, especially in regard to the odor. Yes, it was a hard thing to mention to Livia, but it was too important to go on covering up. When Nancy did get up the nerve, Livia was shocked, but she listened and said, 'I didn't realize I was doing it.' She agreed to wear the special disposable product Nancy had bought her.

"The family was relieved that they could, once again, have friends in the house, but they also needed to establish some privacy guidelines. For example, Livia did not always have to be included in Nancy and Jake's entertaining. And the girls could have *their* friends over without having to be too quiet on certain days, when Livia would either go to her room and turn on the air conditioner or go to the senior citizens' center.

"Late nights were still a problem for Nancy, who wanted to be there for Livia, no matter what the hour. I urged her to set a curfew for Livia: no showers after eleven at night.

"Livia accepted the restriction, but once again, Nancy felt guilty. I tried to reassure her that there is no way to get through this process without feeling guilty, because no matter what you do, there's always more to be done. Doing things *will* conflict with somebody's needs—including Nancy's own. I told her that it would be good for her to accept that instead of wasting energy by fighting it.

"Nancy did find that once she was relieved of her 'night-watch' duties, she could get enough sleep, *and* regain the intimate time with Jake that both of them had missed.

"Last week was Hilary's birthday, and her favorite present was from Granny: a bouncy black and white puppy from the animal shelter. Nancy could hardly describe her daughter's joy—or Livia's.

"After just six weeks of counseling, the Barneses' problems *had* eased. Still, in my last session with Jake and Nancy, we discussed the fact that there will be more problems down the road, that grandparents are living longer and they can get really frail—even to the point of needing 24-hour care. At that point, I told them, nursing homes can serve a purpose and should not be viewed as a betrayal.

"But no matter what lies ahead, the Barnes family will be able to cope because they've learned the good survival skills for any family crisis: to be assertive, to be prepared to get outside help when they need it, and most important of all, to stay in loving touch with one another."

DEATH,

DYING,

AND

BEREAVEMENT

*My husband, Dan, has cancer—and
less than two months to live. But
instead of being extra loving to their
dad, the children are avoiding him.
How can I help make things
better—before it's too late?*

Carol's Story

"When Dan came home from the hospital two weeks ago, I expected the kids to jump up and down," said Carol Tucker, 30. "But Andrew, eight, only said hi, and even Maggie, five, who's never been shy a day in her life, just stood there and stared.

"Dan had been away in the hospital for six weeks—a wrenching and chaotic period for all of us! The children *had* missed him desperately. I'd done what I could to comfort them, but I know it wasn't enough, what with my working and spending the rest of my time driving back and forth between the hospital and home, trying to cover both fronts, but mostly just being exhausted.

"When Dan was about to start a new, risky course of chemotherapy, I managed to sneak the children in for a visit, shushing them as we quickly passed the rooms of people even sicker than Dan. So at least they got to see their father before the nurses chased us out. Then I literally had to drag them back to the elevator and the parking lot for the long, sad, rainy drive home.

"But those treatments failed—and there was nothing left to try. Dan said, 'I just want to go home.' His doctor nodded and suggested that we might want to contact a hospice for help, but Dan said no thanks and I agreed: we have always been a very close family, and we'd manage on our own.

"Then Dan was home, but where was the closeness? Why were the children treating him so strangely? I thought it might have been because he looked so different—so much thinner now, and missing his hair. Or were they confused by the fact that Dan was home not because the doctors had made him well but because they hadn't succeeded in curing him?

"Certainly, I'd tried my best to help them understand. Dan and I had always believed in telling them the truth. I told them that their dad had tried very hard to get well, and all the doctors had tried, but some sicknesses are too hard for anyone to cure . . . and that was why, soon, we would have to say good-bye to him.

" 'Do you understand?' I asked them, and they nodded. I said, 'Good, this is why we need to use this time now to help Dad feel close to us.' I hugged them both and cried. 'This will be a time you'll always remember—and treasure,' I told them.

"But when was it going to start? Even on the weekend, instead of clamoring for Dan's attention as they used to do, the kids weren't even going to say good morning to him.

"I kept telling Dan I was sure that it wasn't that they didn't care. It had to be the opposite, that this standoffishness was their way of protecting themselves from the pain of losing him. Dan smiled. 'I guess they have to do what they have to do,' he said regretfully.

" 'You're throwing something very important away,' I warned Andrew when he phoned from down the street to ask if he could sleep over at his friend Chris's house. And why was Maggie following *me* from room to room, barely giving me privacy to brush my teeth or make a phone call? 'Why don't you do something with Dad?' I suggested.

" 'Why, Mom?' she asked. 'Because you won't always have him, Maggie.' She just put her thumb in her mouth and her head on my shoulder.

"Meanwhile, Dan was having more pain by the day. 'Can't you take something?' I asked, in anguish myself, but he shook his head. He was determined to tough it out, not succumb to medication that might not only ease the pain but also make him groggy. 'I told you,' he said firmly, 'the last thing I want to do is sleep my life away.'

"Sleep! That was just what I needed. Since Dan had been home, I'd averaged three or four hours a night. I had so many things to think about—so many worries. Each night, I'd go from the big ones like, How will I live without him? down to the smaller, practical matters like, How will we eat? We still had medical bills coming in, enormous ones, and I wasn't sure how I'd pay them or when I would even be able to go back to work. An then there was always the worry of why the kids were hanging on me or getting out of the house—and ignoring Dan.

"It's true, Dan wasn't at his best. In fact, he could get quite sarcastic and irritable. He wanted so much to go out and shovel the driveway and steps, but he couldn't, so he told me what a lousy job *I* did of it. And his patience with the kids was becoming badly frayed.

" 'When someone's in a lot of pain, it's just impossible to be nice all the time,' I told both children, adding, 'It's perfectly natural for Dad to be annoyed when people yell when he's trying to nap.'

"This past weekend was particularly hard. On Saturday, it was snowing again, and the kids were running in and out all day with a couple of neighborhood kids and forgetting to close the door. They were making so much noise and commotion; snow from their boots was melting in puddles. I knew how much it was getting to Dan when I heard him fuss at Andrew for 'clomping around' and then later at Maggie for leaving wet mittens on the coffee table.

" 'Do you want me to send them next door?' I asked. But Dan shook his head emphatically. He didn't want to admit that he was having a hard time with them. But later, when Maggie was bringing him soda, she did her waitress routine—with the little tray up high—and ended up spilling ginger ale and ice all over him.

" 'What in the hell are you trying to do?!' he yelled.

" 'Nothing.' Maggie looked scared. 'I was helping.'

"Dan muttered a four-letter word as he tried to wipe up the mess all over his lap.

" 'You're mean,' Maggie said, her cheeks burning. 'I'll be glad when you die.' 'Maggie, NO!' I shouted, and forced a stammering and frightened apology out of her before she ran off to her room. But Dan, who had tears in his eyes, just shook his head and said,

'Forget it, Carol. I had no right to lose my temper.'

"All that night, I was haunted by the simple cruelty of Maggie's words. And I ached more than ever for Dan. He had always been a caring and connected father, and it broke my heart to think that he would have to die without getting a decent good-bye from his kids.

"The next day was Sunday, and I made duck, Dan's favorite dinner. But by evening he was in so much pain that he couldn't even join us at the table. I sat with the kids in a kind of terror: we *were* losing Dan, and it was starting to happen! I kept staring at the empty chair. The children didn't seem to notice.

"It's hard to accept that the children have grown indifferent. Maybe they think, If I don't acknowledge what's happening, then it *can't* happen. But that's so wrong! I learned the hard way, at twenty, when my own father died, that the things you don't get to say you end up carrying around forever!

"Yesterday, I was thinking about all this as I stopped to get some groceries, and when I came out of the store, I saw our car being towed! 'Wait! Stop!' I screamed, trying to run and skidding on the icy pavement. But they didn't stop. When the cab I called finally pulled up—some 25 minutes later—I was fit to be tied.

" 'I'm awfully sorry, ma'am,' the gray-haired woman driver said, jumping out to help me with my groceries. 'I'm sorry, too,' I said. And then, without warning, I started to cry—a flood of tears—and I couldn't stop.

"Haltingly, I poured out the story of Dan, and what was happening at home. She said, 'You poor thing, I know what you're going through.' She handed me a slip of paper with the number for the Hospice of Northern Virginia. She said they helped her cope, two years ago, when her sister was dying of leukemia. She said they really understand and they can probably help. I'm not sure what they—or anyone—can do for us, but I know I can't handle this alone anymore."

The Counselors Reply

With the aim not of curing but of easing the patient's suffering and helping to reduce emotional stress for the entire family, the Hospice of Northern Virginia, located in Arlington, is designed to serve the pa-

tient who knows he or she hasn't long to live but wants to spend that time at home instead of in a hospital. Members of each patient's resource team include a chaplain, a doctor, a nurse, a social worker, and other professionals and volunteers who are available according to individual need.

Sister Catherine Higley, home-care nurse and primary contact for the Tuckers: "Although the reality of having someone terminally ill is inherently stressful, I felt that the Tuckers were having an even harder time because Carol and Dan were both straining themselves to do what they *thought* was right. Dan was suffering unspeakable physical pain, refusing medication because he felt he ought to be alert for the family. Carol, meanwhile, was making herself incredibly anxious because she felt that it was her job to bring the children close to Dan—and it wasn't happening.

"After reviewing the Tucker case with our physician, I told Dan we could make him much more comfortable with palliative medication. He was against it at first, but when I explained that it would definitely not sedate him but would allow him more freedom and control, he agreed to try. 'If I don't like it, I'll throw it away,' he warned.

"I also spent time with Carol, who told me how much she had wanted this to be a rich, fruitful time for the family, but that it was turning out just the opposite. Carol's anxiety on this issue was so intense—in part because she had never fully resolved old feelings of guilt and regret from when her *own* father died—that I felt she could benefit from regular counseling and a social worker. Carol was eager for this, and I made her an appointment with Gretchen Lane, a social worker at the Hospice."

Gretchen Lane, M.S.W.: "I was happy to be able to meet with Carol and explain to her that the warm good-bye scenario she'd imagined for the children and Dan did indeed sound wonderful and loving, but considering the children's ages, it wasn't very realistic.

"At five, Maggie was developmentally unable to envision death as final—and therefore she couldn't say good-bye. But that didn't mean she was rejecting her father. In fact, I explained to Carol, when Maggie had said, 'I'm glad you're going to die,' she may have meant, 'Boy, you're a grouch in *this* episode. Maybe next time you'll come back the way you were before.'

"I went on to tell Carol, 'If Maggie's clinging, it's most likely just because she's picking up on *your* anxiety and craves security, which is understandable and normal and not something to worry about or to try to change.'

"Andrew, on the other hand, *was* old enough to sense that he was losing his father—but like Maggie, he still wasn't old enough to know in advance what this would mean to him or how he would feel. Therefore, Andrew's grief—and Maggie's—would best be handled later on, in one of the Hospice's age-appropriate bereavement groups.

"I suggested that Carol give both children more permission to be with their friends if they felt like it. 'They need—and deserve—whatever fun they can find,' I said. As it was, putting pressure on the kids to 'make this time count' had only served to confuse them and convince them that there was *something* expected of them—something undefined, grown-up, and mysterious that they couldn't deliver.

"I explained to Carol that it might help her to spend some time talking about her father, so that she could sort some of those feelings out and keep them from making her current tasks even harder. But what about the children and their feelings? Carol still felt that they were emotionally blocked and would suffer drastically later if they kept all their love for Dan—and their sorrow—inside. 'I've talked myself blue in the face, but they won't open up,' she said.

"I told Carol that she had been right to explain a lot of facts to the children—such as the fact that nobody could catch Dan's disease like a cold and that no one had made their daddy sick. I said, 'It *is* good to be able to discuss death and dying instead of creating a wall of so-called protective secrecy. But in terms of the emotional issues, words are not always adequate.'

"With this in mind, I suggested art therapy for Maggie and Andrew. The next day, with Carol's consent, we called on Anita Epstein, a free-lance art therapist who has had much success in working with the children of Hospice patients."

Anita K. Epstein, art therapist: "Arriving at the Tucker home with two big bags full of art supplies, I was able to establish an immediate rapport with the children. I had them sit at the kitchen table with me and draw what they felt like drawing, then I had them do specific assignments, such as drawing the whole family or a picture of 'what might feel good,' and finally, I asked for a drawing of 'something that's different now, since Dad became sick.'

"Sometimes the drawing sessions led naturally to telling stories about the picture, but even when the picture itself was the only statement to come out, something constructive was happening: the children were letting their artwork express the frustration, sadness, and anger that had been bottled up inside them.

"I also encouraged Maggie and Andrew to draw scenes of how things were *before* Dan got sick. And what poignant memories emerged! Not just memories of major events like birthdays and a family trip to the Grand Canyon, but also day-to-day small events they'd shared with their father, like throwing a football and going to the beach and making spaghetti and meatballs together.

"These pictures—which the children clearly enjoyed and took pride in—came to serve two important functions. They reminded the children of their legacy: the many warm moments they had spent with their father and what he had taught them. And in addition, the pictures became something tangible—a kind of icebreaker gift the kids could bring in to their dad and say, 'I made this for you.'

"By the sixth session, the den walls were filled with the children's artwork, and the whole mood in the household was noticeably more relaxed. Dan—who, I learned, was now on regular pain medication—found that he had more energy and patience with Maggie and Andrew because he was comfortable. The children, quick to note that change, now felt free—and welcome—to dash in with a new drawing or two and even to scramble up on the couch or the bed to 'help' their father admire it. And he always did."

Sister Catherine: "In the four remaining weeks of Dan's life, members of our Hospice team, including a chaplain and a trained volunteer, continued to lend many kinds of support to the Tuckers—from increasing Dan's pain medication to helping Carol file insurance claims, and also just by being there as sounding board, expert, and friend.

"When Dan died—nine weeks after leaving the hospital—Carol

41

looked at the walls of the room so colorfully filled with her children's memories of their father. And she realized that even though the children's heart-to-heart talks with their father had never taken place—nor had there even been a lot of tearful hugging—nevertheless, the children *had* let their father know that they loved him . . . and they'd done it in a way that was unique and personal.

"In a crisis, it's easy to get stuck on what we *think* is the right and appropriate way for our children to show feelings. But as Carol Tucker discovered, sometimes it's *not* the official 'I love you' but something more spontaneous and unexpected that gets a child's real message across."

We thought that Kim, four, was coping well with the death of her newborn baby brother, but she's become anxious, afraid to sleep at night, and very touchy. Is Kim still in mourning—or is something else going on?

Deryn's Story

"It was January 4, and what began as one of the happiest days of our lives became one of the saddest," said Deryn Colwell, 29. "Our baby, Matthew, was fine all through labor, but during delivery, the umbilical cord got wrapped around his neck and strangled him.

"Devastated, Peter and I decided not to tell our daughter, Kim, right away. We just couldn't. We'd be home in a day, and we decided that we'd break it to her then. Peter did call his mother, Frances, who was staying with Kim. 'Oh, my God!' Frances grasped at the news, but she promised not to say anything to Kim that might upset her.

"A nurse brought the baby in and urged us to hold him. She said it would be therapeutic for us, but we found the experience wrenchingly sad. Maybe if the baby had been born too deformed to live . . . but this child was perfect, and he looked just like Kim.

"We made the customary newborn burial arrangements: no funeral, just a tiny coffin to contain a life that ended just when it should have begun.

"The doctor told us that this 'sudden unexpected demise,' as he called it, was nobody's fault, but I couldn't accept that. I blamed myself; had I gone to too many exercise classes—or too few? And I felt angry at Peter for even less reason. Somehow anger and guilt felt better than the thought that such a cruel trick of fate could just happen.

"The next day, we'd barely pulled into the driveway when Kim bounded out of the house and nearly knocked us down with her hugs. Then she peered into the car. 'Where's the baby?' she asked.

"Peter and I explained to her that Matthew had died. 'But when is he going to get better and come home?' Kim persisted.

"Then Frances came out of the house. 'Come, Kim,' she said. 'Your mommy and daddy are very upset now, so let's go inside and finish breakfast. Okay?'

"Poor Kim! This had to be hard for her, too. As an only child, she'd so looked forward to this baby. Sometimes we'd worried about how well she'd manage to share us. But she had been as excited as we were the first time she felt the baby kicking.

"She was disappointed to learn, after I had amniocentesis, that the baby would be a boy. (Her best friend down the street has a sister.) But we told her that brothers are just as nice as sisters. When Kim still seemed unhappy, we told her that this would be her baby too; and to draw her in, we even asked her to help us choose a name: We all liked 'Matthew' best.

"As the time drew closer, we went through cartons of Kim's old baby belongings trying to determine what would be appropriate for a boy—and also what Kim would be willing to part with. Kim felt that we really ought to buy him some 'boy stuff.'

"I was superstitious and didn't want to buy anything before the baby was born. But Peter said, 'Don't be silly. Kim's interested now; let's encourage her.' And so we went out and bought everything— including a beautiful little stuffed bear that Kim was *sure* Matthew needed.

"We felt happy and close that evening as Peter set up the crib and I put Matthew's new clothes away. Kim sat on her bed and watched us, cuddling the new bear. 'I know this cost a lot, but he'll take good care of it,' she promised. 'I'll show him how.'

"But three weeks later, all I wanted to do was escape. I was depressed, drained of energy, and spent the days sleeping and the nights pacing. Kim wanted me to play with her, but I couldn't. I felt as if I were in a shell. I thought, Why have fun? Why do anything? Why even live when I've lost my baby?

"Peter was in somewhat better control. At least he could answer Kim's persistent questions, and he tried to put the baby's death in terms she could deal with. But Peter became restless at home and soon went back to work, often staying late.

"I felt bad that neither of us was really there for Kim. 'Now, stop; there's nothing to worry about!' Frances said. She insisted that I was the one who needed healing and that Kim was doing fine.

"And apparently she was. Often I'd hear her playing outside or watching TV, very much as usual. Perhaps this wasn't a real loss to her, considering she hadn't actually known Matthew.

"There wasn't any reason to keep her home from preschool; I felt sure that she was better off there than she would be staying home with nothing special to do. Not only was Kim coping well herself; she was even showing a remarkable amount of sympathy for both of us.

"One time she found me crying and asked if I was chilly or if she could do anything. I was touched but still so sad. I hugged her, but I couldn't stop crying. Sometimes I wondered whether I ever would.

"But everything runs its course, and after several weeks I actually did feel myself beginning to recover. It was a tremendous relief, and now I looked forward to spending more time with Kim and becoming close to her again.

"But it was strange: The more available I was, the more Kim seemed to withdraw. Sometimes when we played a game, I felt that she was just going through the motions and that she was not really involved. And she was so touchy—crying over the slightest thing.

"Her tension showed mostly in the evenings, and I noticed that she even had trouble sitting through a TV show. When I asked whether she was feeling sad about Matthew, she nodded or shrugged but didn't elaborate.

"Kim had always fallen asleep right after her bedtime story, but now she didn't want us to leave her at bedtime. Most nights I'd end up lying down next to her, and we'd fall asleep in each other's arms.

45

"When Peter tucked Kim in, he tried to joke and tease her into a good mood, and sometimes it worked. But an hour later, she'd wake up and call out for me.

" 'Something is bugging her,' Peter agreed. 'Maybe it's the room.' Matthew's crib was still up, and the new dresser was filled with his clothes. Peter was right; I just hadn't been able to face the finality of putting everything away.

"But now I knew we had to, for Kim's sake. She watched as we took the crib apart and packed everything away. 'But what if he comes?' she asked us.

" 'He won't, I told her, trying not to cry. I picked up the bear. 'Here, honey,' I said. 'I know Matthew would have wanted you to have this now.'

"Kim held the little bear, and that made me feel good. Maybe this was just what she needed—something cuddly, something connected with the baby we all missed so.

"But when I went to tuck her in that evening, she didn't have the bear. 'Where is it?' I asked.

"Kim said, 'The bear died.'

"I said, 'Oh, Kim, you know stuffed animals can't die.' Thinking she'd misplaced him, I looked in her closet and in the bathroom—and there it was, stuck in the toilet! I pulled it out, assuming it had fallen in by mistake. But then I saw that the bear had been slashed across the chest, its ears partly torn off. And something red—paint or nail polish—had been splotched all over it.

" 'Kim! How could you?' I cried. 'You didn't have to destroy it.'

"But there was no answer, and when I went back to Kim's room, she wasn't there. Calling her name, I checked downstairs, and then I saw the back door—wide open.

"Terrified (Peter wasn't home), I ran outside, calling, 'Kim! Kim!' I must have been screaming, because all the neighbors came out. And then I spotted Kim, huddled in the snow, shivering and crying.

" 'Kim!' I scooped her up and headed for the house. 'Why did you run outside—and in your pajamas, too?' I held her tight. My heart was beating very fast, and so was hers.

" 'You were mad at me,' she said when her teeth stopped chattering.

"When we got inside, I put Kim in warm, dry pajamas and tried to reassure her. But in my heart, I knew that Kim needed more help than we knew how to give her."

The Counselor Replies

Elliot M. Kranzler, M.D., a child and adult psychiatrist in New York City, is assistant professor of psychiatry at Columbia University College of Physicians and Surgeons, as well as a leading authority on child bereavement.

"Deryn said when she called, 'Kim's behavior is so extreme. I know it's because we've been so wrapped up in our own grief, and Kim has needed us!'

"I told Deryn that her feelings were understandable, but I urged her not to blame herself or Peter. 'When you're in a crisis,' I told her, 'it's almost impossible to give to a child the way you normally would.'

"Yes, it was also a crisis for Kim, but as I explained, the fact that she had her parents' full attention and devotion for all of the preceding years would stand her in good stead now—and I would help them too.

"I set up an appointment for both parents, without Kim. In that session, I had Peter and Deryn tell me the entire story of Matthew's birth and death, with all the details they could remember about the day before, the day it happened, and the day after.

"They both cried as they talked about what a tough—and lonely—time it had been for them. 'I wish we'd talked more to each other,' Deryn said. Peter nodded and held her.

"Then we went over the details of Kim's questions, her various attempts to comfort her parents, her tension, and her new fear of being left alone in her room at night.

"I explained, 'Nighttime is when normal defenses are relaxed, and fear and sadness surface. For a young child, going to bed usually means separation. Going to sleep, to a preschooler, can seem almost like a nightly version of dying.

"'Of course, we expect to wake up again, but a little girl like Kim, who has lost her brother, may be afraid that she'll lose her mother or her father in the night—or that she herself will die.'

"Peter frowned. 'Are you sure? She hasn't seemed consistently upset.'

"I said, 'For adults, grief is usually constant and unrelenting, while for children it occurs in bursts that come and go. On the surface Kim seems okay, but I suspect she's been as deeply affected as you have.'

"I asked to see Kim, and the Colwells brought her in. They had explained to her that I was a doctor who talked to parents and kids about feelings and that, since they were all feeling sad and upset about Matthew's death, it would help them if we could all talk about what had happened.

"At first Kim sat quietly, but once she saw that her parents were comfortable talking to me about Matthew, she asked, 'Where *is* he?'

" 'I told you, in heaven,' Peter said.

" 'But where is *that?*' Kim asked.

"Peter and Deryn looked helplessly at each other. We talked some more, and later, when Kim was out of earshot, I said, 'Parents hate to share the pain of a death with a much loved child; but when you hedge, you convey anxiety.' I told them that before Kim could deal with Matthew's death emotionally, she needed more concrete answers.

"In our next session, instead of trying to comfort her with talk of angels and heaven, we discussed what had caused Matthew's death, how his body had stopped working, and how he wouldn't get hungry or cold or lonely under the ground.

"Finally we talked about the fact that death is irreversible and that Matthew can never come back, no matter how hard anybody wishes that he would.

"At my suggestion, the Colwells brought Kim back for one session alone, which proved very productive. Kim played with a dollhouse and a set of family dolls that consisted of two parents, a girl, and a boy.

"Kim quickly set the girl doll aside, explaining, 'She was bad and she died.' I asked Kim what the little girl had done that was so bad, and she answered without hesitation, 'She got mad at her brother for taking all her toys.'

" 'Sometimes brothers and sisters do have a hard time sharing, and they often get angry at each other,' I replied. 'But that doesn't mean that either one is bad or that one dies.'

" 'I know,' Kim said. 'But this mom and dad don't know it.'

" 'Why not?'

" 'Because they cry so much!'

"I told her, 'Moms and dads feel very sad when a child dies, even if it's a very little baby. But that doesn't take away from the love they feel for a big sister. And it *definitely* doesn't mean they think the big sister did anything wrong.'

"Kim suddenly became very busy sweeping the dollhouse with a little broom. 'But what if she didn't want her baby brother?' she asked, without looking up. 'What if she didn't want him to share her swing set?'

"I said, 'Lots of children don't want to have to share with a new baby, and they don't even know whether they're going to *like* the new baby.'

"Kim asked, 'Aren't Mommy and Daddy mad that Matthew died and I'm still here?'

"That was a powerful question, and I answered carefully: 'Do you know how much your mom and dad love you?' Kim nodded slowly. 'Their sadness about Matthew doesn't take away from their love for you,' I continued. 'But sometimes it's not easy to show love for one child when you're feeling so sad about another.'

"Kim sighed. 'I really *did* want the baby,' she said. 'But I didn't want him to have my stuff—or even that new teddy bear.' Kim looked ashamed. 'Lots of times, I wished that Mommy wasn't going to have a baby.'

"I said, 'Feelings can be very strong and very real, but they can't kill. And you know what? You can have a lot of very different kinds of feelings, all at the same time.'

"Kim looked relieved. 'Then this girl didn't die,' Kim said, picking up the dollhouse figure. 'She just went to sleep in her bed—and then she woke up in the morning!'

"Later I met Deryn and Peter, and we talked about how Kim's ambivalence toward the baby (both during the pregnancy and after) had translated into action in her mind. In the absence of much real information about what had happened to Matthew, she had drawn her own guilty conclusions.

"I told the Colwells that Kim will sometimes need to ask more

49

questions—not just now but in the future—about what really happened. She will also need continued reassurance from her parents that they love her as much as ever.

"I advised Deryn and Peter to try to be especially available to Kim at night rather than say, 'It's bedtime; we'll talk tomorrow.'

"I also recommended that the family do something special to memorialize Matthew, such as putting his birthday on the calendar or letting Kim make a book of pictures of things she would have wanted to show him.

"Life at home became more comfortable as Kim felt free to air what was on her mind; before long, she could once again easily fall asleep at night and not wake up until morning.

"In a final discussion, the Colwells and I talked about what they could expect in the future. 'I wouldn't say that everything is fully resolved,' I said. 'Kim may become anxious sometimes, especially when she's playing with dolls or visiting a friend with a baby. And if you become pregnant again, Kim will have many feelings to deal with, and it will be important for you to continue to talk.'

"The Colwells had tried to counter anxiety—both Kim's and their own—by softening the truth. But children need facts; and once we are able to level with them, we can help them make sense out of even life's most painful and confusing events."

It was an accident that killed our son Reed, but his brother, Larry, feels so guilty! We keep saying, "It wasn't your fault"—but can we ever reassure him enough?

Linda's Story

"It was the day after Christmas—one of those very cold mornings that seem to sparkle," said Linda Douglas, 34. "The boys—dressed in jeans and flannel shirts—had wolfed down their breakfast and were bugging me to take them to the skating rink. Reed, seven, had his first hockey stick, and Larry, eleven, had new skates.

"But when we got there, we found the rink was closed for repairs. 'Oh, drat!' Reed said. 'Hey! wait!' Larry had an idea: 'I bet the lake is frozen.' 'Well,' I thought, 'we could check.' Sure enough: the lake where we picnicked and fed the geese in the summertime was frozen solid.

" 'Awesome!' Reed shouted excitedly. 'Look, Larry. It's all ours.' He flung the car door open, and both boys were scrambling out.

" 'Just a second,' I called. 'Your grandma wanted to come by this morning. Let me just go call before . . . ' 'Oh, Mommy . . . ' Reed cried impatiently. 'Look,' I said. 'I guess you don't have to come. You can start to put your skates on, but *don't* go out on the ice until I come back and make sure it's safe.' 'Okay,' they called, eager for me to get going. '*We know.*'

"But when I got back, no more than five minutes later, I saw

51

Larry with his skates on, running toward me. 'Is that the way he treats his new blades?' I thought impatiently. But then I realized something was wrong! I looked around, but I couldn't find Reed.

"As Larry got closer, I could see that he was crying. 'Where's Reed?' I yelled. 'Where's your brother?' Larry cried harder and struggled to talk. 'Where is he?' I was growing frantic. 'WHERE IS REED?' 'He fell,' Larry gulped. 'Through the ice.'

" 'NO!' I screamed as I ran to the shore. I saw a big dark hole, about ten feet out. 'Oh, Larry. I *told* you to wait. You promised!' Wildly, I looked around for a branch—anything. But the ice was cracked; it was too risky. And I couldn't see any sign of Reed. Heart pounding, I left the car and ran the quarter mile back to the phone, Larry running after me. I dialed 911 and the police said, 'Wait by the phone.' In moments they were there with the rescue squad. Back at the lake they took some grappling equipment and almost immediately, they found Reed, unconscious, and wrapped him in a blanket.

"Suddenly I couldn't find Larry. I called him and called him, and then saw him, cowering behind a tree. 'Come on,' I said, grabbing his arm. 'They're taking Reed to the hospital and we're supposed to follow.'

"In the car, Larry said, 'Is he going to live?' 'I don't know,' I answered grimly. 'Let's not talk; let's just pray.'

"But Reed was dead on arrival. A tall nurse put her arm around me and said, 'Who else needs to know?' I had to call my husband, Gil, at his office.

" 'I'm at the hospital. It's Reed. Oh, Gil, it's so bad. Can you get here very quickly?' I was crying too hard to say anymore.

"As I put the phone down, I saw Larry, sitting on a bench in the waiting area. He still had his skates on and looked really petrified. I wanted to comfort him, but somehow I couldn't. When the nurse asked me if I wanted him with me, I shook my head. 'I can't now,' I said.

"She walked over to Larry, and I heard him ask her fearfully, 'Is my brother okay?' 'Honey, the doctors are trying their best,' the nurse answered.

"Gil got there fast, and trembling, I told him what had happened. Then Larry came over and said, 'Where is he?' 'I'm afraid he died,'

Gil answered softly. The three of us were silent on the way home. Back at home, Gil said, 'We've got to talk, Larry. Can you tell us how it happened?'

"Larry looked furtive. 'It wasn't my fault,' he said in a trembling voice. 'I tried to stop him.'

"'Why didn't you grab him?' I demanded. 'I didn't even hear you yell.' 'I *did* so yell,' Larry protested, wiping at his tears. 'I told him you'd be mad, but he just kept going. I even started to go after him, but I could see the ice cracking and I got scared. So I ran for Mom.' He paused, 'I want to know,' he asked shyly. 'What's going to happen to Reed?'

"'Not much,' I snapped. Gil put a calming hand on my shoulder. 'This is hard for all of us,' he said. 'You think it was all my fault,' Larry said. 'No, no,' Gil answered. 'Of course we don't blame you. It was just a very, very terrible accident.' But Larry—in tears—had bolted to his room.

"Larry wouldn't come out of his room for supper. 'Please, honey,' I called. 'Honestly! We know it wasn't your fault.' In my heart, I still thought, This accident should never have happened! But I also ached with compassion for Larry. Something horrendous had happened. He had seen it and hadn't been able to stop it. I could only imagine what he was going through—and how this day would haunt him, maybe for the rest of his life.

"Later in the evening, our neighbor, a clergyman stopped by. When I pointed to Larry's room and said, 'I'm scared for him,' he nodded and said, 'Me, too,' adding that we might find it helpful to talk with someone skilled in helping children cope with the death of a sibling. He gave me several names, and I decided to call one the next morning—for Larry's sake."

The Counselor Replies

Sandra S. Fox, A.C.S.W., Ph.D. (deceased), in human development with a master's in social work, was director of The Good Grief Program at the Judge Baker Children's Center in Boston.

"When Linda phoned, I praised her sensitivity in seeking help for Larry then, instead of waiting for ominous symptoms.

"I agreed with her: the fact that Larry was *there* at the lake when Reed died justified counseling. Linda asked if I would see him right away, but I said no, he doesn't need strangers today. I would see her and Gil as soon as they wanted, and I would see Larry sometime later. I believe that parents, first, and also teachers and other familiar adults are usually the most appropriate people to help their children through major crises. I would see the parents on a weekly basis and advise them, but I would only have them bring Larry with them now and then as long as he seemed to be okay.

"The Douglases' immediate concern was whether to let Larry come to the funeral home. Larry wanted to go, but many relatives and friends were lobbying against it.

"I said, 'I wouldn't force any child to go, but since Larry wants to, why not let him say good-bye?' I suggested that they take him over before the official visiting hours—so that Larry could have privacy as well as his parents' full attention.

"At the funeral home, Larry signed the guest book and asked if he could put Reed's rocket transformer toy in the casket. His parents said it was a good idea.

"By the New Year, I had seen Gil and Linda twice, but I had still not seen Larry. Now he was refusing to go back to school, so I suggested a conference for all of us, including Larry's teacher, Mrs. Roselli. 'I can't go back,' Larry told us, sounding desperate. 'Everyone's going to think it was my fault, and they'll all stare.'

" 'They will be curious,' I agreed. 'But you know what? You can decide whether to answer—or to say, "I don't feel like talking about it." ' Together, we came up with a plan: on the first day back, Linda would drive him, and Mrs. Roselli would be at school, by the front door to meet him.

"I said, 'Larry, probably something should be said to your class. Do you want to do that?' 'No!' he said. He wanted Mrs. Roselli to tell them. She agreed, and they planned the 'speech'—that this sad thing had happened in Larry's family, that Reed had died, and how it was hard for Larry to talk about it, but he would when he was ready. In the meantime he needed to know that his friends cared about him.

" 'But what if I cry? They'll think I'm a baby?' 'Not really,' I said. 'Maybe some people say that older boys aren't supposed to cry, but that's not true. Anyone who hurts, cries.' 'Even me, son,' Gil said.

" 'And, Larry,' Mrs. Roselli added. 'If you feel very sad and need to leave the classroom, you can go to the principal's office and there will be someone to sit with.'

"I was very happy to hear that the day went much better than Larry had expected. Kids did stare at first, but then everyone got busy, and several boys asked him to eat lunch with them. He called his mother and said, 'You don't have to pick me up. I can ride the bus home.'

"But as things went relatively smoothly at school, they were anything but smooth at home. 'We've told him not to feel responsible, but I think he still does,' Linda told me. Larry, she said, was having terrible nightmares—groaning and crying out, 'No! It's too cold!' in his sleep.

"Gil was disturbed by Larry's apathy. 'He's just so passive,' Gil said. Larry—a previously eager and energetic kid—was unwilling to take on the slightest responsibility, even refusing an easy three dollars for feeding the neighbors' cats when they went away for a week. 'I just don't want to risk it,' Larry told his father.

"The Douglases were also disturbed by the loss of closeness they felt with one another. Linda found she was furious with Gil because he wouldn't even look at the sympathy cards she kept by the bed and read constantly. 'Quit bugging me,' Gil would explode, turning his back. 'I don't need strangers to tell me what was special about my child.'

"Two months later the cards stopped coming, and Linda became very depressed. Some days, she didn't even get dressed, much less fix dinner, which made her feel guilty. Larry, sensing his mother's distress, tried to comfort her, but Linda could not accept it. 'I don't want to push him away,' she said, 'but I can't stand his hovering.'

"Meanwhile, Gil was trying hard to be the understanding one—after all he was the only one who *hadn't* been there that day. But it was hard: Larry grew sullen whenever Gil tried to draw him out about his feelings. And Gil was so sad every morning, that some days he didn't even go to work. Noting this, Linda began staying up nights, worrying that Gil would be fired.

" 'I guess we're falling apart,' Linda said, beginning to weep. But I said no, not at all!' This, I told the Douglases, is exactly what acute grief looks and feels like—the nightmares, the sense of isolation, the confusion and emptiness. It's all very normal.

"In addition, Gil and Linda were grieving out of synch with one another; when one had an 'up' day, the other was down—and vice versa—which left them both feeling misunderstood, resentful, and abandoned. 'This is very, *very* common,' I told them. 'In fact, research has shown that over 70% of the couples who lose a child have serious marital problems afterward.'

" 'Does it feel like this *forever*?' Linda asked. 'No!' I told the Douglases. 'A lot of this—like the nightmares—will go away soon. Acute grief goes on until we accomplish certain tasks. First we need to accept the reality of the death, next to experience the pain. The third task is to live in the world without the person you've lost, and the final task is to begin to be able to love and trust again, even if it's not the same world.'

"Linda frowned. 'Isn't there *anything* we can do that will help us get on with our lives?' 'Certainly,' I said. 'Be tolerant—both of yourselves and one another. Realize that there's no right or wrong way to go about healing. Do give yourselves permission to feel down. If you can't cook, send out or have sandwiches. If it's too hard to concentrate on work, then ask for a temporary leave. And as for Larry's trying to comfort you, don't just avoid him or suffer it in silence; instead, you might say, 'Larry, I appreciate what you're trying to do, but take care of *you*; don't think you have to take care of me.'

"Apparently that took some pressure off, and the Douglases were able to go out for a drive together or see a movie.

"But then, late in May, something happened in school. Larry, trying to focus the microscope in science class, brought it down too low and broke the slide. He burst into tears and ran from the classroom, sobbing, 'I can't do anything right.' Mrs. Roselli caught up with him and said, 'Larry, it's okay about the slide, but this tells me you're still having a hard time, and I'd like to tell your parents.' She did—and that afternoon, Linda called me.

"I, too, saw the incident as a sign that Larry had still not made peace with his own role the day his brother died. Despite his parents' loving and tactful insistence, 'It was an accident and we don't want you to feel bad,' Larry still blamed himself.

"In his mind, there was something he had done—or failed to

do—that day that was too terrible to talk about, but the secret had been building up inside him, and it had to come out before he could feel better.

" 'I blew it,' he said with a shrug. 'Reed would still be alive if it wasn't for me.' I listened—careful not to reassure him too fast. Larry needed to know that I (and his parents) could listen to whatever he had to say.

" 'You don't know the worst of it,' he went on, his eyes squeezed shut in anguish.

" 'Then tell me the worst part,' I said. 'I WASN'T WATCHING!' Larry cried. 'I was looking at a squirrel and I didn't even think about Reed . . . until he was already out there on the ice, too far for me to grab him back. Then I heard the ice cracking.' He hung his head. 'Now you all must hate me.'

" 'Oh, Larry!' Linda cried, running over to hug him. 'I'm the one who made a mistake! If anyone did wrong that day, it was me. You've always been *very* responsible, but you were only eleven, and I should never have left you in charge of such a rambunctious little boy. I guess we all use bad judgment at times, but usually we get away with it.'

"Larry looked astonished. His parents *knew*—and they still forgave him! 'You know, son,' Gil said. 'You had the good sense to run for Mom. That was smarter than trying to save him. How do you think we'd feel if we had lost both our sons? We think you're just fine, and you're going to be a good adult, too.'

"That session proved to be a turning point, as the Douglases could finally put the hows and whys to rest, and start moving forward. In June, Reed's second grade class donated several books on rockets to the library in Reed's memory. The whole family came to the ceremony. It was the first time they could share warm memories of Reed without the crushing sadness.

"The next week, Linda was finally able to pack up Reed's clothing and toys to donate to a center for the homeless. Larry helped. 'But I'd like to keep a few things for my own kids,' he said, and his parents were pleased.

"By the end of summer, Larry had become the official neighborhood dog-walker, cat-feeder, and plant-waterer for vacationing neighbors, and he was sharing a paper route.

"The following Christmas was predictably painful for the Douglases, but they went away to visit friends and they coped well. At that point we ended treatment, but I encouraged the Douglases to call on me at any time—not just with problems but with good news, too.

"Linda called one day in April and told me that Larry, now a seventh grader, had drawn Reed in art class. He had told the teacher that it used to be hard to talk about his brother's death, but now it was 'easy.' I was delighted. We as adults can talk about a child 'getting better,' but Larry's saying so himself was more convincing!

"It isn't easy for parents who are, themselves, going through enormous loss and grief to think about their child's needs; but the Douglases are a great example of the strength and generosity that parents can give a child . . . so that he *can* negotiate that long, painful, and often confusing process of healing."

> *Ryan, eight, has always been daring, but since the bus accident that killed a schoolmate, he's been taking worse risks. Is this his way of trying to master his fear—or does he actually want to get hurt?*

Linda's Story

"My husband, Max, says that Ryan's the same as always, but I see a change in him," said Linda Hobson, 33. "Sure, I realize we're talking about a kid who climbed his bookcase when he was fourteen months old and tried to drive to his grandmother's when he was five and always thought it was hilarious to take a flying jump from the sink to the overflowing bathtub. He's still driving us crazy, and we're still trying to keep his spirit of adventure from doing him in.

"But ever since the accident, Ryan's been taking different kinds of risks—risks that seem less joyful and are much more worrisome.

"The accident! It's hard for *me* to put it out of my mind, so it must be twenty times harder for Ryan, who was there when it happened. It was just a little more than a month ago, on the way to school, when Ryan's bus hit and killed a little boy named David O'Callahan. The driver (a fifteen-year veteran with a perfect safety record) swore that he saw David safely on the bus; actually David was still outside, picking up something he'd dropped.

"The driver knew he'd gone over 'something,' but he thought it was a rock . . . until he saw the feathers from David's down jacket flying up in the air.

"Ryan was very, very sad that night. But *why* did it happen?' he kept asking. 'David was *nice.*'

" 'Someone was careless, that's how it happened,' Max said grimly. 'In fact,' he went on, 'this is a perfect example of what we're always warning you about. I mean the way you're always climbing a fence or fooling around with some dog up the street instead of standing at the bus stop like you know you're supposed to.'

" 'Dad . . . '

" 'No, I've seen you,' Max persisted. 'The bus pulls up and honks, and you have to run to catch it, with your sneaker laces all undone to trip over. What happened to poor little David could have happened to you.'

"That night Ryan woke up with a nightmare. 'It was a bus crash,' he told me. 'And every single person on the bus got killed.' I held Ryan tightly as he cried.

"The next morning, I asked if he'd like to come to David's funeral with us, but he just shook his head. I didn't want to force him, but I think it would have been better if he had come. Ryan spent that morning at his baby-sitter's house. When he heard us coming to get him, he ran down her stairs in his socks—falling at the bottom and bumping his knee. 'You could have cracked your head open,' Max told him. 'Haven't we told you a hundred times not to run in your socks? Why can't you ever slow down, Ryan?'

"But instead of slowing down, Ryan kept doing more things to himself . . . like riding his bike where he shouldn't and falling off and chipping a tooth. 'You're being careless,' Max said. 'I'm all for adventure and having fun, but no kid has this many accidents unless he's just plain dizzy!'

" 'Maybe we shouldn't let him ride his bike at all,' I suggested.

" 'No.' Max shook his head. 'We can't seal him in plastic. He's got to learn. How is he ever going to make it in the world if he doesn't learn how to pace himself and how to take care of himself?'

"But I couldn't see that Ryan was learning any restraint or caution. One day, I walked into his room and caught him leaning way, way out his window. I grabbed him and yanked him back by his arm.

" 'Ow,' he said.

" 'You were about to fall out and get killed,' I told him. 'I don't

60

know what's been going on lately, but I don't want to be picking up pieces of you, that's for sure.'

"The next day, I saw him up on the top of our next-door neighbor's jungle gym—swaying there, not holding on. He said, 'I'm Superman.' I said, 'Just get down here.' And when he did, I sent him to his room.

"'He is really an accident waiting to happen,' I said to Mary Ellen, my neighbor. But she just laughed. 'Ryan's only eight,' she said. 'My boys had their share of scrapes and gashes and bumps and even a broken collarbone, but they all turned out okay, and so will Ryan.'

"Was I just being a worrywart? I didn't think so. On top of everything else, Ryan had received two warnings from his new school bus driver for yelling and climbing on the seats and sticking his head out the window.

"'You'd better stop that behavior right now,' Max told him. 'You may think it's a joke, Ryan, but if you distract the driver like that, you could cause another accident.'

"Ryan muttered that it wasn't his fault, that the bus driver picked on everyone.

"'He's just being careful,' Max said.

"'*Why is everyone so worried anyway?*' Ryan demanded.

"'Now I think I see what he's been up to,' Max said later that night, when Ryan had gone to bed. 'Did you hear the way he said, "Why is everyone so worried?" As if another child hadn't died in front of his eyes! Well, it happened, and it's obviously still on Ryan's mind because he's still having nightmares about it. Don't you see? I bet all of this is his eight-year-old macho way of denying what happened by saying, "Hey, *I'm* not scared."'

"'But what should we do? How can we stop it?'

"'We just have to accept it and let him be a little brash and dangerous for a while . . . until he gets that helpless feeling out of his system. He's a smart kid, and I think we can trust that he has the sense not to go *too* far.'

"Max's theory made sense—or at least I thought so until the following Friday afternoon. I'd picked Ryan up at a birthday party and had to stop at the repair shop on the way home to get our vacuum cleaner.

"Ryan wanted to stay in the car and listen to the radio instead of

61

coming in. 'Okay,' I said. 'I'll just be a minute.' But as I waited for the clerk to find our vacuum, I heard a commotion outside and went to look.

"There, unbelievably, was Ryan—standing right in the middle of the fast-moving traffic as drivers swerved sharply to avoid him. One driver stopped just inches from Ryan, rolled down his window, yelling, 'Wanna *die*, kid?' and made an obscene gesture before speeding off.

" 'Ryan!' I screamed. I got outside just as the light changed and the cars slowed to a stop. 'Why did you cross that big, dangerous street—*and against the light?*' My voice was a terrified croak.

" 'I just wanted to look in that video store,' Ryan said calmly—as if that could explain or justify the fact that he had just risked his life.

"I'm absolutely terrified! I don't know if Max is right or not about why Ryan's doing all these things, but at this point, I know that Ryan is in serious trouble and that we need help."

The Counselor Replies

Sandra S. Fox, A.C.S.W., Ph.D. (deceased), was director of The Good Grief Program, a bereavement program, at the Judge Baker Children's Center in Boston.

"I met with Mr. and Mrs. Hobson, and they filled me in on their son's early history, the school bus accident, and the trouble that Ryan had gotten into since then—including the incident near the vacuum shop. 'It was such a senseless thing to do,' Linda said with a shudder. 'Unless he actually *wanted* the cars to hit him.'

" 'Well, you are right to seek help,' I assured her at the end of the session. 'I'd like to meet with Ryan and see if we can reduce his risk-taking behavior and also understand what might be causing it.'

"When Ryan did come in, he was hesitant to talk, at first. I said, 'It sounds like you've been doing some scary things. Your parents are worried and don't want anything bad to happen to you.' I also mentioned that I knew about the school bus accident. 'Could you draw it?' I asked.

"Ryan nodded and drew an elaborate picture of a bus on fire

with a child lying under it, flat as a pancake. 'Too bad that kid didn't follow the rules,' he said. In that session and the two that followed I could see that Ryan was confused over how—and why—the accident had actually happened. But through his drawings and play one strong theme emerged, and that was that you have an accident when you're bad and don't behave correctly.

"Ryan seemed to believe that people who don't follow rules *deserve* to have accidents and get hurt—that, in effect, the injury they receive is their punishment. But here was a big problem for Ryan: David, the boy who died, had been obedient and quiet, while Ryan, the 'wild caveman,' as his parents called him, hadn't been hurt in any way.

"Ryan seemed to have gotten the message that the world is a dangerous place in which you follow the rules or you are bad and must be punished—severely. And since Ryan saw himself as bad and unable to follow rules, he had been—and apparently was still—going around inviting the worst to happen.

"With Ryan's permission, I showed Max and Linda some of his drawings, and they noticed, as I had, that the victim of all the lurid accidents he drew was starting to look more and more like Ryan.

" 'Does that mean he's trying to hurt himself?' Linda asked.

" 'He might be, and that's why you will need to watch him pretty carefully until he's worked this through,' I said. 'But there are things you can both do to help Ryan feel less guilty—and be less self-punishing.'

" 'Well, what do we do when he doesn't follow rules and gets too rambunctious?' Max asked. 'We try to let him have the freedom a child needs. But when he goes too far, we have to crack down. We have to punish him. Otherwise we wouldn't be doing our job as parents.'

"I said, 'Perhaps the key here is setting limits: discussing and figuring out and defining just how far you feel he can safely go. You need to work that out—and then convey it to Ryan—but *not* with punishment or by threatening him.'

"For example, I suggested that instead of an angry 'Don't jump off that high board, you could drown,' a better approach might be, 'Ryan, you need to swim in the shallow end of the pool until you pass the test and the lifeguard okays you to swim in the deep end.'

"I told the Hobsons that simply reminding Ryan not to run down slippery stairs in his socks would be more effective than highlighting the gruesome accident he could have.

"I said, 'The idea is to help Ryan build in his own controls. But that is a slow, gradual process, in which he will need a lot of parental guidance.'

"Over the next several weeks, some important changes took place: In one of our sessions, Ryan said, 'How come my mom and dad get so mad when I have fun?' That gave me an opportunity to discuss safe fun and dangerous fun, and how—especially when you're young—it's hard to tell one from the other. 'That's what safety rules are for,' I told him. 'Sometimes even when we're careful, accidents happen, but *that doesn't mean that the victim deserves it.*'

"At home, the Hobsons outlined specific rules about where Ryan could and couldn't go on his bike. They even made a map and put it on the refrigerator so there'd be no confusion. After a week, Ryan 'forgot' and ended up on a steep, curving road with fast traffic that was definitely off his list of safe routes.

"Calmly and with no anger (nor any conjectures on what could have happened), Max took the bike away and said, 'Ryan, eventually you'll be able to ride wherever you want, but not yet. You can have your bike back as soon as you can remember where you are—and where you aren't—allowed to ride.'

"Linda had another good idea—signing Ryan up for a gymnastics class at the local Y. There, Ryan could have fun and test himself by climbing ropes, using a trampoline, and balancing on a narrow beam, all with padding on the floor and under the careful watch of a skilled instructor.

" 'This is great,' I said, 'you're breaking the equation now in Ryan's mind that brash or wild behavior automatically deserves punishment. Ryan, after all, is a curious, bright, and active little boy, and he'll make some mistakes. You and he will have to work together. But now, more than ever, he needs to know that he doesn't deserve to be punished in the ways he's been worrying about.'

"Right around then, Ryan's nightmares stopped, and he started to talk a great deal about David, the little boy who had died. Ryan expressed regret that he hadn't gone to the funeral. 'I was scared to,' he admitted. Apparently Ryan had not felt able to face David's parents before. But now he asked if it was too late for him to make them a card.

"I assured him that it was never too late to do something so kind. Ryan drew a picture of two boys. 'That is me and David,' he wrote at the top. 'We were friends.' At his request, Linda took Ryan over to deliver the note personally, and David's mother gave Ryan a hug. 'He admired you a lot,' she said. Ryan felt really good.

"To everyone's relief, Ryan's behavior improved by 'at least 200 percent,' according to his mother. Ryan, she said, was still energetic, eager, and sometimes quite exasperating, but now it seemed more like normal, active kid's stuff than panic material. 'I guess he will always have 50 more things to do than he's ready for,' she remarked.

"When Ryan's ninth birthday came, his parents got him a large and boisterous black puppy. Ryan was ecstatic and showed impressive responsibility in caring for Blackberry.

" 'Ryan did forget to feed him once,' Max told me. 'I was tempted to warn him that the dog could starve to death, but I stopped myself and said, "Ry, Blackberry's dish looks empty to me . . . ," and Ryan went down to the basement and fed him, and he hasn't forgotten since.'

"And there was another bonus: In helping to watch that Blackberry doesn't run out into traffic, Ryan has begun to see safety from a different perspective. And as a result, Ryan has calmed down both on the school bus and at the bus stop.

"When we see a child's behavior out of control, it's sometimes hard to know if he's doing what he's doing out of foolish bravery or out of fear. But once the Hobsons got to the bottom of the problem, they were able to give Ryan just the kind of support that he needed, and you can't ask for more than that."

My husband Alex's death was a terrible blow, and I'm afraid that Patty, eight, isn't getting over it. Will time and therapy lessen the pain—or is a father's suicide one hurt that never goes away?

Mia's Story

"Right after it happened, I thought we were doing so well," said Mia Browne, 33. "I fell apart—briefly—but Patty didn't. Even at Alex's funeral, she was calm and brave, and I thought, Yes, we'll make it through this!

"We'd already been through a lot in the past three years, watching a wonderful, loving husband and father sink into deep, unrelenting sadness. 'I'm worthless,' he would say. I tried so hard to convince him that it wasn't true. 'You and Patty would be better off without me,' he insisted over and over again.

"Alarmed, I made him go for help, and he was hospitalized. That was when I learned that depression could be traced back three generations in his family. 'It's genetically loaded,' the doctor said. 'Your husband needs to be on medication.'

"Alex did well on the antidepressant, but two months later, as soon as he came home and was feeling better, he threw the rest of his pills away. 'I'm okay now,' he said. 'Can't you believe me?' And for a short time he did seem calmer, but that must have been only because he'd made his decision to die. Several days later, he went to his office—and shot himself with a hunting rifle.

"Telling Patty was so hard—the hardest thing I've ever had to do. I was tempted to pretend it was a heart attack or at least an accident. But then I realized it would only be more traumatic later, when she learned the truth. So I told her, 'Daddy was very, very sad, and so he decided to end his life.' I stressed that it was nobody's fault, and I assured her that I was still here to take care of her—no matter what—and we would be fine.

"Patty was terrific! I had been working part-time as a nurse, but now I had to work full-time, which meant after-school care for Patty. I felt terrible, but I'd always get a big hug from her—with no resentment or complaints.

" 'I'm proud of you,' I told her, and Patty beamed. But in June, once school was over, I noticed that she wasn't seeing her friends. 'I just want to be with you,' she'd say on the weekends. One week, I was home with the flu, and Patty insisted on staying home to heat up my soup. She proudly brought it in on a tray with a pretty doily she had made out of a paper towel.

" 'Mom, are you okay?' she asked anxiously. 'Yes,' I assured her. Seeing the worried look on her face, I said, 'I'm *not* going to die, honey.' But even after I was well, Patty stuck close by me.

"The time we spent together was precious. But when Patty's birthday came and she didn't want to invite even one friend over, I grew concerned. 'I don't want anybody,' Patty said, in contrast to the year before, when our problem had been limiting the number of friends.

"I said, 'Okay, we'll have a special dinner out—just the two of us.' We went to a Chinese restaurant where the drinks had little umbrellas in them, and ordered a platter of spareribs, some shrimp toast, and morsels of chicken in foil we cooked on skewers in a flame right on our table.

"It was fun—until I said, 'Wouldn't Daddy have liked this place?' Patty stiffened. Her face got blotchy and she turned away. 'It's okay to cry,' I said gently, but she shook her head and pushed her chair back. 'I'm done,' she said. 'Can we go home how?'

"Clearly, talking about Alex was still too painful for Patty, and although it would have made *me* feel better to see her let it out instead of holding in her feelings, I didn't see any point in pushing.

"Was she denying what had happened? That was how my sister, Jenny, saw it. 'Children mourn in their own way,' Jenny said when I telephoned her in Florida, where she lived.

"I tried not to worry, even when I overheard Patty lie to a new kid across the street, saying, 'My parents are divorced too. I might visit my dad this summer.' Knowing I'd overheard, Patty explained, 'Mom, I *had* to say that.'

" 'But why? I told you there's nothing to be ashamed of.'

" 'I know that,' Patty said, 'but the kids act weird.' Patty kicked at some stones. 'I know they're sometimes talking about me because they stop when I get near them.'

" 'Honey, are you sure you're not just imagining . . . ?'

" '*No!*' Patty insisted.

" 'Can't you ignore them?'

" 'I do!' Patty said. 'And don't worry. There's lots of things I can do by myself this summer. I don't need that bunch of dweebs.'

" 'She may have outgrown her old friends,' Jenny suggested. 'After all, look at all she's been through—and look at what *their* big concerns are: TV? New toys?'

"Perhaps Jenny was right, but as the weeks passed, I found myself worrying more and more often. I had taken time off to be with Patty, but she spent most of the time reading in her room.

" 'I thought you missed me, but when I'm here you ignore me,' I said, only half joking. Patty threw her arms around me. 'I *am* glad you're home,' she said. But later, when we went to the lake for a picnic and a swim, I felt as though she was doing it only to humor me.

" 'I had fun,' she said, slouched down beside me, her face barely visible under one of Alex's old tennis hats. 'Really! I had the best time.' She looked up, and her eyes were pleading: Believe me, believe me! Why did her words sound so hollow? She's *depressed*, I thought chillingly. That's why Patty isn't having any fun or hanging out with her friends.

" 'Don't get hysterical,' Jenny scolded me. 'How could Patty not be depressed in that house where the three of you lived? It's got to be hard for you, too, Mia. You could come to Florida—stay with us until you find a place. Nurses are in such demand down here, you could write your own ticket.'

"It sounded so tempting, and as soon as she said it, I knew she was right. I had been naive to think that we could ever get on with our lives as long as every room, every nook and cranny, held reminders of Alex—not just the funny, lovable, endearing Alex, but the bitter, hopeless stranger he had eventually become.

" 'Guess what?' I told Patty excitedly. 'How would you like to move to Florida? We could stay with Aunt Jenny, and you'd have Uncle George and all your cousins to horse around with—and you could swim every day, all year long. Imagine that!'

"Patty just stared. 'For real?' she asked. 'Yes!' I said, hugging her. 'It would be like being on vacation all the time . . . and no flu season! And another thing,' I said. 'It would be a fresh start with all new friends.'

" 'But do you want to?' Patty asked cautiously.

" 'Of course!'

" 'Then let's. I can't wait!'

"After that, it seemed as if we spent every spare moment fixing up our house to sell it, putting aside unneeded items for a garage sale, and contacting hospitals and nursing homes within commuting distance of Jenny's house about possible jobs.

"We set up the garage sale, and to my delight, it was well attended, with lots of people eagerly buying the furniture and other 'junk' we weren't planning to take with us.

"Patty helped all morning, but by noon she seemed tired and edgy, so I urged her to take a break. She did leave, only to come back a moment later. 'Stop! You *can't* take that!' she cried suddenly, grabbing an old, chipped vase out of an astonished woman's hands.

" 'Patty?' I tried to reach her, but she ducked away. And before I could stop her, she threw the vase to the ground, smashing it to pieces.

"Murmuring and shaking their heads, the customers hurried away to their cars. A boy about Patty's age whispered loudly, 'Mom, is *she* crazy too, like her dad?' Patty kicked at pieces of the broken vase and ran into the house.

"I was shocked and scared. Was this a normal part of Patty's mourning—or something more frightening? One thing was certain: My Patty needed help."

The Counselor Replies

Elizabeth B. Weller, M.D., is professor of psychiatry and pediatrics at The Ohio State University College of Medicine, in Columbus. She is also head of the Division of Child and Adolescent Psychiatry and a coauthor of Psychiatric Disorders in Children and Adolescents *(W.B. Saunders Co.).*

"Mia was very concerned as she was telling me the story. I agreed to see Patty right away. I said, 'We'll see what's going on, but if Patty was in sound emotional health before your husband's death, that's a hopeful sign.'

"Nor was I any less optimistic when I met Patty the following day. She was a pretty, well-groomed, and polite little girl who looked very sad. In my office, she had no trouble separating from her mother. When I mentioned her father, she started to cry. She then stopped herself. I told her it was okay to cry. 'No!' she said. 'I've got to be brave—for Mommy.'

"I assured her that she didn't need to be brave for me, that this was a safe place for her to let go of all the feelings she'd been holding back. She burst into tears again and began to tell me how her dad had died and how ever since it happened she had felt terrible.

"I asked, 'Have you told your mom how sad you are?'

" 'Oh, no!' Patty said, wiping her eyes. 'She has enough problems, and she has to work so hard.' Patty said that sometimes she had a nightmare that her mom was dying. 'If only things could be like they used to,' Patty sighed. Over our next few sessions, she talked more about her fears and memories.

" 'Sometimes,' she said during one session, 'when it's dark at night, I think I really see my dad—and it's so nice.' Patty's face clouded. 'Does that mean I'm crazy?'

" 'Absolutely not,' I assured her. 'That's normal, and it just means you miss him and wish he were here.' Patty looked relieved and smiled.

" 'What do you miss most about your dad?' I asked.

" 'Oh,' she said, smiling, 'the hugs! Daddy had a mustache, and it always tickled when he kissed me. We used to go for walks and bike rides, and on Sunday mornings we always made pancakes together, and Mom said they were the best.'

"Now she looked troubled again. 'Do you think if I really wished hard, he'd come back?' she asked.

" 'When somebody dies, he can't come back, but you can hold on to the good memories,' I offered.

" 'But what if I grow up and forget about him?'

"I said, 'I don't think you will,' and suggested that she keep a diary of memories that she could illustrate with drawings and photographs.

"Patty nodded. Then she said, 'If I had done better in school and kept my room neater, then Daddy wouldn't have been so sad.'

" 'Patty,' I replied, 'there was nothing you could have done to help him.' I explained that her father had a serious illness called depression. 'He was very sick,' I said, 'and when somebody is sick and his brain is involved, he gets confused. That was why your daddy did what he did.'

" 'Did he hate us?' Patty asked.

" 'Oh, no!' I said. 'He didn't die *because* of you. When you're sick, you don't reason right. He made some wrong choices. In fact, he might have decided to end his life much sooner if he hadn't loved you. Your mother told me how much he loved you—how he called you his special, wonderful daughter.'

" 'I know he did love me,' she agreed. 'And I loved him! That's why I want to see him. I've even thought about killing myself so we could be together in heaven, but I don't want to die—or leave my mom. But I wish I could see him. I didn't even get to say good-bye to him.'

"Patty had shared a lot of her feelings, and I told Mia what a productive session we'd had. 'I'm so glad—but I'm surprised,' she said. 'She's always reticent with me, and yet she has poured her heart out to a total stranger like you.'

" 'It's *because* I'm a stranger that she feels free to do so,' I explained. 'Patty knows she doesn't have to protect me, because she knows I won't fall apart.'

" 'Does she think I would?'

" 'In a way, yes. Like any child who has lost a parent to suicide, Patty believes she was somehow responsible for her father's death. She's scared that if she isn't careful, she might make *you* feel so sad and overburdened that you would leave her too.'

"I suggested that Patty could now benefit from therapy—to air her feelings. And it would be a way we could keep an eye on her. Mia agreed, and I began seeing Patty weekly.

"During those sessions, Patty talked a lot about her life. She started the diary of memories that I'd suggested, and she found that while many were happy, others were sad and worrisome. Patty remembered her father's erratic moods and how anxious she had often been about him. 'That was hard,' she said, and wondered if now it was 'okay' to feel relieved that she didn't have to worry anymore.

"I said, 'Sure! It's scary even for grown-ups to live with someone whose moods are so unpredictable. *Anyone* in your shoes would feel very sad—but also relieved at the same time.'

"Throughout our sessions, Patty expressed continuing concern for her mother—panicking if Mia was even a little bit late coming home from work for example. 'What if my mom dies? What will happen to me then?' Patty asked.

"I said, 'I don't think it's going to happen, but let's think, What if . . .?' In a joint session with Mia, we discussed that worst-case scenario and what would happen to Patty. Would she live with her grandparents? ('No,' Patty said firmly. 'They're too old, and they might die.')

"Patty said, 'If Mommy dies, I'd like to go live with Aunt Jenny—but not *now!* I don't want to move to Florida.' Hearing this, Mia agreed not to move, at least not in the near future, in order to avoid more stress for Patty.

"Mia said the idea to move had been for Patty's sake. Now she realized that it wouldn't be helpful and agreed to scrap the moving plans.

"This discussion helped Patty regain a sense of control over her destiny and also showed her that there was a backup system to protect her, as well as people out there who cared about her.

" 'Now I see why just reassuring her that nothing would ever happen to me was not enough,' Mia said.

"By the time school started, Patty felt much more relaxed. Her feeling that she always had to prop up her mother was less overwhelming, and at the same time, she was learning to let go of feeling even partially responsible for her father's death.

"But she was still very isolated from the children who had been her friends. Part of it came from Patty herself, since she felt jealous of kids with two parents, and left out. But she was also aware of the rumors that her father had been 'crazy.'

"I suggested, 'Why don't you pick one friend you used to like and trust and see if you can make contact?' I said that maybe Mia could talk to the other girl's mom.

"Patty tried it with her friend Rebecca, who confessed, 'I've missed you, but I didn't know what to say to you, so I didn't say anything.'

" 'But she's just one,' Patty said sadly. 'I can't explain to everyone; it would take too long.' Patty asked whether I could come and talk to her class. I said, 'Why not?' and with her teacher's permission, I did just that.

"The fourth-grade class was very attentive, and very interested in what I had to say. Every one of them had heard of a suicide other than Patty's father. One boy mentioned an uncle, another a neighbor. 'Don't you have to be crazy to kill yourself?' a girl named Amber asked.

"I said, 'No, it's an illness that affects the brain, but if the person gets into treatment, we can usually help him function normally.'

" 'Is it catching, like AIDS?' another child wondered. I said, 'No, not at all,' and I could see many children breathe a sigh of relief.

" 'I'd like to learn about the brain,' Rebecca ventured. 'Why *do* people like Patty's dad think differently—and how can we help them stop it?'

"Afterward, Patty thanked me. 'I think I'd like to be a psychiatrist too,' she said. 'I'd like to be like you and help kids. I think I'd be good at that.'

"Patty continued to feel better, but one day in December she came in quite distraught. 'Mom had a date,' she complained. It was clear that it had been a very casual date and that Mia had been home by eight o'clock.

" 'But what if she gets married?' Patty asked. 'I don't want her to date! That's unfair to Dad.'

"Once again, I arranged a joint session with Mia and Patty to clarify Mia's intentions. 'I'm not really dating yet,' Mia said. 'Todd's just a friend.'

" 'But what if someone else comes along?' Patty wasn't giving up. Mia said, 'You're right, I might fall in love some day.' Patty's face fell. 'But, Patty,' she went on, 'I promise you that anyone I marry would have to be a very good person . . . And also, I can tell you right now, nobody will ever take the place of your father.'

"By early spring I saw a lot of progress. Patty felt better about herself and shared her feelings more easily with her mother and her friends. 'Perhaps you don't need to come in every week anymore,' I suggested.

" 'You mean not ever see you again?' Patty looked stricken.

" 'No!' I told her. I would still want to see her at special times like her birthday, her dad's birthday, and the anniversary of his death.

" 'And for an even longer time,' I said, 'I'd like to see you at least once a year so I know that you're okay.'

" 'Oh, *good!*' Patty said. 'Then I'll always know you, and I won't have to lose you.'

"I felt that this was a very good outcome. Still, I warned Mia that Patty might experience more difficulties during adolescence. 'Patty's still a child now, and she may need help making sense of her loss in a different, more mature way later on.'

"It probably won't be all smooth sailing for the Brownes. Small losses will remind them of what they've gone through and will feel like big ones. But those shake-ups will show them that they can survive and have a life full of love and meaning."

*My daughter, Sarah, had wanted
me to marry Michael after his
family died . . . But now she seems
so edgy and upset. Had I been wrong
to think we could find our happiness
in someone else's tragedy?*

Margo's Story

"I wasn't looking for a second husband," said Margo, a warm, energetic woman of 35. "My first marriage, to John, had been a long-ago disaster, but I just hadn't found a man who was interesting to me *and* could relate to kids. Besides, my life was full—or almost full—enough between my interesting job in the city's consumer affairs department and Sarah, my bright and pretty little blond tornado of a daughter.

"Sarah, who just turned seven, doesn't remember her father, but she's felt deprived ever since she noticed her playmates had moms *and* dads. Her birthday wishes were always for a daddy, and sometimes I would see her looking at someone else's father with a certain longing.

"That was how she looked at Michael Turner, a tall, tweedy man of 40 whom we saw in the park with his 6-year-old daughter, Carly. I could see why Sarah liked Michael. I admired him, too. He was a well-known illustrator, but he was also a fun, wonderful father, who loved children.

"When Sarah said, 'I wish he was my dad instead of dumb old

Carly's,' I tweaked her nose and said, 'Come on, it's not nice to be jealous.' I didn't see the point in her pining over a man who was happily married to a beautiful photographer named Joan. In fact, Michael Turner was a living testimony to the old cliche that 'all the good ones are taken.'

"I didn't know how soon fate would change all that! One rainy Friday at about 5:30 P.M., Joan picked Carly up at a birthday party. They were crossing the street when a speeding taxi ran a red light and slammed into them. Both mother and daughter died in the ambulance on the way to the hospital. I was so shocked—I couldn't believe it. We were all grieving, the whole neighborhood; but while the others sent flowers and notes, they kept a distance from Michael. Nobody wanted to intrude on his grief.

"I was different. Perhaps it was remembering how isolated my sister, Ann, had felt when her baby died of SIDS and her friends were too broken up and uncomfortable even to talk to her. I went to Michael and told him how badly I felt and how I wanted to help. Even Sarah made him a sympathy card with a lot of flowers on it and two angels, one big and one small.

"He was very grateful and welcomed our company—especially on weekends when he didn't have his work to distract him. Then he started dropping in on his way home, and it soon felt natural to cook for three every evening—or Michael would make Sarah happy by bringing pizza.

"After Sarah went to bed, Michael would stay awhile to talk. He said. 'I want to remember all the good things I had with Joan and Carly.' He felt that if he let himself sink into feeling angry and sorry for himself, he would lose his will to live altogether. 'I just need to keep a positive attitude,' he said. 'You don't know how much you and Sarah are helping me.'

"Sarah loved having Michael around—she was more bubbly than ever. One Saturday, we were watching the seals at The Bronx Zoo when she said, 'Michael, will you marry my mom?' We all laughed—I was embarrassed—but Michael said, 'I think that's a pretty nice offer.' Late that evening, he took me in his arms and kissed me, gently and deeply. He said, 'I love you, Margo.' 'I love you, too,' I blurted out—and it was true! In six short months, I had grown to love him with all my heart.

"When Sarah saw how things had changed between Michael and me, she was ecstatic. 'You're getting *married!*' she squealed. 'YIP-PEE! Now I'll have my own dad!' Michael wanted to get married right away. I said, 'Isn't this too soon?' But in my heart, I felt like I'd known him forever. Besides our love for each other, Sarah's joy convinced me *not* to wait. And five weeks later, we were married.

"Michael sublet his apartment and moved into our sunny and spacious one. I was a little surprised that he didn't bring any photographs of Joan and Carly along, nor any keepsakes. I thought it showed incredible tact.

"Life was wonderful! I loved Michael so. Sarah was on a pink cloud—and how she enjoyed it when Michael picked her up at dancing class and she could say, '*This* is my *daddy!*' And Michael was obviously basking in the joy of being a father again.

"You mean you haven't had *any* adjustment problems?' my sister, Ann, asked me incredulously as she helped me prepare an Easter dinner. I shook my head and smiled. We both laughed and she hugged me. 'That's great!' she said. 'You deserve it; so does Sarah.'

"Of course there was one thing I hadn't mentioned. It seemed like a small problem; I didn't even know if it *was* a problem—just that Sarah had started having a little trouble sleeping. I guess it had started about three months after Michael moved in.

"She would wander out of her room—something she had never done before—and say, 'Can't sleep, Mom.' I'd ask her what was wrong, and she'd say, 'Nothing.' I'd say, 'Are you unhappy or worried about something?' and she'd just shake her head. And was it my imagination, or had she also become much more self-critical?—getting tense and even bursting into tears if she made a mistake on her homework.

" 'Oh, come on, let her go through a phase or two,' Michael joked. And I thought, yes, I'm probably worrying for nothing. But when it was time for a conference with Sarah's teacher, I went in expecting the usual raves about how bright and eager she was. This time, however, the teacher frowned and mentioned a lot of daydreaming, in-attentiveness, and small accidents like cutting herself with scissors. 'You know, I've seen other children appear distracted when they're blending into a new stepfamily.' 'Thanks,' I said. 'But it's not like that. Sarah's our only child.'

"That night, Sarah was still up when I got home. 'Is it true that bad people who steal have to go to jail?' she demanded. 'Yes, of course,' I said. A neighbor had been burglarized the week before. Sarah knew that they *had* caught the man, and he was in jail. But she didn't look reassured.

"Hearing about the burglary must have been traumatic for Sarah because she kept referring to crooks and jails in the weeks that followed, and her sleeping got worse. Some nights, if I happened to wake up at two or three, I would hear her opening and closing her closet. If I went in, she would jump onto her bed and pretend to be asleep.

"In the daytime, I found her growing more subdued, less eager to play. What I couldn't understand was why she was reacting with such fear *now* when news of other burglaries in the past had not affected her, and when finally, for the first time ever, we had a man in the family to protect us.

"I began to wonder if her fear had something to do with Michael himself. But that made no sense. Michael was not the type to act seductive or parade around in an open robe. He also never lost his temper with Sarah, never scolded or punished her—even when *I* thought she deserved to be reprimanded: like the time she borrowed some of his art supplies without permission and spilled turpentine all over a magazine layout he was working on.

"I guess I knew that something was really wrong when the hamster incident happened. It was Sarah's turn to bring Mookie, the class hamster, home for the long Columbus Day weekend, and I was pleased to see her enthusiasm as she ceremoniously served him his lettuce and carrots.

"But Sunday morning, Sarah didn't want me to come into her room, and it wasn't until bedtime that I caught a glimpse of Mookie, lying dead on the bottom of his cage. 'Mommy, it's not my fault,' Sarah shouted, trying to push me out the door.

"Michael and I tried to comfort her, to reassure her, but she kept sobbing, and now I was certain that something was bothering my daughter—something she couldn't explain to me. With some trepidation—and hope—I called our family doctor and was given the name of a therapist. I just hoped she could help."

The Counselor Replies

Janice I. Cohn, D.S.W., chief of consultation and education in the Department of Psychiatry, Newark–Beth Israel Medical Center, in New Jersey, is in private practice in New York City and Montclair, New Jersey. She is also the author of I Had a Friend Named Peter: Talking to Children About the Death of a Friend *(William Morrow and Co. Inc.).*

"When Margo called me, I was impressed with her sensitivity and astuteness in recognizing that Sarah was struggling with something that was more than just a passing phase. I said, 'Parents have the best radar,' and asked if she would like to bring Sarah to see me. She readily agreed.

"Sarah, a bright and self-possessed seven-year-old, came in and looked at me shyly. 'I know I'm supposed to talk to you,' she said, 'but I don't have anything to say.'

" 'You don't have to!' I assured her. I showed her the many toys and dolls I keep in my office, and told her that this would be her special time to come each week and do what she wanted to do—talking or not talking, and maybe we could get to know one another.

"Sarah seemed to like that idea. She zeroed right in on the dollhouse, and very soon, I saw a pattern emerging: she would use the little dolls to act out a story, which was always about a bad person who was jealous of the princess, stole all her gold, and went to jail. Sometimes the bad person only had to think about the gold to get it.

"Margo had mentioned Sarah's recent fear of burglary, but I soon began to suspect that Sarah's fear centered more on the punishment than on the crime . . . which tipped me off to the fact that she was feeling guilty! I had a hunch that Sarah felt guilty for having stolen Michael from his daughter, Carly, but I needed to know more.

"Keeping the conversation 'safely' about the dolls rather than about Sarah, I asked her how the 'bad' dolls felt about the punishments that Sarah gave them, which were indeed cruel: some were left alone with no food or warm bed; others were informed that

79

they had to stay in jail forever because their parents didn't want them back. 'They were very bad, so they deserve it,' Sarah insisted.

"Gently, I encouraged her to explore the difference between actually stealing and wishing for something someone else has. She had thought they were the same. 'Wishing really doesn't make things happen,' I explained. 'We are not that powerful.' I told her that if wishing worked, then nothing bad would happen to anyone, because we would all wish only for good things.

"I also explained coincidence . . . the idea that sometimes nice things happen to us out of sad things, but that doesn't mean that *wanting* the nice thing *made* the sad thing happen.

"As we got better acquainted, the weekly play session and the dollhouse folks became an important outlet for Sarah's bottled-up feelings . . . the feelings Sarah had been too troubled to express at home. Margo and Michael were loving and supportive, but Sarah had still felt guilty—believing that her old crush on Michael had in some way caused the accident—and afraid that Michael would 'find out' and be so angry that he would leave and take Margo away, too.

"As Sarah felt more and more comfortable with me, she allowed me to share in making up the doll-play stories. Gently, I encouraged her to think about the needs and feelings of those so-called bad dolls, and as a result she began to experiment with a different kind of ending for her story. Instead of suffering, the little doll would sometimes be forgiven by the grown-ups . . . or would realize that the Bad Thing that happened really *was* an accident and *not* his or her fault.

"I was gratified to learn from Margo that Sarah had begun to concentrate better at school, and at home she was not only sleeping much better but also showing more of her old zest and self-confidence.

"When Sarah mentioned a new class hamster, I encouraged her to volunteer to take it home. She said, 'I'm scared it'll die,' but we talked about how she had done all the right things with Mookie and hadn't caused him to die, that it was, in fact, just coincidence that Mookie had been at her house when he died. At last, she did take Daryl, the new hamster, home and reported proudly that 'his fur got even shinier at my house.'

"During these weeks, I was also meeting regularly with Margo and Michael, not only to convey and interpret what was going on with Sarah but also to give the adults an opportunity to work through their own concerns.

" 'I guess it was my fault for getting married on such a quick rebound,' Michael said unhappily. I told him it was both understandable and very loving of him and of Margo to have wanted to be a family together without delay. Michael acknowledged that he had fallen in love with Margo very quickly—not only because she was a lovely, sympathetic woman with whom he had a lot in common but also because he was in so much pain.

"For the first time in months, he broke down and cried. Now, I told him gently, he would need to confront his own grief and loss, which he had put on hold. It wouldn't be easy—for him or for Margo—as memories of Joan and Carly would come flooding back, but only in doing so would he be free really to let go of the past.

"I encouraged Michael to let Sarah know that he did miss Carly and always would—but that he also loved Sarah very much. One day, when Sarah was mad at herself for a mistake, he sat her down and said, 'You know, Carly did lots of things wrong, and we still loved her.' Sarah was impressed.

"It was months before Sarah fully believed that *this* father wasn't going to leave like the first one had. In the final weeks of treatment, Sarah was making up stories in which the princess could sometimes be a little bratty and the parents angry . . . and *still* nothing terrible would happen.

"Margo showed impressive patience when Michael did allow himself to become moody. She refrained from showing discomfort when he wanted to be alone, and she encouraged him to accept invitations from Joan's relatives and to make them feel welcome. Michael was deeply touched by Margo's generosity and strength, and this, in turn, helped him to get through his mourning without feeling guilty toward Margo—which only would have prolonged it.

"Now the treatment is over. Michael knows there will still be painful moments to be gotten through . . . on Carly's birthday, for example. But Michael and Margo and Sarah are firmly established as a family now; and they know they can count on each other, no matter what."

81

DEVELOPMENTAL

TASKS

*Fourteen-month-old Ben is calm
and self-sufficient, but he seems so
much more interested in things than
in us. Will he be more sociable
once he starts talking—or doesn't
he even want to connect?*

Mara's Story

"Everyone agreed that Ben was the perfect baby," said Mara Davis, 33. "Friends, even strangers, admired his pleasant disposition. 'It's so obvious he's well loved and cared for,' my mother wrote after spending a week at our house. And I felt great!

"My husband, Jon, and I had agreed early on that I would go back to work at the law firm when Ben was three months old, and why not? Many women balance a career and motherhood these days. And we had a place for Ben at the best day-care center in our town.

"Ben was sleeping fourteen hours a night, gaining weight, and looking very healthy. When he was seven months old and starting to crawl, friends warned, 'Now, watch out, once they start moving around, they want to rule the world!'

"But Ben continued to be quiet, easy, and flexible. We could take him to a noisy restaurant or even a concert, and he'd never bother anyone. One night, Jon's boss and his wife were taking us out to dinner. 'Is Ben *always* so good about having a sitter?' Mrs. Greer said, impressed. 'You must make him feel very secure.' Modestly I told her, 'We're just lucky.'

" 'Congratulations! Now you're at the challenging, fun part,' my mother wrote when we sent her a video of Ben—at thirteen months—taking his first steps. She said, 'This is when a baby really starts to be a person and wants to do everything both of you do.'

"That sounded exciting, but as the weeks passed, I became uneasy. The better Ben could get around and do things, the less he seemed to want to be with us. Didn't he *like* us?

"Jon didn't see what I meant at all. 'He's at the age where he's supposed to be busy exploring,' Jon explained. 'That's the way children learn.'

"Well, I understood that . . . but I still felt strange. Perhaps it was that Ben often crawled around aimlessly (and *away* from me instead of *toward* me) when I came home from work. Or maybe it was the way he seemed to ignore me when I spoke to him—as if he didn't like or even know my voice.

"I even wondered briefly whether he was deaf. But no, he loved his music box and his little record player. It was only when *I* sang or spoke to him that he looked bored and indifferent.

"Jon sighed, 'You're talking about the end of the day, when you and I are tired,' he said. 'Doesn't it stand to reason that Ben's tired too and not up for a lot of activity?'

" 'Fine,' I conceded, and it was true: When we got home in the evening, we *were* both exhausted. The three of us usually collapsed in the living room for an hour and listened to music. Jon and I would look at the mail while Ben played on the floor.

"Yes, it was a peaceful, low-key time. But what about the weekends? Even then, Ben wasn't very responsive. He didn't look when I pointed to something, and I couldn't surprise him or make him giggle. Perhaps he *did* dislike me.

"Jon shook his head. 'Ben thinks you're a great mom, but he'll need to be older before he can show it,' he said.

"Okay, I tried to be patient and put my nagging thoughts aside, at least for Christmas—and a long-awaited visit from Rob and Kitty, our old friends from Maine, and their twelve-month-old twins.

"The evening they arrived, I thought the kids could play on the floor while we had some eggnog and talked. But I was mistaken! Ben sat and banged wooden spoons, but the twins, Emmy and Alex, had other ideas.

"Noisy and gleeful, they hung all over their mother, climbing on her lap, sticking their fingers in her drink, wanting hugs, playing with her hair. They were all over Rob, too, one twin exploring his eyes, nose, and mouth while the other one fed him bits of soggy cracker from her own mouth.

" 'Are they *always* like this?' Jon wondered.

" 'What do you mean?' Kitty seemed perplexed.

"Jon laughed and shook his head. 'I just mean they're awfully cute,' he said. Impulsively, he picked up Ben, who was sitting quietly on the floor, and danced him around in the air. Ben, staring off at the wall, jiggled passively in Jon's arms; as soon as Jon put him down, he turned his body away and stared at the wallpaper.

" 'Ben *is* aloof,' Jon admitted to me after our friends had left. 'No matter how energetically I play with him, he always seems detached.'

"We thought his not fussing meant he was a happy baby, but something's been missing all along—either in Ben or in us. I just hope it's something that can be fixed."

The Counselor Replies

Stanley Greenspan, M.D., a child psychiatrist, is clinical professor of psychiatry and pediatrics at George Washington University Medical School, in Washington, D.C. He is a coauthor of The Essential Partnership *(Penguin Books),* The Clinical Interview of the Child, Second Edition *(American Psychiatric Press), and* Floortime, *a videtape (Scholastic, Inc.).*

"Jon said sadly, 'He just ignores us,' when the Davises brought Ben in to see me. Mara nodded in agreement.

" 'The only way to get his attention is with one of these,' she said, winding up a little music box. At that, Ben, who had been playing with the door of a cabinet, turned toward the music and moved his head rhythmically.

"As the tune ended and Ben began dragging a toy phone along the floor, the Davises filled me in on his developmental history, which had been uneventful. 'He's never been anything but super-healthy and very laid-back,' Jon said.

" 'Yes, laid-back,' Mara agreed. 'And *very* remote.'

"After hearing how Ben acted at home and why his parents felt concerned, I asked them to play with him just as they would at home.

"When they did, I noticed that Mara was tense and quiet, neither smiling nor making any chitchat. Her facial expression seemed frozen as she wound up the music box and offered Ben a plastic block. And Ben was indifferent to his mother. He didn't look at her, smile, or gesture.

"When it was Jon's turn, he seemed nervous too. After a moment, he picked Ben up in a rough-and-tumble way and made funny noises. Ben looked overwhelmed and confused.

"Was this typical? I wondered. The Davises said it was. Curious to learn more about Ben, I got down and crawled over to where he was moving the door of a dollhouse back and forth. I looked at Ben and made some supportive comments about his opening and closing the door. And then I made a few gestures, such as holding the house steady for him.

"Ben ignored me. Very slowly, I stuck my finger in the doorway and pretended it was stuck. Ben pulled it out of the way, made a brief sound, and continued to play with the door. This was our first 'gestural' communication. I put my finger back. Ben looked annoyed, and then he just crawled away.

"It was clear that Ben was having difficulty relating to people and sharing interest or pleasure. Most children, by two to four months of age, show enormous joy in relating to others and by fourteen months are mastering many kinds of gestures to express a variety of feelings. Ben, however, was not.

"Mara asked whether Ben was unresponsive because he didn't like one or both of them or whether he might possibly be retarded. I listened with interest and then explained that sometimes babies have special challenges that give them problems in forming relationships.

"For example, some babies are easily overstimulated because they are exceedingly sensitive to one or several stimuli, such as sound and sight. Other babies are undersensitive to these sensations. Also, some babies have a difficult time interpreting their parents' sounds and gestures, thus making two-way communication difficult.

" 'Is there a solution?' Jon asked. I assured the Davises that we would work out an approach, but first we would need to learn all that we could about Ben's needs and his own style of relating.

"The Davises still seemed upset, and I helped them elaborate on their sadness and worry. I didn't want to gloss over fears that had been building up for months. I knew they would need to deal with those feelings in order to be ready for the work ahead.

"Over the next several sessions, I observed Ben and his parents interacting, and I played with him too. I then conducted a complete physical exam, took a more detailed history, and explored the ways the family worked together.

"In addition, I suggested a series of developmental assessments, including studies of his physical health and his various functions: sensory, motor, language, and intellectual.

"Ben was physically healthy, but through the tests, we found that he was *overly* sensitive to touch and *under*-reactive to sounds, and that he had trouble decoding different sounds.

"At the same time, he was interested in what he saw. His gross motor skills (such as walking) were fine, but he was delayed in co-ordinating hand and finger movement and in planning sequential movements, such as stacking three or four blocks by size.

"Ben's speech development was also delayed. His intelligence was hard to assess because of his lack of interest in people, but he seemed to have some of the concepts normally mastered at eight months of age, and clearly had the potential for more.

"As time went on, I noticed that Ben was no more sociable with his parents than he had been on the first visit, and as a result, Mara tended to leave him alone, assuming that if he wanted interaction, he'd initiate it. And when he didn't, Mara felt rejected and retreated even further.

"Jon, who was more assertive, had said, 'Okay, if he won't be available this way, we have to take charge and *show* him we care.' But this determined approach overloaded Ben and left him virtually frozen.

"We needed to find ways to woo Ben into relating, taking into account his unique physical and emotional patterns and strong tendency to withdraw. One thing we noted was that Ben clearly liked looking better than he did listening.

"We also found that he preferred low-pitched vocal sounds to high ones. Also, if the tempo of speech was too slow, he'd lose interest, but if it was too complex (a torrent of words or funny sounds), he would look confused and turn away. A simple phrase repeated in a low-pitched rhythm, however, would occasionally elicit a second or two of attention.

"We worked to find out which sensations Ben liked and which ones were hard for him to tolerate. We learned, for example, that he was disturbed by light touch but enjoyed gentle pressure, like a firm hug.

"Gradually, Jon and Mara got better at noticing what caught Ben's attention, even for a brief second. In fact, it was the Davises who discovered that Ben liked slow, rhythmic rocking.

"Sure enough, Ben's most attentive looking and listening took place when he was being simultaneously hugged, rocked, and spoken to in a low voice, with his parents making especially slow facial expressions.

"Jon was fascinated by the fact that Ben was sensitive to the way other people behaved with him. He still tended to stay in his own world if nobody pursued him, but both parents also realized that too much stimulation would cause him to withdraw. They slowly learned that there was a narrow pathway through which they could reach their son—and that it worked best when they showed a warm and constant level of interest.

"We also discovered together that after he had looked for a few seconds, the next challenge was to see whether a 'circle of communication' could be opened and closed. One day, Jon got results: He noticed Ben turning the knob on his music box. Instead of just admiring Ben or cheering him on, Jon turned the knob the other way. Ben responded to his father's overture by turning it back his way. A circle of communication was completed.

"Ben also looked at his dad with a 'What did you do?' look. Jon gave Ben a big 'I'm sorry' smile. By looking back at his dad, Ben closed another circle of communication, and that signified real progress.

"I said, 'These first circles are the hardest—and the most important—to attain.' I discussed the importance of getting Ben's attention and helping him relate in a warm and trusting way. This first

90

step toward expressing his intentions would help him respond to his parents' gestures and, eventually, to their words.

"At this point, a month after we had begun, I continued to see the Davises twice a week. I also helped them find a speech pathologist, to work with Ben on language development, and a physical therapist, who could give the Davises special exercises to help Ben deal better with physical contact and movement.

"Our goal now was to try and mobilize four critical processes for Ben. The first, already begun, was to help him get into a state of 'shared attention'—looking at and listening to the person on the floor with him.

"I suggested to Jon that he try following Ben's natural interests. I said, 'Sometimes you have to get between him and the thing he wants to look at.' We all felt rewarded one day when the thing that Ben wanted to look at was his father's nose.

"The next part of this process involved helping Ben relate to his parents in simple, pleasurable ways, such as touching his mom's hair or responding to her voice with a smile.

"After that, the aim was to help Ben become engaged in intentional two-way communication. A simple game of peekaboo was a real breakthrough for him. And eventually Ben was able to use much more complex gestures, like taking his mom by the hand, leading her to the refrigerator, and banging on the door for juice.

"The third and fourth steps involved Ben's use of symbols to demonstrate his intentions (like picking up the toy phone and pretending to call someone instead of just dragging the phone around). But Mara and Jon understood that this would take time; under the best of circumstances, most children aren't ready for this stage until 18 to 24 months of age.

"The Davises practiced with Ben, and Mara now felt confident enough to use her voice and body in playing with him instead of relying on music and toys. At the same time, Jon learned to enter Ben's world in a warm, gentle way, following his lead.

"Mara volunteered to take a leave from work. She realized that because of Ben's extreme tendency to withdraw, spending extra time with him at this point could only be helpful, and I supported her decision.

"Relationships are the key to much of the learning that occurs in

91

the first years of life: Trust, intimacy, and self-esteem, as well as verbal and body language, reasoning, and thinking, are all learned through relationships.

"It has been four months since I started working with the Davis family, and Ben has made impressive progress. He smiles and makes many sounds and gestures that his parents understand and respond to. He also enjoys cuddling and often initiates it.

"He can play with his mother and father for fifteen minutes without withdrawing, and his favorite new activity is having one of his parents chase him ... until he gleefully doubles back to 'surprise' them. Ben now seeks out his parents and, if he's worried in a new situation, clings to them.

"Ben's parents have also changed in important ways. Now when Jon is unsure of what to do, he takes a slow and cautious approach. Mara, convinced that Ben loves and needs her, stays involved with him even when he withdraws or seems angry.

"The Davises understand that they will be helping Ben deal with his responses to people for some time. But he is out of the woods, in the sense that he's no longer a child who is too detached to enjoy relationships.

"Ben's problem is not unique. But the special challenges of children like him often go unrecognized until they're two or three years old, when delayed language development alerts everyone to the problem.

"The Davises are to be congratulated, not only for recognizing Ben's problem early, but for providing the intensive help and support he needed in order to progress from someone withdrawn and unavailable to a loving, and lovable, little boy."

> *Jared, three and a half, goes for days at a time without moving his bowels, and the usual remedies haven't helped. Jared claims he wants to go but can't. Is this true—or is he holding back on purpose?*

Sandy's Story

"I was relieved that Jared recovered so quickly," said Sandy Greer, 33. "He'd had a sudden attack of diarrhea at nursery school and soiled his pants. But by the next morning, he was fine.

"Several days later, he complained of a stomachache. I felt his forehead: no fever. I asked whether he needed to go to the bathroom. He shook his head, but from the way he was holding his stomach, I sensed that he had the urge to go. 'No, no!' he denied. 'I want to, but I can't,' he finally admitted unhappily.

"Finally he had a bowel movement. But instead of feeling relieved, he seemed anxious. 'It hurt,' he said.

"I said, 'Maybe you waited too long. That's why it's better to try to go as soon as you have to.'

"Three days later, Jared was having the same problem. 'My tummy hurts,' he said. 'It's too full.' It *did* look round. His sister, Jenny, seven, gave it a pat.

" 'Jared's getting fat,' she said, giggling.

"I took Jared in to the bathroom and sat him on the toilet. 'No,' he cried, 'I can't.' And he tried to wriggle down.

" 'No, just stay here awhile,' I urged him gently. 'Take your time.' But still nothing happened, and all during dinner he was miserable, holding his stomach and refusing to eat.

"My husband, Steve, took Jared to the bathroom again, and they stayed in there a long time. 'Success,' Steve said when they emerged finally. 'Jared just needs a little encouragement.'

"Maybe that was it. Now when Jared danced around or held his stomach, Steve or I would go into the bathroom with him and stay there, reading him stories and singing. It was very sociable, and sometimes it worked, but often it didn't.

"Steve tried sprinkling bran flakes on Jared's yogurt. 'It's to help you go,' Steve explained. Jared took a taste.

" 'I hate it,' he said, making a face and pushing the bowl away.

" 'Eat it anyway,' Steve said. 'Don't you want to make a nice poop?'

"Jenny groaned. 'Dad, that's so *gross*. It's all you guys talk about.'

"Jared's problem *was* becoming a bigger and bigger deal. But what could we do? One morning, he was sure he needed to go—just when it was time for me to drive Steve to the station. Steve missed his train.

"Another time, Jared felt that he needed to go during one of Jenny's soccer games. 'Can't you wait until it's over?' I begged him. Jared shook his head. We found a bathroom, and then he tried to go and couldn't. I was frantic. We rushed back to the game, only to find it was over. Jenny was very upset. 'Next time, can't you just leave him home?' she grumbled.

"Then there was the weekend we visited Steve's sister, Mary, an artist, in her old-fashioned farmhouse. Mary's a real bohemian and uses an outhouse. Jared said he couldn't make a BM with all the spiders, so Steve ended up having to drive him to an all-night gas station ten or twelve miles down the road.

"Mary asked what our pediatrician had to say about what was going on. I realized that we hadn't even mentioned it to Dr. Fane; but of course, now we would. Maybe he could give us some suggestion, some way to get Jared over his constipation.

" 'More likely, he'll tell you to just ignore it and stop catering to Jared so much,' Mary predicted.

"But instead of reassuring us, Dr. Fane pushed the panic button.

He said that Jared could get a blockage and even rupture his intestine. 'He *must* move his bowels,' Dr. Fane warned us, or else we would have to give him an enema.

"An enema? I hated that idea. I'd try something else. I offered Jared a great-looking dinosaur in the toy-store window if he made a BM before dinnertime. To my relief, he did!

" 'No fair,' Jenny protested when Jared showed her his new triceratops. 'You never gave *me* stuff just for going to the bathroom.'

" 'You never had his problem,' I said. I understood how miffed she felt.

"This was also the spring we'd promised Jenny we'd get a puppy, but we hadn't done it yet. How could we? Training puppies takes time, and Jared's problem was taking all the time and energy we had.

" 'Jenny, we will get a puppy soon,' I promised.

"But even bribery worked only sometimes. Each day started with a question mark, and I found that my mood would swing back and forth, based on whether Jared had to go, could go, would go, did go . . .

" 'The doctor says there's no physical reason for this, so why do you let it go on?' Steve's mother, Addie, said, challenging us. 'Don't you see he's just playing games with you?'

" 'That's not *true!*' I told her indignantly. If she thought Jared was playing games, she hadn't seen him sitting on the toilet, struggling, straining—so red in the face, he looked as if he was about to explode. There was no question about it, Jared was trying!

"But privately, I sometimes wondered whether there was a grain of truth to what she said. Jared claimed that coffee ice cream helped, so we let him have as much as he wanted.

"Jared often managed to postpone his bedtime by saying, 'But I almost have to go to the bathroom.' We knew he'd be tired the next day, but of course we let him stay up.

"Steve bought prunes, but Jared wouldn't eat them. Steve tried to persuade him, to no avail. Finally he got furious and threw them away. 'To hell with you,' he said angrily.

"I said, 'Jared, you know Daddy doesn't mean it,' but he cried.

"I had been counting days, and it was the fifth in a row without a BM, so it was enema time. Jared howled when it started and begged me to stop. He said that if I didn't, he'd 'burst open.' I felt so cruel.

"I told Jared that I wouldn't have done it if the doctor hadn't insisted. But I also knew I couldn't keep this up. There *had* to be a better way.

"When I picked Jared up from school the next morning, his teacher asked me whether anything was wrong. 'He seems so stressed,' she said. 'Especially today.' Wearily, I told her about Jared's constipation.

" 'Well, of course I'm not a pediatrician,' she said. 'But I've found very often that this problem is psychological.' I was stunned. Did this mean that Jared had a serious emotional problem? I called Dr. Fane and asked for a referral. I'm worried now, and I don't know what to think. I guess that maybe a therapist can tell us what *is* going on with Jared."

The Counselor Replies

Jan Drucker, Ph.D., is a child psychologist in New York City. She is also professor of psychology at Sarah Lawrence College in Bronxville, New York, and a consultant to the Early Childhood Center there.

"When Sandy phoned, we talked at length, and I told her that I'd like to meet Jared but that I wanted him to see a pediatric gastrointestinal specialist as well. I said, 'His problem may be psychological, but it wouldn't be right to pursue that without exploring organic possibilities first.'

"I suggested that she explain to Jared that he'd be seeing two doctors: one to check the physical causes of his problem and one just to talk and play. I said, 'It might be best if you let him see me first so that we can talk about his physical exam.'

"Sandy agreed, and the following Monday, she brought in Jared, an adorable child with blond hair and big brown eyes. He looked tired, but otherwise he didn't seem to have any problems.

" 'Jared, do you know why you're here?' I asked.

" 'Because you're the doctor who's going to help me make a poop.'

"I said, 'It must be hard for you to imagine how.'

" 'Yeah!' Jared said, laughing. Then he grew serious. 'Do you give enemas?' he asked.

" 'No,' I replied. 'I'm not a body doctor, my job is helping kids and families who are worried.

" 'Also,' I went on, 'you're going to see Dr. Hauser, just to make sure you don't have problems in your tummy or intestines. But I promise you that I'm going to try to help you so that you won't need any more enemas.'

"Jared breathed a deep sigh of relief. Then he looked around. 'Okay, Mom,' he said, 'Where are those toys you told me about?'

" 'Right here,' I said, opening a closet filled with toys. 'Playing would be a good way for me to get to know you. Do you see anything you like?'

"Jared looked in and picked up some toy figures. He played a little with a bunch of things: dinosaurs, a spaceship, a puzzle. Then he found the modeling dough and his eyes lit up. I said, 'I have some tools and a plastic machine that you can fill and squeeze the dough out of.'

" 'OK,' he said. Then he sat down and happily played—stuffing in lots of modeling dough and squeezing it out—until at one point, he filled it too full. The machine got stuck, and the dough wouldn't come out.

" 'I'm all done,' Jared said, and went over to his mother, burying his face against her shoulder.

" 'It is almost time to go,' I said. 'But would you help me clear this out?'

"Of course, the modeling dough getting stuck was symbolic of Jared's problem, but I didn't say anything yet—nor did I just put the toy away. At this early stage in getting to know him, I felt it was more important to reassure him that there would be help for his problem.

"Jared looked dubious, but he watched as I took out some dough so that the rest could come through.

"Jared said, 'I thought you'd have to poke something in, like . . . like with an enema.'

"I said, 'I can see how you'd be worried, but I didn't have to.' Then I said, 'Jared, when you go to see Dr. Hauser, he might poke you a little. Then you'll come back here to play and to tell me how your visit went.'

"Two days later, Sandy called. Jared had been upset about being examined, but the doctor had been gentle and had spent a lot of time with Jared after the physical exam.

"Dr. Hauser explained to the Greers that there was nothing wrong with the way Jared's body functioned. He said he didn't believe in enemas; that the physical and psychological effects were far worse than any problems that might result from infrequent bowel movements.

"He concluded that Jared was experiencing physical distress but had no organic problems, and he prescribed a stool softener for Jared to take once a day in orange juice. Dr. Hauser also wanted to make sure we stayed in touch.

"When Jared came in to see me, I asked him about his visit with Dr. Hauser. 'I hated it, but he was nice,' Jared said thoughtfully. 'At least I don't have to have any enemas.'

"Then Jared asked me whether the modeling dough was okay. 'Did it all come out of the machine?'

" 'Yes,' I said, and showed him.

" 'Good. Then I can play with it again,' he said. 'Okay?'

"This time, Jared played in a different, more confident way, really taking control of the dough: rolling it, pounding it, sometimes putting in too much on purpose, and then taking some out.

"In his first session, Jared had clearly felt like the victim, the one who'd been poked. Now he was playing another role, taking charge and doing the poking himself.

" 'Let's get the bad stuff out,' he said, putting some dough into the machine. 'Watch: We're going to shoot out the bad stuff.'

"Jared was obviously having a good time and didn't need much reassurance, so I was able to ask, 'Why do you call that the bad stuff, Jared?'

" 'It was naughty,' Jared said. 'It didn't want to come out. And that made Mom and Dad really mad.'

"Our time was up, but I told Sandy that Jared should come several more times to play out his problem and his fantasies. I also wanted to meet with both parents without Jared, to help them figure out how to make his toilet-teaching experience less upsetting for the whole family.

"When I saw both parents, Sandy told me that when Jared was an infant, he had had frequent bouts of diarrhea. Apparently this had made his parents unusually sensitive to Jared's bowel functioning. And perhaps that had triggered his intense feelings about the accident in school . . . and his dread of losing control again.

"At that point, Steve said, 'I remember that going to the toilet was always a big deal in my family. Do you think I've conveyed that to Jared?'

"I said, 'All parents' attitudes have some effect on their children, but learning appropriate bowel control is a big developmental task, and it's easy to get off track. What happened to Jared is really not uncommon, especially in boys.'

"Steve said, 'But what do we do now?'

"I said that we might approach the problem in three ways. First the physical: Jared would take the medicine Dr. Hauser prescribed that would eliminate the pain. At the same time, I would explain to Jared about muscles: how he can use them not only to hold in a bowel movement, but also to let it out so that it is not just something that happens to him; it is also an event he can control.

"The second part of the strategy would be the psychological, with Jared coming here to play out his fantasies and thoughts about the troubling experience he'd been through.

"Finally, the Greers would help Jared at home. To defuse the tension, I suggested that they stay low-key in their reactions. 'If Jared says he has to go but can't, remind him that it's okay not to go.'

"I recommended that there be no more special foods and that Jared go back to a normal bedtime. I also urged the Greers to praise Jared each time he made a BM in the toilet.

"I said, 'Put him in charge as much as possible. Let him decide when he wants to move his bowels, and encourage him to wipe himself, even if he doesn't do a perfect job.' I said that this might make him anxious at first but that in the long run, autonomy would be reassuring.

" 'Will we be dealing with this forever?' Sandy wondered. I said there was no reason to think so. Then she said, 'What about Jenny?' She says that she deserves a prize for going to the bathroom.'

" 'Go on explaining, just as you have been,' I suggested. 'Let her know she can help now by getting Jared's mind on other things.' And be sure to thank her for her help. As the focus of your family gets away from this issue, everything will go back to normal.'

"As I predicted, things gradually started to improve. At first, Jared still felt anxious, but less than before; and he was starting to have BMs every two or three days.

"From his play in my office, it was clear that he felt confused about who was good and who was bad. Were his parents bad for hurting him with the enema? Was he bad for not going to the bathroom? And was the BM bad for not coming out?

"Jared began to realize that nobody was at fault. And soon he was able to branch out and play with other toys and to explore other themes, which showed that he was getting back to the usual life of a healthy three-and-a-half-year-old.

"Jared had come in for twelve sessions over a period of three months, and I now felt that he was ready to stop his therapy. Dr. Hauser was also pleased with Jared's progress and reduced the dose of stool softener.

"That was three months ago, and Sandy recently told me, 'Amazingly, several days go by now when I don't even think about it.'

"Jenny just got her puppy, an adorable mixed terrier, and Sandy reports that Jared has been especially helpful in the puppy's housebreaking, since he seems sympathetic to the needs of both the household *and* the puppy.

"Crises around a developmental task such as toilet-teaching can be very upsetting. Jared has emerged with a real sense of himself: not as a baby or a helpless victim, but as a child in charge of his own body. Now Jared is proud and relieved—and so are his parents."

DIFFICULT
BEHAVIOR

Lisa, four, is bright but stubborn—and a holy terror when she doesn't get her way! Why is she always fighting us? And what will it take to get this four-year-old tornado to calm down and behave?

Abby's Story

"Lisa was having fun at the playground," said Abby Hall, 32. "Especially as more children arrived and the noise level rose. But when it was time to leave, she refused to come, and I had to carry her, screaming, to the car.

"The next day, I had a dental appointment, but instead of sitting quietly in the dentist's office and drawing, Lisa threw magazines at me because I told her she'd have to wait until dinnertime to eat. 'No, I want pizza,' she cried, and tugged my arm.

"I tried to reason with her. 'You had pizza three days ago,' I said.

"But she just repeated, 'I want *pizza!*' I warned her to stop or there'd be no TV for a week. But she just kept on saying, 'Pizza!'

"The dentist and his assistant exchanged looks. 'Okay,' I told Lisa, just to get her to stop. 'We'll have pizza.' I knew it was wrong to give in to her tyranny—but what else could I do?

"Dinner that night was another struggle. Lisa didn't want to come to the table. Having had her pizza, she wasn't hungry, and when I insisted she sit at her place, she knelt on her chair and drew a face in her mashed potatoes. I said, 'Don't play with your food.'

"She retorted, 'Drawing isn't playing.'

" 'Anything you do with food besides eating is playing,' I said.

" 'Is cooking it playing?' she asked slyly. A moment later, she coaxed the cat up onto the table. Tim, my husband, yelled at her.

"Lisa looked terrified.

"I said to Tim, 'Don't; you'll give her nightmares.' In general, he had more patience than I did, but when he blew up, he could be scary.

"Not surprisingly, I had to comfort Lisa. When she finally fell asleep at eleven o'clock, I'd *had* it.

" 'She'll outgrow this nonsense soon,' Tim said. He's afraid that if we come down too hard on her, we'll end up crushing her spirit, along with the annoying behavior.

"Perhaps, but all I know is, I'm finding it harder and harder to manage Lisa. She always pushes my buttons. Last week, I got so upset that I yelled, 'You're a brat. I can't stand you!'

"Afterward, I felt so ashamed that I spent the rest of the day trying to make it up to her. 'You're a wonderful girl and I love you,' I told her.

"But in no time, we were arguing again. Tim's mother says I'm not firm enough, but Lisa's very sensitive and doesn't respond well to harshness.

"My friend Mimi, whose kids are great, says that being rigid never works and just makes kids resentful. She says that if the disagreement isn't a matter of health or safety, it's best just to let it go.

"Well, I was willing to avoid unnecessary power struggles. The day after I spoke to Mimi, I took Lisa to buy new shoes, and I didn't scold her for running around the shoe store and rearranging the displays. I just put them back.

" 'You're such a grown-up girl now; you're lots of fun to be with,' I told her, a large exaggeration. But Lisa *was* lovable and cuddly all afternoon, and I thought, Maybe this is the answer—to heap so much praise on her that she won't have anything to fuss about anymore.

"Even dinner was calm that night. So what if she ate spaghetti with her fingers, and the sauce dripped all over the table?

"But the next day, Lisa was a pill again, challenging me on everything—from why she had to eat breakfast to what she could wear to school. 'Oh, no, you'll freeze,' I said to her when she came downstairs in shorts and a skimpy T-shirt.

" 'Why?' she demanded.

" 'Because you'll get cold,' I said. But she refused to listen. Sure enough, later we had to come home from preschool so she could change.

" 'It's your fault,' she raged.

"By the time Tim came home, I was feeling edgy and burned out. All day, I'd been explaining, negotiating, saying no a thousand times, threatening punishment, and finally, just not responding—automatically saying no to everything, even when it made no sense.

" 'You *are* having problems, aren't you?' Tim observed. I admitted that I was getting nervous about our nephew Greg's upcoming wedding—in which Lisa was to be a flower girl.

"I said, 'What if she goes wild and spoils everything?'

" 'She won't,' Tim said. 'Lisa loves Greg, and besides, she's just a child. What do you want to do, wait until she's 21 before we take her anywhere?'

"Lisa was excited about the wedding, and it gave us some leverage with her. Over the next few weeks, all I had to do was remind her that only good girls who knew how to act properly got to be flower girls and she would quickly shape up. 'I know how,' she said gravely. She loved the fancy lace dress she was to wear.

"At the wedding, Lisa looked enchanting—and so earnest! I felt so proud. Maybe this was a turning point, and she'd begun to understand what we expected of her. Tim squeezed my hand as the organ music began and Lisa started down the aisle. And the ceremony was perfect.

"But at the reception, Lisa ran around like a maniac. She got hold of Greg and wouldn't let him go. He picked her up and hugged her, but she wouldn't let him put her down.

"Finally I bribed her away with a soda. 'What a pretty girl you are,' my great-aunt Esther exclaimed. A second later, Lisa spat soda all over Aunt Esther's dress.

" 'It'll wash out,' Aunt Esther lied as I dabbed at her dress with napkins. By then, Lisa was under a table, squealing and tickling people's ankles. I dragged her out, but she was off again, barreling into people and spilling their drinks.

"I caught up with her and told her to sit by herself for five minutes. '*No!*' she screamed, ducking away.

"Tim came up and asked, 'Can't you *control* her?'

"I said, 'I'm trying,' but the next thing I knew, Lisa was taking a large yellow rose from the wedding cake. I said, 'You bad girl!' and she threw the rose, hitting a woman's bare back.

"Tim picked up Lisa and whacked her bottom. 'We're leaving, Abby,' he told me grimly. 'You should have heard the comments! *Your* mother thinks Lisa's disturbed, and *mine* says you aren't raising her right.'

"I don't know what to think! All I know is that Lisa's impossible—and we need help."

The Counselor Replies

Stanley Turecki, M.D., a child and family psychiatrist, is founder and physician-in-charge of The Difficult Child Center in New York City, and is the author of The Difficult Child *(Bantam Books). He is also the father of a once-difficult child.*

"Abby called the center and arranged for an evaluation, which normally takes an hour and a half and involves the child and both parents.

"When the Halls arrived, I observed them in the waiting room, where Lisa played nicely until another family came in and their two children started playing nearby. Then she got excited and threw the blocks she had been building with. 'I want a mint,' she said suddenly, grabbing her mother's bag.

"Abby said no. 'Why not?' Lisa demanded to know.

" 'Because we're going to lunch after this,' Abby said.

" 'But I want a mint right now!' Lisa said, and started butting her mother in the shoulder.

" 'Stop it,' Abby said angrily. 'You know mints aren't good for your teeth.'

" 'Who told you?' Lisa asked, tugging at her mother's pocketbook. '*I want a mint!*'

" 'That's what we go through twenty times a day,' Abby later said, looking defeated. 'Nothing I say or do has any effect.'

"I told Abby that I understood how she felt and would do all I could to help them solve the problem.

"The first step was to take a careful history from both parents and then to talk with Lisa alone to assess her emotional state. Next I would bring Lisa back to the waiting room to play while I gave the Halls some feedback.

"I learned from observing and speaking with Lisa that she is an active and impulsive four-year-old who is quirky about what she'll wear and what she is willing to eat. I also saw that Lisa was easily overstimulated and that once she gets going, she is difficult to control.

"She is also a persistent negotiator, and once she fixes her mind on something, she will not give up.

"I could see that Abby was exhausted and that she felt inadequate, guilty, sad, and angry. Tim and Abby's fundamentally strong marriage was strained by the friction that was occurring, especially at night. Clearly both parents felt that their needs were being compromised by Lisa's tyrannical behavior.

"Abby is a competent businesswoman whose self-image has been damaged by Lisa's ability to make her feel and act like an angry four-year-old herself. Tim tends to be patient and then to overreact. He complains about Lisa's behavior but won't really lay down the law.

"Both parents were raised strictly and want to be open and responsive to Lisa. But in paying her such close attention, they were also tolerating rude and unacceptable behavior.

"Not knowing which traits were 'part of Lisa' and which behaviors they could have some control over, the Halls bounced back and forth between getting angry and being too lenient. This ineffectual discipline and their exasperation led Lisa to see herself, over a period of time, as 'a bad, bad girl.'

" 'Is she disturbed?' Abby asked.

"I said, 'Lisa is *not* disturbed. She is showing symptoms of stress; it's hard to feel good about yourself when you fight with your mom twenty times a day. But I believe these symptoms will disappear as the atmosphere within the family improves.

" 'We can check Lisa out again in a couple of months,' I added, 'but right now I see no need for treatment. You have a great kid, but she's tough, and all of you are caught up in a vicious cycle: The more she misbehaves, the more you react, and the more you react, the more she misbehaves.

" 'I'm going to help you develop an effective system of adult authority. You should be calm but firm. And there will be much more planning; the more carefully the two of you plan, the less punishment Lisa will need.'

" 'I hope we can do it. Sometimes I feel we've ruined her,' Abby said.

" 'You haven't,' I assured her. 'And considering how difficult Lisa is, on the whole I'd say you've done a good job. Look how interesting she is and how well she does at school and with other children. She's very much her own person, too.'

"I saw Tim and Abby each week for a month, and during those sessions, we discussed specifics. I explained that when a child like Lisa acts up in public, it's really not so much that she's deliberately misbehaving as it is a combination of her being an active, excitable, easily overstimulated child.

"I told the Halls, 'The trick is for you to learn to recognize signs of overexcitement before they're full-blown and, when you see signs, to take her to a cooling-off place. Do it *before* you arrive at the dentist's office or the supermarket, and certainly before you try to put her to bed.'

" 'We've tried using time-out as punishment, but it doesn't work,' Abby said.

" 'I don't mean this to be punishment,' I replied. 'This is an early-intervention technique to keep things from escalating.' I suggested that the Halls designate a special area at home for cooling off: perhaps an armchair with a favorite soft toy.

"Tim said, 'What if she loses control too quickly?'

" 'Most parents overreact to a child's loss of control, missing the point that she can't help it—and it's already to late,' I told him. 'So say to yourself, and to Lisa, Bad luck this time, but no big deal. And to let it go. You can't all be perfect or expect never to have a blowup again. If you manage to catch 20 percent of all incipient tantrums, you'll be winning!'

" 'Do we just start doing this?' Abby wondered.

" 'I said, 'No, it must follow a planned discussion, which must take place during a calm phase. Plan what to say so that it's clear. And make it brief, or you'll lose her interest. Choose a quiet time and place for this discussion, and call Lisa in. Your attitude should be friendly but serious; this is *important* business.

" 'You might say to her, "You're a bubbly person, but sometimes you get too excited and misbehave. It's not your fault; we're going to help you. When this starts to happen, we're going to tell you that you need to cool-off. You'll have a special place. What would you like to have in it? Your pillow? A stuffed toy? Some books?" '

"I pointed out that planned discussions also work for specific problems, such as standard dinnertime hassles. They could say, 'Lisa, the new rule in our house is that messy eating isn't allowed. You have a choice: You can eat with us in the dining room and be-have properly, or you can eat alone in the kitchen.'

"It is very important to ask Lisa after each discussion whether she understands. If she says yes, tell her to do her best. Those are powerful words to a child. And, I said, 'Next time you sit down to dinner, don't give her any warnings. Just say, "Remember what we talked about? Do your best." And end the discussion.'

"I suggested that, when a negotiation is developing, they take a stand early on instead of getting caught up in arguing. I said, 'The more it goes around, the more a child like Lisa gets locked in—and digs in.

" 'For example, you could say to Lisa, "You've asked for a mint *twice* already, and both times I've said no. You can ask twice more, but that's all." She'll say, "*I want a mint.*" Then you say, "*That's once.*" Lisa may have a fit, but it will be a less intense fit after the fourth time than it would have been after the tenth.

"I advised the Halls to acknowledge any progress but not to make too big a deal out of it. 'I saw you trying. Well done! Keep it up' is better than 'You're terrific' for a minor accomplishment. If there is too much praise, the child starts feeling entitled to tons of praise for very little.

"Other aspects of Lisa's troublesome behavior required different strategies. For example, it was clear that Lisa had trouble making transitions from one activity to another. I suggested that instead of fighting, they show her a digital clock and say, 'It's six o'clock now. When it says six-twenty, it will be time to come to the table.'

" 'Fine,' Tim said. 'But even if she comes to the table on time, she won't eat what we serve.'

"I said, 'Lisa's food preferences should be respected. And if she's hungry at five o'clock, feed her.'

" 'With clothes, too, let Lisa wear shorts . . . and take a coat along in the car if you think she'll be cold.' Abby asked whether that wasn't giving in. I replied, 'There's nothing wrong with saying yes. It's just as simple as saying no. Giving in is what occurs when you get worn down after a protracted battle.'

"At this point, the Halls had been in to see me four times, and things were improving. Now they had a bedtime routine, and instead of arguing with Lisa about whether or not she was tired, they would tuck her in at eight o'clock, after which she didn't have to sleep but did have to stay in her room.

"Not only did Tim and Abby now have some private time together, but there was also a decrease in tantrums: On average, they were down to one major power struggle a day instead of six or ten, and Lisa was losing control only about once a week instead of twice a day.

"We decided to stop for a month, after which I saw them and Lisa, who seemed happier and less stressed.

"At that time, Abby and Tim observed that Lisa is still a very strong-willed child, prone to flying off the handle; but most of the time now, her parents find her more lively than annoying. I said, 'Often, the traits that give us fits when kids are young become real assets later on.'

"It's very easy to confuse aspects of a child's temperament with deliberate bad behavior and to treat both of them the same way. Once the Halls understood the difference, they were able to transform an impossible child into a terrific one."

Unlike our three older kids, who are all outgoing, Jared, four, drives us crazy—whining, crying, hiding from everything. Why is he so impossible? And what miracle will it take to change him?

Margo's Story

"I'm not even asking children over for play dates with Jared anymore," said Margo Patterson, 33.

"Last week, when Billy, from nursery school, came over, Jared crawled under the dining-room sideboard and wouldn't come out; Billy spent the afternoon playing with me.

"Another time, Christopher, a new little boy in the neighborhood, came over, and Jared hid in bed under the covers with a flashlight.

"Jared wailed when I yanked off the covers. 'You'd better act friendlier, or Christopher won't want to come over again,' I warned. Jared came out, but he was sulky and withdrawn the whole time.

"He wasn't any better at a birthday party down the street, where he hid behind my chair and refused to join the children playing tag.

"'But you play tag in the playground!' I said. This was what puzzled me: Jared was fine in the playground. In fact, he strode around there as if he owned the place.

"'I don't wanna!' Jared said, winding himself around my leg. The more I tried to dislodge him, the more he complained.

" 'Noooo,' he whined, covering his eyes, when the little birthday girl's mother approached him. Everyone was staring, and a couple of the children giggled. I was so embarrassed for Jared—and for me—that I took him right home.

"I'm not saying that our other kids are perfect—far from it! Katy, seven, and the twins, Will and Matthew, eight, can be pretty wild, and they've thrown plenty of tantrums.

"But I can handle that; that's just part of being a kid. They also express a lot of enthusiasm and joy. When Jared goes into his whining routine, though, I feel as if we aren't making his world good enough or safe enough or interesting enough somehow. It wears me out and makes me feel as though I'm not a good-enough mother.

"Recently we went to visit some friends in Connecticut. The entire trip, Jared kept whining. 'Why do we have to go?' and 'How long do we have to stay?'

"There was snow on the ground, and our friends had sleds, but predictably, Jared didn't want to try sledding—until Stan, my husband, *made* him. And then Jared didn't want to stop! He was finding all different ways of going down the hill; headfirst, feetfirst, sitting, kneeling. When it came time to leave, I had to carry him to the car while he wailed.

"What bugs Stan the most is that Jared will almost never do what we ask—like go to bed or come to dinner when we call. And we don't dare interrupt him when he's 'busy' playing. On Christmas Day, Stan's mother came over. When she wanted her glasses from upstairs, Stan asked Jared to go get them. But Jared was on the floor making some kind of pattern with the building blocks his grandma had bought him, and he didn't budge.

" 'I'll go!' Will and Katy both cried, racing upstairs for the glasses. Stan was furious and told Jared that he was selfish. Jared burst into tears.

" 'When will this kid learn to behave?' Stan asked. "I felt a pang then; Jared looked so forlorn and so little. I took him in my arms, and he cuddled against me. Maybe I wasn't giving him enough time; the other kids needed so much attention. I realized I couldn't even remember when I last spent time alone with Jared, and I decided to remedy that.

"That week I bought two tickets for a puppet show that had gotten phenomenal reviews. 'This will be so much fun,' I told Jared the next Saturday morning as we started out.

" 'What is it about?' Jared asked me suspiciously. 'What are they going to do?'

"I wanted to shout, 'Why can't you just trust me and relax?' But instead I smiled and gave his shoulder an affectionate squeeze. 'You'll love it,' I promised.

"He still looked dubious as the lights dimmed and the curtain went up. The show was outstanding. But each time I stole a look at Jared, his face was stony—not a sign of joy or pleasure. When the lights came on for intermission, he whined, 'Is it over? When will it start again?'

"All through the second act, the two children in front of us were laughing and clapping like crazy. But Jared just sat there, showing no emotion. When it was over, he immediately started whining that it had been too short.

"I felt so discouraged. What kind of magic would it take to make him feel joy or wonder? On the way home in the car, he didn't say anything about enjoying the show. He just complained that he was hungry, his shoe was falling off, and he had to go to the bathroom.

"Finally I blew my top. 'Jared,' I cried, 'You are such a sourpuss! I try to do something special with you, and all you do is fuss. You're a very ungrateful little boy!'

"Jared began to sob, and I felt ashamed of my outburst. I don't know why Jared isn't the normal, bubbly kid he ought to be. Maybe there's something wrong with him. That's a scary thought, but I think we need to find out whether he's okay."

The Counselor Replies

Stella Chess, M.D., professor of child psychiatry at New York University Medical Center, in New York City, is a founder of the American Academy of Child and Adolescent Psychiatry and a coauthor of many books, including Know Your Child: An Authoritative Guide for Today's Parents *(Basic Books). Chess, a pioneer in child psychiatry, is known especially for her research into temperaments.*

"When I asked Margo, 'What are the things that trouble you? Why are you here?' she replied, 'My four-year-old, Jared, has always been a whiner. Our other children are positive and adventurous, but Jared resists *everything!*'

"I asked Margo to give me examples of what he whined about.

" 'All last summer and fall, he whined about preschool, but he likes it now,' she answered.

" 'What else?' I asked.

" 'Every time we visit people, he doesn't want to go, and then he doesn't want to leave.' Margo told me about the recent puppet show. 'It meant nothing to him,' she said.

"I asked her if he talked about it afterward. 'Well, yes,' Margo admitted. 'That night I heard him telling Katy the plot as if he'd enjoyed it.'

" 'Maybe he did,' I offered.

" 'He sure didn't act like it,' Margo said.

"As Margo gave me more examples, I came to understand that Jared was generally downbeat. He even expressed his positive moods with low intensity: Instead of smiling or cheering at the puppet show, he had shown that he liked it simply by whining when it stopped.

"As I began to take a history of Jared's development, I learned that as a baby, he had backed off from his first bath and from every new food his parents had tried to introduce him to. The pediatrician had advised his parents to keep trying. They did, and as Jared became familiar with a food, he usually ate it. He also grew to like his bath and would whine when taken out.

"I asked Margo what she liked about Jared. 'Sometimes he surprises me,' she said. 'The other day, he asked me to show him how to sew on buttons. I told him he was too young, but he insisted. He watched while I threaded the needle and sewed one on. I started him off on a two-hole button. To my amazement, he did it, and he did it right. And he kept sewing—for an hour!'

" 'Good,' I said. 'So he's persistent. That will be a boon later, if he's persistent about the right things.'

" 'There's something else,' Margo said. 'The other day, I came home exhausted, and Jared told me I looked tired. The other kids would never have noticed.'

" 'That shows that he cares. It doesn't sound as if Jared is deliberately trying to upset you,' I noted.

"By the end of the session, I had a picture of Jared as a child who was very slow to feel comfortable in new situations and who didn't show positive feelings in a manner his parents recognized. Because Margo and Stan were uncomfortable with Jared's behavior, they had become impatient with him, so Jared was frequently getting scolded for being himself.

"Jared came in with his parents for the second session, and I had a chance to observe him playing. I could see for myself that Jared was coordinated and bright and had no obvious neurological problems. Although he did things slowly, he was persistent and could accomplish tasks above his age level.

"I saw what's called a 'poor fit' between parents and child. These were lively parents who expected free expression of feelings and who accepted big fights as easily as they did open affection. They had a good understanding of their other children, who were expressive, but Jared's inborn temperament was different: low-key, sensitive, cautious.

"By this time, the problem had been compounded by the parents' frustration. Jared was beginning to feel insignificant, since he was being noticed only for what his parents considered negative behavior.

" 'Jared's self-esteem is shrinking,' I told them. 'The more you become annoyed or angry, the worse he probably feels about himself.'

"Margo nodded. 'If we've been so disapproving, he must feel that everything Katy and the twins do is right and he's always wrong. Do you think that maybe whining has been the only way he knows how to express his unhappiness?'

" 'That's very insightful,' I replied. I told the Pattersons that our main goal was to give Jared a chance to be himself, and to show him that his parents could accept him for who he was.

" 'From everything you've told me and from what I've observed, Jared expresses his feelings so subtly that sometimes you don't understand his reactions,' I explained. 'So I'm going to ask you to try to retune yourselves, to try to read him better.'

" 'What do you mean?' Margo asked me.

" 'Look for persistence,' I explained to her. 'Jared expresses his enjoyment by sticking to things. You need to recognize when he's having a good time, and to let him know that his way of expressing happiness is every bit as good as a more demonstrative expression.'

" 'Persistence is fine,' Stan said, 'but I don't think it's great when he's too busy to do what we ask—like when he wouldn't get his grandmother's glasses.'

"I said, 'Perhaps it's a mistake to ask him to do something when he's engrossed in an activity. It's very difficult for this child to be pulled away from a problem he is solving or an activity that has captured his attention. Ask him to do favors when he's not preoccupied.'

" 'If you have to pull him away from an activity—to come and eat, for example—give him warning. Figure out a way of saving what he has done. For example, let him know that you'll protect his blocks while he is away, to make sure that the tower he has built won't be knocked over. He will see that you understand his feelings and that you care.'

" 'Fine,' Margo said. 'But what about his terrible clinginess in social situations?'

"I said, 'Apparently Jared does well in familiar situations but has a harder time when he encounters something new. Try to imagine how you'd react if *you* were in a new situation and wanted to be a million miles away.'

" 'Do you mean we should just give up?' Stan wondered.

" 'Not at all,' I said. 'This is where you and Margo must be persistent.'

" 'Suppose you're taking him to the weekly storytelling hour at the library and all the other children are sitting together in a circle, but Jared is afraid to join them. Instead of insisting that he sit with the group, let him choose a place in the library that he feels is safe. Sit with him there and read together for a while. You can gradually move closer to the group—at Jared's pace. You need to understand how many unfamiliar factors he is confronting at once—the stacks of books, the hushed atmosphere, and so many people he doesn't know. He may eventually learn to love the library, but it could take him six months.

" 'Don't push him,' I cautioned the Pattersons. 'He has to do this at his own pace, and if you become impatient, it will impede his progress. Play games at home with him about having friends over and going to parties. Actually rehearse these situations. Let his brothers and sister participate. That way, everyone will feel important—including Jared.'

" 'I'm not sure I've got the patience for another birthday party,' Margo said.

" 'You need to differentiate between a slow-to-warm-up temperament and bad behavior,' I said. 'You might say to Jared, "I understand you're shy at the beginning, and I'll be there as long as you need me, but you're not allowed to whine or wrap yourself around me like a towel." '

"For the next three months, I met periodically with Margo and Stan—not for therapy, but to help them understand Jared's temperament better and to learn to appreciate him more. At the same time, they also had to teach Jared to live in the real world and to master the normal demands on a child his age.

"After that, I didn't hear from the Pattersons for about a year—until Margo called recently. She sounded very happy. 'I want to tell you that Jared has changed!' she said. 'He came with us to visit a neighbor at Christmastime to help trim the tree. At first he was hesitant, like always, but I let him show me decorations for a while before I encouraged him to join the other kids. Eventually he got right into the spirit of things.'

" 'He seems more expressive these days,' she added. 'I can tell when he's having a good time, and he whines much less than before.'

"I asked Margo to tell me more, and what I heard her describe was not so much a dramatic change in Jared's behavior but the fact that both parents had developed a far greater understanding of him.

"Call it whatever you want; the Pattersons were willing and able to do important work. Each child is unique, and so is each parent. Sometimes a good fit takes place spontaneously, and other times it requires a lot of effort."

Our son Tim, five, was a normal child until he started school—but now he won't talk, except to us. Is Timmy just being obstinate— or is something really wrong?

Joanna's Story

"I was shocked when Timmy's kindergarten teacher said he never opened his mouth at school," said Joanna Sanford, 33. "I'd watch him after school with his brother, Connor, eight, and the two little boys next door, and Tim was just as noisy and playful as the others.

" 'Maybe she's got him mixed up with someone else,' my husband, Kevin, suggested. 'Maybe she's getting old.'

"But the teacher, Mrs. Frank, was only in her twenties, and she knew that Timmy was the boy who had lived in Paris until last May. In fact, it was when she'd tried to get Timmy to tell the class all about living in France that she'd first become aware of his silence.

" 'He just sat there and looked at the floor. He wouldn't answer my questions,' she said.

" 'Perhaps he wasn't feeling well,' I offered.

" 'I don't know.' Mrs. Frank seemed unconvinced. 'Timmy's been in school for a month now, and he hasn't talked at all. I wonder if this could be some reaction to moving.'

"Was *that* Tim's problem? Kevin, who is a news correspondent,

118

and I had moved four times since we'd been married, and twice since Connor was born, but we'd seen it as a real growth opportunity for all of us, especially for the boys. They already had more travel experience than most Americans get in a lifetime, and as a result, they had met and learned to be comfortable with all kinds of people.

"That's why I was so puzzled now. It didn't make sense that Timmy would suddenly get shy. But I *had* noticed him being quiet with strangers in the past several weeks. Recently, when the lady in the bakery offered him a cookie, he barely whispered a thank-you.

"Now, I tried to draw him out and ask if anything was wrong. 'Nope,' he said firmly. But the following week Mrs. Frank called again, because Timmy refused to say his lines in the kindergarten play.

" 'Each child has a small speaking part, but Tim won't speak,' she said. 'I've never seen such a silent child. I wonder if he is having some sort of a problem.'

"Kevin said, '*She's* the one with the problem!' as he reminded me that Tim was speaking not only English but French, too—and clearly—before he was even two.

"Kevin said to Tim, 'Either you cooperate at school or I'll have to punish you.'

"Timmy said, 'Yes, Dad,' and let out a weary sigh.

" 'See?' Kevin said, smiling knowingly. 'It's simple. Kids just need to know what the limits are.'

"At least now, with the long Columbus Day weekend coming up, we would have a little time-out: no school for three days, no pressure on Timmy, and no more of Mrs. Frank's Timmy's-not-talking reports.

"Kevin's boss, Nick Atherton, had invited us all for a cookout. The Atherton home was big and comfortable, invaded by a friendly and spirited army of children, dogs, and cats. 'Come on, we're playing a game we made up,' one of the six Atherton children called to our kids.

" 'Great!' Connor shouted joyfully. 'I'll be on your team.'

" 'You come, too!' Jennie, the Atherton's cute, freckled six-year-old, who had tangly red hair and a long football jersey, nodded to Timmy. But Timmy stood clutching my sleeve.

"Despite my urging him to join the kids, Timmy stayed with the grown-ups, drinking a cola with a cherry in it and playing noisily with the plastic slats on my lawn chair. I had to answer for him when Nick asked him what grade he was in and what sports he liked.

" 'Tim,' I whispered, 'please go and play.' Timmy just shook his head and kept on playing the plastic slats like a xylophone.

"Without a word, Kevin took Timmy by the arm and marched him over to where the kids were playing. 'You take too much from him!' Kevin muttered to me under his breath when he sat down again.

"At nine we were packing up to leave. Connor, flushed and happy, thanked the Athertons warmly. I gave Tim a little reminder poke, but instead of saying thank you, he stared at the ground and moved some pebbles with the toe of his sneaker. 'Tim,' I murmured discreetly, 'haven't you something to say to the Athertons?' Tim picked up a pebble.

" ' 'Say thank you!' Kevin commanded. Timmy dropped his pebble on top of a little pile of pebbles. The silence that followed was embarrassing and very, very strange—until Mari Atherton, Nick's wife, relieved the tension by remembering Kevin's jacket and sent one of the kids into the house to get it.

"Then we were in the car, and everyone (but Tim) was calling good-bye and thank you and come again.

" ' 'See you soon, Connor,' Jennie shouted as we started off. 'And say good-bye to your brother, the one who doesn't talk.'

" ' 'Now I see what Mrs. Frank's been talking about,' Kevin said sadly when the children had fallen asleep. 'I swear I've never come so close to slugging that kid.'

"On Tuesday morning Kevin reminded Tim that he had to be in a play. On Tuesday evening I got a call: 'He got up on the stage, but he still wouldn't speak,' Mrs. Frank said tiredly. 'I really don't even know what his voice sounds like.'

" ' 'Well, I could tape it!' I told her. 'Then you'd know he can talk.'

" ' 'Mrs. Sanford, I believe he *can* talk,' she replied evenly. 'The problem is why he *won't!*' Mrs. Frank recommended a 'mental health consultation,' which is a tactful way of saying 'shrink.'

" ' 'I guess we'll have to do it,' Kevin said. '*We* can't make Timmy stop his foolishness. Maybe this doctor can.' Is it that simple? I hope so, but I'm very concerned."

The Counselor Replies

L. Eugene Arnold, M.D., a child psychiatrist and professor of psychiatry and pediatrics at Ohio State University, is the author of Parents' Survival Handbook *(published by Steve Ramsey, 3286 Kingston Avenue, Grove City, OH 43123).*

"Joanna Sanford was very alarmed over Timmy's not talking, but Kevin said, 'I'm sure there's no serious problem. We just need some advice from you on appropriate discipline.'

"'Oh, *discipline!*' Joanna sighed. 'That's Kevin's approach to most problems.'

"'Well, *I'm* not the one who has trouble getting Tim to behave,' Kevin said dryly. 'Anyway, Doctor, what should we do?'

"I said that I would need more information about Tim's medical and developmental history and to observe him before I could make any recommendations.

"In response to routine questions, Kevin shared the fact that, unlike Connor, Timmy was often 'impossible' and 'stubborn' and usually needed to be told twenty times to do a simple chore, like putting his clothes in the hamper.

"'I don't see what that has to do with his not talking,' Joanna said.

"I said, 'Usually, a child's refusal to talk is part of a larger refusal to do things. It's not a can't-talk, it's a *won't*-talk (except to a very small number of intimates, like family members and a couple of playmates).'

"Kevin said he'd never heard of such a thing.

"'This disorder, which is called elective mutism, *is* very rare,' I agreed. 'In fact, it shows up in less than 1% of the children we see. Fortunately, we're learning more and more about how to treat it. But we can't help Timmy until we begin to see where his refusal is coming from.'

"Two days later, the Sanfords brought Timmy, an appealing child with a mop of sandy hair and dark, brown eyes, in to see me. As I expected, Timmy wouldn't return my verbal greeting or look me in the eye, but he did cooperate—somewhat reluctantly—with a handshake. Sitting with his parents, he did not respond to the routine question that I ask all children of his age, which is, 'What do you know about why you are here?'

"Nor did he answer me, as most children would, when I asked if the visit had been his parents' idea. At that point, just to clear up any questions in his mind about why he was in my office, I asked the Sanfords to say, out loud, why they had decided to bring Tim.

" 'Because you won't talk at school, Timmy,' Joanna said sadly. There was a silence.

"I asked if they had any other concerns that we would talk about.

" 'Well,' Kevin began, 'Tim can be *very* uncooperative at times and very moody. And sometimes he just blows up, over nothing.'

"I said, 'How would you prefer him to act when he's angry?'

"Kevin looked confused. 'But he shouldn't be angry!'

"Joanna put her arm around Timmy. 'That's right,' she said. 'We only want our boys to be happy.'

" 'To be angry or not isn't a choice,' I said. 'Feelings like anger just come sometimes, to all of us—*no matter how wonderful our lives are.* The choice a person has is what to do with those feelings, what action to take.'

" 'For example, we can say that we're angry and tell someone how we feel. We can plan how to get what we want the next time . . . or how to turn the tables on the person we're angry at.'

" 'We can yell and scream or break something. We can hit someone, we can pound a pillow, we can go out and chop wood. But some of us only feel safe dealing with anger in a passive-aggressive way—by pouting, sulking, refusing to do what we're supposed to, or constantly forgetting.'

" 'Obviously, some of these ways of expressing anger are constructive and socially desirable, while others are not,' I went on. 'An adult can choose almost any of them, but kids' options are limited by the ground rules that their parents set. And that may help explain why Timmy has chosen a passive route.'

" 'But I still don't get it,' Joanna said. 'If Tim is so darned angry, why isn't Connor?'

"I said, 'Perhaps what has been stressful for Tim has been exciting and challenging for Connor. Even when children are brought up the same way and in the same home, they may react very differently.'

"I asked Timmy how he had felt about moving. He wouldn't answer, but his father quickly said, 'He took it fine; there were no problems.'

" 'Wait,' Joanna said. She recalled that Timmy had cried for three days before the move—mostly because he hadn't wanted to leave his best friend, Alex. 'But then he never mentioned it again,' she said.

"I asked Kevin if he had been aware of Tim's sadness about leaving Alex. Kevin seemed surprised and asked Timmy why he hadn't told him. Timmy still didn't answer.

"At that point Kevin got irritated with Timmy, and I intervened, suggesting that Kevin share with Timmy how he felt at that moment. My strategy was to promote an honest father-son dialogue on a *feeling* level rather than on an authority-obedience basis.

"Haltingly Kevin told Tim, 'I feel angry and frustrated because I didn't know about your sadness. I feel kind of left out . . . and sorry . . . and kind of stupid.'

"Although Timmy did not respond verbally, he moved over to sit close to his father—and I felt that we'd made a good start in Timmy's therapy.

"The Sanfords agreed to my seeing Tim once a week and seeing them in between, but after his first individual session, Joanna called—leaving two agitated messages before I could call her back.

"When I did reach her, she said, 'This isn't working. Tim told us that you're trying to make him talk, but he's not going to give in.'

"I clarified that I was not attempting to force or trick Tim into talking. On the contrary, I was giving him chances to communicate feelings through play and drawings. 'But I'm sure that there are people trying to trick him into talking, so his expectation of that happening in therapy is very understandable,' I said.

"In my next meeting with the parents, Joanna still seemed tense as we talked about the family's recent move. 'I knew Tim didn't want to leave,' she confessed. 'But I thought the less we let him dwell on feeling sad, the faster he'd adjust. I was afraid that his unhappiness would be bigger and bigger and overwhelm us—to the point where maybe we wouldn't even be *able* to move.'

" 'Please,' Kevin said. 'It's crazy to even think of letting a five-year-old decide where a family is going to live.'

" 'That's right. Parents must be the ones to make that kind of decision,' I agreed. 'Even if that's unfair from a child's point of view. But maybe Tim could have used a little more empathy than he got.'

"I pointed out that sometimes parents are afraid that listening to a child's unhappiness over something the family wants to do means that they must agree or go along with what the child wants, but that is not so. In fact it's the opposite: Just listening to a child can go a long way toward consoling him and taking away the angry, helpless feelings.

"I gave the Sanfords some suggestions: First, I urged them to encourage Tim to tell them when he feels upset or angry. 'Let him know that *any* feelings are acceptable and that you're there to listen,' I said.

"I also asked them to encourage Timmy's sense of autonomy by allowing him to express his feelings and preferences in day-to-day matters, such as how to spend his free time, for example, and what (within reason) to wear to school, and even what he'd enjoy having his mom make for dinner on a certain night.

" 'We haven't done much of that,' Kevin conceded. 'I guess this is a good time to start.'

"The next day, with the Sanfords' permission, I talked to Timmy's teacher. I found that she was eager to learn what she could do to help get Tim to talk. I suggested that she not focus on talking per se but rather on reinforcing Tim with praise for any communication, including gestures—especially when he asks for something. Mrs. Frank agreed.

"Six weeks passed (with reports of better two-way communication at home), and then something unexpected happened: There was a Christmas carnival at school, with a clown. The clown walked up and beeped his rubber nose at Tim—who began to laugh and couldn't stop. 'Look,' Timmy shouted, pointing at the clown.

"The other children all heard this and began saying, 'Wow, you can talk!' and crowding around.

"By the time Christmas vacation started three days later, Tim had made a new friend, answered a question in class, and even told Mrs. Frank how to say 'Merry Christmas' in French. At home, he drew several pictures of the clown.

"'You know,' Kevin told him, 'I'd forgotten, but when I was a kid, I had to move away from my best friend, and I was very lonely—and mad, too.'

"'*You*, dad?' Timmy asked in amazement.

"Through the afternoon, Kevin and Timmy talked, and just before dinner, they walked out together to send Timmy's best clown picture to Alex.

"We had just finished our sessions, a month ago, when I got another good report from Joanna: Timmy is talking at school, and at home he's better at remembering what he's supposed to do and less sulky.

"'We talk things over now,' Joanna said. 'And it's made the world of difference. It's a little bit funny,' she went on. 'But it was only by *not talking* that this child of ours finally taught us how to listen.' "

Adam, six, has always been affectionate, but lately he's been so rude! We've tried ignoring his behavior and reasoning with him, but nothing works. Is he just playing Bart Simpson, or is Adam genuinely unhappy?

Sue's Story

"We felt lucky about having our kids in the most enriched and challenging school in the city," said Sue Malcolm, 33.

"But while our daughter, Sydney, ten, had emerged as a superior—and super-enthusiastic—student, Adam, in first grade, devoted most of his energy to being a wise guy.

" 'I'm smarter than you,' he said, gloating, when I couldn't guess his riddle. He said the same thing when he found the screwdriver my husband, Rick, had misplaced.

"Nor would he accept any advice or criticism. When I tried to get him to slow his piano playing down to the beat of the metronome, his response was, 'So? You're not perfect!' This don't-try-to-tell-me-anything attitude was getting worse by the day, and I didn't know what to do about it.

"Sometimes it wasn't even what he said so much as the faces he made, as if he couldn't believe that his mother could say anything so dumb. But if I tried to call him on it, he was full of denial.

"Adam's teacher, Mrs. Haines, was surprised when I mentioned the problem. 'He isn't rude here,' she said. 'In fact, he's one of my favorite students, if teachers are allowed to have favorites.'

" 'Adam has some good friends,' she continued, 'but he feels he should be able to handle everything, and he hates to ask for help. Sometimes I think he has a lot of self-doubt.'

"I was left with mixed feelings: relief that Adam wasn't misbehaving at school, and yet concern over whether he felt insecure—and, if so, what about.

"That evening, I tried to draw him out. I talked about how we all have problems and how it's better to share them than to suffer in silence. 'You must be feeling something isn't right,' I persisted.

"Adam said, 'Mom, quit it or I'll shoot you.'

" 'Let it go,' Rick urged. A professor of social work, Rick said that the less we reacted to Adam's rudeness, the sooner he would overcome whatever was bugging him.

"Was he right? I had to admire the way Rick could remain unruffled when Adam called him 'Dimwit.'

"One evening, when Rick started playing the piano, Adam howled like a dog and said, 'You stink, Dad.' But Rick went on playing, and sure enough, Adam settled down and even gave Rick a hug.

"Rick could sidestep the rudeness, and Sydney, with all her activities, was gone too much to be a good target. But despite my efforts to play it cool, I was still getting the brunt of Adam's disrespectful behavior, and it was wearing me down.

"Take the swearing, for example. Like Rick, I teach college, but he leaves earlier, so I take the kids to school. One morning, Adam bumped his head getting out of the car, and he swore—at me! As punishment, I told him he couldn't have a friend over after school.

"Adam insisted he hadn't said what I'd heard. He looked so innocent. So what could I do? I tried to reason with him: 'I never would have dared speak to my parents that way,' I said. 'I don't like to punish you, but how else can I make you understand that your rudeness is unacceptable?' No reaction.

" 'You never used to be this way, and you don't hear this kind of talk at home from us—or from Sydney,' I went on. Without a word, Adam dashed away without even closing the car door.

"A few days later, we were at the bakery when the clerk there commented on the necklace Sydney had made me. 'Thank you,' I said, agreeing that it was very artistic. 'She's always shown talent . . . '

"Adam yanked on my arm. 'You don't know what you're talking about,' Adam muttered under his breath. Then, 'Take me home now. Or else.'

"Outside, I said, 'Adam, don't you realize how bad that kind of behavior makes you look?'

" 'She didn't hear it, and she didn't care,' Adam said, scoffing at my concern.

" 'That's not true,' I said. 'It does reflect on you. Don't you want to make a good impression instead of a bad one?'

"Adam sighed and rolled his eyes. His look said, You are so dumb!

"We had a lot of rough days. But as difficult as Adam could be, there were also many times when he was very pleasant and I thoroughly enjoyed his company.

"Was this rude phase on its way out? 'Looks that way,' Rick said, adding that maybe I was handling Adam better. I accepted his remark but sensed that he still wasn't convinced Adam's behavior was a real problem.

"But then there was the game of Monopoly at our friend's house. Rick and Adam were a team against our host, Rick's colleague Dave, and his little girl, Toni, who's five and very shy.

" 'We'll whip them, won't we, Dad?' Adam said, crowing as the game began. But Adam and Rick had to mortgage all their properties to pay the rent, and finally they went bankrupt. 'I could have won,' Adam railed at his father, 'if I didn't have a dad with ravioli for brains.'

"Dave laughed, but Rick was furious! He yelled at Adam, who cried. Rick told him, 'You're going home right now.' But there was nobody there to watch Adam, so we had to let him stay for dessert. Apparently Rick could take what Adam dished out in private, but in public he couldn't handle it at all.

"Rick's visible anger must have had an effect, because over the next several days, Adam was meek and obedient—no cutting remarks, but not much gusto, either. 'Do you think Adam's sad?' I asked Rick.

"He laughed and said, 'You worry when he's rude, and then you worry when he isn't anymore!'

"The next night, I was to host a PTA planning meeting at our house. 'You can say hello and have a cookie, but then it's off to bed for you, young man,' I told Adam, adding that I was counting on his best behavior.

"And he was good! He greeted the other parents, shaking hands and smiling. In the wake of Adam's recent behavior, I'd almost forgotten how charming he could be.

"When I said it was bedtime, Adam scampered upstairs, waving good night, and I blew him a kiss.

"But it was only minutes before he was back for more cookies, and then he flopped noisily into a chair. I gave him a 'what's this?' look. 'Milk!' he whispered loudly. I shook my head.

" 'Mom!' he interrupted. 'Stop talking and get me some milk.'

"I excused myself and turned to Adam. 'You can get it yourself,' I said through clenched teeth, 'and then right back to bed.'

"Adam shook his head. 'I'm comfortable,' he said grandly. 'You go get it.'

" 'Adam, go to bed!'

" 'Why don't you?' he retorted.

" 'Do what I say, or you're in deep trouble. . . .' I didn't know what to do. Then I remembered Rick's advice to ignore him, and I went right back to my proposal for an after-school language club. 'Kids are like sponges for language,' I explained, and told how Sydney had picked up so much French last summer just on our short trip to Montreal.

" 'This meeting is so dumb!' Adam muttered. I tried to ignore him and went on talking, but he ran over and covered my mouth with both his hands. 'Mom, shut up, will ya?' he said. 'I want my milk.'

"The whole committee sat in wide-eyed silence, clearly shocked by Adam's extreme rudeness—not to mention my inability to stop it.

"We thought we were good at raising kids, but we've sure made a mess with Adam, and we need help figuring out what's bothering him."

The Counselor Replies

Russell A. Barkley, Ph.D., is director of psychology and professor of psychiatry and neurology at the University of Massachusetts Medical Center, in Worcester. A clinical practitioner and president of the Society for Research in Child and Adolescent Psychopathology, Barkley is the author of several books, including Defiant Children: A Clinician's Manual for Parent Training *(The Guilford Press).*

"When Sue called, I told her, 'There are many possible reasons for Adam's disrespectful behavior. We will begin, like detectives, with the obvious and, if necessary, move on from there.'

"Both parents came in for the first session, which lasted three hours. From the responses to my questions, I learned that Adam had been a pleasant, easy-to-manage baby with no developmental delays. Toilet-teaching and other milestones had progressed normally. Adam had fit in at nursery school and was well liked by children and adults. He also had a good year in kindergarten.

"It was at the beginning of first grade that Adam had started to treat his parents rudely, especially his mother, calling them names and boasting that he was smarter than either of them.

" 'Is the problem something at school, or at home?' Rick asked.

"First I asked whether Adam was having any sleeping or eating problems, which could indicate clinical depression. (He wasn't.) Nor was he sulky, moody, or withdrawn from activities.

"We went on to explore another possibility: Could Adam have what we call an 'oppositional disorder,' which is characterized by extreme levels of arguing or hostility? 'I don't think so,' Rick replied. 'He very often does exactly what he's asked. He's not stubborn, and he's not antisocial.'

"Sue agreed. 'He does his schoolwork and most of his chores,' she added, 'so I guess he doesn't have that!'

"I posed a third possibility; a posttraumatic-stress reaction. 'Have there been any major upheavals in the family?' I asked.

" 'No,' Sue replied. 'It's been a very smooth period, with no big changes or anything bad happening.'

"Another possibility I always inquire about is marital discord, which can adversely affect a child's behavior. I asked Sue and Rick

130

whether they argued a lot or used disrespectful language toward each other. 'No,' they both said. 'At least *we* don't do that!' Sue added.

"But Sue's smile of relief quickly faded. 'If those are all the possibilities,' she said, 'then we still don't know anything.'

"I said, 'Yes, now we need to look for the less obvious.' I told them it would be constructive to have one session in which I observed all four Malcolms through a one-way mirror. This way, I could see how they interacted as a family.

"The Malcolms agreed, and that session was revealing. Clearly, they were a caring family. But as they began to talk to one another, I noticed that the parents intellectualized a lot, with long and often excessive explanations. Sue, especially, went on and on. For example, a discussion that started with the fact that Adam needed to keep his room clean expanded into a discussion comparing the neatness of one's room with the neatness of one's personality and one's life.

"Furthermore, the parents tended to monopolize the conversation, and I could see the children growing impatient. Sydney was quiet, but Adam showed displeasure with grimaces and sighs.

"After a while, I asked to talk to each of the children privately. First it was Sydney's turn, and I asked her whether there was anything about her family that she'd like to change.

" 'Yes!' Sydney said emphatically. 'I wish my parents weren't so proud of me.' She said she felt embarrassed by how often her parents praised her in public. Was there anything else? 'Yes,' she answered. 'They keep threatening to punish Adam when he's bratty, but they never do anything.' She sighed. 'He used to be okay, but now he's horrible.'

"Next I talked with Adam, who confirmed that his parents didn't follow through on threats, and as a result, he didn't take their scoldings seriously.

" 'They say, "If you do this, blah, blah, blah," but nothing happens,' Adam said. Then he revealed something else: 'School is too hard!'

"Over the next weeks, I met with Adam three times, and with his parents' permission, I contacted his teacher. And it wasn't long before I got the clear impression that Adam was out of his league.

"Apparently, school *was* hard for Adam, who, it turned out, was in the lowest 15% of his class. He wasn't failing, but I wondered whether he felt out of place.

"As an average kid in the highest-achieving elementary school in the city, Adam did feel inadequate because he wasn't doing as well as the brighter students. Curiously, even his teacher hadn't come to that realization until I asked her to rank Adam . . . and then she was surprised.

"I explained all of this to Rick and Sue and offered these recommendations. First, I advised them to cut back on how much they expressed public approval of their daughter. I suggested a rule: Whenever they wanted to brag about Sydney in front of Adam, they had to say something nice about Adam, too. I said that the main thing is to make sure the praise is equal.

"My second suggestion was not to talk too much: 'I understand that you both do a lot of communicating in your work and that you value social exchange, but when you reason too much with children, you bore them to tears.'

"I said, 'If you want to discuss Adam's rudeness, do it after the punishment, and then give only a brief one- or two-sentence explanation. And try, above all, to avoid threats, especially when you don't really intend to follow through.'

"My third recommendation was to establish what we call a pokerchip economy. Rick looked quizzical. I explained: 'Adam gets 50 chips at the start of the week. Every time he makes a face or is rude, you take away a chip. Conversely, you give Adam additional chips whenever he talks pleasantly in a situation in which he would likely have been insulting in the past.

" 'On the weekend, his chips can be redeemed for TV time or a new toy. You might say he needs twenty tokens to get a new coloring book. You can charge him three chips to watch a half hour of TV.'

"Next, Adam got a tutor. I had explained to Sue and Rick that Adam's insecurity at school would only increase as he entered the second and third grades, especially if his teachers knew what an excellent student his sister had been. Initially Adam balked at the idea of a tutor, but when he met Lise and got used to her very nurturing style, he changed his mind.

"After a few months, the Malcolms began to see improvements in Adam's behavior. They concentrated on keeping their praise of

132

Adam and Sydney equal, and they rewarded Adam for his attempts to stop bragging and being rude.

"The tutoring continued until the end of second grade. Then the Malcolms decided to switch Adam to an elementary school where he would have less pressure, and Adam was relieved. Now the whole aura of his sister was gone, and he was delighted to be in what he called 'My own school.'

"Finally, the Malcolms needed to understand that Adam, who was not verbally gifted like his sister, could not express his feelings in words. Because he hadn't been able to articulate his sense of humiliation in comparing himself with his sister, he had been able only to react to it. And that was where all the 'You're so stupid' comments had come from.

"It has been a year and a half since I've seen the Malcolms, but they tell me that Adam's rudeness is, for the most part, gone. Sue reports that Adam still talks back occasionally, but at least now when it happens, they know how to deal with it."

Peter, ten, has always been such a trustworthy child, but lately he has been stealing and playing mean pranks. Why? Is this just kid stuff, being part of the crowd—or does it signal a deeper problem?

Cynthia's Story

"The first time it happened was at day camp," said Cynthia Burney, 30. "Peter and two of his friends took several sheets of camp stationery from the staff's office and used it to write love notes from one counselor to another.

"Peter seemed surprised that anybody thought it was stealing. 'We were just having fun,' he argued. 'Besides, Ben and Scott and I have to apologize to the counselors and wash the tables in the dining hall for the rest of the summer.'

"My husband, Kevin, and I were glad there were consequences, and Peter promised it wouldn't happen again. But almost as soon as school began, he had another incident—with the same two kids.

"This time, the boys, all fifth-graders starting out in the new middle school, stole twenty toilet-paper rolls from a supply room. Then they proceeded to drape a bathroom, clog up the sinks and toilets, and leave a soggy mess on the bathroom floor.

"I was shocked, but Mr. Dickson, the assistant principal, reassured me that it wasn't unusual behavior. He called it 'a harmless ten-year-old stunt' and said that he knew what to do.

" 'These aren't bad or dangerous kids,' he said. 'They're just little boys who are trying to feel big in a new school. They're testing the limits and looking for acceptance with each other.' Mr. Dickson urged us to let the school handle it. 'Peter stole from us and needs to know from us that what he did was unacceptable,' he said.

"For punishment, Peter and the others each had to write an essay on trust, and they had to spend two Saturdays unpacking boxes of textbooks and putting them on shelves. The second Saturday was beautiful and sunny, and Peter grumbled when I dropped him off at the school. 'You should have learned from the episode at camp,' I said rather crisply. 'And if it ever happens again, you won't get off this easily.'

"Things calmed down for a few weeks after that. Peter seemed to be settling down, and I was not the least bit sorry to hear that his friends, Scott and Ben, were grounded on weekends. I thought, Good, let their parents take a hard line. I was sure that they, not Peter, had masterminded both pranks.

"Now Peter had a new friend, Graham, who didn't look like a troublemaker. That's why Kevin and I were so surprised and upset when we got a call from the deli in town: Peter and Graham had just been caught stealing candy.

"This time, we weren't going to go easy on him! We took away Peter's allowance and movie privileges until further notice. 'But why?' Peter complained. He looked angry and defiant. 'It was just two stupid candy bars!'

" 'Because you still think this is all a joke,' Kevin said. Peter took his punishment hard, but we refused to back down, and finally Peter admitted, 'I guess it was wrong.'

"I felt encouraged. But I also noticed that he was starting to lose interest in his schoolwork. I never saw him open a textbook at home, and his first history test came back with a big D on top.

" 'What happened?' I asked. Peter shrugged his shoulders wearily. Even now, he was supposed to be doing his homework. Instead, his books were closed, and he was playing with his collection of World War II medals that belonged to my father.

"I said, 'Put those away until you've done your work.' Peter sighed. He looked so discouraged. I started feeling sorry for him, and I asked whether there was anything I could do to help.

" 'Yes!' Peter answered. 'Just get off my back!' He started to put the medals away, and I noticed suddenly how big-boned and angular he was, no little boy anymore. And I thought, He's getting to be an adolescent! Was that the problem?

"Uncertain, I decided to make an appointment with his teacher, Mrs. Prill. 'I'm just getting to know him,' Mrs. Prill said, 'but I've noticed he's very quiet. He moves slowly from class to class, and sometimes he seems distracted.'

" 'That really doesn't sound like him,' I said. 'He's always been pretty outgoing.'

" 'I'm fine,' Peter insisted when I questioned him at home. But whether he was doing schoolwork or chores in the yard, he seemed sloppy and inattentive.

"Kevin offered Peter a deal: If he did his homework well for the next week, then on our way to visit Grandpa at the nursing home next weekend, we'd stop at the giant new video arcade he'd been begging to visit. And Peter could play as many games as he wanted. Peter brightened immediately.

" 'Deal!' he said happily and shook his father's hand. And Peter came through—all except for one 'forgotten' math assignment. But it was still an improvement, and we figured that it was better to affirm the progress he'd made than to harp on imperfections.

"Peter enjoyed the arcade—at least he seemed to, judging by the way that he kept coming back for more quarters. Ken and I sat drinking coffee and planning how we would tell my father that we'd had to sell his house.

"My father has Alzheimer's disease, and though he shows little response to what we tell him these days, he has lucid moments. I felt we owed him the dignity of telling him the truth.

"Finally Peter had had his fill of video games, and he seemed to be in a good mood. But when we got to the veterans' home, Peter asked to wait in the car.

" 'No,' I said. 'Of course not. Grandpa wants to see you.'

" 'He doesn't even know when I'm there.'

" 'Yes, he does,' I said, surprised at Peter's negative attitude. 'Even though he can't show it, you know how special you are to him! And last time you saw him, you were glad, don't you remember?'

" 'Look,' Kevin said. 'Try to think of Grandpa the way he used to be, when you couldn't wait to see him.'

"Peter nodded. 'Okay,' he conceded, 'but I don't want to stay a long time.'

"I thought the visit went reasonably well. My father even seemed to smile at Peter, though otherwise he was oblivious to us. In fact, he didn't even react when we told him about his house.

" 'See, it wasn't so bad,' Kevin said as we pulled into our driveway. Peter scrambled out of the car and up to his room to watch TV—with the door firmly closed. Yes, I thought, leave-me-alone adolescence strikes early!

"Later that evening, we got a call from Della Lewis, the daughter of my father's 95-year-old roommate at the nursing home. Della sounded very angry as she asked which aide had been on duty with her father. 'Why?' I asked.

" 'His World War I Purple Heart is gone!' she said, and she began to rage about how the nursing-home staff couldn't be trusted.

"I felt uncomfortable. My father's radio had disappeared a few months ago, when he first moved in there, but then it had turned up in a sitting room.

"I told Della that I hadn't seen an aide and that her father had been asleep when we were there. Then I felt a chill: There had been a moment when Kevin and I went out to talk to the head nurse and Peter had stayed in the room alone.

"Now I went to Peter, in the den. Trying to sound casual, I said, 'Mr. Lewis, Grandpa's roommate, is missing a medal. You wouldn't have seen or taken one . . .?'

" 'Of course not!' Peter answered. 'What would I want with something like that?' But his voice sounded hollow, and I had to find out for myself. I headed for Peter's room, wondering what I'd say if he caught me searching. But I didn't have to look far: There was Mr. Lewis's medal, sitting right out on top of Peter's bookcase.

"Quickly, I phoned Della. I told her that Peter had picked up her father's medal up by mistake and that I'd bring it back in the morning. She was relieved, but I was beside myself! I thought, What's going on here? Peter's stealing, and now I'm lying to cover it up!

"Kevin was horrified. We decided to confront Peter together. But instead of being angry this time, Peter hung his head. 'I don't know why I took it,' he said in a shaky voice, and then he started to cry.

"He cried so! No scolding or punishment in the world could have made him so unhappy. I started to cry myself. Finally I put my arms around him. I said, 'Peter, don't worry. We'll get help.'

"He looked at me with such sadness and said, 'Forget it, Mom, it won't do any good.' But we have to do something; we can't give up on him. Kevin and I need to know whether this is just a quirky phase or something much worse."

The Counselor Replies

Jan Drucker, Ph.D., is a child psychologist in New York City. She is also professor of psychology at Sarah Lawrence College in Bronxville, New York, and a consultant to the Early Childhood Center there.

"Cynthia called and told me what had happened. 'Peter's a good kid,' she said. 'I never thought we'd be dealing with criminal behavior.'

"I said, 'Stealing is a symptom. At this age, it's hardly ever related to criminal behavior in adulthood, but I would have to know more about Peter in order to understand what this means for him.'

"The Burneys came in and told me the full story. They also told me about Peter's good behavior in his earlier years. But I still had no idea what the problem might be, and I suggested that they bring in Peter for a couple of sessions so that I could get to know him.

" 'He's not interested in coming,' Kevin said.

" 'That doesn't surprise me,' I replied. 'But I still need to see him if I'm going to help. Let him know that I don't represent the police or anyone who will punish him. Explain that you're asking me for advice and that I have to meet him so I can understand and help.'

"Peter did come in for a private session, looking a little sullen but also embarrassed. He avoided eye contact and sat with his arms folded. To get him to relax, I tried to engage him in talk about school and what *he* enjoyed, but he answered in monosyllables and shrugs.

"In our second session, he was just as unresponsive, and I finally said, 'Look, Peter. Maybe you're not going to feel comfortable with me, but here's how I see the situation: You've been involved in four stealing episodes, and your parents are concerned. The only way we can get through this is to talk.'

" 'I've talked to lots of kids about stealing,' I went on. 'And I've learned that it can mean many different things.'

" 'It doesn't mean anything!' Peter said, looking at the ceiling.

"I said, 'I think it would help if you'd tell me about the day you visited your grandfather at the nursing home.' Peter was silent.

" 'Okay,' I said to Peter. 'Then why don't you go back to before your grandfather went into the home. Tell me, what was he like?'

" 'I don't remember!' Peter said.

" 'Really?' I asked.

"Peter shook his head very slowly. 'I don't like to think about it too much,' he said softly. 'My grandpa was the best.'

" 'It must have been hard for you when he got sick,' I offered.

" 'Yes!' Now Peter was more willing to talk. 'Grandpa was my friend. He'd tell me all the stories about when he was in Europe in the war and he saved people.' Peter talked and talked—about how his grandpa had taught him to swim and juggle and play the harmonica.

"Peter said, 'He taught me to play video games on his TV.' Peter's eyes suddenly filled with tears. 'But then he sometimes couldn't remember what game we were playing.' Peter fell silent.

" 'Then what happened?' I asked.

"Peter swallowed hard. 'He got lost a couple of times. Then there was a fire in his kitchen, and they told us that he had Alzheimer's and he had to go to the veterans' home.

" 'I thought he should live with us,' Peter continued. 'But Mom and Dad said no because they have to work and our house is so small. But he could have lived in my room!' Peter's hands were clenched; his face was red.

" 'Do you think that would have worked out?' I asked.

" 'No,' Peter admitted sadly. 'He pees in bed, and most of the time, he doesn't even know who I am.' Peter grabbed a wad of tissues to wipe his eyes.

"I saw that our time was almost up, but I wanted to make use of Peter's more open attitude at this moment, so I said to him, quickly, 'Peter, tell me about the day you took the medal.'

" 'I don't know,' Peter said. 'It was just a lousy day. The video arcade was fun. But Mom and Dad were talking about selling Grandpa's house, as usual, and I didn't want to hear it. And when we got to the nursing home, I didn't want to go in, but Mom made me. Grandpa was even worse than the last time, and he was wearing a diaper!

" 'When Mom and Dad left the room, I didn't want to look at him. The other guy was asleep—he's always asleep—so I looked at all the stuff on his shelf, and I saw his Purple Heart.

" 'I thought of the story my grandpa told me about when he got his medals. And when I heard footsteps at the door, I just put the medal in my pocket. I didn't know what I was going to do with it. I felt weird!'

"I said, 'It sounds like taking the medal had to do with your feelings about your grandfather. I'd like to discuss this with your parents and also set up a few appointments so that you and I can talk some more.'

"Peter agreed, and I arranged to meet with his parents. I explained that his not being attentive or interested in things lately, and his poor performance in school, were probably signs of depression.

"I told them, 'Peter conveyed a lot of pain about his grandpa's illness. Seeing a loved one lose so much of his functioning is almost like witnessing a slow death.'

" 'Yes!' Cynthia said. She seemed relieved to talk about her father's deterioration, and so did Kevin. 'We've focused so much on the details, the logistics,' she said, 'but we've been sad too.'

"I said, 'Clearly there's been a lot going on for Peter; not just the mourning we've discussed, but also his new school situation. Going from elementary to middle school is hard—especially in your district, where middle school begins in fifth grade. That's pretty young!'

" 'Peter's a bright, healthy boy,' I continued, 'but he seems overwhelmed, and he deserves some help. The better he learns to cope with his stress, the less it will come out in symptoms like stealing.'

" 'I was afraid this was the start of big problems, but maybe it's the start of things getting better,' Kevin said thoughtfully.

"Over several sessions, Peter and I explored many aspects of his life, and he told me that the first two stealing episodes, at camp and at school, had been high points in an otherwise gloomy six-month period.

"Peter found the pranks exciting, and they helped him feel close to his friends. The danger of doing something wrong, and even the drama of getting caught, added to his pleasure.

"In fact, he admitted, the store incident had been an attempt to draw his new friend into that excitement. For Peter, however—and this was important—taking the Purple Heart was not fun at all but was the result of a desperate impulse, reflecting his sadness over the loss of his grandfather.

"By our tenth session, there were encouraging signs. At this point, I was seeing the family together, and it seemed that everybody was dealing better with the mourning process. At first they had found it painful to remember the good times, but I had urged them not to push happy recollections away.

" 'My memories of Dad are precious,' Cynthia said through tears. 'Now I remember some poet saying that God gave us memory so we could have flowers in the wintertime. It applies here, too!'

"In the course of our talks, Peter saw how he had been trying to shut out his sad and worried feelings by seeking high adventure in stealing.

" 'I guess that was dumb,' he said.

"I replied, 'You could call it dumb—or maybe it's just the way a worried boy tried to protect himself.'

"Peter's grief, combined with the stress of a new school, had become more than he could handle. The Burneys were wise to investigate Peter's feelings before punishing him further.

"With help, Peter learned that he didn't have to bottle up his grief. It was a tremendous relief for him to get his feelings out in the open. He began to return to the happy kid his parents had always known him to be. Finally, the family was able to make peace with the events of their lives."

DIVORCE

AND

SEPARATION

*Ted walked out six months ago,
but now he says we owe it to the kids
to try again. Emily and Kate are
frantic—begging me to say yes. Will
they ever understand why I can't?*

Mimi's Story

"Ted never even said goodbye to the kids," said Mimi Foster, 32. "He just packed up and left—like the proverbial thief in the night.

"Was it a shock? Yes and no. We all like to think our own marriage is immune to what ruptures others' all around us. But Ted had never been easy to read. If he seemed self-centered and preoccupied, I didn't know if he was brooding about his thinning hair, the 'arrogant creeps' at work, or something else.

"He had become harder to live with. He could be a warm and responsive father, but for months before his departure he'd been so grumpy with Kate, five, and Emily, eight, that I felt compelled to keep them quiet and out of his hair until I could get them off to bed. Then, when the two of us sat down to dinner, Ted would either be silent—or cranky, complaining that my new chicken recipe was 'strange' or asking why we had to have my brother and his fiancée over on Sunday: Didn't I care that Ted had nothing in common with my brother, Hank, much less his fat little bride-to-be?

"I usually avoided arguing. What was the point? I'd go clean up the dishes—while Ted shut himself up in his study and came to bed after I was asleep.

" 'Don't be so paranoid; nothing's wrong,' he insisted when I begged him to tell me why he was avoiding me. Maybe we should go to a marriage counselor, I suggested. 'That's dumb,' he retorted. 'Okay, then,' I pleaded, 'Just tell me what you want me to change.'

"But it was too late: he had felt suffocated in our marriage, but too guilty and weak to do anything about it . . . until he started talking to a warm, sympathetic 'friend' at the office. And unlike me, she was so in tune with him that he didn't even have to explain things. And, yes, as a matter of fact, they *were* sleeping together—every chance they could, and if he had the guts, he would move in with her.

"I felt like I'd been punched in the stomach. I could hardly breathe, much less think of an answer. For the next week, Ted kept agonizing: Should he go? Should he stay? Should he let this last chance for happiness elude him? By Sunday, I couldn't take anymore. I said, 'GO!' And he did.

"I had dreaded this moment, but now I felt an unexpected surge of energy. It was finally *settled,* and now it would be like an adventure: learning to be happy on our own.

"But even though I tried to reassure the children ('Daddy will certainly come and see you!'), their grief was deep and chilling. There was no laughing, no fun. Emily cried—for an hour—and demanded to stay home from school. ('What if Daddy calls and I'm not home?' she worried.) Kate went to Ted's desk, picked up the clay duck she'd made for Father's Day, and threw it—hard—against the wall. And then she cried and cried.

"When five days had passed without a word from Ted, I called him at the office. 'I put $2,000 in our checking account,' he said irritably. 'That's not it,' I said. 'JUST GET UP HERE AND PAY SOME ATTENTION TO YOUR CHILDREN.' And then I hung up so hard, I cracked the phone. I was furious!

"That evening, he called back and coldly informed me that he had not forgotten the children, that he had been busy, and that if I was going to be so hysterical and emotional about it, he would see them the following weekend.

"After that, our lives did begin to settle down. The children were remarkably adept at putting their relationship with Ted and their relationship with me in separate boxes. I was the comfortable old hat—for six days at a time; then he would come and whisk them away to the magic of New York City—visiting museums filled with dinosaurs and mummies and knights' armor . . . followed by ice cream and pastry.

"At a friend's suggestion, I joined a displaced spouses' workshop at the Y. It felt good to let off steam and share the self-doubt and fear that I didn't want to show the kids. 'I don't mind being a single woman *at all*,' I would tell the children brightly, trying to be a positive role model. But in the workshop, I could admit that I *didn't* feel single: I felt married and deserted . . . and scared.

"The workshop was fantastic. In all that talking and sharing, I realized that Ted's lust for his officemate was not what had made our marriage collapse. Basically, Ted and I were as different as we could be. He was critical and judgmental, while I was soft, flexible—and this had gotten us in trouble. I had willingly dropped out of graduate school to be the full-time Mom that Ted wanted me to be, but then he had railed at me, asking why I couldn't clean the house better when that was all I had to do all day.

"And at the same time, he'd made me feel inadequate for not having all the pizzazz and accomplishment of the women he met at work who *hadn't* stayed home to raise his children.

"Interesting! It was like solving a puzzle, and I started to feel okay about myself in a way that I hadn't in all the years of our marriage. Instead of being the pathetic little tagalong, desperately trying to satisfy Ted's conflicting demands, I could start to be who *I* was for a change.

"I lost five pounds and bought some new clothes, and then I made plans to go back to school and finish my degree in health-services administration. It was funny: Ted had left for *his* liberation, but it was turning out to be mine, as well!

"That was just before Thanksgiving. I was thinking about whether we should stay home or go out when Ted called and announced that he was taking the children *and* me to a country inn in Connecticut for an authentic Colonial Thanksgiving dinner. 'The waitresses are even in costume,' he added when I started to protest. 'Listen, the kids don't want to go unless you come, too,' he went on. 'Please come—for their sake. At least we can *look* like one happy family.'

147

"With a lot of uneasiness, I did go. And, yes, I did feel awkward and phony. The children were jubilant. I never asked Ted if his romance was on or off. And to my own surprise, I didn't even care.

"During his next visit, he told us he wanted us all to spend Christmas together. 'I think it would mean a lot to the kids,' he said. 'Oh, please, Mommy, *please*,' Kate begged on cue, jumping up and down. Later, after the children had been put to bed, I told Ted sharply, 'I'm not sure this fake togetherness is such a good thing.'

"But it's not fake, I'm ready to move home now,' he said. 'That little affair . . . well, it was like this teenage crush. Kind of meaningless. And anyway,' he murmured, slipping an arm around me, 'now we can have the fun of making up.'

" 'No, Ted, I've changed,' I said, pushing his hand away. 'I've noticed,' he answered in a low, caressing tone. 'You've lost a little weight and you look fantastic. Come on, sexy lady, give me a kiss.' 'Don't you ever touch me again,' I said—and I meant it. A month or two earlier, I might have been grateful; but now I could only wonder how I'd lived with this man—a stranger—for nine years.

"Evidently stung by my rebuff, Ted spent his Christmas visit playing dirty pool: 'Oh, I miss you guys *so much*,' he told Emily. 'If only we could get your mommy to change her mind!' He'd bought me an embarrassing number of presents—from lingerie to a microwave. The girls kept glancing at me hopefully, as if to say, 'Now isn't *this* enough to melt you?' I wanted to scream.

"When he finally left, I called the kids over and explained that I just didn't love their daddy anymore. 'But Daddy *said* he's sorry,' Kate cried. In her five-year-old world, a simple apology could still work magic. 'I think you're the meanest person,' Emily shouted, stamping her foot in utter frustration. 'Mommy, I hate, hate, *hate* you!'

"In the weeks that followed, both of the children grew alarmingly sullen. They rejected everything I offered—from a ride to school on a rainy day to a game of cards. They wouldn't even accept a good-night kiss. And they were unforgivably rude to Jon Meeks, a friend I'd begun dating, who was always warm and friendly with them.

"I tried to ride it out for a couple of weeks, but it only got worse—especially with Ted frequently showing up to fan the flames.

148

" 'Well, *I'm* not the one who's being unreasonable and stubborn and selfish,' Ted offered with a shrug when I accused him of inciting them. But the last straw was the note I found this morning, signed by both kids: 'We hate you!!!' it said in a fierce, black marker. 'This is your last chance.' At the bottom of the page were two broken hearts. I knew Ted was behind this!

"I felt like strangling Ted! All this time, I've tried to be patient, to explain, to say the right things, but he's sabotaging me all the way. Now I know we need help."

The Counselor Replies

Janice I. Cohn, D.S.W., chief of consultation and education in the Department of Psychiatry, Newark–Beth Israel Medical Center, in New Jersey, is in private practice in New York City and Montclair, New Jersey. She is a special consultant to New Jersey courts on the impact of divorce on parents and children.

"Mimi was understandably distraught: would her children ever forgive her? 'They will understand, eventually,' I assured her. But she had her work cut out for her—especially when Ted was working so hard to give the children the opposite message: that '. . . if we just work a little harder, we can break down Mom's resistance, and then we'll all live happily ever after.'

"I suggested that instead of arguing or trying to convince the children, it would help for her to acknowledge and validate their feelings by saying, for example, 'Emily, this must be so hard for you' and 'Kate, I'd feel mad, too, if I were in your shoes.'

"I also suggested that Mimi explain that the marriage had never really been happy by using an analogy the kids could relate to, such as: 'You know how great it is to have a best friend to laugh with and to go to when you're sad or upset? Well, Daddy and I never could be each other's best friend even though we tried.'

"That night, Mimi did what I suggested. Had she gotten through? Well, Kate *did* allow her to tuck in the covers. And Emily actually smiled at breakfast the next morning. Mimi allowed herself to hope that things were taking a better turn, but the following evening, Ted took the children for burgers and evidently told them, 'If Mommy won't let me come home, I might go far, *far* away to live, like to Egypt with all the mummies.'

"He claimed that it was meant to be a joke, but the children went bananas! Kate clung to his leg and wouldn't let him leave. Emily wept and sucked her thumb—something she literally had not done in five years. 'Ted, can't you see what this is doing to them?' Mimi's voice was shaking. 'Please, Ted, for their sake, can't we try to work *together?*'

"Apparently for the first time, Ted realized how his comments and behavior were affecting the children. Ted tried to comfort Emily, still sobbing. 'Okay,' he said. 'I'll try to do whatever will help.'

"The next afternoon, when Mimi came to see me, Ted was with her, looking resolute and a little nervous. I told him how difficult it must have been for him to come, and I said, 'This shows me how very much you care about the children.'

" 'Well, that's it!' he said. 'I know how much a divorce would hurt them. That's why I've been badgering Mimi. I thought she'd agree to reconcile if she saw how much the children want me to come home.' He paused. 'I really love them.'

"I listened, and then gently, I tried to explain to Ted what it was like for children to be in the middle, and what a frightening responsibility it was for Emily and Kate to have to think, 'If only *I* could get Mom to change her mind. . . .'

" 'Are you asking me to leave them?' he asked, obviously frightened. 'Oh, no!' I assured him. 'They need you. But they also need to know that you won't be living with their mother.' I explained that sometimes letting go—just a little—can be a better gift than being around all the time. 'You don't want to keep their hopes up. Maybe it's time to let them start to deal with the truth,' I said, 'even though it will hurt them.'

Deep down Ted understood that it was futile to keep pushing Mimi to get back together again. He was also now able to see the toll that putting the children in the middle was taking on everyone involved, especially on Kate and Emily. Ted and Mimi agreed when I suggested that it would be constructive for all of us to talk together. When we did, I was deeply impressed with Ted's response.

" 'Listen, kids,' he said. 'I'm afraid I've been a little unfair to you.

All these weeks, I've been playing a game—wishing and pretending that we just needed Mom to say yes and everything would be perfect. But here's the truth: for years now, Mommy and I have loved you both very much, but not each other. And it does hurt now, but I agree with your mom that we really can't stay married. It just won't work.'

" 'But I hate divorce, I hate it.' Emily burst into tears. 'What part frightens you the most?' I asked. 'The choosing,' she sobbed. 'I just don't know how I can choose!'

" 'But you don't have to choose between us,' Mimi said. 'It will be different from now on. Maybe you kids will spend some of your holidays with Daddy and some with me. But you'll always have both of us—no matter what.' Emily looked relieved and even began to smile. 'I thought it would be like on TV,' she admitted shyly. She had seen a television program that explicitly portrayed a battle over a child that even included a suicide threat and a kidnapping. If it was certain that she and Kate wouldn't be subjected to a similar drama, then maybe it *wasn't* the end of the world, after all.

"Now the ice was broken and the children both felt free to talk about specific fears. Kate needed to be told—in so many words—that she was not the real cause of the split, that she had never done even one thing to make her father mad enough to leave . . . even back when Ted used to tell her to shut up. 'I was taking my own bad mood out on you, and that was unfair,' Ted admitted. 'I'm very sorry for that now.'

"Both children also needed to be told that there were no bad guys—and nobody to blame. It wasn't Mommy's housekeeping that made the marriage collapse. And it wasn't even Daddy's other lady, because that episode had been more a result than a cause of longstanding unhappiness between Mom and Dad.

"As the children began in the next weeks to accept the inevitability of Ted and Mimi's impending divorce, their anger toward their mother subsided, and they felt safe, once again, to enjoy her friend Jon Meeks. (He wasn't Dad, but he *could* burp the alphabet, and he did throw a mean Frisbee.)

"Ted was right. Dissolving a marriage is always painful, as it involves loss, sadness, and a great deal of guilt and suffering. While Emily and Kate would have opted for a more traditional happy ending, they are feeling much less anxious these days, knowing that they haven't lost their real security—their two loving and devoted parents.

Kim, nine, has always been a sweetheart, but lately she's become so belligerent and mean! My ex-husband, Nick, says we should ignore it. But will that make the problem go away or make it worse?

Linda's Story

"Until recently, I've heard nothing but praise for Kim," said Linda Franklin, 33. "But lately I've had one bad report after another from her school.

"It started a month ago. Kim's teacher, Mrs. Gibbs, said that Kim was becoming edgy and confrontational. Several times Mrs. Gibbs had taken Kim aside—and even sent her out of the classroom to cool off.

"One day Kim was reading her book report to her third grade class, when she stumbled on and mispronounced a word. Garth, who sat behind her, started to giggle—at which point Kim grabbed *his* book report and crumpled it up.

"Garth was upset and cried over the ruined project he'd worked so hard on. But Kim refused to apologize. 'I don't care,' she insisted.

"I was worried, but when I talked about it with my ex-husband, Nick—we were divorced eighteen months ago—he said, 'If that kid laughed at me, I'd crumple his paper, too!'

"But there were other incidents that were harder to dismiss. Even the school-bus driver called one day to complain that Kim was bullying younger kids on the bus.

" 'You can't do that,' I told her. But Kim, insisting on her inno-cence, said, 'Those little kids are the troublemakers, *not me*.'

"I wanted to believe her, but there had been so many confronta-tions lately. At least there was one comfort: Kim was as sweet as ever at home.

" 'That should convince you it's nothing to worry about,' Nick said, satisfied. He and Erika, his girlfriend, had just brought Kim home after a Sunday afternoon at the zoo with Erika's two-year-old son. 'You should see how wonderful Kim is with Ricky,' Nick said to me. 'Isn't that right, Kim?'

" 'Sure,' she said.

"That night at bedtime Kim wound up her music box, a gift from Francine, her longtime baby-sitter, who had left just five weeks ago.

" 'You must miss her,' I said. 'I know I miss her.'

" 'Umm,' Kim answered. I wanted to add, 'But weren't we lucky to find someone as nice as Anna so quickly?' But Kim's eyes were closed, so I just tiptoed out of her room.

"The next week was blissfully uneventful. When Kim came home from school on Friday, she was ecstatic: They were having a recital, and she would play a solo on her flute. 'I want it to be just perfect!' she said, skipping off to her room to practice.

"But if I thought that music would soothe the savage beast in Kim, I was mistaken. Two days later the girls from down the street brought their dolls to play in the yard with Kim—a favorite activity. But almost as soon as they arrived, I heard angry shouting.

"I went to the window. There was Kim yelling, 'Get off my prop-erty, you stupid geeks.' She was throwing handfuls of dirt at the girls, who were shrieking and running away.

"I said, 'Kim, what on earth has gotten into you?'

" 'They tried to use *my* stuff,' she cried, pointing to her carton stuffed with doll clothes and accessories.

" 'But you have plenty. You could share your things with them.'

" '*No!*' Kim insisted.

" 'Now, look,' I said, 'you know you love to play with Ann and the twins. But if you don't apologize, they won't want to play with you anymore!'

" 'Who cares?' Kim grumbled, yanking off the wedding dress that her doll was wearing.

"I'd rarely seen her so angry, but when she came inside a few minutes later, she was serene again and asked if we could bake something. I said, 'Honey, not today.' I hated disappointing her, but I'd slept even worse than usual, and I was exhausted.

" 'That's okay,' Kim said kindly. 'Here, Mom.' She patted the pillows on my bed. 'You lie down, and I'll close the curtains and sit over here in this chair and play my flute for you.'

"I was touched and grateful, as always, for this wonderful child and her understanding.

" 'I told you: She's a very together kid, and there's nothing *going on,* as you put it,' Nick said. 'So what if she's feisty? Isn't it better than hanging on to every little grievance, the way you always do?'

"I had to admit he was right about Kim. I remembered how worried I'd been two years ago, when Nick and I were separating—only to find in the end that Kim had coped beautifully!

"She'd had trouble sleeping for two or three weeks, but then she recovered and seemed to take it all in stride—even accepting Erika, which was more than I could have done!

"Perhaps Nick did have the right idea now—that Kim's 'short fuse' was part of just a harmless passing phase.

"Then it was the day of the recital, and Kim could hardly contain her excitement. 'Mom,' she said on the way to school, 'didn't you bring a camera?'

" 'I'm sure your dad and Erika will have one,' I assured her. And I felt so civilized when they arrived and the three of us sat together. 'Kim will really shine today,' Nick said.

"But almost before the lights were out, I could hear a commotion backstage. There were muffled voices and the sound of something heavy falling—and then a wail, and then Kim, loud and clear, saying, 'No fair, she started it!'

"Then there were some more muffled voices and then silence, and the concert began.

"But Kim never appeared! 'It's so unfair,' she sobbed when the concert was over and the lights had come on. 'I *didn't* push Sarah Jane. She pushed *me!* It's her own stupid fault if her cello fell and broke. She deserved it!'

"Kim's face was hot and streaked with tears. I asked her if she wanted me to see the teacher and straighten things out, but she said

155

no, and Nick said, 'Don't force her.' Kim and I drove home in silence.

"I don't know what's going on, but I'm going to call our pediatrician and ask for the name of a child therapist. Nick is still saying, 'No big deal!' but now it seems to me that Kim needs professional help."

The Counselor Replies

Janice I. Cohn, D.S.W., chief of consultation and education in the Department of Psychiatry, Newark–Beth Israel Medical Center, in New Jersey, is in private practice in New York City and Montclair, New Jersey. She is a special consultant to New Jersey courts on the impact of divorce on parents and children.

"Far from being sullen and defensive, Kim appeared calm and self-possessed. She was polite and articulate as she told me that everything was fine and nothing bothered her.

"I said, 'That's good, but as long as you're here, I thought we could make up some stories together.' Kim looked surprised—and interested. (I used a therapeutic technique called mutual storytelling with Kim. I would start a story and have her finish it, or she could start one and I would suggest a variety of possible endings that we'd then discuss.)

"Kim has a flair for storytelling and a fine sense of fantasy, and when I began a story and then invited her to go on with it, she joined in eagerly.

"As she spun out her tales, some strong themes emerged. Many of the characters she made up were cruelly abandoned. And when that happened, those characters would feel that they had done something wrong but didn't know what. As a result, they felt very out of control.

"Sometimes we switched back and forth between storytelling and just talking. I learned Kim had been very upset about her babysitter Francine's recent departure. Even more significant, that event apparently reawakened painful buried feelings in Kim about her parents' divorce.

"Clearly Kim felt abandoned—first by her dad and then by her sitter—and now she wondered, Why *me?* What did *I* do to deserve this?

"It seemed unfair to Kim, who had always tried hard to be a good girl. Convinced (as many children are) that she was somehow mysteriously responsible for what had happened, she worried that it would happen again. Would her mother leave her? Would her father move to California, as a friend's father had?

"And on top of these worries, Kim was still very angry inside: angry at her father for leaving and at her mother for letting him go. 'Everything was fine before Mommy and Daddy got divorced,' she told me. 'But now everything's bad.'

"A few days later I had a session with Linda. I told her that Kim's anxiety seemed to stem in large part from feelings about the divorce.

" 'But that can't be,' Linda said. 'We handled it so well: Everybody said we did!' I asked what she meant. 'We followed all those good rules,' she explained. 'You know, what they say in books about how to make it less traumatic for a child.'

" 'For example,' she went on, 'Nick and I went to Kim and told her *together.* Also, we stressed that it wasn't her fault and that we both still loved her and always would. We were also careful not to disparage each other.

" 'In fact the day Nick left, he could see I was upset, and he said, "Kim, I'm counting on you to be good and to take good care of your mom." And all that worked,' Linda added, 'because Kim got over it quicker and a lot better than *I* did!'

"I said, 'I understand how much you want that to be true. But I don't think Kim really got over the divorce quickly. In fact it's not unusual for children to seem fine initially, only to have a more severe reaction later.'

"I explained that Francine's leaving would probably not have been so traumatic under normal circumstances, but in this case it kicked off unresolved, long-smoldering feelings of loss for Kim. It was my belief that the loss of her much-loved baby-sitter was the trigger for Kim's new, explosive feelings and behavior.

" 'But why does she take it all out on her friends?' Linda wondered.

" 'All that pent-up anxiety and tension has to come out somewhere,' I said. 'Some children turn it inward and get depressed, but Kim turns it on her friends because they seem like a safer target.'

" 'Safer?'

" 'Yes,' I said. 'Kim doesn't dare express such "unacceptable" feelings directly to you or her father: She needs you badly and doesn't want to risk the possibility of your becoming even sadder and even less available. Nor can Kim bear the thought of losing her controlled good-girl image in her dad's eyes and driving him even further away.'

"A month after I'd started meeting with Kim, I felt that it would be helpful to meet with Nick and Linda together. I told them, 'Kim still feels anxiety and confusion, but I think, together, we can come up with some relief for her—and all of you.'

"Most of all, I explained, Kim needed permission from her parents to talk about her feelings. 'Do you mean we should let her know that she doesn't have to be good all the time?' Nick asked.

" 'Yes!' I said. 'Definitely! Kim's anger never came out against you—or against anyone until recently—so you didn't know what a burden it was for her to strive for that unrealistic perfection.

" 'What parents say to a child is very important, and you were right to say the things you did at the time of the separation. But *listening*—and taking cues from a child to pick up on her concerns—is more important than following a script.'

"Nick and Linda were responsive and eager to help Kim, and after several weeks, many good changes occurred. When I told Nick that Kim was upset that she never got to spend any time alone with him, he adjusted his schedule to make time.

"Now Kim felt free to say things like 'I want you to come back—and I don't understand why you had to leave.' And Nick, in turn, was able to explain, 'Sometimes people grow apart; your mom and I did. But when I'm with Erika, I feel happy.'

" 'Oh,' Kim said, with new understanding. All she'd heard before was 'It's not your fault.'

"Nick's style had been to deny any uncomfortable feelings, but in our sessions he learned to help Kim by saying things like, 'I bet you feel sad' or 'Did that make you angry?'

"For the first time, Kim had the courage to say, 'I don't like Erika,' and while Nick was tempted to jump in and say, 'Sure you do! She's great, and she loves you,' he simply said, 'I understand.' And that was a real breakthrough for everyone.

"There was also progress made between Kim and Linda. One day Kim was able to say directly to her mother, 'You used to be fun, but now you're always so sad.' That jarred Linda, who hadn't been aware of how much her own depression had been affecting Kim.

"She was unable to just 'snap out' of her depression at that point. But once she understood know Kim was feeling, she started to make more of an effort to recover—including going into therapy herself to deal with her own unresolved disappointments, anger, and self-doubts.

"It's been three months since I've seen the Franklins, but I recently received a note from Linda, and I learned that things are going well. Kim is, once again, a friendly child. 'She seems more relaxed and spontaneous,' Linda wrote. 'Now Nick and I both see how much she needed that.'

"Separation and divorce are always complicated and painful when a child is involved, and for many, the pain never fully goes away. But at least for Kim, the process of healing has begun, and she is free to move on."

Sallie, seven, has fallen under the thumb of a sneaky little troublemaker named Jill. Why is Sallie so passive—and why does she leap to Jill's defense when I say what I'm seeing?

Diane's Story

"I was delighted when Sallie went to visit Jill Reed, a new girl at school," said Diane Potter, 39. "Up until this year—second grade—Sallie had many play dates, but since my husband, Jack, moved out, Sallie was clingy and had wanted to be home with me every day.

"Even when she missed her dad, she would call and he'd come right over, but even then she would hang on to me and be afraid to leave with him, or even stay at our house unless I was there, too.

"So it was certainly a breakthrough when Sallie went to Jill's huge, impressive Fifth Avenue penthouse for a whole Saturday and had such a great time that she said, 'Sure!' when Jill invited her to come again after school on Monday.

"In almost no time, Sallie was spending most of her time at Jill's. I said, 'Sal, why don't you have her over here for a change?' Sallie agreed and we planned a special Saturday: Jill would come over in the morning and they'd play together. Then they'd have fried chicken for lunch (Sallie's favorite), and after that, I'd take them to the circus.

"Sallie could hardly wait; she kept saying, 'It's going to be perfect!' But when Jill arrived, she seemed to have her own agenda: She didn't want to play; she only wanted to rummage through Sallie's closet—and then watch TV.

"When I told them lunch was ready, Jill took a look at the chicken and said, 'I hate when it's all brown like that. I'd like a taco.'

"Quietly seething, I said we didn't have the ingredients.

" 'Well, I bet they have them at the store,' Jill said.

" 'Can you, Mom?' Sallie asked.

" 'No! And there wouldn't be time,' I said firmly as I put the chicken away and made peanut butter sandwiches.

" 'Well . . . I guess maybe on second thought I'll have the chicken,' Jill decided, and Sallie said, 'I guess I'll have it, too,'

"I'd thought that things would improve when we got to the circus, but fifteen minutes into the show, Jill was whispering, 'I'm bored—can we go home now?' And before long, both girls were saying it—and I was ready to wring their necks.

"What bothered me even more than Jill's rudeness was the way that Sallie had accepted it all without protest. 'Why did you let her call all the shots?' I asked. But Sallie said, 'I didn't let her!'

" 'But Sal,' I insisted, 'you did. You let her push you around all day.' But if I felt upset that evening, I felt a lot worse the following week, when I got some feedback from Sallie's teacher, Ms. Duffy.

"Apparently Jill was also dominating Sallie at school—and seemed intent on turning Sallie against the other girls who had been her friends in the past two years before Jill arrived. 'Sallie's still friendly with others when Jill's not around,' Ms. Duffy said thoughtfully. 'I've moved them to opposite ends of the room, but it hasn't helped much.'

"I told Sallie clearly that I didn't like what was going on, but she insisted that none of it was true. 'You believe her just because she's a grown-up,' Sallie complained. Well, I wanted to believe in my daughter's own good sense. But how could I ignore what was going on? Even that day at the circus, I had heard Jill say things like, 'Let's not play with Ellen on Monday,' and 'Don't forget—we're not talking to Pam.' And I'd seen Sallie nod obediently.

"I said, 'Sallie, Jill is using you, and you're going to be sorry when you don't have another friend left.' But the warning only seemed to infuriate Sallie, who ended up in tears on the phone to her father.

" 'Diane, you're making her very unhappy,' Jack told me afterward. Hadn't Sallie been through enough already with all the separation upheaval, he asked—without my 'heaping more pressure' on her? I felt like screaming at him. Maybe Sallie was too young, but why couldn't Jack understand that all I wanted was to see our daughter stand up for herself?

"Jack saw Jill Reed as a cute, spunky little second grader, but to me she was as bad as she could be—cynically manipulating Sallie and turning her into a dancing puppet.

" 'Why do you let Jill take over and make rules for you?' I railed at Sallie. 'Don't you know that *your* feelings matter?' Jill, on a whim, had just pulled apart Sallie's ancient and beloved rag doll, Beezee, which was now beyond mending. 'You should have told Jill to stop,' I said.

"Our Jill discussion quickly deteriorated into a fight, with me trying to talk about dignity and Sallie defending this brat she called her best friend; and then, as usual, Sallie went to phone Jack and tell him how mean and unreasonable I was.

"But at least there was something good coming up—Sallie's birthday party; and it was a joy for us to plan special games and activities together and to see Sallie getting excited about something involving all the girls instead of just Jill.

"For party favors, I had gone all out—spending many, many evenings making adorable little stuffed animals. Sallie loved them and spent a great deal of time choosing who would get which.

"During the party, Jill kept asking Sallie what the favors were. 'Remember—they're a surprise,' I said pointedly to Sallie, and she nodded. But when the party was nearly over and the mothers had arrived, I called Sallie to bring out the favors—all lovingly wrapped in colored paper and curling ribbons.

"But instead of finding those attractive packages as I had left them, they'd been raided! The animals were scattered on the floor amid a mess of torn paper—all my wrappings strewn and crumbled, and there was Sallie—trying in vain to hide the evidence, as Jill stood and watched.

" 'What's going on?' I demanded.

" 'Jill decided to switch,' Sallie began as I exploded in a tirade of anger and disappointment.

" 'You're just—DUMB!' Sallie retorted—loud enough for everyone to hear—as Jill slipped innocently out of the room.

"There were quick and embarrassed good-byes, and after everyone had left, I tried to talk to Sallie, but she wouldn't listen. 'My daddy is coming,' she said haughtily.

"When Jack arrived, he comforted Sallie and said, 'For heaven's sake, Diane, can't you even let up on her *birthday?*' It was as if I, not Jill, had been the one violating Sallie's rights.

"So much for Jack's insistence that I'm making a problem where none exists. We had a couple of consultations with a child psychiatrist a year ago, when we decided to separate, and I'm going to call him now. Jack will go on denying it forever, but it's obvious to me that Sallie needs *real,* professional help."

The Counselor Replies

E. Gerald Dabbs, M.D., clinical associate professor of psychiatry at Cornell University Medical College, practices child, adolescent, and family psychiatry in New York City.

"When Diane called and told me about the birthday party incident, I agréed to see Sallie to determine *why* Sallie was allowing Jill to dominate her.

"Sallie was a pleasant, friendly child, but she quickly became defensive about the party favors—insisting that Jill hadn't done anything wrong: 'Jill never even touched the wrappings,' she said. But when I asked Sallie why *she* had torn the wrappings off, herself, she admitted that Jill had demanded it.

"When I asked why she let Jill tell her what to do, she tried to rationalize it by saying, 'She's my best friend,' and 'She always has cool ideas.' But the bottom line was that Sallie didn't understand why herself, and she acknowledged for the first time how helpless she had felt all along with Jill and how hard it was to say no to Jill's incessant demands.

" 'I wish this was me,' Sallie said, picking up a She-Ra Princess of Power doll.

" 'We all feel powerless at times,' I told her. 'But maybe you have more power than you think.' Putting it in the context of play, I suggested a game of checkers and set up the board. Sallie played thoughtfully and well, until I said, 'Now, what would happen if I decided to jump sideways to take that piece of yours?'

" 'That wouldn't be fair,' Sallie said quickly, as I took her piece. 'You can't do that in checkers.'

" 'You're absolutely right,' I said, putting it back. 'And you know what? You can also tell Jill that she can't destroy your doll or make you unwrap party favors. You can say no to Jill or anyone else you don't happen to agree with.'

"Sallie looked troubled. 'I'm not so sure,' she said—and began to tell me how helpless she had felt in the past year when her parents had fought all the time and then made the big decision to separate. 'I begged and begged my daddy to stay, but he left anyway,' she said miserably.

"At that point, Sallie had felt convinced that the only way to get what she wanted from her parents was to be upset and seem helpless. Then her parents would both be there, and she'd feel, once again, as though she had them still together.

"Hearing Sallie talk, I was certain that she had unconsciously been using her helplessness with Jill to control her parents: The friendship drove her mother crazy, while it elicited a strong sympathetic response from her father. The whole Jill issue had succeeded in getting her parents 'back together' in Sallie's mind, as they now fought and argued—almost as much as when they had been living together.

"The fact that Sallie was now saying that she didn't really see Jill so much now—or miss her—confirmed my hunch that Sallie *had* been glad enough to withdraw from that friendship once she saw Diane and Jack reinvolved with each other as a result of the relationship.

" 'Well, isn't it okay if it works?' Sallie asked me ingenuously.

" 'But, Sallie, it doesn't *really* work,' I told her. I carefully explained to her then that she had not been responsible for her parents splitting (even though children typically feel that they are), and by the same token, she could not be responsible for 'making' them get back together.

"Sallie cried a little—with a mixture of disappointment and relief. 'I guess I knew inside, but I still kept hoping,' she admitted.

"In between sessions with Sallie, I was also talking to her parents to help them gain a more balanced and realistic perspective. Jack, initially, had felt that everything was fine with Sallie . . . or at least it would be 'if Diane would just relax.'

"Diane, on the other hand, had been frantically convinced that Jill was evil and that Sallie's ego was in perilously bad condition.

"I said, 'I can see how you might hold those views, but actually it appears to me that Jill is not an ogre, simply a child accustomed to always getting her own way.' And if Jill 'ruled' Sallie, I went on, she was probably just taking the power that Sallie had given her.

"I said that there were probably good reasons why Sallie had been vulnerable. First, there had been the obvious allure: Jill was forceful and dynamic, and with her brashness and her big house and her let's-exclude-the-others possessiveness of Sallie, there was prestige—and at least an illusion of security—in being Jill's best friend.

"In addition, I pointed out, Jill had come along at a time when Sallie was feeling uncertain about herself because of her parents' separation; she was experiencing frustration in not being able to do anything to prevent it or even get her parents back together again.

"I observed that Sallie had been trying to rescue the Potters' marriage, while Diane was trying to save Sallie from Jill, and Jack was trying to protect Sallie from Diane. Now, I assured the Potters, Sallie would benefit greatly and they would all feel better when this well-meaning but controlling action stopped.

"I acknowledged to Diane that it is painful to see a beloved child caught in a domineering relationship, but the more we try to correct the situation, the more we end up reinforcing it.

"I also reminded Diane that it usually takes some trial and error for children to learn to relate to peers in the best possible way. I said to her, 'As Sallie gets older, you probably won't approve of all her relationships, but this is a part of the letting go (and letting grow) that parents must learn to accept.'

"Jack continued to see himself as the voice of calm and reason in a turbulent situation, but I told him that his habit of minimizing Diane's concerns over Jill was more provocative than helpful and escalated conflicts instead of resolving them.

"I also spoke again with Sallie and suggested that when she had problems with her mom in the future, it would help to stay and talk things through instead of always calling her dad. And at the same time, I suggested that the Potters develop—and stick to—a predictable program of custody and visits, so that Sallie would know what to expect. I said that this would reinforce for Sallie the idea that she had a right to express her feelings, but that when all was said and done, she was still not in control of her parents.

"After just eight weeks, we ended treatment. The Potters *did* feel better—and Sallie reported that while Jill was no longer a best or only friend, they did things together occasionally, and Sallie was beginning to experiment with saying no and seeing that it meant something.

"As loving parents we are often tempted to 'save' our children when we see them in 'impossible' situations. But both the Potters are finding that the less they try to 'rescue' Sallie, the better she is learning to handle things herself."

When Paul left, I thought I'd be okay as a single mother. But now I feel so drained and so alone! I know how much the kids need me— but does that mean I can't ever have what I need, too?

Linda's Story

"Ending my marriage made sense, but I was concerned about our children, Jason, five, and Heather, eight," said Linda Carpenter, 34.

"As a teacher in a small private school, I'd seen children suffer terribly when their parents divorced.

"Paul kept saying that our situation was different: Our divorce was not a war, just a case of two civilized adults who couldn't live together. And that was true; we'd kept our problems private and hadn't even argued in front of the children. We were hoping Jason and Heather could come out of this unscathed.

"Sure, the kids cried the morning he left, but he reassured them, 'You still have both of us.'

"To my surprise and relief, things did go smoothly. On weekends, the kids would take their little duffel bags to Paul's new loft-apartment. In fact, they were seeing more of him now than they had before!

"Maybe everything would have stayed okay—if it hadn't been for Paul's new job. He got an important management position that re-

167

quired a lot of traveling, sometimes over weekends.

" 'The kids know perfectly well that I'm not ditching them,' Paul insisted. 'They understand.'

"Maybe. But I saw changes in them that made me uncomfortable. Jason was back to sucking his thumb and acting helpless, calling me into his room just to take off his socks and shoes.

"Heather sneered and called him a baby, but in her own way, she was doing the same thing. 'Who stole my sneakers?' she cried, when they were on the floor right behind her. If I was cooking or on the phone, she would whine, 'Help me!' and thrust her homework in front of my face.

"I was careful not to react negatively, to be calm and nurturing. My children were obviously needy, scared—and testing me: Would I be a fair-weather parent, like their dad? Did I really love them?

"I told them that I would always be there for them, and I tried my best to prove it. For example, I gave up my Thursday-night exercise class. Yes, it was relaxing and wonderful for me, but it wasn't worth all the upset the children went through each time the sitter came.

"Those kids needed me so much, and I gave to them willingly, but they were bottomless pits. One night I invited a friend of mine over for dinner—and the children were awful!

"They made a point of ignoring my friend, talking only to me and interrupting freely. I was annoyed and embarrassed, but this just proved how vulnerable the kids were if they couldn't let anyone else have even a little of my attention.

"Paul's travel schedule picked up steam, and things got worse. More than half the time now, he was canceling his visits with the kids, often at the last minute. One Friday, early in November, he called me at school. 'Sorry,' he said from his plane to Los Angeles. 'It's a three-day meeting. I couldn't get out of it.'

"Fran, the school secretary, saw my face as I put down the phone. 'Bad news?' she asked.

"I shook my head and smiled. 'Not really,' I said. 'I'd planned to go to Boston for the weekend, but now my ex-husband can't take the children.'

" 'So, go!' she said. 'I'll take the kids.' I thanked her; I was really touched and grateful. But I knew the children would feel doubly rejected if I left them too. So instead I planned a jolly, busy weekend of biking, a picnic in the park, and a trip to the zoo.

"But it rained all weekend, and there were no movies to see. By Sunday my resolute cheer was no match for the children's boredom. No, they didn't want to play a board game or draw or help me bake a cake. Instead, they followed me from room to room, complaining that there was nothing to do.

"Just then, the phone rang. It was someone from the city university, asking me whether I'd participate in a series of workshops on young adolescents. There would be a small honorarium, I was told. And a plaque. And I'd be working with a great group of professionals.

"I was thrilled—especially when this person said I had been recommended as 'a super teacher with enormous empathy for young people.' That made me feel so good. But there was a catch: The workshops would be held two evenings a week. The only way I could do this would be if Paul helped me out.

" 'Hey, I'd love to spend more time with the kids,' Paul said when I called him. But he was up to his ears in work. 'Try me another time,' he offered. 'I'll send some extra money if you need it.'

" 'Money! Did he think that was the only thing that mattered? I felt a surge of resentment. Why did I need his okay to do what I wanted? He hadn't needed anyone's approval or help when it came to accepting his new job!

"But the answer was obvious: I was the mom, and it made no sense for me to neglect my own kids in order to teach other parents how to nurture theirs! Your plate is full enough anyway, I told myself, between working and taking care of the kids, cooking, cleaning, laundry, and grading papers.

"Not to mention the phone! Strictly speaking, students at my school weren't supposed to call teachers at home, but I'd never enforced that rule. I knew they wouldn't call unless they needed me.

"But those calls took time and energy, especially with my own kids always pulling on me and asking for my help.

" 'You were on the phone, so I get to stay up extra,' Jason would argue. And it was hard to put my foot down. Evening was the time they needed reassurance most.

" 'If Daddy loves us, then why isn't he here?' Heather had asked me, in tears.

"The week before, she'd written a story for school about a house destroyed by a cyclone and the children who had been lost. Clearly, that was how she felt!

"And poor Jason! 'Our dad divorced us,' I heard him explain to a friend. Us! After I'd told the children so many times that it was their father's and my divorce, not theirs. How could I ever give them enough support to make them feel okay?

"I felt I couldn't call a sitter unless it was a real emergency. These children needed a devoted parent, not just someone to watch them. I couldn't even count the times I'd had students describe to me how lonely and abandoned they felt when their folks split and neither parent had time for them.

"Still, as pressed as I felt, that workshop series—and the plaque I could have had—still haunted me. Why couldn't I do it? I was doing everything with the kids, while Paul skipped around the country.

"Oh, stop the self-pity, I told myself. Sure, Paul's job was too demanding; I knew that. And he loved the kids; I knew that, too.

"Suddenly I found myself crying. I caught myself in the mirror: huge bags under my eyes, hair desperately in need of cutting, and blotchy skin; I hated the sight. Just pull yourself together, I kept thinking.

"But what bothered me even more was the way I'd started snapping at Jason and Heather. 'Leave my stuff alone!' I yelled when I found Heather kneeling in my closet.

" 'Mom, I was just lining up your shoes for you,' she said, clearly hurt, and I felt so ashamed! Earlier I'd scolded Jason just for being noisy. Well, what did I expect from a five-year-old, anyway? I felt like the ogre in a Halloween book I'd read to him. Wouldn't I rather that he be noisy than depressed? What had happened to my patience?

"The harder I struggled for self-control, the more I seemed to lose it.

" 'You're just stressed,' my mother said sympathetically on the phone. She was looking forward to our visiting for Thanksgiving, and I could hardly wait! Thank goodness for family, I thought as we got off the bus to smiling faces, hugs, and shouts of welcome.

"It was wonderful to be there—with a bonus: My parents had

invited a guest to share our Thanksgiving dinner, a writer from England named Austin. He was interesting and funny, and I found myself extremely drawn to him.

" 'I can tell, he likes you!' my father said in the kitchen. And the next morning, Austin called to ask me out to dinner.

"How perfect, I thought. With my parents here, the children wouldn't even need a sitter. I couldn't remember the last time I had spent a private evening with any man, let alone one as attractive as Austin, and I was excited. So was Heather, until she realized that she wasn't coming along.

" 'But why?' she argued.

"Jason clung to my arm. 'Don't go,' they both pleaded through the door while I showered. My mother offered them ice cream and cookies as a distraction, but they ignored her.

" 'Stay,' they pleaded.

" 'They're manipulating you,' my mother whispered. But I heard real pain in their voices, and real panic, too; and as much as I wanted to go with Austin, I couldn't do it. I canceled the dinner.

"I just knew I could never enjoy myself if it meant making my children so miserable. So now, what does that make me? A wonderful mother—or a sap? Will these kids ever feel safe enough to let me get on with my own life? I'm totally exhausted, and I've run out of solutions. I think I need help."

The Counselor Replies

Janice I. Cohn, D.S.W., chief of consultation and education in the Department of Psychiatry, Newark–Beth Israel Medical Center, in New Jersey, is in private practice in New York City and Montclair, New Jersey. She is a special consultant to New Jersey courts on the impact of divorce on parents and children.

"Linda seemed very sad when I met her. 'I need help; I'm not myself; I'm crying a lot,' she admitted. 'And I never dreamed I'd need a therapist! I've helped other children cope after divorce, and I thought I understood all the issues,' she explained. 'Why am I losing it now?'

"From listening to Linda, I could tell she was very astute, responsible, and caring, and I told her so. I pointed out that she was keenly aware of other people's needs—her children's, and even her ex-husband's.

"I said, 'It's wonderful to have so much empathy for others; that's what makes you such a sensitive teacher and mother. But in understanding others so well and identifying with them, you're ignoring yourself.'

" 'I can't be selfish,' Linda said, folding her arms.

" 'Wait,' I said. 'Forget reality for now, and don't censor yourself. It's important for you to know what you yearn and long for. In the best of all possible worlds, what would you like for yourself right now?' I asked.

" 'Oh,' she answered without hesitation. 'I'd like more time for myself . . . just to sit. I'd also like to socialize a little, maybe go shopping. Go to a play. Have time to exercise and get my hair cut.' She smiled. 'I'd like to call a sitter up without feeling guilty, and I'd like to have a boyfriend.'

"Suddenly animated, Linda went on: 'I just feel guilty for complaining. Yes, the kids are a lot of responsibility, but they didn't ask for the divorce! Friends always tell me how lucky I am. I know it! So many divorced women have problems with money or abusive ex-husbands; some have rotten kids or difficult ex-in-laws, hateful jobs, or no decent place to live.'

" 'I have everything,' Linda continued. 'But I'm resentful just because I don't have enough time. Doesn't that sound stupid?'

" 'No,' I replied. 'Not having any time to yourself is almost guaranteed to cause resentment. Even a saint would feel the way you do.'

" 'But I can't act selfishly,' Linda repeated firmly. 'I've seen at school what happens to kids when their parents make themselves a priority.'

" 'One of the most difficult things after divorce is to find a balance,' I explained.

" 'That's impossible for me,' Linda argued. 'There are only so many hours in the day. Who am I supposed to shortchange?'

" 'You want your children to feel secure, but the ultimate security for kids is seeing parents having their own lives and being happy. We have to find out what is possible; and it might not be a bad idea to have your children come in to discuss this.'

" 'No!' Linda protested vehemently. 'This is my problem, not theirs.'

" 'This is a family issue,' I explained, 'and they may want to be part of the solution. If not now, perhaps they will later.'

"When I asked whether Paul could be involved, Linda smiled and said, 'Sure, but good luck getting him here!' And she was right: Although I subsequently found Paul likable and very agreeable on the phone, he never managed to keep even a single appointment.

"Still, the eight sessions Linda and I had without him accomplished many things. First, Linda learned that she did not have to feel guilty about being so 'lucky.' (Just because her situation wasn't horrible didn't mean it was perfect or that she wasn't entitled to her feelings.)

"Linda also understood that she tended to overidentify with everyone, especially her kids. Now she needed to acknowledge that her kids were, in fact, not having as hard a time as others she knew.

" 'I guess I was reacting more to fear than to reality,' Linda said. 'But sometimes Jason and Heather are angry or sad or scared.'

"I said, 'I'm sure that's true; kids will be upset in any kind of divorce, even a civilized one. But the fact that they're dealing with powerful feelings of anger, sadness, and resentment does not mean that they will suffer some kind of permanent damage.

" 'As long as you are sensitive to their feelings—which, clearly, you are—kids can cope and recover, and sometimes they end up stronger.'

"We talked about Linda's disappointment over the workshop series.

" 'Why does it still bother me?' she asked.

" 'We all need affirmation of our hard work,' I said. 'Especially when so much of what you do at home isn't recognized—like all the ways you've sacrificed for your children's emotional comfort. The workshop was recognition, at last, and of course it hurt you to give that up.'

"Linda smiled. 'It helps just to know I wasn't crazy,' she said.

"Linda and I discussed her recent trouble setting sensible limits for Heather and Jason. We decided we needed to reduce the pressure that was causing Linda to snap at her children and then overindulge them to compensate.

"With my help, Linda set down some new house rules. Instead of being constantly available to her students, she made one night a week 'calling night.' This alone relieved some of the stress.

"Also, as she and I worked together, she felt more comfortable asserting herself as a parent. She began to enforce a reasonable bedtime for the children, which was something both of them needed.

"Linda still felt it was unfair to the kids to make backup arrangements with a babysitter in case Paul canceled. When we analyzed it, however, she saw that her children did not feel rejected by her—even though they balked at her going out. In fact, she had a very solid relationship with them.

"I told her to make it clear to the children by saying, 'If Dad can't come, we can call on special sitters we love and trust.' But when she tried it, both children objected. Linda was upset, so I again suggested bringing the kids in, and this time, she agreed.

"I chatted with Heather and Jason about many things, and then I said, 'Parents want to take care of their children, but you should know this: Just as your dad has to travel, your mom sometimes needs to go out too, and that's why she's made some new decisions.'

" 'What decisions?' Heather asked suspiciously.

" 'After divorce, it's a tough time for everyone, and there are changes. Some are good; they help you grow and learn. But other changes may feel uncomfortable,' I said. 'Here's the deal: You have two parents who love you. Dad can't be there much. Mom's there a lot. But just as you need friends, so does your mom.'

"The children weren't thrilled, but that was the start of a dialogue that Linda continued at home. Linda later told me that the kids understood her predicament. 'It's so great to know that taking an evening off every now and then won't destroy them,' she said, relieved. And as she felt less trapped and helpless, her crying spells stopped.

"With my encouragement, Linda learned to build in private time for herself, even on busy days; if she couldn't take an exercise class, she could put an exercise tape in the VCR. In time she became less irritable with the kids, which eased her guilt and, of course, made the children feel better.

"Linda Carpenter needed to learn that too much sacrifice isn't good for any parent, married or single. In a crisis, parents may feel that there is no leeway, that their needs can't be met. But when they look at the situation realistically, they can almost always improve things. And as happier parents, they invariably find themselves raising happier children."

EATING
PROBLEMS

Robby, three, was sick a lot last winter, and he's painfully skinny, but he won't eat unless I'm there to urge and coax him endlessly! It wears me out and irritates my husband, but what other choice do I have?

Emily's Story

"Robby had one of those little coughs that turned into something very serious—a case of viral pneumonia," said Emily Chase, 32. "It seemed to take everything out of him; even when he was officially over the illness, he remained pale and listless and alarmingly thin.

"The doctor urged us to 'feed him up' so he wouldn't get sick again, but Robby—who had never been much of an eater—had no appetite at all.

" 'Too much,' he'd protest when I put one scrambled egg on his plate. I felt so sorry for him because I know how hard it is to eat when you simply aren't hungry.

"Still, he had to eat more, so I tried to tempt him with pieces of fruit or slices of cheese cut up and arranged to look like sailboats and clowns. He liked my creations—but just to play with, not to eat!

"In fact, he ate only crackers and cream cheese, certain cereals, hot dogs, apple juice, and—thank heavens—milk. He didn't even care much for ice cream or cake.

"My husband, Nick, was so anxious when the doctor said, 'Feed him—he's got to gain some weight!' He tried everything from force-feeding (a disaster!) to persuasion, as in 'Come on, take a bite; just look how thin your arms are' or 'Rob, please! Don't you remember how your body needs fuel or the engine breaks down?' to bribery: 'If you eat all your supper, you'll get a new dinosaur.'

"One Sunday evening Robby said he was done and tried to leave the table when he'd only had two bites of his cut-up hot dog.

"Nick said, 'Come back here,' and held out a forkful of bean salad. Robby ducked his head away, but Nick grabbed him and got a few beans into his mouth. Robby chewed a little, choked, and ended up spitting them into his father's hand.

" 'What now?' Nick said, looking totally demoralized.

" 'Maybe we could try to make eating seem like less of a battle,' I suggested. The next morning at breakfast I read a story to Robby while he ate, and I made a point of *not* complaining when he got up to run around and play between bites. It seemed to help.

"Encouraged, I started to make up games—like the one in which the spinach on Robby's plate was grass and Robby was a horse. It took a lot longer than I'd planned, however, because Robby, a bright and imaginative child, had to make sure we both agreed on what color horse he was and whether he lived in a barn or out in a pasture.

" 'Are we really making all that much progress? I can still see his ribs sticking out,' Nick wondered aloud one morning when I let Robby run off to play after eating only one spoonful of his cereal.

" 'He'll be back,' I said. 'Yesterday it took forever, but he finally ate a whole bowlful!' It wasn't that I liked spending all that time; but wasn't it worth it if it meant getting Rob to eat even a little bit more?

"In fact, I also stopped enforcing Robby's seven forty-five bedtime. I thought, Why make an issue of it if he actually *wants* to eat at ten or eleven—or anytime? Yes, fixing late snacks for Rob and sitting with him to make sure he ate them did take away my precious private time with Nick; but for now at least, Robby's eating had to be our top priority.

"That's why I didn't want to rock the boat and protest, even when those little games we played got more and more cumbersome and annoying. 'No, no!' Robby complained at supper one night. 'You're supposed to say, "Grr! I'm a dinosaur."

"A couple of times we'd hired a baby-sitter, but Rob would hardly eat anything if I wasn't there myself to keep after him. Of course, I was beginning to feel tied down, but I didn't realize how much so until Nick invited me to go with him to Colorado for a presentation he was giving for his company and I couldn't go.

" 'Why can't you go?' my sister, Hilary, asked.

"I said, 'If I'm not around, Robby just doesn't eat.'

"Hilary said, 'I know how to get kids to eat! It's my specialty. Why don't you bring him to my house?'

"It was a great offer! Robby loved his Aunt Hilary—who made her own bread and muffins every day and whose own kids were wonderfully solid, well built, and happy.

"Nick said, 'If anyone can get Robby to eat, she can.'

"I felt happy and hopeful during those four days, but when we went to pick Robby up, our bubble burst.

"Hilary had given Robby what she had cooked for her own kids. Robby had not demanded the special treatment he gets from me— but he hadn't eaten or played, either.

" 'He wouldn't even touch my blueberry pancakes,' Hilary said. 'All he had the entire time was milk and apple juice. He didn't even like the kind of hot dogs we had. I hate to say it, Emily, but I've never seen such a spoiled little boy!'

"I felt angry, embarrassed, disappointed, and more tied down than ever. This was the year I'd planned on going back to work so we could save money toward buying a house, but now I felt I couldn't dare think of leaving Robby!

"On the way home Nick drove silently as Robby sang the same TV commercial over and over, then insisted that I sing it—and laughed when I got the words wrong.

"Nick said, 'This kid needs to learn some manners.'

"Robby said, 'If you say mean things about me, I won't eat any of my supper.'

"Nick said, 'You damn well *will* eat when it's time!'

"Robby stamped his feet and said, 'No, I won't.'

"Nick said, '*You will!*' and suddenly I felt so overwhelmed and discouraged I started to cry.

"Rob looked startled and stopped stamping his feet. 'Don't worry, Mommy, I'll eat something,' he promised.

"But the next day he didn't, not until I'd replaced one slightly broken cracker and then spent ten minutes searching for *Fox in Socks,* which he wanted me to read to him as he ate.

" 'Now read,' Robby said, like a little prince. I wanted to tell him to get off his high horse, but I looked at that skinny little boy, and I didn't say anything because I knew he needed that cream cheese and cracker sandwich desperately!

"Suddenly I realized what a mess we were in, with Robby using food to control us—and knowing very well that he could! At this point, it's obvious we need some kind of help."

The Counselor Replies

Ellyn M. Satter is a certified social worker, registered dietitian, and psychotherapist specializing in the treatment of eating disturbances at the Family Therapy Center in Madison, Wisconsin. Satter is the au-thor of How to Get Your Kid to Eat—But Not Too Much *(Bull Pub-lishing).*

"Emily and Nick were feeling guilty and discouraged, fearful that they hadn't done enough to help their son.

" 'On the contrary,' I told them, 'I can tell you're very caring par-ents, and you were just doing what you thought was right. In fact, if anything, you've worked too hard: You've actively tried to get Robby to eat, instead of expecting or trusting him to do his part.'

"Emily frowned. 'But how could we?' she asked.

"I said, 'I can understand how frightened you were that Rob would get sick again if he didn't eat more—and your doctor cer-tainly amplified that fear. But even though Rob has been eating poorly, he *is* eating enough to keep going and even to grow. So this might be a good time to try a different way, without all the pres-sure.'

" 'Pressure?' Emily said, looking surprised. 'I wasn't exactly standing over Robby with a whip.'

" 'You *were* very thoughtful and creative in the ways you tried to get Rob to eat,' I agreed. 'But the trouble is, pressure is still pressure, even if it's cheery and disguised as play. And putting pressure on a child's eating always invites resistance.'

" 'Yes,' Nick agreed. 'Rob's really letting us have it in the rotten-behavior department! Like this morning, he was standing on his booster seat, leaning all over the table, yelling, "Where's my food?" Emily had rushed to prepare his cereal and juice, but when he got them, he pushed them away. Finally he ended up under the table eating crackers and putting crumbs in my socks.'

" 'Well,' I said, 'you can't really do a thing to make Robby eat. But what you can control is his behavior *concerning* eating.'

"I explained that we could teach Robby the eating behavior skills that a child his age needs, such as coming to the table when he's called, sitting quietly in his chair, accepting the food he likes and turning down other foods politely, eating in an orderly way without fussing or complaining, and, when he has had enough, politely excusing himself.

"Nick said, 'That doesn't sound like the kid I know.'

" 'I didn't mean this would happen all at once,' I replied. 'But if we take a step at a time, you will start to see some very positive changes.' The first step, I told them, would be just to establish consistent times for meals and snacks.

"I said, 'Reassure Robby that he doesn't have to eat *anything* at those times if he doesn't want to, but if he does get hungry in between meals, he'll still have to wait for lunch or his afternoon snack or whatever scheduled meal comes next.'

"Emily looked troubled: 'Does it make sense to *limit* Robby's access to food?' she asked.

" 'Yes,' I replied. 'This way, Rob is free from having to think about food, except at those times, and so are you!'

"One week later the Chases reported that Robby had eaten almost nothing at the official mealtimes and snack times only to whine and cry for food in between. 'There has been so much tension this week I thought I'd go nuts,' Emily said.

"Meanwhile, Nick had been fighting with Robby, trying to get him to sit still at the table, not to stand up on his chair, and not to keep running away and coming back. 'Now that we're not making mealtime a circus anymore, he doesn't want to stay,' Nick said.

" 'I didn't mean he has to sit there with you for a full twenty minutes,' I said. 'If he really isn't hungry, then he may lose interest in five minutes—and then it's okay to let him go. Many times parents will ask kids to stay at the table longer, hoping they'll eat more, but it only invites bad behavior.'

"Nick rolled his eyes and said, 'Don't I know!'

" 'But what if he's only eaten a bite or two?' Emily said worriedly.

" 'If he makes a mistake and doesn't eat enough this time, then next time his body will remember, and he'll eat more,' I explained.

"The next time I saw the Chases they were feeling much more successful. Robby *was* behaving properly at the table for brief periods, but then he'd keep leaving and coming back to the table—pestering his parents for more food.

"I said, 'Don't let him! Once he's left the table, that's all. Don't allow him to spoil your meal.'

"The following week the Chases reported they had tried what I suggested. 'There were a lot of tantrums,' Emily said. 'But we've all survived.'

"Nick said, 'We do have more sanity at meals now, and we're grateful. But Rob is still eating poorly, and I know you say not to worry, but really I can't help it when I see him eating less than our cat eats.'

"I said, 'I'm surprised. Usually, once the pressure is off, children will become more adventurous about food and more interested in eating.' In Robby's case it appeared that his food intake had actually fallen off rather than increased, even though his weight remained stable. I wondered what was going on.

" 'We *have* been giving him a lot of apple juice,' Emily offered. When she stopped to add it up, it appeared that Rob was drinking between fourteen and twenty ounces of juice a day.

"I said, 'This may well be interfering with his curiosity about food.' I suggested that Emily limit Robby's apple juice to snack time, and even then to only a cup.

"Robby was upset at first, but Emily gradually got him off the juice, and apparently my hunch was correct, because for the first time ever Robby was showing some interest in what his parents were eating. One night he even asked to have the serving dish near his plate.

" 'Looking at food is a good way to get accustomed to it,' I said at our next session.

"Shortly after that Robby began to tease his parents, pointing to the different foods on the table and saying, 'Do you want me to eat some of that?' Nick and Emily realized that this was a power game, and they played it cool, saying, 'Only if you want to, Rob.' Robby stared at them in disbelief.

"The Chases also realized how Robby's refusal to eat was an attempt to get attention at meals. 'Most of our dinner conversations *have* centered on Robby's not eating enough,' Nick admitted.

"Now, at my suggestion, they began to make an effort to include Robby in the conversation—not in the sense of 'entertaining' him or urging him to eat, as they had done in the past, but talking about things of mutual interest on a level that all three of them could appreciate.

"Following my advice, Rob's parents encouraged him to try some of the foods they were having, while allowing him one food of his own choice at each meal. I urged the Chases not to become short-order cooks and not to go overboard in indulging Rob's whims. Rob was still subsisting largely on cereal and cut-up hot dogs, but now he wanted to have some of the food his parents were eating put on his plate. He said, 'Can I just have it without eating it?' and Nick and Emily said yes.

"One night he tried a little bite of baked salmon—and then spat it out. His parents were disgusted, but instead of reacting strongly, they told me about it, and I was glad. 'This is a good thing he's done,' I told them. 'In a child's mind, tasting is not the same thing as swallowing; this is all part of the process of learning about food.'

"At that point the Chases went away for a two-week vacation. When they returned, they were delighted. Emily told me, 'We ate in restaurants and at our friend's house, and Robby was fine!'

"I said, 'Great! So tell me what he had for dinner last night.' Nick and Emily tried to answer, and then they both looked surprised—and sheepish. 'Gee, I didn't notice,' Nick said. 'Did I see him eating some chicken?'

" 'I don't know about that,' Emily replied. 'But he must have had potatoes and green beans because I remember he made a little volcano out of mashed potatoes, then filled it with beans, and ate the whole thing.'

"I said, 'It's great that you didn't really notice what he had. That shows me that you're trusting Rob to eat a variety of food, and that's very appropriate because children *will* eventually come up with a balanced diet—automatically—if they have healthy, balanced choices.'

"And Robby did! 'We're not struggling anymore at mealtimes,' Emily reported back to me recently. 'I think we have a whole new attitude toward food now. I put out the food, and Nick and I try to keep the mealtime pleasant and civilized, but that's all. The rest if up to Rob.'

"This was a major breakthrough for the Chases and very much what I had hoped would happen. Like so many other parents, Emily and Nick had been pushing and pulling Rob to eat because they felt his health depended on it. But it was only when they relieved all that pressure that Robby was free to approach food in his own way and start to eat in a way that was right for *him.*"

> *Jamie, four, is getting fat, but the more I try to control his overeating, the worse it gets! My husband, Tim, thinks I'm not forceful enough, but how can I win—when Jamie's appetite is so much stronger?*

Annette's Story

"Even as a baby, Jamie wanted to eat all the time," said Annette Cowles, 27. "My mother warned me not to let him. 'That was the mistake I made with you,' she said. 'And you looked like a sausage.' I winced at the story, which I'd heard all my life. Of course I intended to keep my child from getting too heavy. But what could I do? Jamie was hungry, and he'd cry inconsolably if I tried to give him water in his bottle instead of milk.

"By the time Jamie was two, my husband, Tim, thought he was getting 'chunky-looking.' I asked our pediatrician, Dr. Butterworth, what to do, but he said not to worry, that potbellies and hefty appetites are perfectly normal at the toddler stage.

"It still seemed to me that Jamie liked to eat too much. And it kept getting worse. Last Thanksgiving, at Tim's mother's house, everyone thought it was cute that Jamie, who at four was the youngest one there, was eating more than anyone else. But I felt mortified for Jamie as I watched him shovel in turkey and sweet potatoes with both hands. And he was still eating long after all the other kids had gone out to play.

"Obviously I couldn't make an issue of it *then*, but at home the next evening, I told Jamie that he had to stop eating so much. He wanted his supper early, but when he saw the plain broiled fish and apple slices I'd fixed for him, he started to cry. I felt so bad, so I tried to comfort him, but nothing worked, and I ended up—reluctantly—letting him have some leftover fried chicken . . . and then a little more. Jamie was my child and I hated to see him unhappy. But wasn't it part of my job as a parent to see that he grew up to be normal and didn't end up overweight?

"The next weekend Tim tried to help. 'Hey, son,' he said at the table, as Jamie was helping himself to more meat loaf, 'that's enough! You don't want other kids to make fun of you.' But Jamie kept right on eating—noisily and with both hands—until Tim got so frustrated that he called Jamie a pig. Then Jamie screeched, 'NO, I AM NOT, YOU ARE!!'

" 'Well, it won't work your way,' I told Tim. I knew from experience that humiliation never helps a child. 'It will only make Jamie feel rotten about himself,' I said. 'Okay, you're right,' Tom conceded. 'But what have *you* managed to do about it?'

"Before I could even reply, Jamie was back, asking for a Popsicle. 'NO!' we shouted in unison. But he was so persistent that even Tim finally let him have cheese and crackers—something healthy, at least. Still, this had been the one day in ages that I'd gotten him to settle for a small lunch, and I hated to lose even *that* little bit of progress.

"The following Friday Jamie had a checkup, and this time Dr. Butterworth took a look at Jamie—and a look at his percentile charts—and decided that Jamie *was* a bit too heavy. 'Let's let him lose about five pounds,' he suggested. 'Fine,' I agreed, 'but *how?* I've already been *trying* not to feed him so much.' Dr. Butterworth shrugged and said, 'I guess you'll have to try harder.'

"So I became the mad slasher, cutting calories wherever I could. Only broiled white-meat chicken with no skin. Only raw or boiled vegetables without butter. Just skim milk and no sugar on Jamie's cereal. But what *I* tried to save him in calories, Jamie still made up for in his snacking—which I just couldn't seem to control.

"I asked the neighbors not to give Jamie fattening treats. But I'd still find candy wrappers in his pockets. I told Jamie that we weren't punishing him, just trying to help him, but he still looked so sad—and puzzled—that it really broke my heart.

"I told Tim how drained I felt from the task of trying to turn our voracious child into a normal eater, but Tim had a theory. 'Maybe Jamie's picked up this whole food preoccupation from you,' he said. 'You eat two bites at dinner—and then you stand in the kitchen afterward, eating cookies. And you're constantly on the scale, vowing to starve yourself! If you didn't have so much trouble controlling your own eating, maybe Jamie wouldn't either.'

"I couldn't deny it. I *do* think about food and dieting a lot, but I have to because I've always had a weight problem. I'm weak. And when I do gain weight, I get angry at myself and have to go on a real crash diet.

"Tim has so much self-control; he doesn't understand dieting, any more than his mother can fathom why I would 'let' Jamie get so heavy. Now, Christmas was coming—with another family party, and a new chance to try and show that I *could* conquer Jamie's over-eating once and for all. And I could also make Tim feel better about both of us!

"But the first week of my slim-Jamie-down-for-Christmas campaign was a bust. I told Jamie that snacks were *out*, but he sneaked whatever he could snatch from the fridge. Scolding didn't help, nor did threatening. 'Don't you want to look nice at Grandma's?' I pleaded when I caught him raiding the hidden box of chocolate cookies. But Jamie's mouth was too full of cookies even to respond.

"So then I resorted to bribing him: ten cents for every hour he could manage to go without a snack. He said, 'Goody! I'll get rich!' But in that first hour he did so much whining, so much asking what time it was, that I finally just sent him out to play. 'Nothing till lunchtime,' I called.

"At noon, I went to get him, and I found him with his little friend, Stevie, devouring a carton of ice cream and a huge bag of taco chips. 'Jamie!' I knew my voice was sharp, but I was upset. *'Don't you care about being too fat?'*

" 'You're *stupid,*' Jamie retorted. I said, 'Don't you dare speak to me that way!' and I half-dragged him home and up to his room. I don't know what to do anymore. I feel so disappointed—and so defeated."

The Counselor Replies

Ellyn M. Satter is a certified social worker, family therapist, and registered dietitian specializing in the treatment of eating disturbances at the Family Therapy Center in Madison, Wisconsin, and the author of How to Get Your Kid to Eat—But Not Too Much *(Bull Publishing).*

"The Cowleses were understandably upset and worried as they described the terrible battle they were fighting with Jamie's overeating. But I told them that their problem was not an uncommon one.

" 'Is it because we've neglected him in some important way?' Annette wondered. On the contrary, I said, she and her husband had been working too hard! I said, 'Feeding requires a division of responsibility. Parents *are* responsible for providing regular meals and snacks, but that's where their feeding responsibility must end. Within that framework, it is the child, not the parent, who must decide what and how much to eat.'

" 'But Jamie would never stop,' Tim protested. I said, 'The reason he seems that way is because you have always been so concerned about his weight. Maybe he *was* a hefty eater, and perhaps you assumed that he would get fat if you didn't do something. Perhaps, even without realizing it, you withheld food a little bit and didn't feed him as much as he was hungry for.'

" 'That, in turn, most likely frightened Jamie. So that instead of calming down and eating less, he put more pressure on feeding, and it got to be a cycle—with you doing everything to restrain his eating, and Jamie looking for opportunities to fill up.'

"Annette looked stunned. 'You mean *we're* the cause of his overeating?' 'Perhaps, in a sense,' I said, 'but I don't think I'd beat up on myself. What you did was natural, and you did it with the best intentions. This is a miscalculation that many parents make, *especially* now, with all the excessive emphasis that's placed on dieting and slimness in our society.'

" 'Well, what do we do now?' Tim asked. 'He has this *appetite.* . . .'

"I said, 'The reason he's been eating so much—and sneaking snacks—is not so much appetite as fear that he won't get enough to eat. That's why he tries to grab every chance he can to stuff himself until he can't take another bite.' I offered to work with the Cowleses

190

for the next few weeks, and I assured them that if they stuck with the plan, they would soon find Jamie's so-called hunger decreasing.

"The Cowleses seemed grateful and eager to cooperate as I laid out the ground rules: three meals a day with planned snacks in the morning, afternoon, and at bedtime. I explained that Jamie's stomach was small and his energy needs were high, and he really might not be able to get from one meal to the next without refueling. But I encouraged the Cowleses to have him sit at the table for his snacks, which should consist of something that they had helped pick out.

" 'When Jamie is at the table, he can have as much as he wants,' I said. 'But there is to be no panhandling—and no snacking in addition to the meals and official snacks.' 'Well, I hope it works,' Annette said with a sigh as they left.

"The Cowleses seemed tense when they returned the following week. Jamie had eaten more than ever before, filling up so much on 'the wrong parts of the meal' that they couldn't help urging him to leave the potatoes alone and have more salad. I told them that I wasn't surprised that Jamie was still eating a lot of food.

"But I mentioned something else that I had forgotten to tell them the week before. They must not push the veggies and salad while subtly discouraging so-called fattening items like bread and potatoes. I said, 'Even subtle pressure about food will feel like deprivation to Jamie, and *that* is what activates his overeating.' Once again I assured the Cowleses that they could afford to trust Jamie to do his *own* regulating.

"Annette still looked worried. 'It's hard for me to believe that,' she said. 'I've had experience in overeating myself, and it's dangerous.'

" 'Maybe you also need to give yourself permission, along with Jamie,' I suggested. 'It sounds like you've been a restrained eater all your life, and you've been behaving like Jamie in the sense that you can deprive yourself for only so long before you give in and indulge in foods you normally avoid. Then you feel guilty and bad, and try to make up for it with even harsher deprivation.'

" 'I think you'll find,' I went on, 'that if you're kinder to yourself and more positive about your own eating, you'll discover your own ability to regulate the amount you eat—just as Jamie will.'

"The next week, Annette had something good to report. Jamie

still wanted a lot of food on his plate, but now he was leaving some of it uneaten. He was doing much less panhandling, and one day he had gotten so absorbed in playing that he forgot his snack!

"Annette also found that even with permission to eat more than a tiny portion, she still felt unsatisfied after meals, because the food she was serving was not very appealing. 'But I hate to add anything fattening,' she said.

"I told her that perhaps she'd been overdoing the low-fat effort in her cooking, and particularly so in Jamie's case (because children need more fat in their diets than adults do). I encouraged Annette to use a little more fat—and make her menus a lot more fun. Stuffing the turkey, making gravy, a little margarine on the vegetables, and a dressing on the salad were just a few ideas.

" 'I thought we were here to get Jamie's weight down—as fast as possible,' Tim put in. 'I'm still worried about his future health.' I told Tim that his concern was valid and suggested three things for him to think about. First, I said, fatness at Jamie's age is not a predictor of fatness in adulthood (especially now that the Cowleses were letting go of the restrained feeding pattern that makes kids fatter).

"Second, I said, it is better if Jamie slims down slowly, so that it doesn't impair his health or normal growth. 'As he grows in the next years, we'll see real results,' I assured him, adding that my own son was chubby at Jamie's age, but that now at age fifteen, he's a bean pole.

" 'However,' I said, 'if you are still concerned about heart disease in your family, you might want to consult with a cardiologist or a registered dietitian, to see if there are extra risks—and recommendations—in Jamie's case.'

"In the next session, Annette said that Jamie's interest in food had dropped off dramatically. He was routinely leaving food on his plate and beginning to take less. He was also eating smaller snacks, and in between times he was out of the kitchen and away from food.

" 'But he still wants dessert,' Annette worried. 'So far, that's something I've tried to avoid.' I told her that a simple dessert—and maybe once in a while, a rich one—would be fine. I suggested putting a serving of it at each place and letting Jamie eat his when he wanted to—even if he started with it. 'He'll still be hungry for his meal,' I assured her. I also urged Annette not to use dessert as a reward for finishing the 'good' food. 'He might overeat twice,' I told her. 'Once to earn his dessert, and again when he gets it!'

"And how was Annette doing? 'I'm beginning to give myself permission to eat what I want, but it's scary,' she admitted. 'Jamie's way ahead of me.'

"In the next session it was Tim who brought up Jamie's 'uncivilized' table manners. 'He's not eating so much,' Tim admitted. 'But he chews with his mouth open, eats much too fast, and uses his fingers more than he should.' I said that four-year-olds do have some eccentric table manners and will continue to for some time because they're not as dexterous as they eventually will be. But I did agree that Jamie's habits sounded a little beyond the range of even four-year-old eating.

" 'Do bring it to Jamie's attention,' I said. 'Try to teach him a different way of eating, but not in the sense of putting him down. And do reassure him that he can have all he wants and take as long as he wants, so he doesn't need to hurry so much.'

"This advice seemed to help, and in the next three weeks Jamie's progress continued—and so did Annette's. She said, 'I'm enjoying meals more now that there aren't so many restrictions on what I can cook.' Annette was surprised that she wasn't gaining weight while satisfying her hunger and decided that it was because now the old forbidden snacks like brownies and cheesecake were not so tempting.

"Clearly, both Jamie and his mother were finding that they each had a 'stopping place' they could trust, so that it wasn't a battle between going hungry and getting stuffed. 'It's made things a lot pleasanter and more relaxed at meals,' Tim reported. 'Amen!' laughed Annette, and she added that she no longer felt so embarrassed and apologetic, and that this was great for all of them.

"For Annette another eye-opener was coming across a long-forgotten album of her own baby pictures and seeing that she looked robust and healthy, but nothing at all like a sausage! 'Maybe *my* mother was kind of brainwashed and overreacting, the same way we were,' she mused.

"At that point I could tell that the Cowleses didn't need any more help from me. In just eight sessions they had found their way from a chaotic and highly charged struggle with their son and food to a comfortable acceptance of Jamie as the only *real* authority on his own hunger.

"As parents, it's natural to fear that letting go of the 'controls' will bring chaos. But as the Cowleses found, sometimes just giving a child a chance to respond to his own internal hunger cues is the best and most helpful 'direction' of all."

FEARS
AND
FANTASIES

Four-year-old Holly has always been gentle, but her imaginary friend is pushy, aggressive, and cruel. Is Holly just playing, or is Barney showing us something new and frightening about our daughter?

Jean's Story

"Holly called, 'Hang up the phone! Quick! Barney's caught in the dryer,' but there was no need to panic," said Jean Thomas, 31. "Barney was Holly's creation, her invisible friend. And he was becoming a real and growing nuisance.

" 'Don't sit there, you're sitting on Barney,' Holly would say, or 'You can't take a bath, Barney's still in the tub.' My husband, Graham, thought it showed wonderful imagination. But he wasn't with her half as much as I was, and he didn't see how relentlessly she insisted that I recognize Barney's existence.

"Barney always needed to have his shoes tied or his seat belt fastened or his teeth brushed, or he had to be rescued from the supermarket freezer. In fact, he stopped at nothing to get attention. 'Barney says the meat loaf looks like when Muffin threw up,' Holly said, giggling. But then she said, very quickly, 'He's naughty, but I'm a good girl, right, Mommy?'

"Smiling, I hugged her and said, 'Yes, you're good—100% good. You're Mommy's little dream girl.'

"And the game continued. Sometimes Barney's mischief was

197

playful: like licking all the stamps in the post office because he had to mail an elephant. But other times Barney could be very provocative. One Sunday morning, while on the phone with Graham's mother, Holly said, 'Barney doesn't like you, Grandma. He says that you always stay at our house too long.'

"Embarrassed and shocked—this was so unlike Holly—I stammered an apology. And then I said, 'But, Holly, you love your grandma.'

" 'I know,' Holly replied. 'But I was just telling you what Barney said.'

"And then there was the reading incident. Holly was choosing her two stories for bedtime, when she suddenly looked impish and said, 'Barney wants 45 stories tonight.'

"I smiled. 'That's too many stories. But maybe we could read five,' I suggested to her. 'That's part of 45.'

" '*N-O* spells no,' Holly said, looking furious and stamping her foot.

" 'But, Holly . . .'

" 'Barney says to just shut up!' she screamed at me.

"I'd never heard that kind of talk from her. Again, I was shocked. I said, 'Now, listen, Holly . . .,' but she put her hands over her ears.

" 'Barney hates you!' she said, flopping over onto her stomach and covering her head with a pillow. And I just stood there and thought, What's happening? Is this Holly or an entirely different child?

"I just didn't know what to make of all this: Holly couldn't really have expected me to read her 45 stories. So where had her explosion of anger come from? What did it mean? And how were we supposed to handle it?

"I started sending Holly to her room every time she was fresh. But instead of helping, punishing her only seemed to escalate Barney's outrageousness. 'Barney says you're dumb, and he's going to throw all your dresses in the garbage,' she called to me down the stairs.

"I was becoming very, very upset, but Graham said, 'You're losing control; calm down.' And I knew what he meant. Even before we were parents, we'd seen friends in battles with their children, and we agreed not to get into that. And indeed, we had found that being warm and super-patient was the best way to deal with Holly. Weren't we the family that made it through the Terrible Twos without so much as a tantrum?

"So I did try not to react too much, but if I thought that would solve the whole problem, I was wrong! I discovered that one Saturday at the playground. Holly was in the sandbox when a little black girl with a pail and shovel ran over to join her.

" 'No,' Holly said, standing up. 'Go away!' The other little girl drew back.

" 'Barney says only blond kids can come in here,' she said in a voice that surely carried, booming and imperious, to the bench where the child's mother was rocking a baby.

" 'Holly, not everyone looks alike . . .,' I began. I felt so ashamed at her words—they made no sense! We live in an integrated neighborhood, and Holly has been exposed to children and adults of other races since infancy. We'd raised her to be 'color-blind,' and we'd thought she was!

" 'Holly, how could you say such a horrible thing?' I demanded.

" 'Barney doesn't like her hair,' Holly said. 'It's too frizzy.'

" 'But what you said was cruel.'

"Holly nodded. '*I* know that,' she said, 'but Barney doesn't.'

" 'Can't he learn?' I asked. Holly shook her head.

" 'Okay,' I said. 'Then I suggest that you try to control him. Because if you can't, then you're going to get in trouble right along with him!'

"I was certain that Holly had gotten the message at last. I was in bed with the flu for a week, and all that time she was like her old self: affectionate, calm, and reliable. Holly said, 'I love you, Mommy; here's an extra kiss,' when Graham carried her off to bed. Holly even skipped her 'Wait, don't close the door on Barney's fingers' routine after I was back on my feet and again driving her to school.

"And I was delighted the following week, when Holly invited a new friend, Tiffany, home from nursery school for a play date. As I watched the two girls running hand in hand I thought how nice it was to see Holly having so much fun with a *real* child for a change.

"But my relief was short-lived. After they'd played for a while, the girls decided to paint, and I set them up with smocks and lots of newspapers. Suddenly I heard a yell. 'My shoes!' Tiffany cried. 'Holly put paint on my new white shoes.'

" 'No, I didn't,' Holly retorted, giggling. 'It was Barney!'

"I sighed and cleaned up Tiffany's shoes. 'Maybe Barney shouldn't be here,' I suggested.

"Ten minutes later the girls decided they were done. 'Look, Mom. It's a war of dinosaurs,' Holly said, holding up her picture. 'Daddy's going to say it's creative.'

" 'Mine is too,' Tiffany said.

" 'Yeah?' Holly peered at her friend's painting. That's supposed to be a dinosaur? Yuck! Barney says it's a big mess!'

" 'Holly!' I said sharply.

" 'Oh, I like it, though,' she went on elusively and insincerely. 'I love it! But Barney thinks it looks like . . . diarrhea!' Holly laughed.

"I said, 'Holly, remember what we talked about?'

"Sullen, Holly went over to the sink, where Tiffany was washing her hands. Suddenly Tiffany flew back from the sink, screaming. It took me a moment to see what had happened, but then I saw Tiffany's left hand was as red as a lobster! While she was washing, my daughter had turned the cold-water tap off.

" 'I didn't do it!' Holly shouted, trying to drown out Tiffany's crying. 'It was Barney!'

"Thank goodness Tiffany's hand turned out to be fine, but I could still feel my heart pounding. All along, Graham had been saying, 'It's only words,' but this was too much.

"Are we breeding a monster? And if so, what can we do about it? On top of all that, I just found my favorite photo of the three of us with holes poked through the eyes. I don't even need to ask who did it.

"I've read about a therapist who works a lot with preschool kids, and I'm going to call her. I just hope she can figure out what's going on—and explain it to us."

The Counselor Replies

Jan Drucker, Ph.D., is a child psychologist in New York City. She is also professor of psychology at Sarah Lawrence College in Bronxville, New York, and a consultant to the Early Childhood Center there.

"When the Thomases told me their story, I assured them that none of the incidents they described were necessarily as ominous as they sounded.

"Even the unfortunate playground incident, which still bothered Jean, could be seen not as the cruel racist comment it had sounded like but rather as typical four-year-old behavior. Four-year-olds will often exclude another child because he or she has short hair or long hair—or anything different from the one who's calling the shots.

" 'But it was still mean,' Jean insisted to me.

" 'Anger and impulsive behavior are quite common in four-year-olds, even when those children have not shown signs of it before,' I said. 'Still, considering the whole succession of events, there may be something going on with Holly that we don't understand.' I asked if I could meet and talk to Holly.

" 'What will we tell her?' Graham wondered. 'Won't she think she's crazy if we tell her what kind of a doctor you are?'

" 'A child Holly's age wouldn't really think that,' I said. I suggested that the Thomases acknowledge the problem, since Holly already knew that her parents were exasperated with Barney.

"Holly did balk when her parents said that I would be able to help her deal with her anger. 'It's not me, it's Barney,' Holly said.

" 'Dr. Drucker will help with Barney's problems,' Graham said. 'But you'll need to go along to talk for Barney.' When he added that I worked with other kids who had friends like Barney and that Barney could play with toys in my office, Holly agreed to come in.

"During our first meeting, Holly was shy and polite as she sat and drew pink-and-purple rainbows. I said, 'I understand you have a real good friend named Barney.'

" 'Yes,' she replied, with a mischievous glint. 'He always gets in trouble.'

"I said, 'He sounds like he's a lot of fun sometimes, too.' At that Holly described Barney in a playful and affectionate way. Then she said, 'But he doesn't get along with Mommy and Daddy—*especially* with my mom.'

"I said, 'I wonder why.' Holly shrugged. I said, 'Maybe you and I can spend some time together and try to figure that out.' When I invited Holly to play, she went over to the dollhouse and told me it was a castle. 'The prince is very naughty,' she said. 'Sometimes the queen gets mad, and then she wants the king to be really mad, too.'

"As Holly described the prince's naughtiness, he sounded much like Barney. At one point she said, 'The princess is being bad again'—and then quickly corrected herself—'I mean the prince,' she said.

"I said, 'Princesses misbehave also. I know girls who think that being naughty isn't allowed for girls, but that's not true.'

"Holly looked at me with interest. 'But then she'd be a bad princess,' she said. 'And the king and queen would run away from her.'

"Now I had enough clues to meet with Holly's parents. I told them that I thought Barney's actions were indeed expressing impulses and feelings that Holly was having trouble dealing with herself. I said, 'How has Holly usually expressed her anger in the past?'

" 'She never has,' Jean said. 'She's a great kid, and we've always tried to be responsive parents. So everything's gone smoothly until now.'

" 'We all like to keep things peaceful,' Graham added. 'We try to be calm and rational. I'd always rather pick up a book and read when I felt tense, and we make sure that we *never* fight in front of Holly.'

" 'There's no point—and it's hurtful,' Jean said with a small shudder. 'I should know: I grew up with parents who were always angry at each other. I used to sing to myself in bed so I wouldn't hear them fighting.'

"I said, 'That must have been awful. I know you've wanted to keep things pleasant for Holly, but because Holly hasn't seen either of you get angry and then resolve that anger appropriately, she apparently has no idea what to do with her anger, and that's why she put it onto Barney: She thinks it's okay for him, but not okay for her.'

"I suggested that we schedule some play-therapy sessions for Holly. 'Four-year-olds have strong impulses, including angry ones, and Holly needs to learn how to express those feelings,' I explained.

" 'But won't that just make her wilder?' Jean worried.

"I said, 'I can understand that fear, but Holly's learning to express strong feelings safely, first in play, then in words, and your being able to tolerate it will provide a real safety valve for her.'

" 'I think I'm beginning to understand,' Jean said and explained some important things about herself. Having been raised in a chaotic, unpredictable atmosphere, Jean had grown up equating perfect even-temperedness with safety. 'I thought we could just avoid all that nasty stuff,' she said.

"I said I could understand that wish but that in my judgment, Holly had been feeling that in order to please her parents—and especially her mom—she had to be as good and controlled as she saw her parents being. 'Now,' I said, 'she'll be able to express some of her stronger, so-called unacceptable feelings and get help with them.'

"As I worked with Holly and continued to advise her parents I saw many changes. Holly was still showing anger and defiance, but now she wasn't pinning it all on Barney.

"And though it went against Graham's nature at first and created considerable anxiety for Jean, the Thomases helped by accepting Holly's words of anger but setting limits on physical expression.

" 'We never set clear limits when she was younger because she never pushed us to limits,' Graham observed. 'But now we're learning.'

"I said that was very constructive. 'Holly needs to be angry, but she needs her parents to help her keep it in bounds,' I explained. 'For example, Holly would feel very, very frightened if she wanted to wreck her room or really injure someone, and you *let* her do it.'

"In therapy, Holly talked about Barney infrequently. Clearly the dollhouse family offered more of what she needed now in order to express the fears and tensions that were still giving her trouble. One afternoon she seemed particularly tense. She said, 'The princess wants her mom to go on a business trip so the princess can be queen for a while.' Then she looked frightened. 'But what if the mom's plane crashes?'

"I quickly reassured her: 'All princesses may wish to be queen sometimes, but it almost never happens,' I said. 'And even if it did, the princess would still be a little girl, and the adults would still be adults.'

"Now the boundaries between permissible and impermissible behavior and between fantasy and reality were getting clearer for Holly, and I could see her begin to relax. At home Barney was still around, but not so outrageous, and sometimes he would disappear completely for several days at a time. And Holly was beginning to show much more interest in real friends.

"When Holly and I were ready to talk about stopping treatment, she seemed nervous. 'What if Barney gets naughty again?' she said.

"I said I didn't think it would happen because she'd learned to deal so well with her feelings and Barney's, but if it did, or if she just wanted to come and talk to me, I told her I would be here. Holly was content with that, and I felt certain that she'd weathered her struggle and was ready to move on.

"Holly was a bright and emotionally sound little girl who was dealing with all the issues that four-year-old girls normally do, but those issues were more loaded—and more difficult—for Holly to work through because of a strong pattern in her family of keeping anger in.

"No parent is happy when a 'dream' of a child becomes grumpy, contentious, and impolite. But it was only when the Thomases learned to accept and live with the inevitable ups and downs of their daughter's feelings that Holly could give up Barney, stop trying to be perfect, and just be herself."

*We know our six-year-old, Jason,
is bright, but he's doing so poorly
in school this year, especially in
reading, and nothing seems to help.
What can his problem be?*

Rona's Story

"It was a real surprise to learn that Jason wasn't keeping up with his first-grade classmates," said Rona Curtis, 34.

"He'd been right on top of things in kindergarten: he was curious and imaginative. But now it was spring, and his teacher, Mrs. Gorton, said that Jason was the only first grader who wasn't reading yet. Nor did he show any interest in books—not even in the stories read aloud in class.

"Just the other day, she read a particularly exciting story about pirates, and she went around the room, asking questions. The other children could tell her what the problem in the story was and how the characters solved it. But when Mrs. Gorton asked Jason which character he liked the best, he looked startled, almost tearful and said he couldn't remember any of them.

"Poor Jason! I'd heard him tell his grandparents that school was too hard, but I thought he'd said that just to imitate his sister, Alison, nine, who really does get hard assignments. Now, hearing what his teacher said and looking at samples of his work, I could see that Jason *was* having trouble in school.

"I suspect he just hasn't settled down yet. Some of the active little boys take longer,' Mrs. Gorton said kindly. 'But I'd like to send him to the resource room once a week. Then he can get the kind of focused attention I don't really have time to give him.'

"But instead of feeling bolstered by the idea of getting extra help, Jason felt stigmatized, especially when Alison called it the dummy room. My husband, Peter, corrected her sharply, and Alison took back her comment, but the damage was done. And although we tried to tell Jason he was lucky to get extra help, he cried and begged me not to make him go.

" 'If I need the help, then *you* help me, Mom,' Jason pleaded. And although I had some misgivings (I'm not a teacher!), I gave in.

"With Mrs. Gorton's blessing, I stocked up on workbooks, flash cards, and special games designed to help the not-quite-ready reader.

" 'We'll have you reading, and it'll be fun, too,' I promised Jason. And it was. At first, at least, he liked the extra attention, the special daily time for just the two of us.

"But Jason didn't like the work part and did everything he could to avoid it. 'I hate this book,' he'd say. He seemed to hate *all* books. He didn't even want to go to story hour at the library anymore, something he always used to enjoy. And now he was even asking for extra TV time instead of a bedtime story.

" 'Of course a child will hate books if he's frustrated when he tries to read,' Mrs. Gorton explained. But the more I tried to engage him in learning games and very easy study drills, the more he balked.

" 'I hate school so much,' Jason said, sobbing over one exercise that Mrs. Gorton suggested—cutting out magazine pictures of anything starting with the letter *B*. 'Look at this,' I said, handing him a magazine open to a picture of a boy on a bike in front of a building.

" 'There's nothing here,' Jason wailed. 'I'm quitting school! I've had it.'

"Still, I wasn't about to give up. Shamelessly, I resorted to bribery. Peter disapproved, and Alison was jealous. 'You mean he gets a toy for just doing that?' she cried, pointing to a half-done workbook page. I told them both, 'If it gets Jason to read, then it's worth it.'

"I tried not to miss any opportunity. 'I know you know this word. Try to sound it out,' I urged Jason, pointing to the word 'cake' on the recipe card I was using.

" 'No way,' he protested. When I said, 'Won't you even try?' he muttered, 'What's so great about reading, anyway?'

" 'It's a wonderful part of growing up,' I replied.

" 'Maybe I don't want to be a grown-up!' he yelled.

"Later Peter said, 'Sounds like a tug-of-war. Don't you think it's time to back off?'

" 'Maybe he doesn't love tutoring,' I conceded, 'but if he needs help . . .'

" 'Oh, come on,' Peter said. 'Don't you always say each child develops according to his own schedule?'

" 'Well, yes.'

" 'Okay,' Peter said, 'we both know Jason's extremely bright and well-adjusted. He has friends, he plays sports. Why don't we just quit pushing him for a while and see what happens?'

"Spring vacation was coming up, so I agreed to drop the tutoring for those twelve days. I had to admit that Peter was right: without the pressure of lessons, Jason was like a new kid.

"I noticed, too, how competent he really was: initiating great adventure games with his friends and building complex structures with his plastic construction blocks. Maybe I *had* overreacted to his problem. Perhaps the reading *would* take care of itself.

"But all too soon the vacation was over and Jason was back at school—with a new problem: homework. And he was frantic. 'I can't do it,' he whimpered daily, and every evening Peter or I would end up doing it for him.

"For the next three weeks, Jason did everything he could to avoid going to school, claiming he had a stomachache one day, a scratchy throat the next. 'Look, this can't go on,' Peter said. And it was true. By missing school, Jason was falling even further behind his classmates.

"One afternoon I went to see Mrs. Gorton. 'Jason is so bright, but his skills are still so poor,' she said. 'And that combination usually points to a learning problem.' She gave me the name of a psychologist who could test him. 'Jason may need more special help than he can get here—or even at home,' she explained.

"Special? It sounded ominous. Would Jason be transferred to a special school? How he'd hate it if he had to leave his friends!

" 'Oh, no, most children with learning problems are relieved when they're placed in an appropriate educational setting,' the psychologist, Susan Goodale, informed us.

" 'Sounds as if she'll find a learning disability whether Jason has one or not,' Peter commented wryly. All during Jason's testing I sat in the waiting room, feeling guilty: Was his failure to read our fault? Had we let him watch too much TV?

" 'He's within normal range for his age,' the psychologist concluded. 'However,' she went on, 'he does seem very stressed and anxious—which makes me wonder if his problem may not be emotional.'

" '*Emotional?*' I exclaimed, feeling really shocked.

" 'Yes, depression in a child can look like many things—including a learning disability. Emotional distress can hurt a child's ability to concentrate, and impede his learning.' She handed me a list of phone numbers. 'I only evaluate children. I don't treat them,' she explained. 'I suggest you consult a child therapist.'

"Peter and I are very alarmed. Jason's always been fine until this year. What could his problem be?"

The Counselor Replies

Cynthia R. Pfeffer, M.D., is professor of psychiatry at Cornell University Medical College and chief of the Child Psychiatry Inpatient Unit at The New York Hospital, Westchester Division. Pfeffer is also a co-author of Difficult Moments in Child Psychotherapy *(Plenum Medical).*

" 'I don't know,' Peter told me at the beginning of our first visit. 'I'm sure we'd have noticed if something was bothering Jason. Alison doesn't always show her feelings, but Jason does!'

" 'Perhaps the stress isn't obvious to you—or to Jason,' I replied.

" 'Then how will we ever find out?' Rona wondered.

" 'Through playing and talking, we can begin to understand what a child is feeling and what's causing the conflict,' I explained, and suggested that Jason see me a few days later.

"When I met Jason, he just sat there, until I showed him my office closet filled with toys and told him he could play with anything.

"When he picked up a baby doll, I was surprised. Wondering if a baby had anything to do with his conflict, I asked Jason if he knew any real babies. He shook his head, held the doll for a while, then tossed it back on a shelf and sat down.

"Then I asked Jason what he liked to do best. He became more animated as he mentioned baseball, soccer, and bike riding with his friends.

"I asked him how he was getting along at school. As I'd expected, he was vehemently negative. ' I hate school! It's the pits!' he told me.

" 'Why is that?' I persisted.

" 'I don't know . . . I guess it's because I'm so dumb,' Jason said sadly.

" 'You certainly don't *seem* dumb,' I told him. 'You strike me as being a very smart boy. But I can tell you are having a tough time at school, so we're going to work together to try to make school easier and more fun.'

"The following week, when Jason arrived for his second session, I had a pile of drawing paper and a few markers on the table. He took some paper and markers and drew what he told me was his mom on a golf course, holding a club. Then, with a red marker, he drew blood, first trickling out of her arm, then gushing out.

" 'My mom plays golf a lot,' he said.

" 'Oh,' I replied. 'But what's all that blood? Did your mom ever get hurt?' Jason shook his head.

" 'I guess that mom in your picture got hurt,' I observed.

" 'Yup!' Jason nodded. Then he swept the picture away and started drawing a boy. 'That's Gary,' he said, 'a kid at day camp last summer.'

" 'Is he a friend?' I asked.

" 'Used to be,' Jason said. 'My mom asks why he doesn't come over, but I don't like him anymore.'

" 'Why is that?' I asked. Jason shrugged. 'He tells gross stories,' Jason said, squirming and looking uncomfortable. 'Is it time to go yet?'

" 'Not yet,' I replied. 'What stories?'

"Blushing, Jason pointed to the baby doll. 'You know, babies and that stuff,' he said. Then he told me about the day last summer when he had been at Gary's house and Gary had given him a very graphic 'explanation' of where babies come from. The trouble was, Gary's version was very distorted and made the whole thing sound extremely brutal and painful for the woman.

"Shocked, Jason had said, 'I don't believe you,' but Gary had produced a book with pictures of naked men and women engaged in sex. To Jason, they certainly looked as if they were fighting—maybe to the death! 'Your parents do it, too, everybody's parents do it!' Gary had chortled at Jason's discomfort.

"Looking at the pictures, Jason had felt disgusted and frightened—but at the same time oddly excited, almost breathless. Jason was in turmoil. He'd wished—desperately—that he could read the words, but he'd also felt ashamed. In fact, he'd felt so ashamed and upset, he'd phoned his mother and asked to be taken home, and threw up twice on the way home.

"He 'forgot' the incident—only to have it resurface in September when school began. Then Jason found that whenever his teacher read a story or tried to teach him to spell a word he would think about Gary's book—and become so flooded with feelings that he would lose track of what he was supposed to think about.

"This is a classic example of how an emotional problem can masquerade as a cognitive one. By avoiding words and books, Jason avoided a recurrence of the feelings of shock and pain he had experienced over Gary's impromptu sex-ed course.

"In this way, Jason apparently developed what we call a learning inhibition—a sense of danger, wondering what other horrible, overwhelming surprises might be lurking in books. Not that Jason was aware of that on a conscious level: all he knew was that school (and anything like school, including his mom's tutoring) made him anxious, inattentive, and forgetful.

" 'But he knew about how babies are born,' Rona said when she and Peter came in a few days later. 'Jason was three when our cat had kittens, and we talked about it then.'

" 'Yes, and that was the last time we mentioned the subject,' Peter added ruefully. 'I was planning to talk to Jason, but I thought there was time. Were we wrong to wait?'

" 'There is no correct time,' I said. 'Each family handles the subject differently, and it's rarely a problem—even if the child does get some misinformation from his friends along the way. But in Jason's case, it happened to stir up a lot of conflict. However, now that we know what the problem is, we should be able to resolve it.'

"I suggested a few more meetings with Jason so that I could help him unlearn the wrong information and replace it with correct ideas about intercourse and birth.

"I asked the Curtises to tell Jason that what he and I talked about was important and that he would soon feel better—and do better in school.

"During the next three sessions, Jason and I talked together, and he asked interesting, curious questions. I was able to explain many things to him: for example, that sex is pleasurable and loving, not exploitive or hurtful; that couples have sex not only to make babies but also as a way of expressing love and closeness.

" 'Oh!' Jason said, clearly relieved, as I refuted all of Gary's alarming 'facts.' In addition to just talking, Jason and I also looked at some books, but these were special books for children, explaining and illustrating aspects of human sexuality in a way that a boy of six could understand without feeling threatened or overwhelmed.

"Finally free of the shame and anxiety that had triggered his learning inhibition, Jason was eager to start reading—and frustrated that it wasn't happening more quickly.

"This was when Mrs. Gorton, his teacher, took over, setting up many situations that gave Jason the message 'You can handle it, you can accomplish it, you can do it.' These gave Jason confidence and the freedom to pay attention and learn.

"When Jason did become anxious over something he was asked to do in class, Mrs. Gorton gave him an alternative assignment. She set things up so that there were no wrong answers, and gave him choices; and if he forgot, she would tell him the answer.

"Now, without fear of failure, Jason was eager to try sounding out words when his parents read to him at home. And he actually initiated trips to the library. One day, passing a rack of children's paperback books at the supermarket, Jason picked one out and asked his mother if he could have it. Rona said of course.

"Even Alison got involved and was quick to correct her younger brother when he made a mistake. 'Being critical won't help,' Rona explained.

" 'But I *want* to help Jason,' Alison insisted.

" 'If you really want to help, don't criticize,' Peter said, and suggested that, instead, Alison could help Jason with some of his learning activities, games, and puzzles that he'd shied away from earlier.

"Now it was working! And Jason was the one to pester Alison, begging her to play a rhyming game or test him on his flash cards.

"The really big breakthrough came when the family went away to Massachusetts over Memorial Day weekend and Jason found that he could read at least one—and often several—words on every billboard and sign they passed. Flushed with his success, he soon became a full-fledged reader.

" 'If Jason does a little extra work over the summer, he'll be ready for second grade with his classmates in the fall,' Rona told me delightedly in their final, follow-up session. She said that she had enrolled Jason in a summer program at a nearby college campus that included sports, reading, and even a class in magic—and he was very excited.

"This was wonderful news. Jason had always had the potential to learn to read, but his fears and fantasies had prevented him from doing so. I was glad for the chance to relieve him of these conflicts, allowing him finally to hit his stride at school and go full speed ahead."

ILLNESS IN THE FAMILY

Cheryl, eight, has been tense and self-centered since my brother died of AIDS. Is this just part of the process of mourning her Uncle Paul, or is there something else wrong that Cheryl can't talk about?

Nina's Story

"Saturday was a perfect example," said Nina Hoyt, 32. "Cheryl spent most of the day by herself, cutting out paper horses and watching TV on the old set in the basement. Several times I heard her tell her sister, Stephanie, who is nineteen months old, to go away and leave her alone.

"Then we had watermelon for dessert. Cheryl took a bite and pushed hers away, but when I offered it to Steph, Cheryl grabbed it back and threw it in the garbage. Cheryl said, 'I don't like to have to share with her.'

"But why now? She had gone through an earlier period of not sharing for almost a year! But for the past eight months she'd been a wonderful big sister, warm and nurturing, and I was proud of her.

"I wondered if the change had something to do with my brother, Paul. Paul, 29, a lawyer and a writer on gay-rights issues, had just died of AIDS. He had been close to us and very important to the girls, whose dad, from whom I'm divorced, lives far away and is rarely in touch.

"As Paul had become incapacitated, the girls and I had spent a

215

lot of time with him, visiting and helping with his laundry and preparing his meals.

"Were these visits frightening for Cheryl? If so, she never expressed it. She always wanted to be at Paul's house, telling him jokes and pouring his tea. She would get out the silver polish and shine up his old swimming trophies. And he'd always say, 'Cheryl, what would I ever do without you?'

"But then he died—with a suddenness that shocked us. 'AIDS is a time bomb; you never know when the patient will die. The progress of each case is unique,' the doctor explained. When I told Cheryl, she was devastated, and angry at me. 'But you said I could see him next Saturday,' she sobbed. *'You promised!'*

" 'I was wrong,' I told her sadly. But Cheryl wasn't listening. She was holding her hands over her ears, and I couldn't blame her. All this must have been so confusing, with nothing in her own experience to hang it on. And how hard this little-understood illness had been to explain to her: 'Yes, this *is* a deadly contagious disease, but, no, *you* can't catch it.'

"When I had first heard that Paul had AIDS, to reassure Cheryl of her own safety, I'd explained that Paul had gotten it from sleeping with his friend Barclay, who had AIDS but didn't know it at the time.

" 'Besides,' I had told Cheryl a few weeks before Paul's death, 'we're very careful when we go to Paul's, and we don't take any chances. . . .' I searched for an example. 'Like . . . oh, we'd never eat from his plate.'

"Cheryl had nodded. 'Maybe he won't die,' she'd said hopefully. 'That was my wishbone wish on Sunday.'

"But Paul had died in spite of all her wishing, and Cheryl was crying her eyes out.

"I was almost afraid to let her attend the funeral, but it went well. It was only that night that she seemed to be very troubled by something. 'How much does it hurt to die?' she asked. 'How do they know dead people don't get hungry or cold or lonesome?'

"It was eleven o'clock when the questions ran out, but instead of getting into bed, Cheryl took her pony-decorated sleeping bag into the hallway. 'I don't like all the shadows on the ceiling in there,' she explained, pointing to the room she shared with Stephanie.

" 'Fine,' I told her gently. 'You can sleep in the hall if you like.' Why not? I bent down to give her a kiss, but she pulled away and burrowed into her sleeping bag.

"I expected that kind of behavior to last only a night or two, but Cheryl was still sleeping in the hall a week later, and that was when I started to notice the selfishness. Now she wasn't even willing to let her sister have a sip of her soda!

"I said, 'Cheryl, this isn't a happy time for any of us, and I know you feel cheated in losing Uncle Paul. But acting piggy won't help. In fact, this is when we really need to be kind to each other.'

"Cheryl just blinked at me. But she must have taken my words to heart, because the next day I didn't hear a single 'Go away' or 'Hands off.'

"In fact, she spent two hours stacking boxes and neatening shelves of toys, not just her own, but Steph's, too. 'That was so nice of you,' I told her warmly. But I wondered if I'd praised her too much, because she became really intense about keeping everything orderly. And when she wasn't tidying up, she was playing with cards.

"She was playing some kind of solitaire she'd made up herself. It involved dealing the whole deck out in rows, then mixing the cards up and doing it again . . . and again.

"It was hard to get her to stop. 'I *have* to win this two more times before it gets dark,' she explained. 'I *have to!*' Once Stephie grabbed some cards, and Cheryl exploded. 'You ruined everything,' she cried. 'Now I have to start *all over.*' Nor would she take a break to help me make brownies or to lick the bowl.

" 'It's a way of letting off tension,' our pediatrician, Dr. Oppenheimer, assured me. And once again I felt relieved and hopeful that the old, cheerful Cheryl would soon come back to us.

"A week later Cheryl woke up with a sore throat. 'It doesn't look bad,' I said, checking with a flashlight. She had no temperature. 'Go to school, and if you feel bad later, they can call me,' I suggested.

" 'No!' Cheryl sobbed. 'Mommy, don't you get it? I have AIDS!'

" 'Oh, Cheryl!' I said, kneeling down beside her. 'You do *not* have AIDS; you just have a little sore throat.' Cheryl pulled away.

" 'I understand you're upset,' I said very calmly. 'But you haven't done anything that could make you get AIDS. So just put it out of your mind.'

"Cheryl begged to stay home. I said, 'I don't think you need to, but okay. You can go out and play and get a little sunshine. But you go to school tomorrow, okay?'

"I expected her to jump at my generous offer, but she didn't. 'I don't want to go out and play,' she said sadly. 'And I'm never going back to school! And I do *so* have AIDS!'

"Now I'm really frightened: Something is definitely up. I met a child psychologist a while ago, and I'm going to call her. At least she can tell me whether this is normal mourning behavior for an eight-year-old or something really to be alarmed about."

The Counselor Replies

Jan Drucker, Ph.D., is a child psychologist in New York City. She is also professor of psychology at Sarah Lawrence College in Bronxville, New York, and a consultant to the Early Childhood Center there.

"I was interested in what was going on with Cheryl, and I confirmed for Nina that it sounded like more than the usual reaction to the death of a relative.

" 'Why don't you bring her in?' I suggested, hoping that meeting and talking to Cheryl would shed some light on why she was convinced she had AIDS despite her mother's assurance that she couldn't have it.

"When mother and daughter came in two days later, I noticed that Cheryl looked pale and moved slowly. She looked as if she felt very fragile as she sat down in a chair across the room. When I moved closer, she said, 'You'd better not get too close.'

"I asked her why. She looked surprised. 'Didn't my mom tell you that I have AIDS?' she said.

"I said, 'Your mom told me that you're worried about it. Why don't you tell me what's happened to make you think so.'

" 'I got it from my Uncle Paul,' she answered gravely. 'He was my favorite uncle. But then he died, and I'm going to die just like he did.'

"I said, 'But how could you get AIDS from him?'

"Cheryl looked troubled, and for a long time she just sat there, not saying anything. Finally she took a deep breath and said, 'I ate the cookies.'

" 'What do you mean? What cookies?' Nina asked.

" 'Chocolate chip,' Cheryl said. 'At Uncle Paul's. I kept hoping I wouldn't get sick, but when I got the sore throat, I knew it.'

"I began to understand. 'Cheryl,' I said, 'are you also worried that you will give it to others?'

" 'Yes!' Cheryl answered quickly.

" 'And that's why you don't want to share with your sister?'

"Cheryl nodded and looked at her mother. 'It's also why I don't want to kiss you, Mom.'

"Nina looked stunned. 'But I've been telling you over and over there's no way you could have it, Cheryl. Why won't you believe me?'

"Cheryl looked at the floor, and tears rolled down her cheeks.

"I said, 'Kids don't usually give up ideas they have just because we tell them to.' Instead I suggested first that Cheryl come in again so we could talk more and go over what was bothering her, and second that Nina take her to the pediatrician for a blood test, to give Cheryl tangible 'proof' that she didn't have AIDS *and* a sense that her concerns were being taken seriously.

"In ten days, when I saw her again, I wasn't surprised that the test results were negative. But Cheryl still looked dubious as she sat in my office. 'Sometimes they can't tell from tests,' she insisted.

"I told her that I thought we could trust the results and that I wanted to know more about what she had been doing and thinking.

"Cheryl explained to me that she had felt very guilty when her mother said, 'We don't eat Uncle Paul's food,' because she had already eaten some cookies he'd left on his plate.

"Feeling like a bad girl, Cheryl had imagined that AIDS would be her punishment. But then she had tried being very good about keeping toys off the floor. And with her eight-year-old imagination, she thought if she won enough solitaire games, she could magically control her health.

"Cheryl had hoped that doing those things would reverse her fate, but then when she woke up with the sore throat, she 'knew' that she had AIDS and would die, just like her uncle had, and that there was no hope.

"Cheryl looked embarrassed but relieved at finally having the secret out. 'You know why I sleep in the hallway?' she asked.

" 'Because those shadows on the ceiling are scary?'

219

"Cheryl shook her head. 'Mommy said Uncle Paul got AIDS from sleeping with Barclay. Well, I don't want *Stephanie* to get AIDS from sleeping with *me*.'

" 'Cheryl,' I said, 'I think there was a misunderstanding. When you heard about Uncle Paul sleeping with Barclay, what did that mean?'

"Cheryl shrugged. 'Sleeping!' she said. 'Like you go to sleep.'

"I said, 'Did you know that the term "sleeping together" is also used to describe a special thing grown-ups sometimes do when they love each other? Having sex is different from kissing or anything that they would do with kids or that kids would do.'

" 'Oh, I get it!' Cheryl smiled knowingly. 'Like making a baby, right?'

" 'Something like that.'

" 'But Uncle Paul and Barclay were both men!'

" 'Yes,' I said. 'But sometimes men have those feelings for each other.'

" 'Oh,' Cheryl said. 'But that still doesn't mean that I didn't get it from the cookies.'

" 'In a way it does,' I replied. 'AIDS is hard to get. There are only a few ways that someone can get it. One way is by being born to a mother who has it; another way is by receiving a blood transfusion from someone who has it; the third way is by taking illegal drugs with a dirty needle; and the fourth is by having sex with someone who has it.'

" 'Now, you *know* your Mom doesn't have it, and you've never had a blood transfusion.'

" 'Are you *positive* I couldn't have gotten it from the cookies?'

" 'Yes,' I said emphatically. 'Despite what lots of people think, we can't get AIDS from hugging or kissing or getting coughed on by someone who has it. Nor can we get it from eating someone's food!'

"Cheryl looked scared. 'But my mommy said we shouldn't,' she said.

" 'Cheryl,' I said gently, 'sharing food *isn't* a way to get AIDS, I promise you. And I'm pretty sure your mom really knows that, too! But sometimes, even when we know things with our head, we still feel worried. It's just like now: The blood test proves that you don't have it, but you're still worried, anyway.'

"'We can talk again when I see you next week. But I think you're feeling a little bit better already, aren't you?'

"Cheryl agreed, and for the first time, I saw her really smile.

"The following day I met with Nina. I told her that Cheryl had been worried about having AIDS for a long time, even before she said anything about it. I confirmed that Cheryl's apparently selfish behavior had indeed been a secret attempt to protect her mother and sister.

"I explained to Nina that eight-year-olds are very concerned about right and wrong and the consequences of breaking rules. When Nina had tried to reassure her daughter by saying, 'We don't eat Uncle Paul's food,' Cheryl saw that as an important rule—one that she had already broken. Cheryl then tried to compensate by making up her own new, much stricter rules.

"'Which rules were they?' Nina wondered aloud.

"'Telling herself, I *must* keep toys perfectly neat and even. I *must* win so many solitaire games in a certain amount of time, or else,' I replied.

"'Oh, my gosh,' Nina said. 'Here I tried to be so straight and honest with Cheryl, to avoid misunderstandings, but it all got twisted anyway. I feel so incompetent!'

"I said, 'I think you handled things extremely well considering the stress you were under—going through all this as a single parent while coping with your own grief about your brother. And you still had time to be concerned with Cheryl.'

"'Thanks!' Nina said and smiled. I told her I thought that things would go more smoothly now. But I said I'd like to see them both once more in a couple of weeks. 'Feel free to call if anything comes up or if you have questions in the meantime,' I said.

"Two days before the appointment I got a call. Nina said that things had been much better, but now she had a new concern. The third grade was having a cookout the next day, and the kids were preparing the food. Cheryl was wondering if she could dare to go and help.

"I asked Nina to put Cheryl on the phone, and I said, 'I hear you still feel a little bit worried, but if you go, I bet you'll be glad.'

"When we met for that final session two days later, Cheryl was beaming. 'You were right,' she said happily. And then, more soberly, she said, 'I guess you must think I was pretty silly to think I had AIDS.'

" 'No, you weren't being silly,' I assured her. 'It *is* a scary disease—so scary that it's easy to panic and feel like you have to do anything you can to keep from getting it or giving it. Sometimes that fear makes even grown-ups do unusual things or worry unnecessarily . . . or even hurt people who have it by avoiding them more than we need to.'

"Cheryl nodded. 'I'm glad we didn't do *that* to my uncle,' she said. 'Right, Mom?' And Nina said, 'Right!'

"Some things are hard to explain to kids because certain subjects are so controversial and confusing that even the right words can easily convey a wrong meaning. Thanks to Nina's sensitivity and good judgment in asking for help, we were able to turn a child's fear and confusion into genuine understanding."

> *Suddenly Stevie, our eight-year-old, can't walk—and the doctor thinks its emotional! Why would it happen to a normal child in a close, loving family like ours? And what will it take to get him well?*

Emily's Story

"My sister Alice's first thought was to have us fly home right away," said Emily Jansen, 31. "Stevie had come down with a temperature of 105 degrees and pneumonia—while my husband Nick and I were away at a travel agents' meeting in the High Sierras.

"But finally, Alice (who has been through lots of crises with her own five kids) decided not to call and scare us to death when we'd be home so soon anyway. Besides, Stevie was in excellent hands with Dr. Bacon and the hospital staff, who saw the problem as routine and fixable—not like the old days when a child's pneumonia could be deadly.

"Apparently Alice was right: By the time we got to Stevie, his fever was gone, and he looked no worse than if he had a cold. Dr. Bacon said we could take him home—with a mild warning not to let him run around too much.

"But Stevie, who was normally such an energetic kid, just wanted to lie in bed—the whole week! He didn't want to see friends or even get dressed. 'He's so droopy,' I told Dr. Bacon on Saturday at the time of Stevie's checkup.

" 'I wouldn't worry,' Dr. Bacon replied. 'His blood count is good and his chest sounds fine. Sometimes kids get hospitalitis—a little mild hypochondria. It's normal and goes away soon . . . if you don't indulge it.'

" 'You're all better,' I told Stevie on the way home. 'Dr. Bacon said you can even go to Cub Scouts!'

" 'I don't know,' Stevie said. 'I might still be sick.'

" 'You had a sickness, but you're well now, Stevie. That's the truth!' It was six the next morning, when his screaming woke us up.

" 'Help!' he cried. 'I can't move.'

" 'What do you mean you can't move?' Nick asked, pulling back the covers on Stevie's bed.

" 'MY LEGS!' Stevie said, frantically pointing down. 'They won't move; they're dead.'

" 'It's probably just a cramp,' I said soothingly, and started rubbing one of his feet. 'You probably just slept funny.' But Stevie shook his head.

" 'I can't move them,' he insisted. 'DO SOMETHING!'

" 'Take it easy, Steve,' Nick said. 'Just relax. We'll help you.'

"For half an hour, we tried everything—from massaging Stevie's legs to standing him up and moving his legs for him. 'It's not working,' he sobbed softly.

"Dr. Bacon came over at ten o'clock. 'I don't get this,' he said. 'I think we had better put him back in the hospital for tests.'

" 'Please, not again!' Stevie whimpered. 'I really hate hospitals.'

" 'Well, he *could* have the tests as an outpatient,' Dr. Bacon relented. He would arrange for Stevie to have a complete neurological workup, and he advised us to rent a wheelchair.

"All that next week, we showed up at the hospital once and sometimes twice a day to keep all Stevie's appointments: the CAT scan, his skull X ray, a lumbar puncture, and the other high-tech procedures Dr. Bacon had ordered.

"We tried to joke about the wheelchair—calling it Stevie's sports car—but its huge, gleaming presence, inviting curiosity and pity in the street and blocking our path at home, mocked our efforts to pretend that things were fine. Things were terrifying!

"Stevie, of course, was having the hardest time. 'But *why* did I get sick?' he'd ask over and over. Well, how could a kid understand when even the medical experts were stumped? He hung on me, which wasn't usual and only showed how upset he was. 'Don't you even care anymore?' he'd demand if I didn't appear two seconds after he'd summoned me.

" 'Try to be patient,' I'd urge him. 'Soon we'll find out how to get you well.' But when the tests were completed, we were still in the dark: They were all negative. And while it *was* great that he definitely didn't have meningitis, for example, or brain cancer, he still couldn't walk—and *we* still didn't know why.

"Dr. Bacon suggested that we talk with a child psychiatrist. 'His symptoms aren't following anything usual. We can find no physical cause for Stevie's paralysis,' Dr. Bacon explained. 'So we need to consider the possibility that this is psychological.'

"Psychological? But that made no sense. How could a child who's always been happy and healthy get so disturbed as to become paralyzed—and so suddenly? Wouldn't any reasonably sensitive parents have had some clues?

The Counselor Replies

Cynthia R. Pfeffer, M.D., is professor of clinical psychiatry at Cornell University Medical College in New York City and chief of the Child Psychiatry Inpatient Unit at New York Hospital, Westchester Division. Pfeffer is also a coauthor of Difficult Moments in Child Psychotherapy *(Plenum Medical).*

"Emily and Nick Jansen were obviously caring, intelligent parents—struggling to understand what was happening to Stevie, and wishing that I had some ready answers or theories.

"I questioned both parents extensively, and Emily was right: there were no 'red flags' in their family life or in Stevie's early history. Nevertheless, I felt there still might be a 'reason' for his not walking.

" 'Stevie,' I said when he arrived, 'I understand you were sick recently, and one day you found that you couldn't walk.'

"Stevie nodded. 'Today was my last chance,' he said sadly. He said he hoped to be back to normal by this very morning, but since he wasn't, that 'proved' he must die.

" 'Stevie,' I said after a silence. 'What would you say if I told you I believe we can help you get well?'

" 'Sure, I wish,' he said softly. 'But I don't think the doctors know how.'

"Afterward, I spoke with his parents. 'I'm not sure whether there are any physical or neurological avenues left to explore,' I told them. 'But Stevie is talking in a strange way about his difficulties, and that in itself is worrisome. He thinks that he's going to die soon. So I don't know if he might try to hurt himself.'

" 'I'm not trying to scare you,' I went on. 'But I really think he belongs in a hospital.'

" 'Oh, no!' Emily looked distraught. 'Stevie's had too much already! Can't he just come to you for some therapy?'

" 'He *could* stay at home,' I said. 'But I feel it would be better to have him come in—not to the general hospital, but to a small psychiatric children's unit, where he can be given physical therapy and, at the same time, we can try to find out more about his emotional state. I think this may be a very serious situation, one which requires the kind of intervention that only residential treatment can provide. The hospital is a very warm and reassuring environment—and a 'normal' one, in that Stevie will be with other children, attending classes right in the hospital. And of course, you can both visit him every evening.'

"Emily and Nick looked devastated. This was clearly a most difficult decision, but at last they agreed. I phoned the hospital and learned that a bed would be available.

"I arranged for Nick and Emily to see the facility and meet with staff. 'It's certainly friendlier and smaller than I expected,' Emily commented, peering into the unit's sunny, modern schoolroom. The Jansens were clearly heartened to see that the children's unit of the hospital was not some dreary, institutional-looking building, but a bright, pleasant cottage with flowerbeds and an apple tree in front and a large jungle gym and swing set out back. Inside, everything was clean and cheerful, with cozy private bedrooms and a living room filled with comfortable furniture, patchwork quilts hanging on the walls, and loads of books and games.

"Two days later, the Jansens came back for another tour—this time with Stevie. 'Did you notice all those great art materials?'

Emily asked. Stevie nodded. He was cooperative but very quiet.

"Three days after that the Jansens returned and Stevie was admitted. 'We'll be back this evening,' Emily promised when Stevie had trouble letting go of her. A nurse helped Stevie unpack and talked to him about the various activities he could choose, apart from his schoolwork.

"By suppertime, all ten of the other children in the unit had introduced themselves, all wanting the privilege of showing Stevie around—and trying out his wheelchair.

"Stevie seemed tense that night, and the next day, too, but once he got into the routine of the unit, his nervousness about being there seemed to vanish. 'The other kids are nice,' he told his parents.

"This was a relief to the Jansens, who had worried that Stevie would only get more upset around children with problems. 'Actually, the opposite is true,' I told them. 'The children come with a range of emotional problems—from Jimmy, a twelve-year-old who had tried to kill himself, to Cindy, six, a little girl suffering from depression, and Toby, a nine-year-old who experienced hallucinations—but in this environment, they all seem to be able to empathize and support one another.'

"Stevie was also comfortable with the adults: the nurses, the teachers, and other staff people he saw every day, and especially his therapist, Dr. Gill, a young psychiatrist who made it clear that he was there just to listen, to understand, and to be with Stevie and make no demands.

"Stevie talked freely to Dr. Gill about all kinds of things, including his premonition of death. 'I don't feel so scared here, like I did in the other hospital and at home,' Stevie said—and then, hopefully, added 'Maybe I won't have to die soon.' Dr. Gill asked if Stevie had ever known or visited anyone who was very sick. Stevie thought for a moment and then shook his head.

"Nick and Emily were also seeing Dr. Gill regularly. Emily said, 'I keep thinking it was our fault, maybe because we chose the wrong day camp when Stevie was five . . . or because we wouldn't get him a dog when he wanted one . . . or maybe because of how tense and angry both of us were the year Nick changed jobs and we were deep in debt.'

"Emily found some relief in Dr. Gill's assurance that no childhood is perfect, no matter how hard we try to make it so. But she felt a lot calmer the following evening when she and Nick joined the parents' group that meets to talk and share encouragement. 'Oh, I hear you,' another mother said. 'But there's a lot in our kids— good and bad—that we didn't put there.'

"Gradually, Stevie began to remember 'a weird story,' something from years ago, when he was only four. He remembered going out with his grandma, expecting to see his grandpa; but instead, they went to a big, unfamiliar place and took an elevator and then walked down a busy hallway . . . and into a room where a very old and very skinny man lay gasping on a bed with bars around it.

"The man—as white as paper—couldn't move, and a nurse had to move him. It was only then that Stevie recognized his grandpa! Stevie remembered feeling very upset—especially without his mother there to comfort him. Stevie's grandpa had suffered a severe stroke. Stevie remembered his parents telling him that, but he'd had no idea what it really meant.

"He was scared to ask what had happened. As a typically egocentric four-year-old, Stevie was certain that it was something *he* had done or failed to do that had caused this shocking change, and Stevie felt like a bad boy with a secret that even he didn't understand.

"This was Stevie's memory—long 'forgotten' but never resolved. And it was only when Stevie found himself with pneumonia, *gasping in a hospital bed* (and again, without his mom there), that his traumatic visit of long ago came back to haunt him.

"The Jansens were amazed: Stevie's cousins had all seen Grandpa. The family had agreed that it was better for the kids to see their beloved Grandpa dying than not to see him.

"In discussing it further, Dr. Gill explained that Stevie had probably experienced what's known in psychiatric terms as a conversion reaction, or hysterical paralysis, in which his unconscious memory of that day got channeled or changed into his physical symptom of not being able to walk—just as his paralyzed grandfather couldn't walk and had to be moved by the nurse.

" 'But Stevie didn't say anything to us or seem upset,' Emily said. 'So how could we have ever protected him enough—or known the kind of problems it would cause him later?'

" 'I'm not sure that anybody could have predicted this,' Dr. Gill assured her. 'It's like when you send four kids out on their bikes, and nobody falls off. How could you know in advance that the fifth kid will hit a rock, fly off his bike, and break his nose? You can be a very careful parent and still not be able to prevent every possible accident.'

"Once Stevie's painful and potent memory was out in the open, where he could talk about it, he was no longer stuck. And three weeks after he'd arrived at the unit, he scrunched forward in his wheelchair, grabbed hold of a nurse's hand, and took a step forward. 'Look, I'm walking,' Stevie shouted, and everyone cheered.

"At that point, I knew we were ready to plan for Stevie's discharge. 'Does this mean Stevie's all well now?' Nick asked.

" 'It would seem so,' I told him. Stevie's particular conversion reaction had been more extreme than others I had seen, in which only pain in a limb, rather than paralysis, had occurred. While conversion reactions occur only rarely in children, they are considered to be a real psychiatric emergency. When a forgotten fear or traumatic event manifests itself in a real physical symptom, pain, or even paralysis, the root cause must be uncovered and consciously dealt with. But Stevie had been a well-adjusted, well-functioning child, which pointed to a good prognosis.

"His particular symptoms—the paralysis and anxiety—had been acute and specific to a certain event, as opposed to something chronic. Stevie had finally been able to talk out his scary feelings and impressions, and this further defused the likelihood of more trouble in the future.

"I suggested that Stevie keep seeing Dr. Gill for a while on a weekly basis, just to make sure that the troubling issues in Stevie's mind had been resolved. I also recommended a follow-up session in six months, perhaps, or sooner if they felt the need.

" 'I thought that putting Stevie in this hospital was like the last resort,' Emily admitted sheepishly. 'I didn't expect the results to be this good—and this fast.'

" 'It's a terrifying prospect for most parents,' I told her. 'But it can actually serve a fine purpose in treating kids.' For Stevie, the round-the-clock care in a therapeutic setting with a highly trained staff and the fact that he could be involved in normal activities, not fall behind in his schoolwork, *and* see his parents every day proved to be ideal.

"It is now six months later. Stevie Jansen has been home, enjoying life and playing soccer on an all-star team. Emily just sent a local newspaper photo of Stevie's team to his friends at the hospital—along with a special and heartfelt thank-you note.

"We always try to prevent bad things from happening to our children, and most of the time we succeed. But as the Jansens discovered, sometimes it's not the absence of problems—but our open-mindedness and courage in seeking the right solution—that makes all the difference in the world."

Gwen's cancer is gone, and we should be the happiest family on Earth! But Gwen, nine, and Liz, thirteen, resent each other; my husband Dan's a stranger; and I just feel empty and scared. What's wrong with us?

Christina's Story

"Gwen's cough had gone on for a long time, almost half of first grade. But it was never bad enough to keep her home from school," said Christina Read, 36. "So how could this doctor be saying that our child has cancer?

" 'Lymphoma, cancer of the lymphatic system, often strikes with unimpressive symptoms,' Dr. Merritt, the pediatric oncologist, explained. 'I know it's a shock,' he added sympathetically, 'but most childhood cancer *can* be cured, and Gwen has an excellent chance.'

"That was the beginning of a two-year struggle—a devastating time for our family, during which all normal life, normal feelings, normal *everything*, was put on hold.

"Gwen was treated with a combination of brief radiation therapy and long-term monthly chemotherapy. Those assaults on the cancer did terrible things to Gwen. She lost her rosy look, her stamina, and even her ability to fight off simple infections.

"We had to be super vigilant. For example, a normally inconsequential ear infection could turn into meningitis if it wasn't treated quickly and aggressively. At one point, Gwen got a bladder infection

231

that required a stay in the hospital and intravenous antibiotics to keep it from causing her chronic kidney damage.

"To protect Gwen, I had to see that she ate enough and didn't overtire herself. It was also important to keep her from becoming upset or stressed, as that too would affect her ability to fight. And whenever she was battling one infection, it was vital to keep away all other sources of infection.

" 'I'm so sorry,' I told Liz, our thirteen-year-old, when I couldn't let her best friend in because she had a runny nose. I felt bad for Liz, who wasn't getting her fair share of anything but hardly ever complained. When I told her how mature she was, she shook her head and said, 'I just want Gwennie to be okay.'

"Would Gwen *ever* be okay? I'd look at her—bald, skinny, and exhausted—and I'd feel so awful; I'd think, maybe if we'd recognized the problem sooner, we would have spared her all this.

"Each two-day treatment made her so sick that she'd be in bed at home for a week afterward. By the time she recovered, it would almost be time for the next round; and then she'd be so scared that she'd throw up when we got to the hospital, before she and I even went in.

"Besides all that, Dan didn't like to talk or even read about Gwen's illness. While I was always reading medical journals and questioning the doctors, Dan's attitude was, 'We can never know enough, so why should we try? All we can do is find good doctors for Gwen and trust them.'

"I felt I couldn't share with Dan everything that was happening. He and I had always been able to talk, but it didn't seem fair now to dump any more stress on this man who was already overloaded. He was working six days and two evenings a week to pay all the bills that were now coming in so fast, since I had had to quit my job in public relations to care for Gwen.

"So I got used to keeping my darkest feelings to myself, and somehow—miraculously—we survived; just over two years after starting treatment, Gwen was cured!

" 'Just bring her in for a checkup in six weeks and, after that, once every six months, Dr. Merritt, the oncologist, advised. Was that *all?* We were elated! No more cancer, no more treatments! Now we could all start enjoying our lives again.

"But it wasn't long before I learned that returning to a normal way of life was easier said than done. Over and over I asked myself, how do we know the cancer won't come back? Each morning I drew Gwen close—and checked her lymph nodes. 'Quit it,' she complained, pushing my hands away. Obviously *she* felt safe. Why didn't I?

"Superstitiously, I felt that as soon as I stopped worrying, the cancer would return. I didn't tell Dan for fear he'd think I was morbid. All he talked about was getting on with our lives, making up for lost time.

"I knew that was what I should want too, but I was scared. One morning Gwen woke up with a sore throat. Heart racing, I called Dr. Merritt, but he said to take her to our regular pediatrician. 'We're quite busy here today,' he said when I protested.

"So we didn't warrant his concern anymore! Intellectually I knew that was good, but emotionally I just wasn't sure. I'd so come to rely on those special cancer-fighting doctors and their treatments: Even with Gwen's hair falling out and the incessant vomiting and the doctors practically running our lives—all that had made Gwen well. Without that support, I felt shaky and alone.

"Relax! Get back to normal, I chided myself. But it was hard to reinstate old rules, and in some ways I wasn't even sure we should. Gwen was still thin, and if she didn't like her dinner, I'd make her something else and let her eat it in her room.

"Was she taking advantage of my anxiety, insisting that she 'needed' the TV in her room and that she could take gym but didn't have the pep to change the cat's litter box? I wasn't sure how flexible to be, and I found it hard to draw the line, even though Liz kept saying we were letting Gwen get away with murder.

"One day I said, 'Liz, what's happened? You were so understanding when Gwen was in treatment.' Liz glowered. 'Sure! But at least she was nice then; now she just acts like a selfish *brat!*'

"Dan made light of the girls' bickering. 'Aren't you glad you get some peace when they're at school?' he said. I smiled, knowing he would really think I was nuts if he knew how much worse I felt when I was alone! I knew it was time to return to work, but I felt scared. What if Gwen needed me?

"I wanted to enjoy myself: While Gwen was sick, I'd had no leisure time to garden, shop, see friends, or read a novel. But now that

I had time, those activities all seemed meaningless . . . and so I did virtually nothing.

"In truth, I missed the hospital—desperately. I'd grown so close to the nurses, and I'd felt needed then and important. Of course, I didn't want Gwen's cancer back; but now that she was well, I felt let down.

"Was I crazy—or did others go through a similar 'withdrawal'? I asked Terri, a friend from the hospital, whose son, Eric, had also been cured of cancer.

" 'Depressed? God, *no!*' Terri sounded incredulous. 'We're the lucky ones! Just think about the parents of the kids who didn't make it.' So I *was* alone in this, not grateful enough, weird.

"Ashamed, I tried to be upbeat when Dan asked me out that night for a 'catch-up' anniversary celebration. It had been so long since we'd had the luxury of some private time together.

"We went to a romantic little restaurant on the water, but our attempt at an intimate evening fizzled into small talk—and too much silence. When I mentioned the word 'hospital,' Dan demanded, 'When will you ever be done with all that?'

" 'Why should I? At least *they* cared about Gwen!' I flung back unfairly. We argued some more and then settled back into silence. Life is so tense at home, and it's all in such contrast to what I'd expected. Even Dan agrees that something is definitely wrong. But what?"

The Counselor Replies

Gregory K. Fritz, M.D., is director of child and family psychiatry at Rhode Island Hospital and professor of psychiatry at Brown University, both in Providence. He specializes in treating psychological problems in families in which a child has been seriously ill.

"Dan and Christina's first session was a draining one as they recounted the history of Gwen's illness—and found that just telling the story brought them both to tears. Increasingly, they began to comfort each other.

" 'I thought we could put all this illness behind us,' Dan said, in pain. 'Won't it ever go away?'

" 'Why can't we just be grateful and happy?' Christina wondered, wiping her eyes.

"I assured the Reads that their anxious and depressed feelings were normal. 'Just because you were spared the worst doesn't mean you'll be perfectly happy. In fact,' I went on, 'it's often the most competent and committed families—the ones who worked hardest to fight the disease—who have the hardest time getting back to normal when the crisis is over.

" 'You've been through enormous and unusual stress,' I pointed out, 'and abnormal situations often generate abnormal responses. I'm not making light of it,' I assured them. 'But you're far from crazy, and if I were in your shoes, I expect that I'd be going through the same turmoil.'

" 'What about my friend Terri? Her son Eric had a bout with cancer, but she isn't having our problems,' Christina protested.

"I replied, 'The response to a serious illness is individual; it varies. There's no prescribed pattern of reaction, no formula for putting this kind of intense and traumatic experience behind you. It just isn't useful to set standards or deadlines for getting over it. You need to trust and respect your feelings.'

"As we talked, Christina learned that Dan, too, had kept a lot of his feelings inside; each had been making a stoic effort to 'spare' the other. Now they both realized that those efforts hadn't really helped and had actually deprived them of the closeness they needed.

" 'It's not too late to start communicating,' I said, and urged the couple to continue talking to each other at home. I also encouraged them to get back into another way of communicating; to return to the close and rewarding sexual relationship they'd given so little time to since Gwen had gotten sick.

"Both Dan and Christina found it a great relief to express their real feelings once again, but as they grew closer, certain buried resentments surfaced. Christina said, 'There were so many times when I felt you didn't care enough—that you were glad to have all that work to hide behind.'

"Dan retorted, 'Of course I cared. But sometimes *you* seemed so wrapped up in the hospital I felt you didn't care about *me*.'

"I asked Christina, 'What if Dan hadn't been willing to work so hard? What would you have done if you hadn't been able to quit

235

your job to care for Gwen?'

" 'I'd have gone nuts!' she admitted, looking gratefully at Dan.

"I asked Dan, 'And what if you'd had to be on the scene every day and take care of all the details?'

"Dan shuddered. 'No,' he said, 'I wouldn't have had an easy time with that. I guess we both did what we had to do . . . and it worked pretty well.'

" 'But what about now?' Christina wondered. 'Dan wants me to forget the hospital experiences, but I can't—I'm not even sure I want to.'

"Again I urged the Reads to recognize that there is no right or wrong way to feel. I said that Dan's desire to get back to normal activities is healthy and does not show any lack of feeling.

" 'However,' I added, 'Christina's missing the hospital, and her involvement there is just as legitimate.' I suggested that Christina, instead of trying to get rid of that yearning, channel it into volunteer work—either through fund-raising or by becoming a resource person for those parents just beginning the kind of ordeal that she and Dan had gone through.

"Christina liked that idea. 'Yes,' she said. 'I could go back to work four days a week and give one day to the hospital.'

"But even though some of the tension had eased, the Reads still had two major issues to deal with: first, a nagging fear that the cancer would 'sneak' back if they dared to relax; and second, the ongoing animosity between Liz and Gwen.

"On the first issue, I urged them to try taking one day at a time and to focus on the visible improvements in Gwen's health: her increased energy level, the way she'd bounced right back at school and with her friends. I reminded them both that being hypervigilant and overprotective would just end up making Gwen unreasonably fearful—or rebellious.

"Instead, I suggested that Christina take an evening course on keeping children healthy that the community college was offering. 'It may not teach you anything you don't already know, but it will help you rebuild confidence in your own skills.'

" 'That's a great idea!' Christina said, relieved that there was something constructive she could do.'

"But there was the other major problem: Their two girls were still not getting along. I suggested they start holding structured family meetings, an important tool of family communication.

" 'Isn't that a little hokey—or forced?' Dan asked.

" 'Not if it offers everyone a chance to say what's really on their mind,' I said, and the Reads agreed to try it. They began with some good, open-ended questions, such as 'What would each person here like all the others to know?' and 'How can we all get back to normal in terms of rules?' and even 'Does Gwen have any leftover privileges that aren't fair anymore now that she's all well?'

"At the first meeting, Liz admitted, 'You guys have been acting so weird since Gwen went off treatment!' Liz felt confused: Her parents *claimed* that Gwen was well, but they treated her as if she were still fragile. 'If Gwen really is well, then why is she still acting like a privileged character—and why are you two letting her?' Liz demanded.

"Christina now realized how her inconsistency and strategy of making allowances had ended up compounding the problem, making Gwen even more demanding, and Liz resentful.

"The Reads responded wisely, bringing more structure back to the family—which led to more normal expectations. 'The doctor says there's nothing Gwen can't do now,' Christina pointed out—'including changing Muffy's litter box.'

"As for privileges, Gwen could no longer keep the television in her room or expect room service. Nor was she to be exempt from punishment. The same consequences of inappropriate behavior that had applied before her illness would apply once again.

" 'Was Gwen angry?' I asked at a follow-up session.

" 'No,' Dan reported. 'Surprised, for sure, but basically relieved. It seems she wanted desperately to get back to normal, to prove to herself that she really is well. In fact, her chief complaint at that point was, 'Liz never argues with me anymore.'

" 'I guess I was scared to,' Liz admitted. 'You may have gotten a little bratty, but I didn't want to hurt you.'

"It's been almost a year now since Gwen completed her treatment, and her checkups have all been perfect. The Reads don't have family meetings very often anymore. According to Christina, they don't need to.

" 'We no longer keep important feelings from each other,' she told me recently. That was what their counseling had really been about: both cancer and family communication. Through it, the Reads learned to recognize that family members need to express their emotions in an honest, forthright way, just as much as they need to share everything else."

I'd thought Amy, thirteen, had accepted her diabetes, but now she refuses to take proper care of herself and insists that I "butt out." Why can't she see that this game of hers is foolish—and deadly?

Charlotte's Story

"Amy was just eleven when her diabetes showed up, but she accepted it like an adult," said Charlotte Gordon, 36. "She gave up all the sweets and junk food she loved, and she exercised diligently. And though she'd always been terrified of injections, she now took her morning insulin shots like a real pro.

" 'Dr. Stein says nobody ever gets rid of diabetes, but I'll bet *I* can,' Amy told me after a checkup. Well, she *had* conquered her nail-biting habit, and maybe she had willed away that funny little wart on her knee, but didn't she understand that this was different?

"Dr. Stein had told us that Amy's type I, or insulin-dependent, diabetes was serious and chronic. Amy's body was unable to produce insulin, which is a hormone we all need to process our food and maintain a normal blood-sugar level. Amy would need to take insulin shots for the rest of her life.

"The problem, he went on, was not taking the shots, it was having to constantly adjust and readjust the dosage, as too much or too little could cause big problems. That's why Amy would have to be extra careful with her diet and exercise, and why she had to draw a drop of her blood several times a day to check her sugar level.

"Dr. Stein said that type I diabetes requires vigilant care and monitoring. By the time she was thirteen, Amy needed more frequent shots of insulin, and the whole task of keeping her blood-sugar and insulin levels in balance was getting harder—for both of us.

" 'It's just not fair,' she said, cranky and despondent. 'I've tried so hard to be good and I still have it, so what's the point of going through all this?'

" 'There's lots of point,' I assured her. She couldn't get rid of her disease, but she could lead a happy, normal life if she just kept her food intake, her energy expenditure, and her insulin level in balance.

"And it *was* a daily balancing act! Too much food, too little exercise, a case of the flu, or too little insulin would make her hyperglycemic. She would feel nauseated and maybe vomit. And if left untreated, her condition could lead to a coma—and even death.

"The opposite problem—hypoglycemia—is also a complication of diabetes that comes from too little food, too much insulin, or too much exercise. And it comes on more acutely. The symptoms of this include sweating, trembling, anxiety, confusion, and blacking out.

"And the really scary part, we were learning, was how many things could affect the delicate balance. Like Amy's worrying about a test at school or staying up too late or having a little sore throat. All of those had given her symptoms.

"And now, with her body growing and changing so rapidly, her vulnerability was higher than ever. 'Adolescent growth spurts and hormone changes will make her diabetes harder to control,' Dr. Stein had cautioned us.

"But now, instead of understanding that all this meant we had to be extra careful, Amy seemed more and more casual—and sloppy—about her health. Often, I found that if I didn't remind her to test her blood, she would forget—or not bother. And while I tried to make sure that she ate the right things in the right amounts at the right times, I'd find all these hidden bags of potato chips and other evidence of cheating, and I'd feel so helpless!

"Here I was, a single parent caring for a child with a life-threatening illness. But she wasn't a little kid anymore; she was an adolescent and she was resisting my help.

"Amy was at that age of terrible insecurity—dressing like all her friends and afraid of being one tiny bit different—she forbade me to tell anyone about her disease.

"I'd say, 'But, Amy, if you're going to dinner at Meg Johnson's, I'll have to tell her mom so she can give you a snack if supper's going to be late.' But Amy would command me to stop worrying.

"Well, I *wanted* to stop worrying! I wanted Amy to take the responsibility herself. *But she wasn't doing it!* Like that night she went to the Johnsons': Amy said nothing and waited politely for dinner. At seven-thirty, Mrs. Johnson noticed Amy drenched with sweat, confused, and shaking—and immediately brought her home.

" 'All I needed was some orange juice and I would have been fine in ten minutes,' Amy said, crying tears of embarrassment and anger.

" 'But this will happen again and again if you won't let me tell people what you need or if you won't tell them yourself,' I pointed out. The next day was cold and drizzling. 'I'll go for that run with you,' I offered. But she said, *'You go,'* and went into her room and slammed her door.

"I hated Amy's making her illness a power struggle when we needed to work together. I thought that if she didn't want to listen to me, then perhaps she would 'hear' the facts and warnings better from strangers.

"So I signed Amy up for a weekend conference on learning to live with diabetes, and I was hopeful, but as soon as she got home, I could see from the look on her face that I'd made a mistake. 'It was like being in the army. They gave us our food all premeasured, with no choices or seconds.'

"Even my hope that meeting other people with diabetes might make her feel less ashamed and alone was dashed. 'They were such *nerds!*' she said when I asked. 'And I hope I never meet another one again.'

"After that, our relationship became more strained than ever. I tried to give her the 'space' she demanded, but when she went on a junk-food binge or forgot a shot for the third time in a week, I got upset. 'Don't you understand you're on your way to serious complications?' I demanded. But she just seemed to ignore me.

"And then a very frightening thing took place. Amy had gone to her eighth-grade party at a nearby park. I expected to pick her up at seven, but at six, I got a phone call—from the hospital emergency room.

"Apparently, after playing and swimming in the pool all afternoon and not eating, Amy had become hypoglycemic and confused. When she began staggering and slurring her words, her friends assumed that she was pretending to be drunk, or had actually had some beer. They laughed at her antics—until she passed out.

"Luckily, one savvy teacher-chaperone, Mr. Henchey, suspected the problem and took Amy to the hospital. She looked so thin and pale, I started to cry.

" 'It can be rough,' Mr. Henchey agreed, and asked if I knew of Hertko Hollow in Boone, Iowa, the special camp for diabetic children and teens. He said the camp had been great for his neighbor. I don't care if Amy hates the idea. I would rather send her and risk her anger than let her stay home and risk her life."

The Counselor Replies

Cece Carsky, R.D., a free-lance counselor to diabetic teenagers, is an administrative dietitian for Open Kitchens, a food-service company in Chicago. Carsky, who has worked at Hertko Hollow and does extensive consulting on camp diet planning for the Illinois chapter of the American Diabetes Association, has diabetes.

"When Amy arrived at camp, she clearly didn't want to be there. 'I already know all this stuff,' she told me sullenly. Yes, she knew the facts. But I hoped we could chip away at some of the anger that was making her job of coping much harder than it really needed to be.

"After sports, in the bunk that afternoon, I sat my seven twelve- and thirteen-year-olds down and asked them all to tell what they each hated most about their disease. A couple of the girls began by mentioning the shots and the food restrictions, but then deeper issues started to emerge, like feeling weird and different—not being able to trust their own bodies and then, more emphatically, the sense that a mother feels her child's diabetes gives her the right to run the child's life, to pry, and to say no to everything the child wants to do.'

"I saw Amy wipe tears away, relieved to let strong negative feelings out and to find support and empathy.

"I said, 'All your feelings are valid, but now you're old enough to make a choice: You can go on feeling helpless and victimized, resenting your disease and your parents, *or* you can put your energy into really helping yourselves—to be independent, to be free, and to feel good, too.'

"The girls, including Amy, looked interested. 'Great!' I said. 'Tomorrow, we'll get down to specifics.' And we did. We talked about food—how a person with diabetes doesn't have to be rigid or bored to eat right.

"Clearly, the major topic of interest was 'how to get Mom off my back.' 'You've only got one parent, but I've got two,' a girl named Peregrine said to Amy. 'Yes,' Amy replied, 'but maybe it's even worse when there's only one—she *really* feels she's got to do everything!'

" 'I'm not sure it makes a difference,' I said. 'It can be hard either way. Parents *all* think they're helping! You need to tell them—lovingly but firmly—when they've embarrassed you. And explain that you need to be able to take care of things on your own.'

" 'Will they accept that?' a girl named Maureen asked dubiously.

" 'Maybe not at first,' I said. 'But they'll get the message a lot faster if you make it your business to demonstrate how responsible you are. After all,' I went on, 'they're hovering because they love you, not because they hate you. If they feel that you are safe, they may be very glad and relieved to get off your backs.'

"At that point, I asked the girls if they could see anything positive in having diabetes. Two or three of them laughed. 'No, I mean it,' I said. 'None of us would have asked for it, but it's given me a real opportunity to be who I am with my friends without being apologetic or insecure.'

" 'But I *hate* for my friends to know,' Amy said. 'Give them a chance,' I urged. 'I suspect you'll find, as I did, that they'll appreciate your trusting and confiding in them; and instead of thinking it's gross when they hear about shots and blood tests, they will respect you for being able to handle all that.'

" 'And another thing,' I added, 'if you let your mother know that

243

you *are* telling friends, then she won't bug or restrict you so much.'

"They all smiled at that. 'But wait,' Amy said. '*My* mother wouldn't feel better. She gets frantic when my blood tests aren't totally perfect. That's why sometimes I just feel, I can't be perfect, so why even bother?'

" 'None of us is perfect,' I said gently. 'That's why it's so important to do three things: First, learn as much as you can about your disease. Your local chapter of the American Diabetes Association is a great source. Learn how the disease affects you so that you can recognize and promptly treat even your subtlest symptoms. Frequent testing is important, and keeping a diary can help you learn whether it's anger, for example, or boredom or loneliness that triggers your "forgetting" insulin or going on food binges.'

"The second thing, I told them, was always to be prepared for the unexpected—by wearing a Medic Alert bracelet, always having an emergency snack in your pocket, and letting your teachers and coaches know that you are diabetic, so they can help if necessary.

" 'And the third thing,' I said, 'is to keep expectations realistic on both sides: to be tolerant when your parents are a little protective and also to be willing to say to your mom or dad, "Look, I'm not perfect. I might cheat on my diet and forget my shot sometimes, but I'm still coping well with a lot of responsibility. And the more you can focus on that and notice when I *haven't* had trouble, the better we'll all feel." '

"The two weeks of camp seemed to fly as the girls in my bunk tried out new sports, developed skills, and made some lasting friendships. On the last day, Amy hugged me and promised to let me know how she was doing at home.

"Here's what she said in a recent letter to me:

> *Dear Cece,*
>
> *Things are better at home—a lot better. Mom's not so bossy, and I've gotten her to say "Can you have that piece of pie?" instead of "Don't touch that!" She even amazed me by letting me spend a whole weekend at Peregrine's house, and she only called twice!*
>
> *I'm pretty good about my exercising. Still, I don't always have perfect blood sugar, but now I don't give up—and Mom*

doesn't panic and put me in a cage. I guess you could say that we're working together, and we laugh a lot more than we used to. Thanks for everything!

Your friend, Amy

"Rebellion—like Amy Gordon's—was a natural response to feeling helpless. She couldn't cure her diabetes, as she had once hoped, but thanks to camp and all the people she met there, Amy is coping responsibly and feeling like a competent young woman instead of like a victim."

PARENTING
DILEMMAS

Julie's a devoted mother, but she's scared to let the kids do anything without her! Can't she be more sensible . . . or is she caught in something that's beyond her control?

Julie's Story

"Julie was actually scared to have kids," said David Hoffman, 41." " 'Oh, I love them,' she would say, 'but there are so many things that can go wrong. I mean, how do we know the world will even be here in twenty years?'

"It sounded strange from Julie—a person who was rarely even moody, but I could understand where she was coming from. Julie's parents were survivors of the Nazi Holocaust, and I assumed that it must have had some effect on her growing up. Not that she ever said it did. 'My parents put all that suffering behind them,' was the only comment she'd made about it. I'd thought, What a courageous family! and left it alone. No more questions.

"But Julie did become pregnant. Then all her apprehension seemed to vanish, and she glowed. So did I!

"Kenny was a beautiful baby, but he spat up like crazy and slept for only an hour at a time. I was grouchy and exhausted, but Julie never complained or even seemed to get tired. She would hold him in her arms—all night if necessary—just to soothe him so he'd keep the formula down.

" 'Julie's a natural,' everyone said, and I agreed. The demands on my time at the law firm where I worked were ridiculous. Most nights, I didn't get home until ten or eleven. But Julie didn't seem to feel 'stuck' with Kenny. In fact, she even wanted to have another baby right away.

"Melissa Amy was born a year later. I thought she looked like one of those Cabbage Patch Kids, but Julie said she was beautiful—even when red in the face and screaming her head off, which was most of the time.

"By the time Melissa was ten months old and sleeping through the night—more or less—I thought it would be a treat for Julie and me to get away for a weekend together, our first without the kids. But Julie said, 'Oh, I couldn't go. Melissa would cry all night.' She squeezed my hand. 'The kids won't always need me so much,' she said. 'Okay?'

"I tried to be patient. But as time went on, I sensed that Julie wasn't teaching the kids to do without her at all. I mean, she never put Melissa down to play. And did she really need to stay at Kenny's side when he had a play date? Weren't other five-year-olds comfortable without their mothers around?

"I felt that Julie went overboard to accommodate the kids. I don't think they ever had a chance to be angry or bored—even for a moment. Julie swooped in to cheer them up at the first whine or whimper, to the point where they expected her to 'fix it, Mom!' whatever it was. When I remarked on this, Julie said, 'Oh, come on, David. *My* mom spent a lot of time with me and I turned out okay, didn't I?' I didn't argue.

" 'Julie's a *perfect* mom,' our friends would say, and I really did agree—most of the time. But I couldn't help remembering how much more freedom I'd had . . . how much I'd enjoyed biking around the neighborhood at the age of six and seven, and going to day camp. But Kenny didn't get to do anything alone! Instead of sending him to day camp, Julie joined her mother's beach club, where she could take both children every day. ('There are nice kids there,' she said, 'so why bother with day camp?')

"It was Julie's decision not to let the children have a skateboard, even though it was the fad of the moment on our block. 'They're really dangerous,' Julie insisted tensely. 'I've read about them . . .'

But nobody had any accidents—until Hiroki, the boy next door, broke his nose. 'Now, will you please stop acting like I'm nuts?' Julie pleaded.

"By the time Melissa was in kindergarten, she and Kenny could have walked to school together, but Julie drove them. I said, 'Don't all their friends walk to school? But Julie bridled. 'Why shouldn't they have a ride? she demanded. 'They like it, and I don't mind.' I just shrugged and shook my head. It didn't feel right, but I couldn't explain it.

"But something else disturbed me: the children were so demanding with Julie, expecting her help with things that they definitely should have been able to handle on their own. For the life of me, I couldn't see why Kenny—at age nine—should interrupt Julie in the middle of a phone call to help him find his spelling book. He always wants her to stay in the room when he does his homework—and she does! He thinks he *needs* her.

"And what about Melissa? She wants Julie to stop making dinner and play a game. And Julie gives in! Melissa never did become pretty, but she's cute and smart and could have friends if she weren't so whiny. When some little girl in the neighborhood has a party and doesn't invite Melissa, Julie buys a present—for Melissa!

"I think one of the most upsetting incidents was last month, when Kenny's class went to Washington, D.C. Julie had worried about the food on the trip, but she'd finally signed the permission slip, and he had gone. But that Saturday night, at eight, Kenny called collect to say he had a stomachache. Kenny's teacher assured me that Kenny seemed fine. But Julie wasn't convinced.

" 'What if it's his appendix?' Julie worried. 'Maybe I should fly down . . .' In the end, I managed to talk her out of it, but it involved several more phone calls and even a doctor's visit. And he *was* fine.

"That night, I felt confused: Was I wrong? Was one of us crazy? How could we both love the same kids—and have such opposite ways of looking at them? Julie calls me insensitive, but sometimes she can be such a stone wall—shutting me out and not even showing me what she's feeling inside. Everything is always fine . . . as long as I let her dote on the kids.

"Sometimes I feel so superfluous. I even look at other women and fantasize—a lot. But I don't do anything about it because the

251

only one I really want is still Julie. That's why it seemed so fantastic last week, when I picked up one of those scratch-and-win coupons at the bank and won a trip to London for two! This was exactly what we needed.

"Julie and I were like kids that night—planning all the plays we'd go to see, the dinners in cozy pubs, the walks past Buckingham Palace. I knew this was the trip that would bring us close together again.

"But when I got home the next night, reality hit. Julie had thought about the children . . . and couldn't go.

"Well, I am very disappointed, and really scared that she's never going to feel that they're 'old enough.' All you have to do is look at Nora, Julie's mother, who is delightful and generous but is wanting us to come for dinner *all the time.*

"I'm not saying that togetherness is wrong. But it's just too much! Julie still disagrees. But at least she feels badly enough about the trip that she's agreed to go with me for counseling. I may be kidding myself, but I think I've found a person who can help us—if anyone can!"

The Counselor Replies

Esther Rosenthal, M.S.W., B.C.D., A.C.S.W., is a family therapist in Belle Harbour, New York, who has specialized in treating Holocaust survivors and their children.

"After he had described the problem in detail, David said, 'Julie's afraid of letting go—as if the children would die without her.' Julie sighed. 'It does feel that way sometimes,' she admitted. 'I guess it's the arrogance of the supermom's "no one can take care of them like I can!" ' She smiled ruefully.

" 'Maybe there's another reason,' I offered. 'Julie, David mentioned on the telephone that your parents were in one of Hitler's concentration camps . . .'

" 'Yes, yes,' Julie interrupted irritably. 'But I've told him a dozen times that they *never talked about it*—and they certainly never frightened me with any nightmare stories or made me feel guilty and vulnerable for being alive when so many others died. Listen,' she went on angrily, 'My parents gave me everything I asked for. So how can you possibly say they traumatized me?'

"Julie crossed her arms and glared. 'I understand why you're upset, and it's okay,' I told her. 'But I think you should know that many survivor families behaved just as yours did—saying nothing. But silence doesn't heal . . . in fact sometimes it has just the opposite effect.'

"Julie stared. I said, 'Chances are, your parents didn't want to hurt you . . . and you didn't ask because you didn't want to hurt them. But they couldn't help transmitting nonverbal signals, signals that said, 'Being apart is like death' and 'Being a good parent means having kids stay very close and taking no chances.'

"I said, 'The trouble is that when you grow up that way—overprotected but underinformed (because *something* happened that's considered much too terrible to talk about)—you naturally do the same with your own kids. It gets set up without anybody wanting it to be that way. The hard part is changing.'

"By this time, Julie wasn't angry anymore. She looked fascinated—and a little scared. 'It's a very common problem,' I assured her. 'So many people think they've gotten away unscathed but still feel troubled. They don't connect their current problem with its real source.

" 'Well, what is there to do about it?' Julie asked. 'I can't go back and undo what's happened.'

" 'No,' I agreed. 'But one thing you can do is break the silence—and its hold on you.' I knew that for Julie, going to her mother and asking questions would not be easy; but Julie had opened her own mind, and once that's happened, it's hard to close it again.

"Julie did meet very strong resistance. 'Herb (rest his soul) and I *promised* ourselves that we'd never make you unhappy with our past,' Julie's mother, Nora, said firmly. But Julie would not be put off, and little by little, the stories came out.

"Nora told about herself at age fourteen, being literally torn from her mother's arms and tossed in a truck, while her mother was pinched and whistled at—and then raped by a succession of pink-cheeked soldiers until she was dead. Julie began to cry and found she couldn't stop. But then she said, 'I need to know everything—about Daddy, too. Please tell me the rest.'

"In her next counseling session, Julie told me that she felt regret that it was too late to talk to her father, who had passed away ten years ago. But Nora did tell her—for the first time—that Herb, Julie's wise-cracking father, had been married first to Nora's elder sister, Leda. And they had an adorable little boy they called Wolf. When Herb was captured in front of their door, Leda grabbed Wolf and ran to hide in the woods. But Wolf, who was only two, had cried for his papa. This made it easy for the SS to find and shoot the two of them.

"Julie felt enormous sorrow for what her parents had suffered and for those relatives she would never know or even be able to see pictures of; but she also felt a new sense of continuity with the past, as her mother shared earlier happy, and sometimes funny, memories of aunts, uncles, and grandparents.

"Julie's hunger for details began to surpass her mother's ability to recall—as well as her tolerance for delving into her past. Julie felt frustrated, but I suggested two things: first, sharing her feelings with David, who welcomed her confidence, and second, joining a support group for children of Holocaust survivors. 'You grew up learning not to talk about painful things,' I said, 'but silence caused your problems, and talking will help to free you.'

"Julie was touched by how supportive David was, and realized for the first time how distant she had been to him all the years she'd been so focused on the children. As she became more expressive and warmer, he gave her the encouragement and reassurance that she needed.

"The support group filled a different need: as Julie sat and listened to other children of survivors, she saw things in her own history that she'd never recognized. Julie remembered how hysterical her mother used to get when she fell and scraped her knee, so Julie had given up the roller-skating that she loved. Now it had come full circle as she tried to trouble-proof Kenny and Melissa.

"Julie remembered feeling guilty that her parents had numbers on their arms, which showed that they had suffered even if they didn't tell about it. And she made herself responsible for being extra good and always meeting their needs—*just as she was now doing with her kids.*

"Julie said, 'David was right! I *have* smothered the kids. But how can I stop worrying?' I told her that it would be a very slow and undramatic kind of progress, like *any* unlearning, but I knew she had the guts to do it. I would give her suggestions and moral support along the way.

"I asked her to search for a sitter, and after weeks, she found one she trusted. Then she made a standing date with David to go out one night a week. At first the children, accustomed to having her at their disposal, tried to make her feel like a deserter—and succeeded. But Julie stuck with it, and within just two months, she was willing to go away for a night with David, and she didn't phone home until morning.

"Another important task for Julie was allowing the children to make more of their own decisions and take responsibility for their behavior. I was pleased when, instead of buying a new toy as a consolation prize, she told Melissa, 'Honey, if you let Sally share your toys and stop calling her names, she might invite you to her party next year.'

"Gradually, Julie developed an ability to listen to her children in a new way—*reflecting* any sadness, self-doubt, or anger, without feeling that it was her job to make the bad feeling go away. Julie said, 'I was trying to live their lives for them!' I assured her that she had only been doing what she had thought was right. Now she was finding that the less she hovered, the more the kids could go about *their* business (without clinging, which they had done partly because they'd sensed *her need* for them to cling). And the less demanding Kenny and Melissa became, the more time Julie had—both for David and for herself.

"Julie has come a very long way, but she and David both need to continue to be patient when she worries excessively. Lately, Julie has managed to discuss those feelings with her children and to explain the reason behind them, which is important because the Holocaust is also their legacy as well as hers.

"Julie and David are leaving soon, for their first real trip without the children. It isn't London, this time. It's only Long Island—just 100 miles away. But as Julie herself said, you have to walk before you can run.

"It's very hard to look at the world without distortions when something very tragic has happened in the family—even very long

255

ago and far away. But Julie is an example of the freedom we can gain when we're ready to stop leaving well enough alone."

Jim's wonderful with fourteen-month-old Scott, but he's so tense and impatient with four-year-old Cindy. Will this ever change, or will Cindy grow up feeling not quite good enough to please her dad?

Melissa's Story

"Jim brought home a new book for Cindy, and she was thrilled," said Melissa Bowen, 36. "He tried to read it to her, but he got so exasperated with her running off to pet the cat, constantly interrupting, and grabbing the book to see a picture on the next page that he finally gave up. He flipped the book to me and said, '*You* read it! I'll go and give Scott his bath.'

"Later, when we were alone, I asked Jim why he always got so annoyed at Cindy.

" 'I don't,' he said. 'But even Scott can sit still and listen to a story. Why can't she?'

"*Was* it just about the book? It seemed that so many of these incidents ended up with Cindy feeling rejected, and it bothered me terribly. Maybe she's hard to handle (and all the more so lately, since Scott has been on his feet and 'talking'), but Cindy is also an exceedingly warm, enthusiastic, and loving little girl. It hurt me that Jim didn't seem to see it.

" 'If you could only be a little less judgmental,' I suggested. 'Instead of thinking, Oh, that's such annoying behavior, why don't you try to accept that it's her style? After all, she's only four.'

"Jim said he would try, and he really did: I could see it the following weekend at his mother's seventieth-birthday party.

"Cindy—excited to see all her relatives—was jubilant and very noisy. She pushed ahead of the other children in her eagerness for one of her Uncle Phil's piggyback rides. After all the kids had had their turns, and Cindy had had two, she still clung to him, pleading for more.

"Then, when Jim's mother sat down to open all her birthday gifts, Cindy yelled, 'No, Grandma, not that one, open *ours* first! You have to!' And when it was time to eat, Cindy, in a rush to sit next to her grandpa, knocked over a pitcher of milk and sent it crashing.

" 'I know, it was an accident,' Jim agreed that night. 'But it's so embarrassing. How come all the other kids in the family can sit through a meal without jumping or causing a disaster but Cindy can't?'

"In the weeks that followed, Jim managed to keep his temper in check, but even though he didn't yell at Cindy too much, he seemed to stiffen every time she approached him. It seemed as if he were enduring rather than enjoying being with her, the way he clearly enjoys spending time with Scott.

"And all the while Cindy kept right on pursuing him. I felt sorry for her and tried to fill the gap. 'Honey, Daddy's busy reading now, but I'll play with you,' I'd offer when Jim would hide from her behind his newspaper or his book.

" 'Don't you think I *try* to get along with her?' Jim would protest when I confronted him. 'I try all the time.'

" 'They need a little father-daughter magic,' my friend Molly suggested over lunch one day when I poured out my concerns.

" 'Be serious,' I said.

" 'I am,' she said. 'When I was little, my dad used to take me to the ballet, and it was magical. For years it was something special we loved to share together, just the two of us.'

"So I bought two tickets to a brand-new ballet written especially for children. Maybe this special afternoon would bring Jim and Cindy a little bit closer.

"Jim took Cindy to a restaurant for lunch. But according to Jim, instead of loving it, Cindy complained loudly and refused to eat. Afterward she begged for candy. Reluctantly (but thinking it would help her be quiet at the ballet) he gave in. 'We'll enjoy this,' he promised her as they entered the theater.

"Cindy was bored and restless and spent the first half hour climbing all over Jim and dropping the candies he'd bought her on the floor, then scrambling over people's feet to retrieve them. Later, in the middle of the second act, she had to go to the bathroom. Jim was mortified, pushing past people to get out and then pushing back in again. He was especially embarrassed when Cindy kept whispering loudly, 'Dad, when will this dumb ballet be over?'

"Finally the lights came on for intermission. Jim told Cindy, 'It's over,' and took her home.

"When he got home, he admitted, 'I didn't really enjoy it much myself. But of all the hundreds of adults and children there, Cindy was the *only* one in the audience who was creating a disturbance.'

" 'Oh, come on,' I protested. 'It couldn't have been *so* terrible.'

"Then Jim said, 'I don't think you understand how bad it was. I was so embarrassed! Everybody was giving me a dirty look.'

"The next day Molly called to say she remembered that she had fallen in love with the ballet when she was much older than Cindy—eight or nine at least.

"Besides, I realized, it was my mistake: Even if Cindy had liked it, Jim wouldn't have—and he, not Cindy, was the one who needed wooing. So didn't it make more sense for them to do something together that Jim already enjoyed?

"It was unseasonably warm. Jim was still going fishing out at the lake on some weekends, so I suggested that he take Cindy along. He thought it sounded like a great idea. And so did Cindy.

"But that didn't work, either. Cindy couldn't sit still in the boat— or keep quiet. She was hungry; she was hot in her jacket, freezing without it; she was thirsty; she was too tired; she wanted Jim to read her a story; she had to go to the bathroom.

"Then she started to play with Jim's tackle box. He told her not to, but she did it again—and got a hook caught in her hair. Jim managed to remove it without any damage, but Cindy's screams were so loud and lasted so long that they seemed to echo all over the lake.

"They came home cold, bedraggled, and miserable. Cindy said, 'Daddy was really *mean*. He kept yelling at me the whole time.' I glared at Jim, and he glared back at me.

" 'Why do you *assume* that I was mean? Just because she said so?' he demanded. I shrugged.

"Jim waited until Cindy left the room. Then he said, 'I just don't know how you can stand being with her all day, every day.'

"I didn't like his tone. I said, 'She's your daughter, and you sound as if you don't even like her!'

" 'Maybe I don't!' Jim flung back. Then, more calmly, he said, 'It's just that with Scott, well, I like him, and I like spending time with him. He's only a baby, but I can relate to him. But Cindy puts me on edge. Friends at work say it's so much fun to have a four-year-old, and sometimes I pretend I feel the same way—but I don't! When Cindy starts whining or jumping up and down and getting intense . . . I just want to get away from her. I really try not to get mad at her. And when I do, I feel like such a failure as a dad. I know it sounds awful, but there are times when I wish we'd never had her.'

"Suddenly I heard a loud sob from the doorway. It was Cindy. Jim saw her too and said, 'Oh, Cindy! You know I didn't mean that . . . '

"But Cindy shook her head and yelled, 'You don't like me! You just said so! I heard you!'

"Jim looked at me helplessly. He had tears in his eyes, but he didn't even try to follow Cindy to her room. I feel so awful—for all of us. I want us to be such a happy family, but somehow it's just not working."

The Counselor Replies

Jan Drucker, Ph.D., is a child psychologist in New York City. She is also professor of psychology at Sarah Lawrence College in Bronxville, New York, and a consultant to the Early Childhood Center there.

"When Jim and Melissa Bowen came in, they both seemed very sad as they told me their story. 'I just don't know where we've gone wrong,' Jim said. At that point I asked them to tell me how things had been at the beginning—when Cindy was a baby and even before that.

" 'We both wanted her so much,' Melissa replied. 'In fact, when I was pregnant, Jim was so involved he used to measure my belly every couple of days. It was an easy pregnancy. Everything went smoothly, and when Cindy was born, the pediatrician said she was perfect.

" 'Actually,' Melissa went on, 'everything was just fine until Scott was born fourteen months ago.'

" 'Wait a second,' Jim interrupted. 'Don't you remember? Even when Cindy was an infant, she was impossible. We were frantic— Cindy woke up every hour on the hour. She cried to be held all the time. We never had a complete dinner without at least one interruption.

" 'The pediatrician said at the time that there was nothing wrong with her, but it wasn't until we had Scott that I began to compare and realize how difficult Cindy had been.'

"Jim looked thoughtful. 'Scott's whole development has been so different from how Cindy was when she was little,' he said. 'He's a dream. . . .'

" 'That's the whole problem,' Melissa stated. 'Jim thinks that Scott's such an angel—and that Cindy's a monster, and I'm starting to see real hurt in her eyes.'

" 'Of course I don't want to hurt Cindy,' Jim retorted. 'But it's clear that she would much rather play with you than with me.'

" 'That's obviously because you always reject her.'

"At that point I cut in. 'I'd like to meet Cindy and get to know all three of you better,' I said. 'Perhaps then we'll be able to figure out how to make things better for all of you.'

"The Bowens agreed, and one week later Cindy came in. She was a very intelligent, active little girl, quite sturdy, articulate, and curious about my office. After exploring the room, she wanted to know where the toys were kept. 'My mom said you have lots of toys,' she explained.

" 'Yes,' I said, opening a closet, 'I do have some toys here.'

"Cindy immediately chose a baby toy: a transparent plastic ball with a bright butterfly spinning around inside. 'Even big girls can play with this,' she said. I agreed. A moment later Cindy put the ball down and picked up a baby doll. She proceeded to play with it in appropriate four-year-old fashion: pretending to feed it and changing its diaper.

"In response to my questions, Cindy said that she loved nursery school and that her brother was a 'googoo silly head' and her mommy sometimes yelled too much, 'but not as much as Daddy.'

"Cindy's activity level was unusually high—not hyperactive in any sense, but she did have a need to keep moving. I could imagine that if crossed or upset, she could be quite a handful. Indeed, when it was time for them to leave, she started to fuss. But Melissa was skillful in getting her moving.

"The following week I had sessions with both parents individually, during which I learned some facts that helped to explain the heightened tensions at home.

"Jim had come from a very quiet, serene, and rather formal household, in which even the youngest kids were expected to control themselves. Recalling his mother's birthday party, Jim acknowledged how edgy he had been, anticipating that Cindy's behavior would upset his parents. It actually hadn't. Jim said that as grandparents, they had mellowed, but he still 'heard' their reprimands in his mind.

"As for Melissa, she felt sorry for Cindy over the father-daughter issue because her own father, who had died five years earlier, had been emotionally erratic: sometimes warm and affectionate, but frequently distant and cold. Melissa had expected better for Cindy and Jim, but it just wasn't happening.

"But although she agreed that her own past experience played into her sensitivity and fear that Cindy would be hurt and damaged by her father, she still saw it as a real and pressing problem. 'Jim *is* cold toward her. How can that not be a problem for her, later in life if not right now?' Melissa wondered.

" 'I'm not saying that there isn't a problem,' I replied. 'But Cindy's just getting to the point where little girls really turn to their daddies. It's not too late to work things out so that they'll both be able to benefit fully from their relationship.'

"After two more sessions alone with Cindy, I met with both parents. I said, 'She's basically a very healthy, normal child, but on a behavioral continuum, she is at the more difficult end. Like all children, Cindy needs to learn self-control, but apparently it's coming slower to her. That's something I can work on with her,' I assured them.

"Jim frowned. 'But why do *I* have so much more trouble with her than Melissa?' he asked. 'It isn't lack of love.'

"I said, 'It may be that your wife has a threshold for noise and activity that is different from yours and doesn't feel as swallowed up in meeting Cindy's needs. Still, there are lots of things you can do that will help—like giving Cindy more of your attention.'

"Jim looked nervous.

" 'I don't mean any more fishing trips or ballets,' I said. 'But instead of always keeping Cindy at arm's length, pick her up or get down on the floor with her; make eye contact, hug her, and, above all, *listen* to her. It won't make Cindy more voracious; if anything, it will help you both relax and get closer.'

"I added that when dealing with a child as difficult as Cindy, it's a good idea for both parents to always try to support each other rather than blame each other or themselves when things aren't going well.

"Jim affirmed that he wanted to have positive experiences with Cindy, just as much as Melissa wanted him to. 'But how?' he wanted to know.

" 'Start small,' I suggested. 'Ten or fifteen minutes of real fun together is better than a cumbersome five-hour outing of any kind if the conditions aren't right.'

"We also discussed limits of tolerance—both Jim's and Cindy's—and the important need to plan ahead. That meant anticipating Cindy's physical needs: her hunger, thirst, fatigue, and even boredom before she had a chance to become disruptive. For Jim, it meant keeping track of his feelings so that he could say enough is enough before he lost his temper.

"Jim liked these specific suggestions. He gradually began to apply them and reported glimmers of success. For example, he started taking Cindy to a nearby high school field to run and play ball on Saturdays. Both Jim and Cindy enjoyed the physical activity—and the fact that Cindy didn't need to be quiet or to perform in a prescribed way. Jim genuinely admired her coordination and physical stamina and told her so. Cindy was pleased.

"Building on a new feeling of success, Jim took Cindy to a fast-food drive-in place a few times. By avoiding situations in which Cindy would act up, Jim began to find her energy a plus instead of a problem.

"And once the struggle and tension between the two of them eased, Jim began to enjoy his conversations with Cindy. 'She's not only smart, she's very funny, too,' he said delightedly.

"As Jim stopped seeing Cindy as a 'bad kid,' he experienced less need to idealize Scott, so there was less of a split in his feelings for his family.

"These changes were reassuring to Cindy and to Melissa as well. The whole household atmosphere became calmer and much friendlier.

"At one point, six weeks after the Bowens had first called me, Melissa telephoned and said, 'I'm really happy that Jim is getting along better with Cindy, but I also have a sense of loss. I have to get used to not being the only big love in Cindy's life anymore.' I assured Melissa that her feelings were natural and, most likely, temporary. And, as it turned out, they were.

"One Saturday Jim took both children to a new children's museum. Scott toddled around happily, but Cindy soon got bored and started whining. But Jim didn't go bananas. He just scooped up both children and took them to a nearby playground to let off steam. 'And you know,' he told me proudly, 'we all ended up having a really great time.'

"Jim looked thoughtful. 'Cindy's behavior hasn't really changed all that much,' he said. 'But I'm learning to handle it and accept her better.'

" 'Aha!' he added, laughing. 'I'm beginning to see what this therapy business is really about.'

"Jim had become aware that children differ greatly in style and temperament and that parents differ, too, so family interactions can be very complicated.

"Cindy will always be a challenge to her father, but thanks to a brief period of intervention, the Bowens no longer feel pulled apart by the fear that there might not be enough love for everyone."

> *Robby, seven, is a wonderful kid.*
> *I can't stand the thought of losing*
> *his respect. But how long can I*
> *go on pretending before he*
> *discovers that I've been fired—*
> *and that I'm a failure?*

Neal's Story

"In one day my whole life changed," said Neal Morton, 38. "I'd gone to work one morning as vice president of a textbook company and had come home that night unemployed.

"Ann, my wife, was more distraught than I was. 'But they can't fire you!' she said. 'It's not fair.'

" 'Don't take it so hard,' I said. 'I'll find something else.' Maybe it hadn't hit me yet, but I felt that the less we made of this problem, the sooner I'd be able to solve it.

"I didn't even want to tell Robby what was up. Why get him all upset? He couldn't help, and he would only suffer worrying about the future and wondering what kind of dud he had for a father.

" 'He wouldn't think that; you know he looks up to you,' Ann said.

" 'That's the point,' I replied. 'I don't want to take that respect away from him—a boy needs that.'

"We agreed that we would tell him the truth only after I had found a new job; now it would simply be 'Dad will be working at home for the time being.'

265

"Robby didn't take the news lightly. 'But they still have to pay you, right?' he asked. And could he still come to visit my 'real' office sometimes, to use the computers?

" 'Sure!' I said, praying that I'd have a real office—and a real salary—before he asked me for proof.

"That evening Robby made me a sign for my desk. It said, 'Dad the Grate.' Touched, I told him it was wonderful, and the next day I set to work with a real determination.

"But I couldn't even write a resume. How could I make myself sound good when I'd been given the royal shaft? I honestly didn't know where to begin and spent the day drinking coffee, tidying drawers, and filling pages with nervous doodling.

" 'Is that *work?*' Robby asked, catching me after school.

" 'Yes,' I replied. 'It's thinking.' But my thoughts were anything but productive. I kept playing the 'what-if' game. What if I'd been smarter? What if I'd done things differently?

"I knew it was my own fault that I'd been fired: There had long been rumors of cutbacks, but I'd ignored them. Like a real sap, I had put my energy into the job at hand, when I should have been worrying about furthering my career by lunching, hustling, and cementing alliances with all the 'right' people in the business world.

"Well, now it was too late. I'd blown it, and I really wasn't sure if there was anything out there for me. In a tight job market, companies don't exactly line up to hire an almost-40-year-old has-been.

"I didn't want Ann to know how helpless I felt. When she suggested that I call some of our friends for advice, I said, 'No need. I have my own ideas.' Actually I was too embarrassed to tell anyone I was out of work, let alone ask for help.

"In fact, I didn't even want to see our friends—and bowed out of a couple of dates by claiming I had a stomachache. Even on Saturdays, when Robby had Little League, I'd snatch him away right after the game. I didn't want to hang around with the other fathers; they were all successful guys, like Jack Gardener, with his new sports car.

" 'Isn't that an awesome car, Dad?' Robby asked one day. 'Sure,' I sneered, jealous and defensive. 'If someone is really *that* desperate to impress other people.' Robby looked deflated, and I felt like a fraud, a complete phony.

"One day Ann told me that the library where she worked mornings would love to have her work full-time. I told her it was absolutely out of the question. We'd agreed a long time ago that she wouldn't go back to work full-time until Robby was older; besides, I said, 'by the time you paid a sitter, there'd be very little left.'

" 'Still, I'd really like to help out somehow,' she offered.

" 'There's no need,' I said with finality. I just can't help but feel that it's my responsibility to support my family. 'Have a little faith in me, Ann,' I said. 'These things take time.'

"Dinner was tense that night. Ann barely spoke to me. Instead, she picked on Robby, who wasn't eating the steak I'd bought. He said he wasn't hungry.

" 'Well, we can't waste such expensive food,' she said angrily.

" 'Leave him alone,' I cut in. Ann glared at me. Robby took another small bite.

"At breakfast the next morning she was on his case again. 'Robby!' she cried. 'You're wasting the syrup. You don't need to use that much.'

" 'For God's sake,' I said, disgusted, 'if we're being so conservative this morning, let him have my share. I'll eat my waffle dry.' Ann got up and left the table. Robby looked at me, upset. 'Never mind,' I said, feeling beaten. 'Your mom is just being sensible. Now go ahead and eat your waffle.'

"Of course she was being sensible! I knew that. With my severance pay all gone, we were already living on savings. But instead of galvanizing me, this new cause for panic had the opposite effect: I was paralyzed! Each day I'd plan to make a lot of calls and go see people, but then I'd get cold feet and end up doing nothing.

"I did a lot of daydreaming, fantasizing that the company would realize they'd made a mistake and beg me to come back. (They'd even give me a raise and throw in an extra two weeks of vacation.)

"Just a couple of days earlier Robby had asked when we could go to Disney World. 'Not this year,' Ann had said in a voice that seemed to say, 'Maybe never.'

" 'Hell, no!' I'd said. 'We'll go next year—unless we do something even more exciting!' I gave Ann a dirty look. Why did she have to undermine me all the time in front of Robby?

"Then there was the issue of the baseball glove. Robby needed a

267

new, bigger glove. Ann sighed. 'Can't we just borrow a glove from Adam and Eddie next door?' she suggested.

"I said, 'No way!' and went out to a sporting-goods store and bought Robby a real top-of-the-line pro-style glove. 'This is just like the ones the Red Sox are using,' the man in the store assured me.

"Ann looked as if she wanted to cry. 'I can't believe you spent *a hundred dollars* on a glove that doesn't even fit him yet!'

" 'He'll grow into it. He'll love it!' I insisted, and I was right. 'Wow! It's great, Dad. Thanks,' Robby said, clearly awed; for the first time in weeks I felt good.

"The next day after Little League practice, Robby said he was starving and asked if we could stop for pizza. I said sure, and we ordered the kind he likes best, with everything on it. But when I went to pay, I was two dollars short.

" 'No problem!' said Gino, the owner. Being regular customers, we could pay the rest next time, he told me. 'I must have left all my money in another jacket,' I said. 'Sure, Dad,' Robby agreed.

"That night I was sitting in the den when Robby came in. 'Here,' he said shyly, handing me his piggy bank. 'I've only got $6.29, but I want you and Mom to have it.'

" 'No thanks,' I said, quickly handing it back. My voice was unsteady. I felt touched by his gift but also humiliated. Here I'd been, trying so hard to keep things looking normal, but Robby had obviously seen through 'Dad the Grate.' My seven-year-old thinks I'm a deadbeat who needs to be rescued! Ann's been talking about some guy she heard on the radio who counsels people who've lost their job. I'm not sure he can help me, but I'm willing to give it a shot."

The Counselor Replies

Barrie Sanford Greiff, M.D., a psychiatric consultant for Harvard University Health Services, in Cambridge, Massachusetts, is a coauthor with Nick Kates, M.B.B.S., and Duane Q. Hagen, M.D., of The Psychosocial Impact of Job Loss *(American Psychiatric Press).*

"Neal's self-esteem was badly tarnished. He had lost his job and needed to find a new one, but feeling inadequate and scared, he had done little but procrastinate.

"I said, 'It sounds to me as if you've lost your confidence, and that's what's really hurting.'

" 'Well, not really,' he said.

" 'I think you *have!*' his wife, Ann, interrupted. 'Whenever I suggest calling someone for advice, you say that it would be a waste of time.'

" 'So maybe I'm not so confident!' Neal went on the defensive. 'What category does that put me in?'

" 'Hold on,' I said. 'I'm not judging or trying to put you in a category. I'm here as your ally, and I want to help you.' I told Neal that it's not unusual for a man who's lost his job to feel so ashamed and worthless that all he can do is sit around and berate himself. However, I told him, 'it's possible for anyone to lose a job, no matter how good he is. Still, that doesn't have to be the end of everything.'

" 'You may feel as if you don't have any resources,' I went on. 'But you do.' Apart from this one negative event, Neal's work history showed talent, accomplishment, and steady progress. 'It might help you to focus on that,' I suggested.

"Another problem was that Neal had been trying to heal his injured pride by keeping Ann at arm's length, denying the real extent of his worry, and refusing her help. 'It's *my* problem to solve, not hers,' he said. 'A man is supposed to take care of his wife, not be a burden.'

"I said that sounded very lonely for both of them. 'You're not operating in a vacuum,' I said. 'What happens to you affects Ann, too. She's your partner—and she loves you.'

" 'That's true,' Ann said. 'You won't let me help, and you won't even share how you feel. Don't you know I *want* to be there for you?' Neal took her hand. 'I tried to be a tower of strength,' he said sheepishly. 'I realize now I was just being a jerk.'

"I asked the Mortons how much Robby knew about their situation. 'Nothing concrete,' Neal said. 'I may have done the wrong thing with Ann, but at least I know you don't burden a child with adult problems.'

"I said, 'You lost your job twelve weeks ago. Don't you think he senses something?'

"Ann frowned. 'Robby does keep a lot inside,' she said. 'But I

269

don't think he could know when neither one of us has told him.'

" 'Children don't need to be told that something's wrong,' I said. 'They feel it. I assume that Robby has some fantasy about what's going on. But fantasy has no boundaries, so Robby's private scenario may be even worse than the facts.'

" 'So not telling Robby might actually be doing more harm than good?' Ann wondered.

" 'Exactly,' I said. 'But there's another reason to tell him. When you can't share embarrassing or painful information with your child, you're setting up situations in the future in which he won't share with you.'

"Neal still felt apprehensive. 'I believe you, but I'm not sure I can bring myself to tell him,' he said.

" 'Then bring him in,' I suggested, and a few days later they did.

" 'Your mom and dad have been concerned,' I said when Robby and I were alone in my office. 'How are things at home?'

" 'Fine,' Robby said.

" 'Are they really?' I asked.

" '*Not* really,' he said. 'I mean, not the same. I thought it would be great with Dad working at home, but it's no fun. He's always so worried.'

" 'Why do you think that is?'

"Robby looked anxious. 'Dad gets stomachaches a lot, and he looks skinnier. Isn't that what cancer does? Dad *says* he's fine, but twice lately he was too sick to go to a party.'

" 'Is he going to a doctor?'

" 'Well, no!' Robby looked relieved, but then his face clouded over. He sighed. 'They're getting a divorce.' He lowered his voice. 'And it's all my fault. A lot of the time they fight about me.'

"I said, 'That's a big worry. Why don't we ask them?'

"Neal and Ann were both shocked. 'Never!' Ann said.

" 'How did you even get that idea?' Neal asked him. Robby shrugged.

" 'But maybe there is *something*?' I prompted them.

"Neal took the cue. 'I hoped I wouldn't have to tell you this, Robby,' he said, 'but I don't have a job anymore. I was fired.' Robby's mouth fell open. 'I don't know when I'll find a new one,' Neal added.

" 'But, Dad, you're great!' Robby cried, relieved. 'Why didn't you tell me? You always said if I was in trouble, you'd be on my side. Well, I'm on yours, too!'

"It was an emotional moment. 'I love you—you're so important to me, and I feel so much better now that I've told you the truth about my job,' Neal said, hugging Robby.

" 'We're sorry we kept this secret; you're a much bigger boy than we thought,' Ann added.

"Robby began to ask a lot of questions. But this time instead of evasions and false reassurances, he got straight answers. 'Yes, we have enough money to live on—for quite a while if we plan ahead and are careful,' Neal said.

" 'Then let's not get that remote-control car for my birthday,' Robby offered. Neal looked amazed. 'It's okay,' Robby said with an impish smile. 'If you'll get me a candy bar!' Neal laughed, and so did Robby.

" 'You know I'll get you the car when I can,' Neal told Robby. 'I know!' Robby said. 'You really are a great kid,' Neal said.

"Because he was now less depressed, Neal began to job hunt in earnest. He combed the want ads and called some headhunters, but the results were disappointing.

"When I asked if he'd told his friends, he shook his head. 'I think you should,' I said. 'Nowadays, being unemployed is really not the stigma that you think it is. Besides, networking is valuable, and many people find jobs through word-of-mouth, not through ads.'

"Cautiously, Neal did tell a friend, and then another . . . and another. But instead of losing face, as he'd feared, he was floored by the outpouring of warmth, encouragement, and potentially helpful contacts.

" 'You'll do fine, Neal,' Jack Gardener (the fellow with the snazzy sports car) reassured him. 'If you were good enough to get the last job, you're obviously good enough to get the next one.'

"Neal said, 'I used to think I had to have supercontrol over my life in order to be liked and respected. I certainly was wrong.'

"But his growing optimism slipped a few days later when a pipe burst in the Mortons' basement—and the plumber presented him with a bill for several hundred dollars. Ann said, 'This time you have to let me help,' and sold a gold bracelet her grandmother had left her.

"Neal was tempted to protest, but when Ann said, 'We're all in this together, and we're going to get through it,' he thanked her with sincerity and love and told Robby, 'I hope you'll be as lucky as I am when you get married.'

"The next two months were like a roller coaster ride for the Mortons: Neal went on some job interviews, and two or three seemed extremely promising—only to result in a 'Sorry' or 'You were our second choice.'

"Then one day Neal got a call from someone he didn't even know—the head of a company that made memory boards for computers. 'I know it's really not your area,' the man said, 'but would you consider coming in for a talk?'

"Neal went to the interview and found it fascinating, 'We can't offer you as much as you were making before,' the man said, 'but we've heard some good things about you. If you come on board, you'll end up making more money with bonuses.'

"Neal knew it was a gamble, but he accepted the job, and that night the Mortons all went out to dinner to celebrate. 'This may not be forever,' Neal said. 'There are no guarantees, but if I ever lose my job again, I know I'll have all the support I need.'

"Getting fired felt like an irrevocable loss to Neal, but in the end he actually came out ahead. While he'd always thought it was essential for a 'real man' to have his act together, he now knows that there's another kind of strength in being able to tell a loving wife and child, 'I need your help' and 'Thank you for being there.' "

PHYSICAL DIFFERENCES

> *We've done everything to help our son, Michael, feel good about himself in spite of his handicap. When did he turn into such a tyrant that even our best friends can't stand him?*

Antonia's Story

"We all felt badly when our neighbors, the Oyamas, moved to Florida," said Antonia Perry, 32. "They were a lovely family with whom we'd shared a lot over seven years. I knew I'd miss them. But the real devastation was Michael's.

"Our son, Michael, who is six, was born with cerebral palsy. Thank God, he isn't retarded, but he limps and wears a brace on one leg. He gets around slowly and tires easily. And he's had only one real friend—Wilson Oyama, who is also six, a bright, funny child who would sit on the porch with Michael, playing endless imaginative games.

" 'Nobody will play with me now,' Michael said as we watched the moving men load the Oyama's furniture into the truck. And with a pang, I knew he was right! Sure, there were boys on our block, but they were too busy playing football and racing bikes.

" 'Maybe there'll be someone at school,' I said hopefully. Michael had just begun first grade. But the dejected look on his face each day at three told me how lonely he was. When he'd ask if we could go to a toy store, I'd say sure, and let him get something. If anyone deserved some fun, he did!

" '*Another* new Jungle Cat?' my husband, Ron, said one evening. I couldn't tell if he was kidding or not. He had a few stuffy ideas about not spoiling kids but I also knew how deeply he shared my commitment to minimizing Michael's built-in unhappiness.

"Now—of all times—with Wilson gone *plus* the transition from a warm kindergarten to the real world of first grade, Michael was extra vulnerable, and I felt that we should be a little more indulgent than usual. Give the treats and hold the criticism: that was my strategy.

"Not that Michael wasn't a handful! Especially in the mornings, when he'd sit and laugh at comic books instead of getting dressed. His excuse was 'I couldn't find any socks.'

" 'Please get going,' I would beg. Ron and Nell, Michael's eleven-year-old sister, would be already dressed and almost done with breakfast. When Michael finally made it downstairs—hair unbrushed and face unwashed—he'd insist on a complicated breakfast, like a bacon-cheddar omelet.

" 'It's not *fair*,' Nell would fuss. 'I clean my room and walk the dogs and everything . . . Michael doesn't have to do *anything* and he's going to make us late *again*.'

" 'SHUT UP, you retard,' Michael would scream, giving his sister a punch. There'd be pushing, yelling, tears. 'Michael would do chores if he could, Nell,' I would tell her firmly.

" 'But he called me a retard!'

" '*Don't* use that word, Mike!'

" 'YOU'RE MEAN AND I'M NOT GOING TO SCHOOL,' Michael would cry, running from the table. The dogs would eat his breakfast while I calmed him down and found his favorite Hawaiian shirt. By this time, Nell would be beside herself, and Ron, having missed his train, would be looking at his watch and softly swearing.

"Ron called Michael's morning behavior 'manipulative,' but I felt sure it was more a case of hating school and trying to delay his arrival. And I sympathized because it wasn't just his lack of friends, it was also the teacher. 'Miss Tower made me miss recess just because I'm not fast enough,' Michael sobbed into my jacket. 'I'll speak to her,' I promised, and hugged him tight.

"In my mind, I felt like throttling that teacher—and also the

276

smug young obstetrician who'd brushed off the damage to Michael as 'minimal.' I wanted to yell, "THERE'S NO SUCH THING AS MINIMAL WHEN THE CHILD IS YOURS!'

"For the millionth time, I relived that hot August day six years ago, when I took Nell for a day of sailing on my sister's friend's boat. I wasn't due for three more weeks, but I went into labor in the middle of that lake. And by the time they could get me to a hospital, Michael had already started to choke on his umbilical cord. Some nights, I still have dreams in which I'm on the phone saying, 'No! We can't go sailing. Maybe next month.' But then I wake up—and I know it's too late.

"That evening, when I phoned Michael's teacher, Miss Tower, and told her—as calmly as possible—that Michael needs encouragement, not punishment, she sighed. 'Mrs. Perry, Michael could be faster if he followed directions. And Mrs. Perry, *he's* the one who's hard to make friends with, not the other children.'

" 'Sounds like a witch,' Ron agreed that evening when I told him. I said maybe it was time to look into a private school, because it didn't seem that this school would ever meet Michael's needs. Ron said there was no way we could afford it.

" 'Oh, school's not the problem,' said Nell, plopping down beside us on the couch. 'It's Michael—he's such a brat! I mean it. Don't you see how he loves to embarrass me?'

" 'Come on, Nell!' I said, putting my arms around her. 'All brothers tease! Besides, things are tough for Michael, you know?'

"So here I was not only Michael's cheerleader but also his public relations department! But in between, I had my own bad days when I'd lose my temper at Michael. Then I would feel *so* bad that I could hardly wait until after school so I could cater and make amends.

"But no matter how generous I was in buying him goodies or in giving him every little smidgen of my time and patience, it was never enough for him—*or for me!* I'd still be left with a little tiny canker sore on my conscience, and I'd think, 'What kind of mother are you, anyway?'

"Just when life seemed hardest, something lovely and unexpected happened: June Oyama invited us to visit them in Florida over the children's winter holiday. 'Please say you'll come,' June urged. 'Wilson can't wait to see Michael.'

"It would be a two-day drive each way, but Ron agreed it was a great idea. And I'll never forget how joyous it was, pulling into the Oyama's driveway, and seeing Ben with Wilson on his shoulders, June waving wildly, and even shy, serious Garrett Oyama, sixteen, with a huge grin.

"But that evening was tense. Michael ignored the wonderful dinner June had made. 'Why *can't* we get pizza?' he whispered audibly. That night, he was too jazzed up to sleep and kept Wilson up until after one in the morning.

"The next day, Michael couldn't wait to hit the beach, but when he got there, he found he was afraid of the water—and didn't want Wilson to go in either. 'Don't be a rotten jerk,' he begged, as Wilson started putting his swim goggles on. Then I saw June whisper something in Wilson's ear, and he dropped back down on the blanket next to Michael.

"I was grateful. The two boys spent the entire day building sand castles—and for a while it seemed almost like old times.

"That evening, Michael—who had fiercely refused any sunscreen—looked like a lobster. 'I can't lift my arm,' he whimpered, and I ended up having to feed him. 'Tomorrow, I want to get a raft,' he announced. 'I saw one that looked like an alligator.' 'Will you go in the water?' Ron asked dubiously. 'Of course, if I get the raft,' Michael answered.

"We did buy the raft, and a pair of goggles like Wilson's, and Michael went in—but only up to his ankles. This time, he grudgingly gave Wilson permission to swim, but not to borrow the alligator raft—until I promised to buy him another, bigger present. That afternoon, one of Wilson's school friends stopped by. 'He's dumb,' Michael stated, livid with jealousy, and sat with me until the friend left and Wilson came over to offer Michael an ice cream cone.

"That evening, there was a lot of screaming: Michael had taken Nell's bathing suit top and dangled it in Garrett Oyama's face. 'Now you see why I hate him?' Nell sobbed.

"I was relieved, in a way, that the next day was our last. 'June,' I said, embracing her when it was time to leave, 'we had a great time, and we really do want you to come to visit us for a while next summer.'

278

" 'Sure,' Ben said warmly. 'NO!' Wilson blurted out. 'Dad, you *promised!* You and Mom said that if I was nice to Michael this time, I'd never have to see him again!'

"There was a silence. None of us knew what to say. 'I'm sorry, Antonia,' June said finally. 'I have to admit it. We did tell him that. I like you so much—all of you! It's just all the fighting, the upsets . . . we just can't deal with it again.'

" 'Yes, I understand,' I said, but I didn't! I felt mortified and stupid! I'd thought we were doing the right thing for Michael—always trying to boost his self-confidence. But, somehow, we'd let him become a brat."

The Counselor Replies

Betty B. Osman, Ph.D., is a psychologist and faculty member in the graduate program at Sarah Lawrence College, in Bronxville, New York, and a psychologist for the Child and Adolescent Services in the Department of Psychiatry at White Plains Hospital Medical Center in New York. Osman is the author of No One to Play With: The Social Side of Learning Disabilities *and* Learning Disabilities: A Family Affair *(Warner Books).*

"Antonia Perry was understandably troubled as she described the visit to Florida and how Michael had acted up—demanding his own way, no matter how much people gave in to him.

" 'I know Ron's always felt I should be tougher,' Antonia said. 'I thought it was just because of his stiff upbringing, but now I'm not sure. Michael *is* hard to live with. He can be very provocative and wearing.'

" 'Let's start small,' I suggested, and asked what one thing at home drove them the most crazy. 'Mornings,' they both said, and they gave me a play-by-play of all the dawdling and yelling. I said I thought we could modify and improve the situation.

"To begin, I urged the Perrys to help Michael lay his clothes out the night before and to wake him up a half hour earlier to allow for dawdling. Then, if he was late coming down, he would have to settle for the simplest breakfast—like toast and juice—and he'd have to take his lunch as is, with no substitutions. 'Buy him a special calendar and give him a star for every day he's all ready by eight. Then,' I said, 'if he comes through—and I suspect he will—you can reward him!'

" 'Well, that *sounds* good,' Ron said. 'But it seems to me he gets too much pleasure out of turning us into helpless, raging beasts,' 'Maybe,' I replied, 'but maybe not.'

"I asked to meet with Michael, and when we were comfortably settled in my office, I said, 'Mom and Dad say that morning is a hard time in your house.' 'No, it isn't,' he said ingenuously, and I felt that he really *hadn't* been aware of the turmoil going on around him.

" 'Isn't there a lot of yelling in the morning?' I persisted. 'Well, maybe,' he admitted. 'I wish they wouldn't get mad at me.' So Michael really *did* want approval! And that was confirmed when he began to earn stars—and wanted more.

"When he came for a session with me two weeks later, he proudly showed me his calendar, all filled up with different colored stars. 'I've only been late one time,' he said with a big grin. 'And that was because Mom and Dad overslept!'

"Michael proved to be quick and imaginative as we worked with puppets to help him tune in to how his behavior affected others. We acted out selfishness, jealousy, and generosity. Michael also tried out empathy and self-control—new concepts for that little boy. And we role-played 'mean-teasing'—Michael's cruel behavior toward his sister and others, which came out of his own sense of fear and insecurity. Together, we gradually came up with other, better ways to feel strong . . . ways that don't leave you feeling so lonesome.

"When he came in and told me how he had 'felt like being mean to Nell three times but only did it once,' I knew he was on the right track.

"Michael, by himself, used a puppet to introduce the 'funny feeling' of wanting more and more, but only liking things for a while. As he acted it out, I could see that it wasn't just greediness, but something else, that fired his insatiable appetite for 'getting something.'

"Acquiring, I saw, was his way of reassuring himself that Mommy cared. But all his mother's indiscriminate buying was a double-edged attempt—to cheer Michael up *and* to make herself feel less guilty.

" 'I understand it's been hard,' I told her. With obvious pain, Antonia described Michael's birth and how she felt responsible for what went wrong. I encouraged her to talk it out. When she was finished, I said, 'Antonia, guilt is not productive. It is important for you to understand and accept your own feelings. And then you will be able to help Michael. We'll never know if Michael's problem was really preventable. The important thing is where you go from here.'

" 'One real gift you could give him at this point is limits,' I suggested gently. 'You've given a lot, but you've let all those powerful guilt feelings cloud your judgment.' I urged her to begin to trust her instincts and not be afraid to say no.

" 'It works,' she told me in amazement two weeks later, as she recounted several grocery shopping trips during which she had not let Michael get toys at the supermarket. I congratulated her.

"I was also delighted to hear that Michael was now expected to do certain chores on a daily basis. At first he had balked and cried, 'I can't do it, I can't reach, *you have to help me, Mom!*' But with Ron's encouragement, Antonia stood firm, and Michael found he could empty the dishwasher *and* put dishes away without breakage.

" 'These activities are so constructive,' I told the Perrys. 'Asking little or nothing of a child only reinforces his sense of inadequacy. But there are few things that children value—and relish—quite so much as their own accomplishments.'

"By the end of the school year, even his teacher, Miss Tower, acknowledged that Michael had made 'big strides in becoming a helpful member of the class.' And Nell was willing to admit, 'He's improving.'

"Michael still has his physical problems—and a lot of frustration. But he's learned to live less tumultuously now that both his parents are convinced that setting limits and saying 'Here's what we expect' is not insensitivity, but a loving and crucial way to help a child grow up."

Our daughter, Courtney, is a lovable child, although she was born with a malformed face. How will she ever develop self-esteem when people are so shocked by her appearance? Will her life ever be normal?

Beth's Story

"The official name for it is hypertelorism," said Beth Lange, 33. "The fact is, our newborn daughter looked like a child from another planet. Her eyes were very wide apart, her nose very broad and misshapen, and there were open clefts at the corners of her mouth.

"I held her gingerly. Was she blind? Retarded? Would she die soon? She was so unlike the perfect baby we had expected; this little one looked hopelessly damaged.

" 'She's normal in every way except for her appearance,' one of the doctors assured us. 'We don't know why it happens,' he added sadly. A surgeon would be able to repair those clefts, and that would help a little. But any real cosmetic surgery would have to wait—ideally for many years if we wanted the very best outcome for our daughter.

"My husband, Drew, who had felt squeamish about being at the birth, hadn't even seen the baby yet. I had begged him on the phone to wait until the clefts were closed. Drew is a loving and wonderful man, but he's very visual and particular about how things look.

282

How could he, of all people, accept such an unsightly child?

"I already knew that my mother couldn't. 'What a shame, what a terrible tragedy!' she cried when she saw the baby. 'I don't see how two beautiful people could end up bearing a child . . . like *that!*' Courtney was her first granddaughter, and she felt cheated. She wouldn't even pick up Courtney. 'I might be getting a cold,' she said.

"That whole night after Courtney was born, I couldn't sleep, dreading Drew's reaction. Would he hate and resent *me?* Would he want a divorce? One of the nurses told me that a teenage couple who had a baby like this some months ago chose to give him up for adoption. Would I do that if it came to a choice between our marriage and this baby?

"I prayed for help, and it must have worked, because when Drew came the next day, he took it all incredibly well, cuddling Courtney, talking to her gently, and even touching her face. 'We'll be okay,' he said, kissing me. I felt relieved and grateful . . . and ashamed of how I had underestimated Drew!

"But almost as soon as we brought our daughter home, all my optimism crumbled. The weather was mild for November, and the first time I took Courtney out in her carriage, people came and peered in, smiling, wanting to say, 'What a beautiful baby!' but not being able to. They looked stricken, embarrassed.

"It occurred every time I took her anywhere. 'What *happened?*' people would ask, horrified. 'What's the matter with her?' One woman at the supermarket said, 'Oh, the poor little thing!' I smiled to put her at ease, but she didn't smile back. 'When they're like this,' she said, 'it's a mercy to let them die.'

"How *dare* she! Courtney didn't have a terminal disease, just a face that upset people. Well, I decided, I would protect my daughter, I would just keep her home. It was peaceful in our own backyard, where there was no explaining to do—or cruel bigots to answer to.

"Courtney was a sweet and responsive child with a face only her parents could love. To avoid exposing her even to subtle disgust or condescension, I avoided most friends and even relatives. Drew said I was wrong to push everyone away, but what else could I do, when my own mother was urging me to have my tubes tied to avoid another 'mistake'?

"Last week we were supposed to go to Thanksgiving dinner at

283

Drew's brother's house, but when I dressed Courtney in the beautiful velour stretch suit with the lace collar that friends in Texas had sent, I just lost heart. The perfect outfit only emphasized Courtney's disfigurement. I told Drew that Courtney seemed feverish; of course, we ended up staying home.

"Drew saw right through that. He said, 'We can't live like hermits,' and I knew he was right. But what was the choice? We'd never give up Courtney—I'm ashamed now that I ever considered that. Our pediatrician mentioned a psychiatrist who works with families like ours. I can't imagine how she can help, but I'm willing to try."

The Counselor Replies

Marilyn Reed Lucia, M.D. (for whom the UCSF Marilyn Reed Lucia Child Care Study Center is named), is clinical professor of psychiatry at the University of California at San Francisco and a consultant to the Craniofacial Center there. She is also a fellow of the American Academy of Child and Adolescent Psychiatry.

"The Langes were deeply discouraged. 'It's depressing staying home,' Beth admitted. 'But it's so exhausting and painful each time some new person sees Courtney—and inevitably reacts.'

" 'I know,' I said sympathetically. 'Our culture is so oriented toward attractiveness. Society says, We can't deal with unsightly faces; we must always keep them hidden.'

" 'Then what are we supposed to do?' Drew asked grimly. 'Keep our little girl hidden away in the house forever . . . or are we supposed to fall apart from all the stress?'

" 'Neither,' I replied. 'You *can* take Courtney out in the world and not fall apart, and you can all grow from the experience.' The Langes looked skeptical. 'Believe it,' I said. 'It will take a lot of strength and energy, but I'll be here to help you get Courtney to a point where she will not be in hiding and will be able to live a normal life.'

"I explained, 'The world makes you feel that Courtney's appearance is unacceptable. It says, Don't show us that face; we'll be too shocked. But you both have to change your thinking and say in your own minds, That's just *tough!* Our child needs to see the world, and we are going to put her needs first.'

"It's a normal tendency to conceal a disfigured child in order to protect her, but that's actually not fair to her. What Courtney really needs is to get out and see the world, and the longer you keep her at home under wraps, the harder it will be to change that routine.'

" 'I guess I know that,' Beth said. 'But she's *so* different . . .'

"I said, 'It's natural to feel that because this child's face is so deformed, everything about her is different. But that's not so. Her facial defect is only a small part of who she is. Instead of focusing on the problem, you need to focus on the things about her that are wonderful and pleasing.'

" 'Do you mean that?' Beth asked, fascinated, hopeful.

" 'Absolutely,' I said. 'Try to think of her as a *normal* child, which she is, and don't be so concerned with protecting the world. People may well be shocked when they look at her at first, but so what? *Let* them be inconvenienced for the minute or seconds that they have to look at Courtney; they'll survive.'

"That was the first of many talks I had with the Langes, dealing both with their feelings and with practical matters. For example, it was vital for them to accept Courtney fully before she grew old enough to notice her disfigurement.

" 'Clearly, you both have good self-esteem, and that will help,' I said. In addition, we spent time working through their deepest feelings and fears about having an imperfect child, and what that actually meant to both of them.

"We explored their feelings about possible reasons for Courtney's deformity—from a painful this-must-be-some-kind-of-punishment misconception to an erroneous concern over 'tainted genes,' for which there is no evidence—and then we examined a more realistic possibility: environmental contaminants. I told the Langes that we are beginning to suspect these culprits more and more as we see increasing numbers of birth defects along with increasing environmental pollution.

"At the end of this discussion, the Langes realized that although they may never know for certain the reasons for Courtney's facial anomalies, they felt less guilty—and, consequently, much more relaxed.

"Meanwhile, I encouraged Drew and Beth to take Courtney out

to restaurants, to visit friends, to do everything they had done and enjoyed before she was born. Beth looked hesitant. 'I hate to subject her—and all of us—to public humiliation,' she said.

" 'People will be curious, but you must get used to that,' I said. 'Once again, it's really for Courtney's sake. I want you to push yourselves and eventually push Courtney in the same direction.'

"By the time Courtney was a year old, the Langes had taken her out a lot. They had been stared at, questioned, and in some cases rejected, but there were friends, relatives, and neighbors who accepted Courtney and saw her not as a freak but as a bright, inquisitive, friendly, and affectionate little girl.

"Beth became newly alarmed when she found fourteen-month-old Courtney stepping on her favorite doll's face one day. 'Did she seem angry?' I asked.

" 'No,' Beth replied. 'It seemed as if she was trying to flatten the nose. I told her no. I said we love Dolly; we don't do that.'

"I said, 'I would allow her to work it out alone. She may just be trying to rearrange her doll to look more like her. That doesn't mean she doesn't like herself; it's just a sign that she's become aware of the fact that she *does* look different.'

"Drew, meanwhile, had become uptight about what he viewed as pity from strangers. For example, an obviously poor man selling balloons had tried to give one to Courtney. Drew's quick, mortified response was to say, 'No, thank you, she doesn't need it.' I helped him realize that accepting it not only would make the balloon man feel good but, more important, would also be nice for Courtney.

"The next problem came some months later. 'I just wish we could go someplace once in a while and not have people ask what's wrong with her,' Beth said. I asked her how she usually responded. 'I say, Please don't ask that, you'll make my daughter feel self-conscious,' Beth replied. 'I guess I sometimes answer them rather angrily,' she added.

"I said, 'I understand how you feel, but you *can* discuss it—and in a friendly way. Tell them what it's called. Let them know that Courtney will have corrective surgery someday but that you want her to have a normal life even *before* she can have a normal face.'

"Again, a relatively smooth period followed. But when Courtney was two and a half, her parents noticed that sometimes at night she would look in the mirror—and hit herself in the face. 'I pick her up and tickle her or kiss her to distract her,' Drew said, 'but it breaks my heart.'

"I suggested that a more constructive approach than distracting her would be to encourage Courtney to talk out her feelings.

" 'How?' Beth wondered.

"I said, 'She needs and deserves a chance to ventilate her feelings. The hardest part for you is just being willing to listen. Naturally, both of you want everything to be right for Courtney, and it's painful to hear that she's aware it isn't.'

"The Langes understood that and became much more receptive to listening to Courtney. One day, for example, Courtney was aiming her little car at the wall and crashing it repeatedly. 'Me!' Courtney said, after a while. 'Went crash.'

"Beth felt a pang. Sometimes people in the street look at Courtney's face and ask whether she has been in a car accident. 'No, you weren't in a crash, honey,' Beth told her gently. 'You were born this way.'

" 'All *broken*,' Courtney insisted, tracing the scars where her clefts had been, and ran to get her Humpty Dumpty book. 'You feel concerned about looking different,' Beth said, hugging her daughter. 'Well, you can always come talk to Daddy and me, because we love you.'

" 'It *is* good that she can express her feelings about how she looks, but that won't fix it,' Beth told me in our next session. 'She has her little playmates on the block and her cousin Patty, but I'm scared that the older she gets, the more different she'll feel and the more she'll be forced to retreat socially.'

" 'Not if you continue to support her and to push her into social situations,' I said. 'That's what will help Courtney the most.'

"Beth gave a weary shrug. 'I don't know,' she said. 'We took her to a playground last weekend, but she was pretty much ignored by the other kids, and when that happens, it always makes her shy.'

"I said, 'Children with visible defects are often ignored—and that's why communication skills are so important. Courtney has a delightful personality, and the quicker she can project that personality, the better.'

"When Courtney was ready for preschool, I suggested that we do

287

some preventive preparation. The Langes selected a fine co-op nursery school for her, and with the school's cooperation, we arranged for Courtney to start a few days after the other children.

"Before that, we arranged for Beth and me to go to the school with a videotape of Courtney to show to the teachers, the other children, and their mothers. This way, any initial shock would be over by the time they actually saw Courtney. They would see all the things Courtney could do and would understand that she wasn't frail or handicapped.

"Also, the children could ask me questions they might be embarrassed to ask in front of her, and they'd know that Courtney did not have a contagious disease, had not done anything bad, and would be a good playmate.

"When we had this session, almost everyone responded positively. But predictably, one mother balked. 'I don't think that little girl belongs here,' she said. 'My son is very sensitive, and I don't want him traumatized. I know he'd feel too frightened—or upset.'

" 'Actually, it's great for young kids to learn that a child who's different has a lot to contribute and that being friends with her won't diminish or threaten them in any way,' I quickly assured her.

"The mother wasn't convinced. 'I still think it's too much to ask of such a young group,' she insisted.

" 'Oh, I understand,' I said sympathetically. 'And you're right, it *is* scary to look at someone like Courtney and have to think, This could happen to me. But it's also reassuring to know that you could experience a catastrophe and still be a human being, and that people would still be able to like and relate to you.'

"Courtney started school the following Monday and, sensing the welcome, settled in beautifully. Enthusiastic, kind, and creative, she emerged as a leader and was such a favorite with the other children that she had almost more play dates than her mom could keep up with. Of course, the Langes were thrilled.

"I had seen the Langes on a monthly basis up until this point, but now I was seeing them only when a specific problem came up. For example, they had seen a wonderful house in a town 40 miles away and wondered whether moving would cause any problems.

" 'It might,' I told them frankly. 'I generally advise families with children who have problems like Courtney's not to change schools or move any more than they have to. Each new contact will stare, react, and need to learn. It's comfortable for all of you to be with people who are used to Courtney and have finished asking questions about her face.'

" 'I didn't really think of that,' Beth said. 'It *would* be nice not having to go through it all again, at least not for a while.' Beth smiled ruefully. 'It's funny, isn't it?' she said. 'We're so hung up on people having to look perfect. But if you consider coins or stamps, it's the one that has the defect that's really valuable.'

"The Langes decided not to move, at least not until Courtney is ready to start elementary school, which will be a big change whether they moved or not.

"Courtney has just turned four. Since her birthday is just a couple of weeks before Thanksgiving, there was another birthday cake and presents for her at the usual family gathering for Thanksgiving dinner. 'I feel so *terrible*; I really wasn't thinking!' Beth's mother cried, blushing, as Courtney opened Grandma's gift: a cassette and picture book of *The Ugly Duckling*.

" 'It's no problem,' Beth assured her mother, smiling. 'Courtney loves that story; it's one of her favorites!'

"The Langes have come a very long way from the days, four years ago, when they were in hiding and not coming to terms with their child's problem. People still stare at Courtney every day. Sometimes she stares back defiantly until they look away, but most of the time she pretends not to notice. And what makes her parents proudest is that she never acts meek or apologetic for the way she looks.

"Courtney is still quite a few years from the surgery that will make a significant difference in her appearance. But for now, her father says, 'She knows she's lovable just as she is.'

"There are many people in this country with some kind of facial deformity, and most are hidden away. That could have been Courtney's fate; but thanks to her parents' courage and to their extensive therapy, the Langes are determined to keep educating those they meet—always directing attention away from Courtney's imperfect face to the lovely and appealing human being who is inside."

SCHOOL
PROBLEMS

Wendy, eight, keeps saying,
"My teacher hates me," but is that
the problem, or is it Wendy's own
defiant behavior that's making this
year at school so unpleasant?

Joanna's Story

"It was obvious right away that our eight-year-old, Wendy, wasn't as happy at school as she'd been in past years," said Joanna Harding, 34. "I could see it in the way she dawdled in the morning—watching cartoons on TV and letting her cereal sit and get soggy.

"Nor was she devoting much care to her homework. Last year, in second grade, she did it conscientiously and almost eagerly—asking me to check her arithmetic and test her on spelling words. But now she would avoid getting to it each night for as long as possible, then scramble to get it done before bedtime.

" 'Honey, don't you want to copy this over?' I asked when she showed me a very messy, pencil-smudged composition.

" 'What's the point?' she said. She sounded so dejected. 'Even when I do something really good, Mrs. Rush doesn't like it. She doesn't like me.'

"Was Mrs. Rush really such a mean, uncaring teacher, or was the 'she-doesn't-like-me' just a figure of Wendy's imagination? I figured I'd find out for myself very soon at parents' night. I told Wendy, 'I bet you're wrong. We'll probably come home with all

293

kinds of compliments about you.'

"But Mrs. Rush, a pretty, smiling redhead, grew cool when my husband, Michael, and I introduced ourselves.

" 'Wendy has a mind of her own, all right!' Mrs. Rush said crisply.

" 'Is that so bad?' Michael asked.

" 'In her case it is,' Mrs. Rush replied. 'She's bossy and demanding. She talks back to me and actually argues with me as if I were someone her age and not her teacher.'

"I was really surprised. Wendy was a willful child, but usually reasonable. At home the next day we warned her that she had better start being more respectful.

" 'I am!' Wendy protested. 'But she always yells at me—no matter what I do. Yesterday Mark was making funny faces, and a lot of kids laughed. All *I* did was smile, but Mrs. Rush said, "Wen-dy!" like I'm the one who did something awful. Then she said "Next time I'll send you to the principal." Mom, I'm telling you—Mrs. Rush *hates* me!'

"Michael retorted, 'Teachers don't hate children. If she's on your case then you must be doing something out of line.'

" 'No way,' Wendy protested. 'Mrs. Rush is the jerk . . . '

" 'That's exactly what I'm talking about!' Michael said. 'You have a real attitude problem.'

" 'Wendy,' I added, 'Dad just means you have to be polite, whether you like her or not.'

"Grudgingly, Wendy agreed to try, but her dawdling continued when she was getting ready—or rather, not getting ready—in the mornings. And she still put very little effort into her homework. In addition, notes began to come home from Mrs. Rush saying that Wendy's attitude had not improved.

"I tried to talk to Wendy, but she was always so defensive, insisting that she was innocent. 'All I have to do is raise my hand and she says, "No!" Mom, now she won't even let me go to the bathroom.'

"Was that true? Sometimes I found myself wondering if Mrs. Rush was too rigid, expecting perfect behavior. Or was she too inexperienced to contain so many bright, lively eight-year-olds without losing her temper?

"I decided to talk to Tom Bates, the school principal, who listened thoughtfully as I told him what had been going on. 'It's hard to judge when I'm not in the classroom,' he said. I asked if he considered Mrs. Rush a good teacher.

" 'Mrs. Rush a good teacher?' Tom said, shaking his head. Then he smiled broadly. 'No, she's not a good teacher. She is a *fabulous* teacher. I wish I could clone her.'

"I went home feeling awful: Apparently Wendy really *was* the problem! Michael said, 'Obviously talking hasn't worked,' and suggested that we punish Wendy by taking away privileges.

"Two days later a note came home saying, 'Wendy refused to clean up scraps of paper on the floor by her desk. She said, "Why me? I'm not your servant," when I asked her to clean it up. Because of this, Wendy will not be allowed to go out at recess for the coming week.'

"Michael put his foot down and told Wendy that she couldn't play with friends after school that week.

"Wendy cried—and I really felt sorry for her. But I knew Michael was right: Talking hadn't changed Wendy's attitude. In fact, she'd drawn some witchlike character in her assignment notebook, labeled 'Mrs. Rush—the meanest and smelliest.'

"I made Wendy tear the page out. I said, 'What if she saw that?'

"At Thanksgiving Wendy's cousin, Meg, eighteen, said, 'Wendy, your mom and dad are right: You can't *win* against a teacher; you'll only end up hurting yourself.' Meg encouraged Wendy to spend extra time on her social studies report.

"Things did get calm after that. I said to Michael, 'Maybe kids can only hear wisdom when it isn't coming from their parents.' But then I had a call from Mrs. Rush. Wendy hadn't handed in her homework for a week—including her report.

"I said that couldn't be, but when I asked Wendy, she admitted freely, 'I was going to hand it in, but Mrs. Rush was so mean that morning . . .'

" 'But you have to hand it in,' I said. Wendy smiled. 'I can't,' she said triumphantly. 'I threw it away.'

"Nor did she seem especially contrite when Mrs. Rush took away her playground privileges for a month and we locked up her bike.

"Finally we requested another meeting, in which Mrs. Rush said that Wendy's behavioral problems were extreme and suggested that we try psychological testing.

"Was the situation that bad? Michael thought not—she was just stubborn. He sat Wendy down and said, 'Every time you get in trouble with your teacher you will find yourself with no allowance, no TV time, and we might even decide to leave you home with a sitter when we go to Florida next month to see Grandma.' Wendy was too shocked to speak.

" 'Bingo!' Michael said to me later. 'This time I think it's finally sunk in.'

"We heard nothing more from school for a full two weeks, and we were encouraged. Wendy seemed quite subdued. 'That's good,' Michael said to me. 'She's thinking.'

"But was it really pensiveness, or was Wendy depressed? She said so little, even at suppertime, and that wasn't like her.

" 'Honey, is something wrong?' I asked. Wendy said no sadly.

"I shared my concern with Michael. 'She's so distant,' I said. 'Do you think maybe all her hostility toward Mrs. Rush was really meant for us?'

"Michael shook his head. 'Now *you're* getting too psychological,' he said. 'Wendy's testing the limits and learning where they are. That's supposed to happen; that's how kids grow up.'

"What he said made sense, as usual. And, yes, it *was* a good sign that Wendy wasn't complaining and being so rambunctious.

"But if we thought that all was well, we were mistaken. The following Monday Tom Bates called, and he sounded grim. 'Mrs. Rush was just here in tears,' he said.

"Apparently Wendy had written a poem, a very, very nasty one, about Mrs. Rush washing her hair in the toilet and eating dead rats. There were graphic drawings to go with it.

"Tom said, 'I suggest you get Wendy into counseling without any further delay.'

"I'm all for that, and now even Michael admits something's wrong. We only hope and pray there's something we can do to help."

The Counselor Replies

Betty B. Osman, Ph.D., is a psychologist and faculty member in the graduate program at Sarah Lawrence College, in Bronxville, New

York, and a psychologist for the Child and Adolescent Services in the Department of Psychiatry at White Plains Hospital Medical Center in New York. Osman is the author of No One to Play With: The Social Side of Learning Disabilities *and* Learning Disabilities: A Family Affair *(Warner Books).*

"Joanna Harding sounded quite anxious on the phone. 'I still can't understand why a nice, bright girl like my daughter would get locked in such a bitter conflict with a teacher,' she said.

"I agreed that it sounded like something to explore, and I set up a meeting with both parents for the following day. In that session the Hardings told me a great deal about their family life and Wendy's early years, and in all that, I heard nothing that would signify a problem.

"Even school had been trouble-free—from nursery school right through second grade. According to the Hardings' recollections and some written reports from teachers, Wendy had always spoke up, but she had also shown eagerness, intelligence, and creativity, and she had been a valued member of the class.

"Wendy did sound quite angry, from her parents' description, and so I asked to see her.

" 'Sure,' Michael said. 'But she'll probably just give you the same tired line, that her teacher hates her.'

"But instead of the sullen, defensive child I expected, Wendy was friendly, warm, and outgoing. I asked her what she liked to do after school, and she said, 'Lots!' She loved to get into her mom's old clothes and put on plays with her friends. She also mentioned riding her bike, painting, playing adventure, and going to the library. Her list was long and enthusiastic.

"Then I asked if she liked school. 'No!' she said emphatically. 'My teacher's horrible!'

" 'Why? What does she do?' I asked.

" 'She gets me into trouble,' Wendy replied. She drew a few pictures of Mrs. Rush and then made her own face look fierce to demonstrate 'how mean she looks when she yells, "Wen-dy." ' Then, as an afterthought, Wendy admitted that sometimes she liked to make her teacher mad.

" 'But then my parents get *so mad* at me!' she said unhappily.

"I suggested that maybe, together, we could figure out a way to make life more pleasant. And so I spent the next four sessions with Wendy learning what was causing her to have such a hard time at school.

"As we talked and did some role-playing, Wendy began to see her behavior in a new light. 'It's okay to have angry feelings and to talk about them,' I explained, 'but not to act them out.'

"Wendy began to see, for example, that not handing in homework or talking back in a rude, provocative way doesn't really win points and only causes more problems.

"But even as she began to see the practical advantages of toning down the way she expressed herself in class, she said, more than once, that she wished she could switch to the other class and have Mrs. Lilliston for a teacher instead.

" 'Wouldn't that simply be running away and avoiding the issue?' Michael asked when I telephoned one evening. I wasn't sure. Perhaps now, with more awareness of her feelings (and of the way her actions affected others), Wendy could continue in her present class.

"Still, I thought it would be constructive to talk to Mrs. Rush, and with the Hardings' permission, I called her. But as soon as I told her who I was and why I was calling, Mrs. Rush went into a tirade about how awful Wendy was.

"For ten minutes she poured out her frustration. Clearly she was a teacher who expected good feedback from her students. But instead of eliciting affection and cooperation from Wendy, all she felt she got was hostility, resistance, and rudeness.

" 'Wendy's the kind of kid who makes a teacher feel helpless and angry,' Mrs. Rush concluded bitterly. 'Maybe I *am* sharper with her than I am with the other children, but Wendy gets to me! Frankly, even her laugh drives me crazy. I hate to say this, but when she's absent, it's like a vacation day for me.'

"So Wendy wasn't all wrong when she said, 'My teacher hates me.' I shared my observations with Joanna and Michael, who acknowledged that they had sided with the teacher.

" 'But whom should we believe in the future?' Michael asked.

"I said, 'It's hard to know, since you're not there—and that's a good reason why you shouldn't punish Wendy for anything that happens at school. It's tough enough to be punished at school for what she's done. Wendy needs home to be a haven.'

" 'Do you mean we should just believe her?'

" 'Yes,' I said. 'Didn't you tell me that she's never been dishonest before? And even more than just taking her seriously, you can help her express how she feels. You don't have to condone anything. Just be open to hearing her side of the story.'

" 'Now I feel so guilty,' Joanna said. 'We've been very critical and not very willing to understand what she was going through.'

"I said, 'Don't blame yourselves. You were only trying to do what you thought was best for Wendy. But now we have an opportunity to help her.'

"At that point I set up a meeting with the Hardings, Mr. Bates, the principal, and both third-grade teachers. I told them, 'Wendy is not without responsibility for much of the turmoil, and she realizes that now.'

"But I went on to say that certain children and adults have trouble relating to each other and that Wendy and Mrs. Rush were one such unfortunate mismatch of personalities. I suggested that we call it a no-fault situation and try putting Wendy in the other class.

"Tom Bates hesitated. 'We've never done this before,' he said. 'But I think there's good reason to give it a try.'

"Everyone agreed. Wendy, on hearing the news, was overjoyed. Mrs. Lilliston welcomed Wendy with a hug, and that afternoon Wendy came home beaming.

" 'How long will this honeymoon last?' Michael worried. And sure enough, two weeks later an incident occurred: Mrs. Lilliston said that Wendy couldn't leave class to get a drink of water, and Wendy flared up.

"But Mrs. Lilliston responded calmly, taking Wendy aside and reminding her that the rules about leaving the room applied to every student in the class.

"The rest of the year went well, but when school began again this past September, the Hardings held their breath: Would Wendy be defiant with her new fourth-grade teacher, Miss Albertson?

"Apparently not! She has come home grumbling a few times, but her parents sit down and listen and don't even make a comment unless Wendy asks them to. 'I guess some teachers have their crabby days just like kids do,' Wendy acknowledged.

"It's often hard for parents to know whose side to take when a child gets into a dispute with an adult. But it was only when the Hardings began to listen to Wendy—and not automatically side with her teacher—that she was free to stop fighting and get on with the business of learning and growing up."

> *Matthew always liked school, but now he won't go at all. He claims it's stomachaches, but the doctor can't find anything. Is Matthew faking—or is this something much more serious? How will we ever get him to go back?*

Gina's Story

"This year it seemed that our life was especially hectic and crazy," said Gina Ballard, 39. "Paul was struggling to build his own law practice, and I was busier than ever—trying to help make ends meet by teaching dance at several different schools, a Y, and a junior college. I always tried to be home for dinner at six but often didn't make it until seven or later, and Paul was much later.

"That was why we went to Vermont to ski over Christmas. It was our first family vacation in two years, and it was wonderful—with all of us together for a change and not rushing off in twenty directions! As I wrote in postcards to friends, it was just what the doctor ordered.

"The morning after we got home, Eric, who is twelve, was ready for the school bus early: he couldn't wait to tell his friends that by mistake he had gone down an expert slope—and hadn't fallen. But our nine-year-old, Matthew, had hardly begun his breakfast. 'Hurry up,' I warned. 'The bus will be here!' But he didn't move. 'I've got a stomachache,' he moaned loudly.

"I called our pediatrician, Dr. Peltz, who said it was going around. 'I'd keep him home a day,' he suggested. Matt got cozy in our bed with the TV on as I scrambled for a last-minute sitter. I had a class to teach at nine and hated leaving him, but when I got home at suppertime, he was drinking ginger ale and reading *Mad Magazine*. I said, 'Great! You're back to normal,' but the next morning he complained of another stomachache.

"Dr. Peltz still didn't think it was anything serious but agreed to see him. He kneaded Matthew's middle and suggested bland food. I took Matthew—and some cans of chicken broth—home and made arrangements to pick up his homework at school. Again, that evening, Matt was feeling better, playing with the dog. 'Looks like you're over it now,' Paul said. But by midnight, the ache was back. I wrapped the hot-water bottle up in a towel for Matthew. He fell asleep after a while but woke me later, to make the water hot again.

"When the ache dragged on for a fourth day, Paul wondered if Matthew was faking to avoid school. I said no, he loves school. 'Hold it,' Paul said. 'Didn't I hear him say that the new gym teacher yells too much? And that he didn't like the kids on his school bus this year?' Yes, there had been a number of minor complaints—but that was all back in September. Why would Matt manufacture an illness *now*, when the year was half over?

"On Friday morning, Matthew lay on his bed and groaned. 'But the doctor says there's nothing really wrong with you,' Paul argued logically. I could see that his attempt to minimize the problem was only making Matthew groan louder. 'I'M SICK!' he told his father. 'Why don't you believe me? *You* wouldn't like it if you felt sick and *I* said it was nothing!'

"Paul nodded. 'You're right, I wouldn't like that,' he admitted. 'And I guess a stomachache that's lasted more than a week *could* be something to worry about.' I called Dr. Peltz, who referred us to a specialist, a pediatric gastroenterologist. The testing on Monday took several hours, but then we had the results: 'Your son has a mild gastroenteritis,' the specialist said. Translation: a bellyache. His secretary handed me a neatly typed bill for $350.

" 'Now we know for sure it's nothing serious, Matthew, so you *can* go to school,' Paul said firmly that evening. Matthew looked at him resentfully. 'Dad,' he said, his lips trembling, 'you don't even *know* how bad it feels. What if I go to school and have to go to the hospital—or die?'

" 'Knock it off, young man. You're fine and you'll go tomorrow or else!' Paul retorted. 'And frankly, I think it stinks for a kid to go on an expensive ski trip and get all kinds of presents for Christmas and then not be willing to meet the very basic responsibilities, including going to school.'

"Matthew's eyes filled with tears. 'Thanks, Dad,' he said. 'Just for that, I won't go to school. In fact, maybe I'll never go!'

"That night, I had one of those anxiety dreams in which I'd gone to work and then realized I'd left Matthew—a newborn baby—home alone by mistake. Of course in real life that never happened! I didn't even think of going back to work until Matthew was three. In fact, my friends used to tease me about the fact that I waited longer to go back to work than any of them—and yet somehow, I was the one who felt the most conflicted.

" 'Try not to worry so much,' Paul mumbled sleepily. The next morning, I heard him speaking sharply to Matt: 'I want you up and dressed right now,' Paul commanded him loudly.

" 'I'm not getting dressed, Dad. I don't feel good.' Matt was whining—something he knows just drives Paul crazy. 'Then you'll go in your pajamas!' Paul started roughly pulling him out of the bed.

" 'NO! Let go.' Matt was kicking wildly. 'Fine!' Paul said, moving back, 'but don't expect ski trips—or *anything*—from me anymore.' 'I don't want anything from *you!*' Matt shot back. 'You don't even believe your own son has a stomachache.'

" 'Matthew,' I said, trying to calm things down, 'Dad just means that we want you to go to school. You've already missed two weeks on top of the vacation.' Matt looked at me thoughtfully. 'Well, okay, maybe I will go,' he said finally. 'But I really, honestly don't feel good. So if I go, you have to come along with me.'

"It bothered me so much to give in. I felt certain it wasn't right—for any of us. But Matt was so insistent I finally said, 'Yes, okay, but just this one time.'

"When we got to school, we went to the office to check in and then to Matthew's classroom. He kept looking around uneasily. I said, 'Honey, I have to leave now.' 'NO!' Matthew grabbed my arm. 'You've *got* to stay.' His voice was tense. 'But I don't belong here,' I said. 'Your friends are all staring.'

" 'I don't care,' he said, holding on tighter. Even his teacher, sparkling, blond Mrs. Wheeler, couldn't seem to entice him to the tables in the back of the room, where the other children were building Egyptian pyramids out of sugar cubes, until I went with him.

" 'You actually stayed in his classroom all day?' Paul was incredulous. I said, 'I know, I feel the same way.' Luckily, Matt's teacher was incredibly understanding. But at least on the way home, Matt had admitted that there was really nothing scary or unpleasant at school.

"But the next morning, Matthew sat in his bed and cried while Paul cursed and tried to manhandle Matthew out of his pajamas and into his underwear. 'Stop it, Daddy, stop,' Matthew sobbed. 'Please don't make me go!' Eric peered in. 'Who's winning?' he asked. 'Guess!' Paul snapped, tossing Matt's jeans on the bed. 'I'm going to work; I give up.'

"I don't know what to do next, and I certainly don't understand what's causing this. I just know we've got a real problem on our hands."

The Counselor Replies

Alex Weintrob, M.D., is a child and adolescent psychiatrist in New York City. He is past president of the New York Council of Child and Adolescent Psychiatry and a fellow of the American Academy of Child and Adolescent Psychiatry. Weintrob is also a consulting child psychiatrist in the Department of Pediatrics at Lenox Hill Hospital.

"The Ballards came in feeling anxious, confused, and out of control. 'I just don't understand how this could happen so suddenly and for no reason,' Gina said. Paul told me that he knew someone at work whose youngest daughter developed school phobia in tenth grade—and never went back. 'Should we make him go tomorrow so this doesn't get worse?' he asked. 'And should we punish him if he refuses? I'd hate to let this develop into a really chronic situation.'

"I assured the Ballards that Matthew's problem sounded manageable, and that if we worked together, we would see good results fairly quickly. While many therapists believe you have to delve deeply into a child's unconscious, I think that's usually necessary more with chronic difficulties. Matt's school avoidance was not chronic, but *acute*—a crisis of sorts, deserving a crisis approach: a swift, immediate, and practical intervention. I would see him twice a week for the next two or three weeks. This, I explained, would let Matt know that he's being listened to and help engage him in a constructive solution.

"For right now, I suggested that instead of pushing Matt to go to school the next day, they back off, at least until I could get to see him.

"'Well, what do we say when we bring him here?' Gina wondered. 'Can we somehow *not* tell him that you're a shrink?'

"I said, 'Why not just say something like this: "Matt, we're all having trouble, with us yelling at you and you yelling at us. You're unhappy and angry, and there's a lot of tension. We're going to take you to talk to someone who can help us." ' I explained that parents often think that bringing a professional helper in will make a child more anxious, but actually it can be very reassuring to the child— first for him to know that you *are* taking steps to get help, and second, for you to say that this isn't just 'your' problem, it's 'ours.'

"The Ballards brought Matt in. He was bright and open. I could sense that he was not depressed, that there were no other areas of difficulty in his life, and that he was pretty good at putting his feelings into words. He said, 'I don't know why I don't like school anymore. I just need my mom there.' When I mentioned the stomachaches, Matt said, 'They don't believe me, but it's true.'

"When I said, 'Matt, would you like to be able to go to school?' he said, 'YES! That's the whole point. I want to go, but I just can't.'

"Later, I explained to the Ballards that Matt's school avoidance seemed to be fueling a family power struggle—in which Matt was losing by winning, and everyone was losing by his not going to school. 'It's true,' Paul admitted. 'The whole thing with Matt has got me upset and angry. And I get even more upset about losing control and yelling at him. I guess there must be some better way.'

"I suggested that we focus on the fact that Matthew wanted to go to school. With my encouragement, the Ballards said to Matt, 'We're going to find ways to help you go. What would you like us to do?'

305

Matt immediately said, 'I want Mom to come with me.'

"I asked Gina to try to adjust her schedule in the next week or so to meet Matthew's needs. Gina looked panicky. 'But I can't keep doing this,' she said. 'I've already fallen way behind in my work.'

"I said, 'I know you've lost a lot of time over this, but that's the whole point. What we're interested in doing is getting Matthew back to school on his own, for everyone's sake, especially Matthew's. I don't think we should worry now about the price of achieving that, or worry that he'll get used to not going. It's a mistake to think if you give in now, you'll have to go on doing it forever. In fact, just the opposite is true: the more responsive you can be in a crisis, the sooner you solve it.' I asked the Ballards to call me whenever they felt themselves tempted to get into the battle again.

"The next morning, Matt and Gina went to school, and Gina reported that everything had been fine—other than the fact that she had had to go with him. I suggested that she reward him for going. 'Why reward him?' she asked. 'I've always thought it was wrong to bribe a child to do what he's supposed to do.' I said, 'Yes, you're right, but this is special because Matt is doing something that is hard for him, even though it seems easy and quite routine.'

"By the end of the week, she was still going with him, but leaving, with his blessings, by noon. 'What if I need you?' he asked. 'Then you can call and I'll come back,' she said. 'After all, we made an agreement.' That seemed to satisfy Matt—until Sunday night, when the stomachache returned.

"Paul was very agitated when he phoned me. 'Is this going to go on every Sunday night, forever?' he asked testily. I said, 'It's only been one week. Let's not panic yet.' In the week that followed, Matt went to school every day, and each day, his mother was able to leave a little earlier.

"The following Monday was another good day; Gina only had to stay for fifteen minutes. But on Tuesday, Gina called me, terrified, at 7:40 A.M.: Matt didn't want to go at all; he said he had a stomachache 'that might get worse.' I said, 'Gina, why don't you let Paul handle this? You're more worried and he's more detached.' Paul did rise to the occasion and handled it well, calmly explaining to Matt that if his stomach bothered him at school, he could go to the nurse and she would help him or let him phone his parents.

"That day proved to be a kind of turning point: Paul took Matt to school, and Matt let him leave right away. And the next day, with only slight trepidation, Matt got back on the school bus. Paul and Gina were very proud of Matt and told him so.

"The Ballards had one last appointment. 'I still don't understand what set this off in the first place,' Paul mused. I explained that this kind of thing often will follow a death, divorce, or separation, or it may result from a major embarrassment at school. But sometimes it happens without any noticeable precipitant. In Matt's case, it seemed that he couldn't bear the fact that the warm family vacation was over. Deep inside, he felt that going back to school again meant losing his mom.

"Gina looked deeply upset. 'I always try so hard to give the boys enough attention,' she said. 'That's why I struggle so to get home at a decent hour, and I get so mad when Paul can't or won't.'

" 'It is really difficult,' I agreed. 'Naturally, you want to have lots of quality time with your children, and you've even tried to schedule it, but scheduling doesn't work. This is typical of many busy families: Mom gets home late—harassed, irritated, and guilty; then Dad gets home even later and Mom's angry and he's defensive.'

" 'I've always tried,' Gina said again. 'I'm sure you have,' I told her sincerely. 'And I think you deserve enormous credit.'

" 'But you're saying to me that I haven't really been home enough!'

" 'No,' I protested. 'Not at all! You're doing a hard job and you're doing it well!'

" 'The problem is that when we try to make ourselves do something, it's always tense, and you've been pressuring yourself and Paul to give more time than you actually have. What you need to do is make the times when you *are* home more valuable to your children. You might have to decide consciously to put chores and irritations on a back burner, so that you can really be there for Matt and Eric. Sometimes just being able to acknowledge a problem can take some of the heat off. Once a family can talk together about the craziness in their lives, it's not quite so awful.'

"I reassured the Ballards that I wasn't insisting they make any major changes in their lives. I pointed out that they had already accomplished a great deal. First, in respecting Matt's anxiety, they had changed the atmosphere at home from combative to cooperative; second, they had been flexible enough to put important business aside for a while and to let Matt know that when he needed them, they would do whatever they had to in order to help.

"Matt has been doing very well for the past month, and his parents report that, even with the hectic schedule, their home life has become a little more relaxed and informal. Wisely, Gina and Paul have begun to put less stress on how many hours and minutes a day they spend with their children and more emphasis on being accessible.

"Parents, like the Ballards, may become frightened of even temporarily 'giving in' to what looks like the tyranny of a child's irrational fear. But as the Ballards discovered, sometimes it's precisely that willingness that can make all the difference in converting a very upsetting and perplexing problem into one that can be managed—and solved."

Valerie, fourteen, is clearly miserable at boarding school. But my wife, Ellen, says it would hurt Val in the long run if we let her quit. How can we tell if it's just normal homesickness—or something much more serious?

Peter's Story

"Valerie, our fourteen-year-old, had never been away from home for more than a night or two," said Peter Whitmore.

"But now, suddenly, we were sending her away to boarding school—something we had never dreamed of doing, but something Val had wanted desperately ever since she'd heard about this unique little school in New England with a truly outstanding music and drama department.

"Val had always starred in school productions and even some local amateur shows, and this school did seem like the perfect opportunity for her to do more.

"Ellen wasn't convinced. She agreed that the brochure looked exciting, but she also felt that living away from home and with mostly older kids seemed 'heavy' for Val. 'I would just hate to see her bite off more than she can chew,' Ellen worried.

"I saw her point, but I couldn't see it as a good enough reason for disappointing Val. I myself had loved the theater as a kid and all

309

through high school. I probably would have tried to make a career of it if my parents had let me. But it wasn't my persuasion that convinced Ellen—it was Val's acting! While we were debating the issue, Val got a starring role in the junior high production of *Grease*, and she was so good—and so obviously gifted—that Ellen finally said yes. Val was ecstatic.

" 'I can't wait,' she told us excitedly. She could work on acting, singing, and dance. 'And best of all,' she said, her eyes shining, 'I'll be with people I can really talk to.' For two years she had complained that the kids at school 'think you're a freak if you don't want to spend every single afternoon at the pizza parlor trying to pick up boys.'

"So we took her up to Massachusetts, helped her unpack, and left her looking gloriously happy and excited. 'Break a leg,' I called—the traditional theater 'good luck.' Knowingly, she grinned and waved. The next day she phoned. 'It's fantastic,' Val reported. But no sooner had we told everyone what a success it was than the unhappy phone calls began. 'It's not like I thought it would be—not at all,' Val said.

"We tried to pin her down: What exactly was wrong? 'Everything!' she said. 'It's just the newness,' we said and told her that she'd probably love it soon. But in a week Val felt just as bad, if not worse. 'I don't fit in,' she said. 'I want to come home.'

" 'Oh, Val! Don't be like that,' Ellen said. 'You have to make an effort.'

" 'You think it's my fault,' Val protested. 'I didn't say that,' Ellen insisted. 'But you'll start having fun sooner if you don't waste time hugging a tissue box and feeling so sorry for yourself.'

" 'All the kids here—they just think they're so great,' Val said, weeping.

" 'Well, you just show them how great *you* are,' Ellen said firmly. 'Don't you remember the show at school, when everyone was applauding?'

" 'But I can't . . .' Val began. 'You sure *can*,' Ellen said decisively. 'We're counting on you!'

" 'She sounds pretty miserable to me,' I remarked. But Ellen said, 'She's got to come out of her shell, and then she'll be fine!'

"We spoke to Glenn Francis, the head of the school, but all he seemed to offer were vague platitudes about growing pains. Would

Val be okay? 'You know how adolescent girls are—everything's bleak one day, heavenly the next.' He said Val *was* quite shy but that we should just give it some time. He also suggested that maybe the phone calls back and forth were making the situation worse and actually preventing Val from adjusting.

"That made some sense. And we were hopeful for the next three days, during which we heard nothing . . . but then the Saturday mail arrived, and there were three six-page letters. 'I'm miserable beyond belief,' she wrote in the first letter. 'This was a horrible, horrible mistake, which I'll regret as long as I live.' Ellen bit her lip and said, 'I just wish she could put all that dramatic energy to work in her acting.'

"Letter two told more of the same. And the third letter—the saddest of all—said, 'I know I'm a failure. I'll never live it down, but I'll die if you don't let me come home *now!*'

" 'I want to go get her,' I told Ellen. 'I thought this would be fantastic, but if it was a mistake, why put her through all this agony?' But Ellen stood firm: 'We know she's got what it takes, right? We believe in her?'

" 'Of course,' I agreed. 'Well, don't you see?' Ellen continued. 'She will never, ever believe in herself or her own ability if we rescue her.' Ellen took my hand. 'Sure, it's hard for *us* to live through. But she's not in a concentration camp, right? She's at a very good, reputable school, and she's being taken care of. For Valerie's sake, we can't give in now. Unless we want her still living home with us when she's 35—and that's only half a joke—we really have to let her tough it out.'

" 'Val will resent us in the long run if we take this away from her,' Ellen went on. 'She's got to stick it out for the first semester at least—if not for the year.' Ellen sat down and wrote a letter reminding Val that she had made a commitment, that we had, too (the first half of the year was all paid for), and that we had full confidence that our bright, beautiful daughter would work things out. She signed it with lots of hugs and kisses.

"I really couldn't argue. Everything Ellen said about encouraging Val instead of undermining her made sense—and why not? Ellen was the one who had studied child development in college while I was preparing to be an engineer. And Ellen had been decisive—and

311

apparently correct—about when to wean and when to toilet-train and even when Ellen could 'safely' go back to work, leaving Val in the capable hands of a sitter.

"During the next two days I began to wonder if something was wrong with me. Why was I in so much vicarious pain? Why couldn't I tolerate my daughter's very normal and inevitable beginning of leaving the nest?

"But Valerie's letters begging to come home still stung me. I simply wasn't accustomed to sitting by and letting her suffer this much, even if it was for her own good.

"The next night we got the 2:00 A.M. call from Glenn Francis. 'I'm sorry to disturb you,' he said and proceeded to tell me about Val: that her counselor had gone into the dorm—where the girls were supposed to be asleep—at 10:30 and Val wasn't anywhere to be seen.

"Moments later, Daphne, the counselor, found Val in the bathroom, retching and vomiting. After saying she was fine—and then half collapsing on her counselor—Val admitted that she had swiped aspirin from the infirmary and taken *twelve* of them 'for a headache.'

"Daphne and Glenn had taken Val to the hospital, where they were now and where her stomach had just been pumped. 'She's fine,' Glenn said. 'But they want to keep her here until you arrive. If you can fly up, there's a plane first thing in the morning.'

" 'Of course,' I said and assured him that we'd be on that plane.

"I know I should probably be angry with Ellen for all her crazy theories about character building. But she's just as anxious and upset—and guilty—as I am. I don't know whose fault this is, and I don't care. We both just want the same thing—for our Val to be okay."

The Counselor Replies

Cynthia R. Pfeffer, M.D., is professor of clinical psychiatry at Cornell University Medical College and chief of the Child Psychiatry Inpatient Unit at The New York Hospital, Westchester Division. A recent past president of the American Association of Suicidology, she is also the author of The Suicidal Child *(The Guilford Press).*

"The hospital in Massachusetts referred the Whitmores to me, and I arranged to see them immediately. All three of them looked tired, shaken, and deeply apprehensive, but still, I could see almost at once that Val would not need to be hospitalized.

"First, I could see how much Ellen and Peter wished to respond and cooperate, and also—unlike many other children who have made suicidal attempts or threats—Val was willing to talk openly about what she had done and why.

" 'I didn't have a headache, and I didn't really want to kill myself, either,' she admitted, even though she had gotten the idea from '*Night, Mother*,' a play in which a daughter committed suicide. 'I was just feeling so trapped, and my parents didn't believe me.' Val went on. 'I thought, Maybe if I hurt myself, I can get them to really pay attention.' Val had made the decision when she got her mother's letter. 'I was so hurt, and all you did was lecture me,' Val said to her mother accusingly.

" 'I know it. I made a mistake,' Ellen explained, her eyes brimming with tears. 'I was just trying to save you from a sense of failure . . . to keep you from quitting . . .'

" 'But you *knew*, I kept telling you!' Val said angrily.

"I said, 'How was it decided that you'd go away to this school?'

" 'She wanted it,' Ellen stated firmly. 'And Peter pushed, too.'

" 'Well, I thought I was good enough to go,' Val cut in. 'But I stunk. I was so terrible, so embarrassingly *terrible*. I knew right away that I didn't belong there, but you kept saying how you were counting on me. I knew that it was impossible, that it was hopeless! But I'm home now, and I don't need to see a psychiatrist,' she said, looking at her parents. 'Everything is just fine!'

" 'Well, I can see that you're feeling better,' I agreed. 'But you did a pretty scary thing, and that tells me how overwhelmed and how lonesome you must have felt.' Val nodded slowly. 'I *was* alone,' she said.

" 'Did you talk to anyone at school?' I asked. 'I tried,' Val said. 'I talked to one girl, Renata, but it didn't really help—or not enough.'

"I asked if she'd tried to talk to an adult. But Val said no, she didn't want to call attention to her problems. In fact, Val said, she was 'really touched and surprised' that when she was leaving the hospital with her parents, Daphne, her dorm counselor, embraced

313

her and said, 'Write to me. I want to know how you are.'

" 'I'm surprised you didn't know an adult would help you,' I said. Val shrugged. 'I learned at home that it's pretty useless,' she answered. 'I know they love me. But Dad thinks I'm just his clone—like he thinks I only have the same feelings he had at my age. And Mom always lectures me. Even if she gives me what I want, it always has to come with a lecture. Besides, what if I did talk to a grown-up? How could I have had the nerve to admit what a failure I was?'

" 'What made you so sure you were a failure?' I asked.

" 'It was obvious,' she said. 'Everyone else was fabulous, and I couldn't measure up—not in a million years. I thought I'd fit in there. At my old school they called me a snob. When I saw what a mistake I'd made, I just felt so alone and so scared . . . I had to do something, so I took the aspirin.'

"This had been the crux of Val's problem: Away from home for the first time, filled with disappointment, loneliness, and self-doubt, she was unprepared to cope. In therapy she and I would work on problem solving, on dealing with stress and looking for options. We would talk about panicky feelings, both in terms of how to avoid them and, if necessary, how to cope with them without giving up and thinking of hurting herself as the only way out.

"But for now, I needed to know that Val would be safe. I asked if she would work with me and, in the meantime, if she'd agree not to hurt herself if she felt upset about anything but to call me or tell her parents. 'Yes,' she said solemnly, 'I will.'

"Two days later Val arrived alone for her appointment, and I asked her how she was feeling. 'Embarrassed,' she admitted sheepishly. 'My mom's friend called, and when she heard my voice, she said, "What are you doing home from school?" and I felt that awful failure feeling again.'

"I said, 'You went to a special school. That school was a place for you to grow and learn, not simply a place to perform. And really, you did grow and learn from the experience. Learning is a process, not an acting contest or a test of success or failure.' With that thought in mind, we began to talk about what Val might have done to improve the situation.

" 'I guess I could have practiced and watched the really good people . . . and maybe I could have asked for help,' she suggested. 'Yes!'

I praised her warmly. 'All of those approaches could have been good.' 'I see what you mean,' Val said slowly. 'Maybe I wasn't as help-less as I felt.'

"During the second week of treatment I met alone with Val's par-ents, who were still troubled as they tried to figure out where they had 'failed' as parents. 'We disagreed about her going away to school,' Peter said. 'And we also disagreed about letting her come home.'

"Ellen closed her eyes. 'I've always been worried about Val,' she said. 'I've wanted her to be strong, not weak and spoiled. I grew up with an alcoholic mother; everything was chaotic. Growing up was very hard for me, and I wanted to do things right with Val. I think this is more important than all the coddling and cuddling and res-cuing that Peter wants to do.'

"I said, 'It's natural to think of our own childhood experiences, and they do affect the way we raise our kids. But sometimes our strong convictions and our wish to give our children what we didn't get can actually hinder our ability to hear our children, to recognize that their needs may be different from what we think they are.'

" 'Perhaps I have been rigid . . .' Ellen said softly.

" 'I always felt she was just like me,' Peter said.

"I said, 'This has been an important event for all of you: It's the first time your daughter was away, and maybe you've all learned something about yourselves and the way you really want things to be.'

" 'But what should we do?' Peter asked. 'Send her away? Keep her at home?'

" 'I wish there were an absolute right answer,' I said. 'Val will need to have more experiences away from the family so she can develop self-confidence. But she also needs protection and nurturing. Breaking away is not an event but a *process*—and growing up is hard work, not just for the child but for the parents, too!'

"We ended formal treatment in late November, and I felt very good about Valerie Whitmore and what she was accomplishing. During our sessions together Val developed new skills and aware-ness that would help her in coping with all sorts of frustrations and trade-offs and other positive elements in what might at first appear to be a 'totally hopeless' situation.

"Val also became better at describing her feelings in specific terms. She found that the more clearly she could tell her parents what was bothering her, the better they could respond.

"After much soul-searching, Val and her parents decided that she should finish her freshman year at the local high school. Val found the hugeness of it somewhat daunting at first, but she was gradually able to see it as a wider and therefore more satisfying world than junior high had been.

"In addition, Val began to test—and recognize—her own strengths, which gave her a more realistic sense of herself: perhaps not as the star she had hoped and imagined herself to be after her junior high successes, but also not as a failure. And as she felt more secure about herself, she found it easier to make friends.

"Perhaps most impressive of all, Val has learned to handle frustrations without falling apart, as she has started to see that bad feelings do arise, but they also pass—and that even if there isn't something she can do about it, she can talk about it to someone who does care and will listen: one of her parents, a friend, or, if necessary, me.

"A child's suicide attempt is always frightening, but if it's recognized and heeded right away instead of denied, there is a good chance that it can lead to all kinds of positive changes—within the family and the young person herself."

SEXUAL
ABUSE

*My husband, Phil, was the last
person in the world to molest any
child, let alone our daughter,
Heather. Was she saying it just
for attention—or was
there something scarier?*

Kay's Story

"When a Mrs. Erickson from Child Protective Services rang the doorbell one Friday, I assumed it had to do with my work," said Kay Hodges, 38. "I'm a pediatric nurse, and just two nights earlier, I'd been the one on duty when a badly battered two-year-old youngster was admitted.

"But Mrs. Erickson had come on a very different matter: apparently our daughter, Heather, ten, had told her teacher that her father had molested her, not once but many times.

"My first reaction was fury. Heather had some weird ways of seeking attention, but this was the limit! She must be crazy to tell such a far-out lie! Hadn't she realized how it would hurt us? Still shocked—but laughing to show the absurdity of it—I tried to tell Mrs. Erickson how Phil was a happily married man, a super father, and about as far as you could get from some pervert!

"She listened, but when she took out her notes and started listing occasions when this thing was supposed to have occurred, my self-righteous anger froze. Was it just coincidence that each of those

319

dates matched up with nights I'd been working? Even Christmas Eve! Of course I hadn't wanted to go, but I'd had to. Had Heather been especially quiet on Christmas morning? Yes, but I'd thought she was just disappointed with her gifts. These kids expect so much!

"Now I didn't know what to believe. If I couldn't trust my husband, what was left? I couldn't question Heather—she was on a Girl Scout overnight. Mrs. Erickson asked if she could wait until Phil came home. 'Good,' I thought. 'He'll deny it.' (I was praying he'd deny it.) Well, he *was* outraged, at first, but when confronted with specifics, he quieted down and said, 'You know how kids exaggerate, misinterpret . . .'

"Mrs. Erickson asked if he would leave home while an investigation was completed, and he said, 'Yes, I can go to my brother's.' I felt my heart thud. The fact that he was willing to go seemed like proof that something *had* occurred.

"That night I tried to figure out a reason, but I couldn't. Phil and I have been married for sixteen years, and he's never run around or acted 'restless.' We've prided ourselves on the fact that we've never even had a fight! If one of us gets irked, I'll just go upstairs to sew or he'll go down and build something in the basement, and then the bad feelings are all gone.

"Not that we haven't had problems like any other couple. Two years ago, Phil lost his job as a foreman for a big construction company. It was a really tough time in that industry, and so for a long time I was the only one with a regular paycheck.

"I know it must have hurt Phil's ego, but I couldn't do much to build it up because, just at that time, I needed a hysterectomy. Phil and I never sat down and talked about it, but he does all this work with Scouts and Little League, and I knew he must have been crushed that we couldn't have more children. I also felt less attractive and didn't know how he felt about me as a woman anymore. It was hard to cope with, and I guess I went into a shell.

"Since Phil was basically unemployed—doing a few odd carpentry jobs—I let him do the shopping and a lot of things for Heather, like checking her homework and making her lunches for school. He was good with her. Besides, it seemed only fair!

"By the time I got home, I was exhausted, and I wanted only to go upstairs and sew or watch TV. Besides, it wasn't as though

Heather really wanted to be close to me. Even as a little kid, she preferred Phil and would shrug off my help when I'd try to button her coat.

"Eventually, about a year ago, Phil did find a good job, but just as he was on his feet, he had another blow; my father died of a brain tumor. I loved him, but this was much more of a trauma for Phil, as his own dad had left when he was eight, and he had become very close to my father.

"Phil looked older and sadder, and I could see he was suffering. At the same time, I noticed how much quieter Heather had become. She wasn't bringing any friends home, and her grades had slipped. I considered saying something to her, but I thought she'd resent my 'intrusion,' so I said nothing.

"That was why it startled me when she came to me one evening when Phil was out bowling with friends. She said, 'Do you have to work tomorrow night?' I said, 'Of course, why?' She said, 'Nothing,' and then, 'Well, Daddy's been bothering me.' I said, 'Do you mean about your homework?' She shook her head. 'No,' she whispered. 'He's been . . . you know, touching me . . .'

"I put down my sewing with a sigh and patted her back. Poor Heather! Now I knew what this was about! The night before, she'd watched *Something About Amelia,* a TV movie about a father having sex with his daughter, and it upset her.

"Heather had always been suggestible, very quick to imagine things. In the past, when she'd wanted attention, she'd said a man followed her home. We went out looking, but there was never anyone there.

"I said, 'Heather, there is fantasy and there is reality. Don't you know your father loves you and would never hurt you?' 'Yes,' she admitted, 'but it's true!' I said, 'Heather, I've had enough of this! Just cut it out and go to bed—now!' She sighed, but she did as I said. Later that night, I said to Phil, 'Are things okay with you and Heather?' and he said, 'Oh, sure.'

"That was enough for me. I didn't want to upset him by telling him what had prompted the question. In fact, I felt sheepish for even asking . . . until Mrs. Erickson showed up. Heather must have told her teacher what she had tried to tell me six months earlier. Except the teacher believed her.

"Mrs. Erickson zipped up her briefcase. 'Here,' she said, handing me a phone number. 'Even if Heather *was* exaggerating, she is troubled, and I urge you to get help.' In a daze, I took the card. But I was sure that there must have been some mistake."

The Counselor Replies

Alan Trager, A.C.S.W., assistant executive director of Westchester Jewish Community Services in Hartsdale, New York, founded the Child Sexual Abuse Treatment Center there.

"I was encouraged that the Hodges came in voluntarily, although an investigation, an official report to Child Protective Services, and perhaps mandatory treatment as dictated by family court were still necessary. Naturally, it was a shocking revelation to Kay, and a major crisis for the family. Fortunately, in this particular case, the sexual abuse did not progress as far as sexual intercourse. It did, however, include long-standing fondling incidents when Kay was out, and one occasion of oral genital contact.

"I explained that while Phil was the offender, all members of the family were affected, and because of that, they could all use help.

"Kay, for example, felt humiliated, deeply betrayed, and angry, which led to a combination of denial ('It couldn't have happened') and insufficient sympathy for Heather ('Maybe she invited it').

"At the same time, Kay felt guilty—convinced that her own inadequacy as a mother and as a wife had caused it to happen. She had so many mixed feelings. She didn't know what to do with her loving feelings toward Phil, whom people were calling a child molester, and who she knew had many good sides to him. And although she was saying the right things to Heather, such as 'It wasn't your fault' and 'You did right to tell,' the words didn't ring true.

"Heather, the primary victim, initially came across as sullen, guilt-ridden, depressed, and reluctant to talk about herself in general, let alone to describe the details of the abuse.

"Phil, on the other hand, was the most able to talk about the fact that at least something inappropriate had occurred. But his treatment was just beginning, and he needed to get past a tendency to minimize what he had done. He needed to acknowledge the full nature and extent of what he'd done with Heather and to take full responsibility for it.

"Why had it happened? This is what we discovered: as Kay had been depressed and had retreated into what she called her 'shell,' Phil and Heather had developed an inappropriate degree of closeness.

"In treatment, we learned that Phil, as a boy, had been sexually abused by his father (something he had never told Kay). Phil's habit of 'keeping things in,' plus a sense of shame, intensified when he lost his job and Kay turned away from him. (He hadn't know that her 'shell' was because of her own low self-esteem, which had been exacerbated by her hysterectomy.) When he lost his father-in-law, Phil felt scared and forlorn.

"He hadn't intended to do anything with Heather, he claimed; one night it 'just happened' when he was kissing her good night as usual. He ached for comfort, and had lingered for a moment, putting his hand under her nightgown and letting it stay there. Though he felt ashamed afterward and tried not to do it again, he found it impossible *not* to be with Heather in this clearly inappropriate way.

"Phil was intelligent and honest, and quicker than many offenders to recognize that—*whatever* his needs and feelings—what he had done was very wrong. At that point, he began to worry about the lasting effects it might have on Heather. It was obvious that he cared about her very much, and hoped it wouldn't ruin her life.

"This concern was sincere. However, like most offenders, Phil's ability to be concerned about his daughter was not a sustained feeling. Although he said, 'I feel so bad, I'll stop!' we knew that this was not enough. Like most incest offenders, Phil had long-standing emotional problems, and without a great deal of therapy, those problems would still be there.

"I explained that he would need to understand more of the feelings that he was avoiding—including the still-painful residue of his own early victimization experience. This would help him not to victimize Heather—or any other child.

"Kay also had work to do—at first, just to face what Phil had done *without* blaming Heather and to understand that it takes tremendous courage for a victim of incest to come forward. Kay also needed to take a look at how arid things had been at home for a long time, as the overrated virtue of 'not fighting' had simply masked the emptiness and lack of sharing in their marriage.

"Kay hadn't realized at all how much she had become aloof—both from Phil and from Heather. Part of it came from feeling overwhelmed, and part from feeling they didn't need or want *her*. I now encouraged Kay to try approaching Heather in a warmer, more interested way and to keep with it even if she wasn't getting much feedback. 'That will come later,' I assured her.

"Meanwhile, Kay made important progress in working through her unresolved depression from her hysterectomy and her father's death (which, at the time, she had pushed off as 'Phil's loss' rather than hers as well).

"With Heather the treatment goal was to help alleviate her depression and guilt, which she felt not only about the sexual contact but also about having told her teacher, which she saw as 'horribly' disloyal. But she was a victim and not in the least responsible for any of what had occurred between her and her father.

"Similarly, it was important to reinforce the crucial point that even though Heather might have experienced some slight physical pleasure, the emotional pain was much deeper, and yes, she had indeed been a victim and never an accomplice.

"In addition to individual sessions, Heather joined a group with other nine- to fourteen-year-old incest victims. She felt happy to 'hear stories even worse than mine' and to 'know I'm not the only one it happened to.' Soon she became less constricted and more talkative. And almost at once, her ability to concentrate at school—and her grades—improved.

"By the end of six months, we saw Kay and Heather's relationship improving, as Phil appropriately backed off from Heather and Kay stepped in. Meanwhile, in special couples' sessions, Kay and Phil learned to discuss important things with each other, to listen, and to follow through without withdrawing to another room.

"Eight months into therapy, Heather began to seek out Kay's advice—something she had almost never done. Kay was touched and, at first, almost scared by the change; but gradually it began to feel natural to them.

"After nine months we felt that Phil could move back home. While the family 'walked on eggs' for the first week, life settled down and even the nights Kay had to work were no longer fraught with danger.

"One year into treatment, the family was functioning better than ever. Phil and Kay were even feeling intimate enough to argue, which showed real growth. Heather had made many new friends, and she was elected class treasurer.

"Formal treatment—as mandated by family court—ended at eighteen months, but the family chose to continue. It is our philosophy that incest offenders—no matter how well intentioned they are—need to view themselves not as 'cured,' but always 'at risk,' in the same way that alcoholics who've been sober for many years still call themselves 'recovering.'

"Phil and Kay joined respective self-help support groups for offenders and spouses, which they attend weekly. Phil will come in for periodic 'booster' sessions with his therapist for years, and maybe forever.

"The Hodges expressed a lot of gratitude to us at the center, but I said, no, it's Heather you must thank. In her disclosure, not only did Heather help herself, she also gave her family a gift: the opportunity to get help and to improve the distorted relationships that allowed the sex abuse to happen in the first place. Thanks to a brave young girl, the Hodges could face the past—and in so doing, find hope for the future."

Pam, eleven, has been so sulky and withdrawn since Joel and I returned from a business trip to Asia. Did Pam miss us that much? Or did something happen while we were gone?

Lucy's Story

"Clay, my father-in-law, had always been the most generous man, and now he was coming through for us again," said Lucy Ingram, 34.

"My husband, Joel, and I had to visit some important clients in several Asian cities, but the baby-sitter we'd been counting on had become ill. We couldn't cancel the trip—it was crucial to our business. Nor were we willing to consider taking our daughter, Pam, out of school.

" 'Why can't I stay at Beth's house?' Pam begged. But I told her I didn't think it was a good idea. 'There's not enough supervision there,' I explained.

"That was when Joel's father, Clay, who had come for Thanksgiving, volunteered to stay on. 'I'd be coming back here for Christmas anyway,' he said. 'This will just save me some traveling . . . and some loneliness.'

"I squeezed his hand. Clay's wife, Mary, had died a year ago, and he still seemed so lost. This arrangement would work out well for all of us!

" 'I just hope Pam doesn't take advantage of her grandfather,' Joel said, laughing, on the plane to Hong Kong. 'If I know Pam—and Dad—they'll be going out for pizza and ice cream every single night.'

"When I phoned home from Tokyo two days later, the connection was poor. 'Is everything okay?' I shouted. I could hardly hear Pam. 'I miss you,' she said, but there was too much static to hear what else she said.

" 'Everything's fine!' Clay shouted over the static. But later that night I told Joel, 'She sounded upset.'

" 'You're such a worrywart,' Joel teased. 'What could be wrong?'

"When we arrived home three weeks later, I ran to give Pam a tremendous hug, but she stiffened. 'Why did you have to stay away so long?' she said sulkily.

" 'Don't you want to see what we got you?' Joel asked—and received a cool, standoffish little shrug and a half smile. She barely acknowledged the beautiful robin's-egg-blue silk kimono we'd brought her. After dinner, Pam headed straight for her room. Later, after Clay had gone to bed, Joel asked me if I thought she was trying to make us feel guilty.

" 'I don't know what to think,' I replied unhappily. 'I never realized this trip would be so hard on her.'

" 'She'll snap out of it soon,' Joel said reassuringly. But Pam remained aloof. She spent most of her time in her room or at Beth's house, and when she was with us, she was surly and argumentative.

" 'Pam,' I said to her one day after dinner, 'you seem so upset and resentful. Didn't Grandpa knock himself out for you while we were gone—taking you to all those movies, even taking Beth along, and buying you all those tapes you were saving up for?'

"Pam picked at a loose thread in her sock and didn't answer.

" 'Well, then why are you so grumpy?'

"Still no answer. I said, 'Did something happen while we were gone?' Pam's guilty look gave me a quick stab of alarm. 'Did anything happen at Beth's house?' I persisted.

" 'Nothing happened,' Pam insisted. 'It's just that I missed you guys. *Okay?*'

" 'Okay,' I said, smiling. 'Case closed.' But I still felt something was wrong.

" 'Sure, some kids of Pam's age still take separation very hard,' said my friend Lois, who teaches psychology. 'Especially when they aren't used to it.'

" 'So we shouldn't have gone?'

" 'Of *course* you should have gone,' Lois assured me. 'Pam's a resilient kid, and it's obvious she had some fun while you were gone. Don't act as if you've done something dreadful. Just try to be matter-of-fact. It will pass.'

"Apparently Lois was right. Two days later Pam's Christmas vacation started, and I could see her getting excited, poking at mysterious packages in closets—and grinning when I caught her.

"And Christmas morning started off as a real delight, too. Joel and I had worried that the day would be hard for Clay this year, thinking of past Christmases, before Mary died. But he'd seemed really fine at breakfast, and now we were all sitting around the tree together, opening gifts.

"Pam pulled the gold ribbon off a velvet box and then lifted the cover. There, inside, was a small gold bracelet, perfectly simple and exquisite. Joel read the card: 'To Pam,' he said. 'Love from Grandpa.' Pam put the box on the coffee table.

" 'It's so beautiful!' I said. 'Put it on.'

"Pam looked at me. 'I thought you didn't like jewelry on kids,' she said accusingly.

" 'This is different,' I said. 'It's so appropriate and tasteful.' I put the bracelet on Pam's wrist.

"Suddenly Pam pulled the bracelet off and threw it on the table. 'I don't want it,' she said and ran out.

" 'Pam!' I followed her up to her room. My heart was pounding. What was *wrong* with this kid? 'I'm *ashamed* of you,' I told her. 'Ruining your grandfather's Christmas—and ours, for that matter.'

"Pam started to protest, but I silenced her. 'I don't care if you hate his gift,' I said. 'There is *nothing* that could justify the way you just behaved toward your grandfather.'

"Pam lay on her bed, her face to the wall, sobbing.

"Later she came down and apologized. 'I'm sorry, Grandpa,' she said. 'I love you, and I didn't mean to make you feel sad.'

" 'It was all my mistake,' Clay told her. 'Why don't we take it back tomorrow and get you something you'd really like?' He's being too generous, I thought to myself.

"The next morning, Joel and I went to work, still wondering what had gotten into Pam to make her behave so outrageously. 'Maybe she's been spending a little too much time at Beth's,' I suggested.

"Joel shrugged. 'Maybe,' he said. 'Or else we've just witnessed her first adolescent mood swing.'

"At noon we decided to close the office. We thought it would be fun to take Pam and Clay to Rockefeller Center to see the Christmas tree.

" 'Hello!' I called when I opened the door. There was silence. Maybe they were still out shopping, I thought. But then I heard the television in the den.

" 'Pam?' I opened the door. And then I froze. There was Clay, half sitting, half lying on our new gray tweed couch. His fly was open, his penis was out—and Pam had just taken her hand away from him! They both looked up at me, stunned.

"I shouted, 'What the hell is going on here?' But my mind still hadn't really put things together yet. Everything seemed to be spinning slowly. I'd been standing there for only a few seconds, but somehow it seemed like a very, very long time.

"Pam started to cry. I must have been yelling because Clay, who had zipped himself up, said, 'What are you screaming about? *What do you think happened?*'

"Before I could answer, Joel was beside me. He said, 'What's going on?'

" 'I don't know,' Clay answered smoothly. 'Your wife here seems to be all upset.'

"I looked at Joel, not sure I could find the words to tell him what I had just seen.

"At that point Pam vanished from the room. '*What?*' Joel demanded. Finally I said, 'Joel, your father was molesting our daughter.'

"Joel looked incredulous. 'What the hell are you talking about?' I described what I had seen.

"Clay shook his head. 'It wasn't what it looked like,' he said evenly. 'You both know I wouldn't do anything wrong.'

"Joel looked at me. He didn't seem to know what to believe. And even I was still thinking. This can't be! But I was sure of what I'd seen, and gradually Joel accepted that it was true.

"For a long moment all I could think was, We have really failed as parents! As I went upstairs to find Pam, I could hear Clay slamming drawers in the guest room. Good, pack up your stuff and get out of here, I thought.

"When I found Pam in her room, she just looked at me. I said, 'Honey, we don't have to talk about it now, but I just want to tell you that I love you.' Pam nodded, eyes red, and put her face down on her pillow. I have *never* seen her so upset!

"What do we do now? We can't call the police and have Clay arrested! It seems that the most important thing is to get help for Pam. I remember a therapist we once met at Lois's house, who specializes in situations like this. I still can't believe this horrible thing has happened to us."

The Counselor Replies

Alan Trager, A.C.S.W., assistant executive director of Westchester Jewish Community Services in Hartsdale, New York, founded the Child Sexual Abuse Treatment Center there.

"The Ingrams came in feeling understandably upset and angry—but also confused. 'We aren't naive about the things that can happen to a child,' Lucy said at once. 'We just never dreamed that someone so close to us, someone we loved and trusted, could be a pervert.'

" 'Our priority is to help Pam—that's our main concern,' Joel said. 'It must have been terrible, or why would a smart eleven-year-old allow it? You know, she never screamed or ran away. Maybe she'd never have even told us if Lucy hadn't walked in.'

"Pam looked at her father. She seemed to be struggling to come up with an answer. 'Dad, I just don't know,' she said in a whisper.

"I said, 'I think that what Pam needs most right now is to know that she has your support. A child who's been victimized needs to be certain that her parents are with her 100 percent. Only then can she begin to understand the situation herself.'

" 'Of course we're with you, honey,' Lucy said. Joel said, 'I'll say we are!' There was a lot of hugging then, and a lot of tears. And almost at once Pam seemed to relax.

"At that point I asked her to tell me when and how the abuse had started. 'It was last year at Grandpa's house in Pennsylvania—right after Grandma's funeral,' Pam said. She had found her grandfather crying in his bedroom. 'Oh, Pam,' he'd sobbed, 'I'm so alone.' He hugged her very hard—and then he took her hand and placed it on his penis.

"Soon he wanted her to fondle him whenever he could get her alone. One time he put his hand up Pam's skirt, but she cried, so he stopped and didn't try it again. But he still wanted her to touch him.

"Pam said that she *knew* it was wrong. She hated touching Clay, and she hated and resented him for making her do it. But she also felt that he was very important to the family. And she believed him when he told her that her 'loving' him was all he had to live for.

" 'My poor sweetheart,' Joel said, shaking his head. 'But why didn't you tell us what was happening?'

" 'I was afraid,' Pam said.

" 'Afraid we wouldn't believe you?'

" 'No. You always believe me. I was scared you'd think that I was bad for doing it. And I thought you might get so mad at Grandpa that you'd kill him—and it would be my fault. Yes, Dad! I've seen you get real mad sometimes! And you always say you won't let any-one hurt me.'

" 'You were putting up with all that so your parents wouldn't feel bad—and your grandfather wouldn't get in trouble,' I commented.

"Pam nodded. She said that she had dreamed of telling the truth to her parents—so that the abuse would stop—but somehow she couldn't . . . even on Christmas Day, when she'd wanted to shout, 'You both think he's so generous, but look what he's been making me do!'

" 'I understand now,' Joel said softly. 'I guess he didn't have to threaten or coerce her. He had this power over Pam just because he is her grandfather—and because he knew that she felt sorry for him.'

"Pam looked surprised. 'That's right,' she said.

"I explained to Pam that her wish to protect the adults in her family was very generous but that she had taken on too much responsibility for a child, and that by being so protective, she had been very unfair to herself.

"Then Pam began to cry, and her tears were obviously tears not just of pain but also of relief; she even managed to smile as we set up our next appointment.

"But as Pam began to feel better now that the secret was out in the open, her parents needed help to sort out their own feelings of guilt and confusion. Lucy felt terrible for having trusted Clay. She also blamed herself for having missed the clues. And she even went so far as to question whether she had overlooked obvious signs because of how much she felt she loved and needed her father-in-law.

"I told her that such feelings were natural but that I saw no evidence that she had been anything other than a normal, loving, caring mother. This assurance helped Lucy to begin making peace with herself.

"Joel, on the other hand, found that this crisis had brought to the surface all kinds of intense, complicated feelings about his father, whom he had looked up to greatly, sometimes resented, and recently felt sorry for. But now he felt utterly betrayed and very angry, and his conflicting emotions made him uncertain about what his next move should be.

"A part of him wanted to punish and humiliate his father, while another part of him was saying, Let's forget we ever knew him! And still another part was saying, Even though he did this to my daughter, he is still my father, and he is very sick and lonely and needs help.

" 'I know it would be pointless to confront him,' Joel concluded. 'He'll just deny anything happened, as he did when Lucy saw him and Pam together. He's always been famous for denying things. He's generous, bighearted, easy to get along with—just as long as nobody ruffles his feathers or says something he doesn't want to hear.'

"At that point I suggested that there might be real advantages— for Pam and for Joel, too—in speaking to his father about what had happened.

" 'What if he hangs up on me?' Joel wondered. 'What do I do then—send the police to arrest him?'

"I said, 'That's one option, but there are others as well. It's important that we gain control over the offender—in whatever way we can.'

"It became clear to me that Joel's strongest wish was to see that his father got help and was made accountable for his behavior. He decided that he would call and insist that his father go into therapy with a child-abuse expert (and that his therapist would contact me).

" 'And if he does refuse to see a therapist,' Joel said, 'I will tell him I'll report him to the police and that none of us will ever speak to or see him again.'

"Joel did call his father the next day. At first Clay denied everything, but when Joel gave his ultimatum, Clay said, 'Okay, I'll do what you say. I certainly don't want to lose the only family I've got.'

"Clay made good on his promise, and now—ten months later—he's the only one in the family who is still in therapy.

"Recently the Ingrams had their first face-to-face contact with Clay. At that time, over dinner, Clay was able to apologize to Pam and her parents—sincerely and with absolutely no excuses.

"He also admitted to Joel and Lucy that he had abused other young girls on a number of occasions. He had never been reported, nor would he ever have gone into therapy if the Ingrams hadn't insisted.

"Clay stayed at a nearby hotel over the weekend, and despite his wishes, no guarantees were forthcoming from Pam or her parents about when—or if—they would ever again trust him to stay in their home.

"Too often, families who find themselves in these situations become confused. They fail to be supportive enough of the victim—or appropriately confrontational with the offender. As a result, everyone loses: the victim, the family, the offender, and even society.

"But thanks to her parents' ability to confront the crisis quickly and sensibly, Pam Ingram's secret ordeal is over. Together, they are rebuilding her shattered sense of trust. And once again she is living in a world that feels both sane and safe."

SIBLING
TROUBLES

Billy, five, and Justin, two, were such loving brothers . . . until a month ago. Now they want to tear each other apart! Is this a normal phase as my husband, Ken, insists, or is it something much more ominous?

Jessica's Story

"Our friends used to wonder if we had a magic formula for peace in our family," said Jessica Miles, 34. "They meant the fact that Ken and I were together not only at home but at work all day, too—as partners in a small consulting firm. But they were also, maybe even more, impressed with the closeness of our children:

"Billy, at five, was gentle and small for his age, but so articulate, you'd think you were talking to an adult. Big, broad-shouldered Justin, on the other hand, was the caveman type—all action, no talk. At two and a half, he was still more inclined to grab and push than to speak.

"But as opposite as they were, our sons were nuts about each other—which is why it was such a shock when the trouble started. The first time I saw it was a Saturday about a month ago when Ken was working. The boys had been sitting on the floor, playing with toy cars. Billy turned his back, and Justin whacked him on the head with a big oil truck. 'OW!' Billy yelled and started to cry. Justin said nothing.

" 'No, no!' I told Justin. 'You must never hurt your brother.' 'I sorry, Mommy,' Justin said, winding his arms around my neck. But it happened again, and kept on happening.

" 'Do something,' Billy wailed when Justin had just bitten him on the hand for no reason. Well, I tried—all kinds of things, from sharp reprimands to spending more private time with Justin, just in case this behavior meant he was feeling shortchanged.

"Each time, I reminded Justin that you don't beat up on your brother who loves you; and each time he'd act as though he got the message. But in no time, he was at it again! And the sad result was that Billy, who had been the world's most adoring big brother, started saying chilling things, like 'I wish he'd get kidnapped' and 'If I could get a gun, I'd shoot him.'

"Ken insisted I was only imagining a problem. 'Younger brothers are *supposed* to be feisty,' he explained. But Ken was rarely around to see the attacks and how random and painful they could be.

"I couldn't imagine where the hostility was coming from, and if Justin knew, he wasn't able to tell me. So all I could do was try to keep the boys apart as much as possible, even having them watch *Sesame Street* in different rooms. And if I had to take one of them for a haircut or a new pair of sneakers, I'd leave the other boy at home with a sitter.

"Ken still wouldn't admit that anything was wrong or agree that we should seek counseling. 'I'm telling you, Jess, you're overreacting,' he insisted irritably.

" 'But it makes no sense to let him go on hurting Billy!'

" 'Hurting him?' Ken laughed. 'Jessie, there's no way a two-year-old can *victimize* a five-year-old, for crying out loud! You should be glad that Justin's a real boy and not some little wimp. And frankly, I don't see why Billy can't manage his little brother without always crying for his mommy!'

"I felt a familiar spasm of anger. Ken has always imagined that he's the expert on all family matters just because he had a lot of brothers and sisters and I had none. It never occurs to him that maybe sometimes he's wrong!

"The children's fighting continued to escalate, and things were so unpleasant at home I decided it might be a good distraction if we went to our little beach house on a rocky point in Rhode Island for a long weekend.

"Ken said he had to work. But the boys were excited as I packed, and I was hopeful, too. Perhaps when they heard the crashing surf and the sea gulls and flew their kite, it would recall the happy feelings of last summer.

"But the peaceful surroundings only made the children's enmity more apparent, and I felt I'd go crazy if they didn't stop. Even on the drive home, I had to stop and move Justin's car seat up front because I couldn't concentrate with all the screaming and hitting going on in the back.

" 'Don't you see how you keep stirring them up?' Ken said. 'Giving them attention when they fight just reinforces it. Why do you think Billy cries so much?'

"All through the next week, Ken and I barely spoke to each other, at home or at work. Everything was icy and polite, and even the boys seemed a little restrained. Then, on Saturday, Justin put his head down, like a bull, and rammed his brother, *hard*, right in the stomach.

"I screamed, 'Justin, NO!' as Billy ran sobbing into my arms. 'Leave my son alone,' Ken muttered angrily as he stepped past Billy and grabbed for Justin. 'Come on, J.M.,' he said affectionately. 'If you're so full of beans, let's go outside and play catch.'

" 'I insist that we go and get counseling,' I told Ken that night. 'No,' he said coldly. 'You've told me how much *you* loved going to a shrink in college, and how it freed you from all the unhappiness in your childhood, etcetera, etcetera. But you make every little non-problem into a psychiatric emergency, and I'm sick of it.'

" 'Well, go away then,' I said. Without answering, Ken got up, took his pillow, and went to sleep on the living room couch. 'I hate you,' I whispered through clenched teeth. And oh, how I did!

"The next day was Monday. I avoided Ken at the office and finally left early. When I got home, our babysitter, Lulu, was waiting for me. 'I'm giving notice,' she told me stiffly, putting on her coat. 'I tried to keep the boys from murdering each other, and Justin kicked me. See that? It's bruised bad!'

" 'Oh, I doubt it really happened,' Ken said dryly when he got home and I told him. 'She probably just wanted a vacation.'

" 'Daddy *home!*' Justin cried, running toward Ken. 'Hi, little guy!' Ken laughed and opened his arms, but instead of hugging his father,

339

Justin leaned over and slapped me on the side of my face so hard he sent my glasses flying across the room.

" 'Justin!' I shouted. But he had scrambled down from Ken's arms and run from the room. Ken picked up my glasses, scratched and bent. 'I guess we really do need help after all,' he said softly. 'Go ahead and call a psychiatrist. It's okay with me.' "

The Counselor Replies

E. Gerald Dabbs, M.D., clinical associate professor of psychiatry at Cornell University Medical College, practices child, adolescent, and family psychiatry in New York City.

"Ken and Jessica Miles came to see me because of what Jessica described as a sibling conflict that started with Justin. 'He's the one of us who definitely needs the help,' she explained.

" 'I don't know,' Ken disagreed. 'I think it's both boys. Billy's such a wimp and a crybaby. I just can't help feeling he asks for those attacks—and then milks them for all the attention he can get from his mother.'

"I said, 'You may both be right, but when children start fighting all of a sudden, it's often a reflection of something else, perhaps some other conflict going on in the family.'

" 'But there's nothing wrong with us,' Ken said sharply.

" 'Oh, yes, there is!' Jessica retorted. 'Three years ago we talked about separating, and now I think we will! But the children don't know that. We haven't said anything.'

" 'Maybe you didn't need to,' I said. 'Even a child as young as Justin can notice tension between his parents and react to it. In fact, what doesn't get talked out in families frequently gets fought out— by the children.'

"I could see that there was a lot of tension, anger, and uncertainty 'under the rug' in the Miles home. Still, I was very optimistic: 'If we all work, I believe we can make some important changes,' I told them.

"Seeing the children was also very revealing. Justin *was* a very physical and active child. He was bright and full of vitality: but he had few verbal skills, and I sensed that, in addition to family tensions, this was a big part of his frustration and his tendency to strike out.

"His parents had denied the possibility of a speech problem, but at my suggestion, they did take Justin to a speech and hearing specialist, who confirmed an 'expressive language delay,' or lag, in Justin's verbal development. Shocked at first, then hopeful, the Mileses put Justin in a three-mornings-a-week nursery school that provided special language stimulation.

" 'I hope he won't feel like there's something wrong with him,' Ken worried. But Justin loved it! 'Big boy—*school!*' he told me proudly.

"Billy, who was three years older than Justin but not much bigger, was very, very articulate. Yes, he was troubled by Justin's attacks and longed for 'some kind of magic protection.' But there was something else that bothered him even *more,* and that was his parents' fighting.

"He'd heard his parents disagree about Justin. 'Daddy always sticks up for him,' Billy said. 'And if they get a divorce, it will be Justin's fault.' I said, 'Billy, divorce is never a child's fault.' But he looked skeptical. The battle lines were drawn, and Billy was on his mother's team. He seemed to feel an overwhelming need for Jessica's support and comfort.

"It also became quite apparent that Billy had *never* liked Justin that much, even though his mom insisted otherwise. I pointed this discrepancy out to Jessica and asked her why she might have needed to exaggerate so strongly the degree of her sons' attachment.

" 'I guess it's had to do with my own mixed feelings,' she said, and told me that when she became pregnant with Justin, she was already thinking of leaving Ken, but the prospect of a second child had made her feel obligated to stay.

"When Justin was born, Jessica waited to feel the same 'perfect' love she had felt when Billy was born, but it didn't happen. And Jessica just couldn't forgive herself. She could keep the guilty feelings under control as long as there was no aggression or rivalry between the children, but now, in the midst of all the fighting, she was finding it intolerable. Also intolerable were the marital tensions, which, she believed, had kept her from bonding 'enough' with Justin in the first place.

"I said, 'Most mothers feel differently about their children, and it doesn't mean that you're depriving either one of them.' Rather, I felt that the problem for Justin and Billy was the growing discord that existed between Jessica and Ken.

"'Whether you stay together or not,' I said, 'I recommend marital therapy. At least it will help you to learn to communicate more directly and more constructively, so that it doesn't fall on the kids.'

"The Mileses agreed. Now they were working together, and I was continuing to see the children, separately and together. Billy still complained about getting 'clobbered' all the time by his brother. But I began to see how often this child, who felt like a victim, was *provoking* his little brother into rages.

"For example, if Justin was playing with a toy, Billy would take it, saying, 'May I have this, please?' and not waiting for an answer. Justin would then scream and strike out. Then Billy would say, 'But all I did was borrow the dinosaur for just a second, and I asked first; I even said please.'

"Seeing this enabled me to work with Billy to show him how he could affect, by not provoking his brother, whether Justin hit him or not. 'It works,' Billy announced, with some amazement. That day, he left my office with a smile on his face. 'Hey, when we get home,' he said to Justin, 'do you want to play something?'

"Justin, too, was making progress. He felt accepted and happy in his special nursery school, and within three months, his language skills had developed sufficiently that he no longer needed to hit and kick in order to make a point.

"By the time our therapy had formally ended, five months after beginning, I saw many encouraging changes that boded well for the Miles family. For one thing, Ken and Jessica were still together—and still in couples therapy—working very hard. 'We really do love each other,' Jessica said. 'I'm so glad we didn't throw it all away.'

"Interestingly, Jessica had left the small firm that she and Ken had started together nine years earlier. Having felt that her whole identity had been tied up with Ken, she now felt a sense of freedom and challenge in her brand new job, and she was touched by Ken's supportiveness and real interest.

"As Ken felt happier and less defensive within his family, he no longer felt the need to 'bury himself alive' in office work, and he began to set aside more time to spend with the boys. His relationship with Billy improved a great deal, as Ken came to terms with his own insecurities and realized that the 'weakness' he had so disliked in Billy was a reflection of what he had always most feared in himself.

"Now he began to enjoy some wonderful conversations with Billy, and Billy was so happy about the new, improved rapport with his father that he seemed to glow.

"Nor was there any longer a need to keep the children apart! I had told Jessica that doing so had only reinforced the idea that the two boys couldn't get along together. At first she had been hesitant to risk more fighting. But now, they were going more places together, and they did sometimes scrap and fight—as almost all brothers do sometimes—but it no longer terrified Jessica to hear the fighting.

"And finally realizing that it's okay and normal to love two children differently (and even to feel a little closer and warmer toward one of them), Jessica lost her compulsion to get involved in the children's spats. She no longer felt the constant need to mediate, comfort, or punish.

"Jessica and Ken had seen a problem that needed fixing. But what they saw were only parts of a larger whole. To have worked with, or focused on, only one or two individuals involved would not have led to any resolution for the whole family.

"It's often upsetting to parents when their children seem to be fighting excessively. But when we can take a step back and see it not as an isolated problem, but as a barometer of family tension, we have the best shot at making *everything* better."

Terry, fifteen, is never satisfied with her grades—or herself—no matter how much we try to reassure her. Why does she feel so bad about herself? Is there something she won't tell us?

Nan's Story

"I wish I could get Terry to stop driving herself so hard," said Nan Rankin, 40. 'You'd think she was in law school, the way she tenses up. But she's only a sophomore in high school. The worst part is that she works and works and still gets only C's—and then she feels like a failure.

"I don't know how many times we've tried to tell her that C's are perfectly respectable—especially when you're taking all honors classes. But she won't listen! She only takes time off for one thing, and that's chess club. If I urge her to take a break, she says, 'I don't have time.'

"It bothers me to see her growing up with the feeling that she's got to achieve, or else. I know what that feels like. I *had* to strive, because no matter how well I did in high school and college—even in graduate school—it was never enough to please my cold, demanding parents. That's why I've always gone out of my way to give both our daughters lots of praise.

"My husband, Alan, doesn't really understand my concern. He's a research scientist, and to him, work is pleasure. He can't wait to get to his lab every day. He's the brilliant one, the one our daughter Kate takes after. Kate's nineteen, goes to Yale, and has always been a whiz in everything. It all seems to come naturally to her.

"But Terry is *not* the same kind of kid. She plugs away at her work and worries. Far from *putting* pressure on her, it's been my mission in life to chase away her self-doubt.

"That's why, even when the children were in grade school, I asked Kate not to show Terry her all-A report cards. 'You just happen to be very gifted,' I explained to Kate. 'Terry would feel sad if she saw what you got.' And Kate was wonderful! She'd say, 'I got about the same as you,' when Terry asked her.

"In eighth grade, Kate did win the Top Student award, which was a desk set. Terry was excited for her and planned to win one herself someday. But of course, she didn't come close to winning. So Alan and I bought her a set. 'But what's it *for?*' she asked, touching the polished wood of the penholder. 'Just because we're sure you came real close, and we think you're great,' I said. But Terry didn't look pleased.

" 'I didn't win this,' she said, and that pen set stayed in its box until I finally give it away to a rummage sale.

"I thought it might be easier for Terry once Kate went to college. But last year she became real intense, and this year has been the worst. We've told her at least a hundred times that it's enough that she's *in* honors classes. She doesn't have to get A's or even B's. But she doesn't hear us. Even when she does get a B, she isn't satisfied. She says, 'Mom, how come Kate always did so much better with less effort?'

"I honestly don't know how to answer. I say, 'It probably only looks that way to you,' but she doesn't buy that; she says, 'Mommy, are you telling the truth?' And I lie through my teeth and say, 'Of course.' I feel terrible about lying, but what am I supposed to say: 'Kate's smarter?' or 'You're not as capable as Kate?' I'd rather lie than hurt her feelings.

"I worry more and more about Terry's lack of a social life. She hasn't started dating, but she should at least have girlfriends. Kate always had a ton of friends but Terry doesn't get a phone call.

"Terry doesn't talk much about not having friends, but recently, when the Curry girls had a barbecue and a backyard dance and didn't invite her, and we could hear the music from down the street, Terry did say, 'Mom, why don't kids like me?'

"I wanted to cry, but I said, 'Oh, darling, they do! But you need to be more available . . .' Terry just shook her head. 'Mom, I don't have time to hang around the pizza place every day and giggle at boys.'

"Alan says it's probably just an awkward phase and she'll out-grow it soon. He loves her, but he's not very tuned in to feelings, and frankly I don't think he's home enough to see how tense Terry's become. I do talk to Kate about it sometimes, and she's really super. But we haven't solved it.

"I phoned Kate after that Curry party, and she said, 'I know what to do.' The next day she called to invite Terry up to Yale for a week-end, to give her some fun and maybe a pep talk. I thought that was so kind! I put Terry on the bus and told her how lucky she was and how much fun she'd have . . . but when she got home, she looked miserable.

" 'Wasn't Kate nice to you?' I asked. Terry said, 'Yes, Kate was very nice.' 'Well, didn't you have fun?' I persisted. Terry just shrugged. 'Did you meet some exciting people?' I asked—and got another shrug. I wanted to shake her and call her ungrateful and cold, but I held myself back. Later that evening, I told Alan.

" 'There's a lot of competition between those two,' he said. 'And the problem is, Terry's always going to lose.' I said, 'That's not so.' I reminded him of when the girls were little: how Terry used to idol-ize Kate to the point that she wanted to copy her in everything—and how sweet and almost motherly Kate was in return. Kate's *never* undermined her sister. In fact, she's always told Terry, 'You can do it, kid, I know you can.'

" 'One thing I learned from looking for research-grant money,' Alan said, 'is how to pick up on competition. I tell you, it's there, and it isn't a fair fight.'

" 'But this is not a fight at all,' I insisted. Alan just shook his head. Terry continued to push herself unmercifully . . . and I continued to worry.

"But last Friday, something else happened—something more upsetting—and I don't know what to make of it. It had started snowing unexpectedly—the first snow of the season—so I decided to pick Terry up at school so she wouldn't have to walk home in her light jacket and without wearing boots.

"But when I arrived at school and found the chess club's meeting room, the faculty advisor, Miss Kim, looked puzzled and said, 'But Mrs. Rankin, I don't understand.' Yes, of course, she knew *Kate* Rankin ('a first-rate play'), but Terry Rankin? 'I'm sorry, I didn't even know that there *was* another Rankin.'

"Driving home, I felt confused and embarrassed, but mostly worried. If Terry wasn't in chess club, where *did* she spend Friday afternoons? Had her school frustrations sent her off the deep end in one way or another? Was she in some kind of trouble? I tried not to let myself imagine awful things, and I tried to stay calm.

"When Terry came in at six o'clock, freezing, with her hair and shoes soaking wet, she said, 'Hi, Mom,' and tried to hurry past me. I said, 'Terry, please. I want you to tell me where you were.'

" 'I don't *have* to,' Terry shot back. 'You can't make me. I'm entitled to a life, too!' Since then, she's been very defiant, very secretive, and I'm frightened. I don't know what's up, but it's clear that Terry needs help."

The Counselor Replies

Philip Diaz, M.S.W., Ph.D., author of Twelve Steps to Self-Parenting (Health Communications Inc.), *is a therapist and consultant specializing in parenting issues. Diaz was formerly Assistant Deputy for Prevention, Office of National Drug Control Policy, Executive Office of the President.*

"Nan Rankin called and told me what was going on. She said that Terry still wouldn't divulge where she'd been. 'Should we all come in as a family?' Nan wondered.

"I said I thought it would be best if Terry came in by herself a few times, so that she and I could get acquainted. Later, we would all talk together. But, Terry had her own plans: for the first session, she sat in my office and worked on her math.

" 'Terry,' I said, 'is this really the way you want to use this time? Or would you like to talk with me about anything?'

" 'No,' she said firmly. 'I'm only here because my parents forced me to come.'

" 'I guess you know they were—and are—very concerned about you, and where you go on Fridays,' I said.

" 'I don't want to talk about it,' she retorted. 'Besides, what's the point? I know why they brought me here. It's not just about Fridays. They want you to fix me—to be like Kate.'

"I asked her what she meant. 'Don't you know about Kate? She's Miss Perfect! I mean she *is* really wonderful. She just makes me mad sometimes. Like she never stops telling me I can do it, that I'm just as smart as she is and I just have to try a little harder. Well, that's a lie! I know because I'm trying as hard as I can!

" 'It's the same with my parents,' Terry went on unhappily. 'They *always* lie. They say, "We're proud of you," but who are they kidding? They can't even face the fact that I'm not another supergenius like Kate. I guess they're so disappointed, so embarrassed . . .'

"I said, 'How do you know that?'

"Terry snorted. 'Mom will say, "Oh, you got a C plus—that's so fabulous!" But she'd never be so condescending to Kate. Can't they just *respect* me? Wouldn't it be fabulous if they could think I'm okay even though I'm not like them?'

" 'What *are* you like?' I said to Terry gently.

"She sighed. 'I don't care about the things they care about. And I don't want to go to Yale like Dad and Kate. I just like helping people.'

" 'Tell me how.'

" 'I go to a hospital—on Friday afternoons—and I just help out. That's where my best friend works.'

" 'Who is that?'

" 'Her name is May and she's a nurse,' Terry said. 'And she's nothing like the snobs my mother teaches with and my father works with and my sister lives with! May doesn't know anything about chess or biophysics or the art-history junk Mom teaches. But she knows how to care for people, and that's exactly what *I* want to do.'

"I said, 'These are important things you're telling me, Terry. Don't you wish your parents could know, too?' She shrugged. 'After all,' I pointed out, 'you really *did* keep this a secret. You can't hide an important part of yourself from your parents and still expect them to understand.'

" 'I guess you're right,' she admitted. The next week, the four of us met, and Terry told her parents about the hospital where she had been volunteering all semester.

"Both her parents were relieved—and very, very touched. 'But that's a *wonderful* thing you're doing,' her mother said.

" 'I'm sorry I lied,' Terry said.

" 'I'm sorry you felt you had to,' Nan answered.

" 'I was ashamed to tell you I want to be a nurse,' Terry blurted out. 'I mean, let's face it. In our house, if you're not going to an Ivy League college and if you're not a big-deal professor, you're nobody—you are just a failure.'

" 'No, darling, *I'm* the one who's a failure if that's the kind of message I've given you,' Nan said unhappily.

"I told them it sounded like the only real failure was a classic failure to communicate. The misunderstanding stemmed from the fact that Nan—because of her own unhappy, pressured childhood and because of Kate's daunting abilities—had bent over backward to reassure Terry that she wasn't second-rate. But Terry had read her mom's concern *for* her as disappointment *in* her. I said, 'Sometimes the more a parent tries to reassure a child, the less convincing it sounds.'

" 'So that's where the pressure came from,' Nan said. 'We kept telling Terry that we weren't comparing her to Kate. We fooled ourselves, but we didn't fool Terry!'

"In the weeks that followed, I met several times with Nan and Alan in order to help them resolve what they saw as 'unacceptable' feelings. 'I *wanted* to feel that Terry was fine,' Nan said. 'But it broke my heart when she didn't just rise to the top of the heap the way Kate did.'

"Alan nodded. 'I guess we take superachievement for granted, so we always regarded Terry—a child who's never failed—as a poor soul, just because she was average.'

" 'How can we change?' Nan asked. 'I know in my head that nursing is a perfectly respectable profession, but deep down, I can't help thinking, Why a nurse? Why not a doctor? No wonder poor Terry felt pushed.'

"I assured the Rankins that acknowledging their disappointment was an important step toward resolving it. To help, I encouraged them to try to redefine success—to see it not just in terms of grades and academic achievement and a high-prestige career, but in terms of personal qualities as well, like compassion. 'Terry is way *above* average in that,' I said.

" 'You're right,' Nan said at last. 'I just hope it's not too late to let Terry know.' Alan agreed, and in the following weeks, some important changes came about. Terry—with her parents' support—agreed to drop her honors courses for second semester; and for the first time, Terry felt so confident and able to master her work that she began to linger after school to play sports or just sit and gab with classmates.

" 'It was weird: I felt sort of guilty at first,' Terry told me, laughing. 'But now I feel good—no more butterflies in the stomach.'

"Terry put off telling Kate what she'd done. And when she finally did level with her, Kate *was* upset that their parents had let Terry 'cop out' on her honors courses. 'You won't even have a chance of coming to Yale,' she warned. But when she began to give Terry another pep talk about trying harder, Terry said, 'I'm not copping out. I think I'm just *finding* out that I'm okay without doing a million hours a week of homework.'

"Kate listened in amazement. 'Boy, you sound different,' she told her sister. 'Listen. Next time I drive myself crazy trying to juggle too many courses and too many commitments because Mom always says I'm supposed to be gifted, well, I'll come to *you* for a pep talk!'

"That made Terry feel good. And as her tension diminished, a whole new sense of humor—and fun—emerged, and she made some new friends. Dating is still in the future, but some of her 'buddies' are boys, and the phone has started ringing.

"Terry is still enthusiastic about the hospital, but she no longer considers it her only joy. She is a faithful volunteer and often recounts her experiences later at home, and her parents listen with interest. Nan and Alan finally got to meet May, and they hit it off so well that May has become a genuine friend of the family. 'Your daughter is fantastic,' May told the Rankins. 'Everybody loves her.'

"Last month, I saw the Rankins for a final session, and I was pleased. 'We're trying things differently at home now,' Nan told me: less dinner-table talk about achievements and more sharing. 'There's a lot more listening—and a lot more laughing,' Nan said. Even Alan has found that there's life beyond the lab and is planning time off for a family trip.

"Nan always meant well when she'd shaded the truth for Terry; but even with good intentions, parental dishonesty does more harm than good because children *will* sense the lack of candor and will mistake the motive for something worse.

"The Rankins have learned how much warmer family life can be without a lot of subterfuge, and I don't think they'll ever be tempted back to the old way."

SLEEP DISTURBANCES

*Getting our son, Stevie, three,
to go to sleep at night has become
a terrible ordeal. Is he just
fighting sleep to see how far he
can push us? Or is he really
terrified—and if so, why?*

Rachel's Story

"It all began last spring, when Stevie graduated from his crib to a bed," said Rachel Wilder, 29. "He knew it was a reward for not needing a diaper at night. 'I'm a big boy now,' he told everyone.

"But the change was more than my husband, Tim, or I had bargained for. Instead of just asking for a bedtime story and a goodnight kiss, Stevie began making repeated demands for glasses of water and trips to the bathroom, more stories, more rearranging of stuffed animals. Each night, bedtime seemed to last a little longer.

"Friends told us it was a normal clingy phase that he would soon outgrow if we were patient. So we came every time Stevie called. And when he came out of his room, we'd gently take him back.

"But the trouble was, he would come out again, insisting that he needed a tissue or another story. One night Tim—who had been extremely patient—said, 'That's it, Stevie. I'm going to spank you if you don't stay in bed.'

"There was silence, but a moment later Stevie was back downstairs. He was crying. 'But I'm scared,' he said in a very small voice. 'Something's in my closet. I heard it breathing.'

"Tim realized Stevie was really fearful and felt ashamed of having yelled. He carried him back upstairs. I got a flashlight, and we shined it all over the bedroom and in the closet. 'See?' Tim said.

"But Stevie's fears persisted. As the weeks passed he needed more and more reassurance to go to sleep.

"Friends still told us not to worry. But they weren't going through those awful bedtimes. One night Tim spent an hour checking all around with the flashlight—not just in Stevie's closet, but everywhere, even outside in the bushes—to prove that there was nothing to be scared of.

"Tired, Tim came to bed. We had barely fallen asleep before Stevie was calling. 'I don't think you really looked, Daddy,' he shouted, at which point Tim awoke with a start, leaped out of bed, and stomped down the hall to Stevie's room in a rage.

" 'Be gentle with him!' I called. But I could hear Tim yelling and Stevie crying. It sounded awful, but I understood. Two nights earlier I had lost *my* temper and screamed like a witch when Stevie woke me for the fourth time in two hours.

" 'Mommy!' he had wailed. 'When you scream, you make me feel like running to another house.' His words hit home. I felt like the worst and meanest mother in the world.

"A few times we got a baby-sitter and went out. But we were too tired to really enjoy ourselves, and when we got home at eleven o'clock or so, there was Stevie, waiting up for us.

"One sitter, Mrs. Kifford, suggested locking Stevie in his room. I was shocked. Sure, it was difficult and frustrating, but how could she even contemplate curing a little boy's fear by shutting a door in his face?

"But Tim actually liked the idea, and one night he insisted on trying it. 'We've been letting him jerk us around long enough,' Tim argued. 'And listen, he's not even calling us or crying.'

"I listened, and to my surprise, I heard no sound from Stevie's room. 'He's probably fallen asleep,' Tim said, satisfied. But after twenty minutes I went to check and found that Stevie wasn't asleep at all. He was just lying there, huddled in his bed, rigid and shaking!

"I picked him up and felt his rapid heartbeat. Poor Stevie, he was absolutely *terrified*. I had to hold him in my arms for an hour until he fell asleep. And then when I tried to leave, he stirred awake and needed me to stay for another 45 minutes.

"The next night Stevie refused to get into his bed at all. I certainly wasn't surprised. 'I guess we could take him in with us,' Tim finally suggested.

"Stevie climbed into our bed, and he was soon fast asleep.

"Just before I drifted off to sleep I thought, Maybe we should have done this a long time ago. But Stevie slept so actively—rolling around and twisting and kicking—that Tim ended up sleeping in Stevie's bed.

"It was hard for us to fathom: How could such a good, happy, and cooperative little boy in the daytime become so frightened (or so manipulative) at night? Was he really that scared? Was he consciously trying to control us?

" 'What's the difference?' Tim grumbled. 'Either way, we're stuck.' And we were! By June, it was so bad I was ashamed to tell friends that in order to get any sleep at all, Tim and I had to take turns 'guarding' Stevie from his imaginary intruders—sometimes for hours!

"I guess I should be grateful that Stevie still takes his afternoon nap. Without it, he'd hardly survive. But what about *us*? We don't get enough sleep, and we don't have nearly enough time alone together. It's impossible to relax, knowing that Stevie could call or appear at any moment.

"And when he does need us, we have to respond quickly. If we wait, he just gets more upset. And besides, there's always that outside chance that if we do what he wants fast enough, he'll go right back to sleep, without another whole production.

"Last week was impossible! Tim was out of town on business, and I had a very bad cold. When Stevie called me, I reminded him that I was sick, that I felt rotten, that I needed to stay in bed and sleep.

" 'But, Mommy, I'm scared,' Stevie whined. 'You *have* to come.' And I felt such a wave of resentment, thinking, Oh, how I hate this kid! and at the same time I felt so guilty for having such a thought, especially when he was so scared.

"I've heard Stevie's nursery school teacher, Mrs. Ball, say, 'It's the parents' job to create a child's emotional security.' Somehow we've failed, or Stevie wouldn't have this problem every night. I feel so bad, but where do we go for help?"

The Counselor Replies

Richard Ferber, M.D., a leading authority on children's sleep problems and director of the Center for Pediatric Sleep Disorders at The Children's Hospital in Boston, is the author of Solve Your Child's Sleep Problems *(Simon and Schuster).*

"Rachel Wilder called me in distress. 'I'm afraid our son has a major sleep disorder,' she said. 'Last night it was one o'clock before I got him to sleep, and he *still* woke up twice.'

"I said, 'A child's sleeplessness is always distressing, but sometimes when we know why it's happening, it can be simple to treat.' Of course, I couldn't know about Stevie's case without more information, so we made an appointment, and two days later the Wilders came in.

"Meeting them, I could see at once that they were a warm, intelligent, caring family and that Stevie was a friendly, outgoing child. What's more, his parents seemed to share in the responsibility of caring for him.

"Stevie's physical exam was normal. Nor was there any red flag in his medical history or psychosocial development. His sleeping had been normal until six months ago, and despite his current problems at night, he was still doing fine in the daytime, both at home and at nursery school, where he'd not had trouble separating from his parents.

"Tim and Rachel explained how hard it was to get Stevie to go to sleep and to stay asleep. I asked them what their routine was. They said supper was a six-thirty. Then Stevie would play, have his bath, and get into his pajamas. One of his parents would sit with him in the living room and read.

"At eight-thirty it was time for bed, and that's when the trouble would start. Stevie would do anything he could to procrastinate, and even when his parents had indulged him in all his requests, he would usually call them or come downstairs, saying he was scared.

"As Tim and Rachel described a typical night I asked if Stevie raced down the stairs or if he walked and whether he seemed terrified.

" 'He usually walks,' Tim replied. 'And he seems upset, but not

358

hysterical.' I asked what happened next.

" 'I walk him back upstairs to bed,' Rachel said. 'We talk for a while—he always has so many questions! I give him another sip of water, and then I leave. But invariably he's back before long, insisting that he "heard something breathing in the closet." '

" 'By the fourth time, we're usually angry,' Tim said. 'I hate to yell at him.'

" 'Me, too,' Rachel said. 'I feel like such a rotten mother, being mean when he's scared. And he really is! In fact, it's gotten to the point where he can't even fall asleep unless he's with one of us, and we all end up exhausted in the morning.'

" 'What happens now?' Tim asked. 'Will Stevie have to spend a night in your lab, hooked up to monitors for you to see what's wrong?'

"I said, 'No, we rarely use the lab for three-year-olds, unless there's a possible breathing disturbance or seizures or if we need to study a child who's unusually sleepy. But clearly that's not Stevie. In fact, I'd say we can treat his problem easily, and with your cooperation, I believe we'll get quick results.'

"I told Tim and Rachel, 'It's significant that Stevie's problem started when he moved from a crib to a bed.'

" 'But why?' Rachel wondered.

" 'Suddenly the bars of the crib that had kept him in bed at night were no longer there,' I explained. 'Yes, he wanted the big-boy status that comes with graduating to a bed, but it also disturbed him. In effect, you were telling him that you expected him to stay put at night.'

" 'Well, what was wrong with that?' Tim asked. 'We've read that three is the right age for that.'

" 'For many kids it is,' I replied. 'But maybe Stevie wasn't ready for that transition. After all, he had only recently learned to control his bowels and bladder. And nursery school requires children to be civilized and to control their angry feelings. Asking Stevie to control his impulse to come out of his bedroom at night may have been just one more demand for self-control than he could handle.'

" 'We knew *something* was making him anxious,' Rachel said. 'That's why we tried so hard to soothe him.'

" 'Of course you meant well,' I said. 'But indulging his demands, then sometimes getting angry and scaring him, *then* feeling guilty and trying to make up for that by indulging him even more gave Stevie the message that his parents had no control, either. And that made him feel even less safe.'

" 'You mean it was wrong for us to sit with him?' Rachel asked. 'Or to let him into our bed?'

" 'Many parents do resort to those tactics, but they seldom succeed. Children tend to feel anxious in bed with parents,' I explained. 'And it's even worse when a child's a wild sleeper, like Stevie, who literally kicked his father out of bed!'

"I explained that sitting in the child's room until he falls asleep can also backfire: The child quickly associates falling asleep with having a parent there, and consequently he won't even try it alone. And even when the parent is in the room, he worries that the parent will leave, so he actually fights going to sleep to keep the parent there for as long as possible.

"I said, 'Stevie needs to know you're there to step in to control what he's unable to control. Once he understands that, he will relax and sleep. But in the meantime,' I went on, 'we need to replace the sense of security and control he lost along with his crib.'

" 'We gave the crib away,' Tim said uncomfortably. 'And the one time I tried to confine him in a different way, locking him in his room, he was so upset. I certainly wouldn't want to repeat that.'

" 'I agree,' I said. 'Locking a child in his room is too much like prison. He doesn't know when—or even if—you're coming back, so you're just trading one kind of fear for another. Rather,' I said, 'the idea of control is to decrease Stevie's anxiety—in a nurturing, supportive way—and here's how I think we should do it.'

"I suggested they buy a safety gate made of nylon mesh for Stevie's doorway. 'This way,' I said, 'his whole room becomes a crib. When you put him down at night, you shut the gate, not to frighten him, but to show him that control is there.'

" 'If he calls or cries, show him that you're there to take care of him, not to give in to his repeated requests. Stay calm, don't make threats, and don't let him draw you into long conversations. Instead, just come back to the gate each time to reassure him, and then leave.'

" 'Each time he calls I want you to wait a little longer before you go to him,' I said. 'Start by waiting half a minute the first time he calls, and on each successive night make the intervals a little longer.'

"I suggested that the Wilders have Stevie go to the bathroom before bed and then let him make only one other trip, and to limit him to only one little drink at bedtime, no more.

"To help ensure success, I made another recommendation. I said, 'Since Stevie never falls asleep until ten-thirty at the earliest, starting with an eight-thirty bedtime dooms you all to two hours of battle.' I suggested that the Wilders say good night at eleven o'clock. 'Don't worry. It won't be forever.'

"I also advised them to wake Stevie at seven instead of eight every day to get him onto an earlier schedule. 'And let's eliminate his nap,' I said. 'If he does fall asleep, wake him after fifteen or twenty minutes. Whether he really needs a nap will become apparent as we go along.'

"I pointed out that Stevie was old enough to make a contract. I urged his parents to discuss the new plans with him and to made a bedtime wall chart. Tell him that if he goes to bed without a fuss and stays in his room all night, he gets a sticker. And if he doesn't wake anybody until morning, he gets another. And when he has enough stickers on his wall chart, he will get a special prize.

"The Wilders liked the idea. 'But what if he doesn't want to?' Tim asked. I said, 'Just tell Stevie, "If you can do this, great. But if not, it's okay, and we'll close the gate to help you." '

"The family's difficulties continued for the first week, but things became much easier when Stevie realized his parents were not about to give in or go back to the way things were before, despite his protests.

"Over the next couple of weeks there were just occasional awakenings, but not much of a struggle about going back to bed. 'A month ago I wouldn't have believed this change could be possible,' Rachel told me. 'It really seems like a miracle.'

"Like the Wilders, many parents have no trouble setting limits for their child during the daytime. But at night they want to sleep and will give in and do anything to be able to do so—not realizing that they're really reinforcing the child's unwillingness to go to bed.

"Once the Wilders understood that allowing Stevie to call the shots at bedtime had *caused* problems rather than solved them, they were able to correct the situation and give their son all the structure and security he needed."

*Tim, seven, is bright and mature,
except that he's still wetting his bed!
We've tried all the sensible
approaches, but absolutely nothing
works. What will this do to his
self-esteem—and our sanity?*

Emily's Story

"Tim was such an early walker and talker I never dreamed he would still be wetting his bed in second grade," said Emily Springer, 31.

"My husband, Paul, kept urging Tim to try harder. 'If you can control it some nights, you can control it every night,' he told Tim. 'And, Tim, you'll really have to stop wetting your bed if you want to go to baseball camp next summer.'

"Tim bit his lip. It had to be hard for him when Paul put the pressure on, especially now that his four-year-old brother, Matthew, was dry at night. In fact, last spring when Matthew made that leap to training pants, we'd hoped that it would motivate Tim—and apparently it did!

"'I don't want to wear a diaper, either,' Tim had said, and we had agreed. But that didn't stop his wetting. The only difference was that I then had a lot of extra bed stripping and laundry to do in the morning before I went to work.

"Paul suggested that I make Tim do his own cleaning up. But I didn't see what punishing Tim for something he couldn't help would accomplish.

"'I went through a bed-wetting phase when I was a boy,' Paul said.

'And so I know: If we don't actively help him stop, we'll just perpetuate the problem.'

"Was that true? Our pediatrician shook his head when I asked him during a checkup. 'All I know is that Tim has no physical problem,' he said. He suggested that this pattern of bed-wetting might simply be Tim's way of clinging to early childhood a little longer.

"I nodded, but it made little sense: Tim loved acquiring new 'big-boy' skills, and I felt sure that he hated his bed-wetting as much as we did. For months he'd avoided having friends over for fear that his bedroom smelled or that Matthew would call him "Peepee-pants" in front of them.

"And I'll never forget Tim's tongue-tied anguish in the school car pool when his friend Teddy asked, 'How come you're the only kid in class who never goes on sleep-overs?'

"Last week my father was here for supper. 'Good night, Timmy, *sleep dry*,' he said when he was leaving. Tim felt embarrassed and upset. 'Do you have to tell *everyone?*' he demanded. That night Tim was already wet at eleven when I went to his room to take him to the bathroom. I changed his bed, but he was soaking wet *again* in the morning.

"Paul sighed. 'This is getting out of hand,' he said. 'The whole house is starting to smell like a zoo.'

"Had Tim overheard? I hoped not! I understood that Paul was upset, but more humiliation was the last thing Tim needed. At least we'd be away for a couple of days, visiting Paul's stepsister, Nancy. Not that I felt so comfortable with Nancy—she can sometimes be so opinionated. Still, I would have gone anywhere, just for a break from the tension at home.

" 'Hi, guys,' Nancy said warmly, hugging the boys. As usual, her house looked picture-perfect.

" 'I think you'd better sleep in a diaper,' Paul told Tim firmly at bedtime. Tim looked miserable. 'I'm not a baby,' he said. In the morning his diaper was soaking wet.

" 'What's *that?*' Nancy teased when she saw me throwing the sodden plastic bundle in the garbage. 'Matthew, I can't believe that a smart dude like you still wears diapers.'

" 'I don't,' Matthew said with a giggle. 'Tim's the one who's a peepee-pants.'

"Nancy looked at me quizzically.

" 'It's true,' I admitted. 'He still sometimes wets in his sleep.'

"Nancy drew in her breath. 'You've got a problem then,' she said. 'Kids his age don't wet unless they're incredibly angry at their parents.'

" 'Oh, come on!' I had to laugh. 'Tim? Angry?'

" 'It's true,' she said. 'Kids are primitive, and they use their bodily functions to express strong feelings. It's a classic power struggle, and right now I'd say Tim is winning.'

"Driving home with the children asleep in the back of the car, I felt really discouraged. What could we have done to make Tim so angry? And how many years of therapy would it take to undo it?

"I vowed to try harder and to be more patient with him. But it was only a few days before my patience snapped. It was around ten o'clock on a night when I'd had to bring a lot of work home and still had hours more to go.

"I was trying to take Tim to the bathroom, but he was putting up a fight. 'No,' he whimpered, burrowing deeper under his covers. 'I already went. I don't have to.' Then the next moment he began to urinate in the bed right in front of me!

" 'Tim!' I was furious. 'How dare you!' I pulled him out and sent him to the bathroom to wash himself. Yanking his soggy sheets off, I said, 'Dad's right. You'll probably stop this when you go to college and have to take care of your own sheets.'

"Tim was silent and sulky. Well, let him be, I thought. Maybe now he realizes that even mothers can get fed up sometimes.

"I went back to finish my work, but I must have dozed off, because Paul was shaking me. 'Tim's disappeared!' he said. 'He isn't in his room; he isn't anywhere!'

"Alarmed, we began to search the house. My mind was racing: Had Tim run away? Would we find him? Would we ever see him again?

" 'Calm down,' Paul said. 'We haven't checked the basement yet.' And that was where we found him, sitting up against the washing machine, fast asleep!

"He seemed surprised when we woke him. 'I tried to stay awake,' he explained. 'That was the only way I knew I wouldn't pee. But when I was in bed, I couldn't keep my eyes open, so I came down here. I thought if it happens, I'll stick my pj's in the wash . . . so Mom won't know.'

" 'But why?' I asked, amazed.

" 'Because I didn't want you to be mad at me, Mom,' he said, lowering his eyes and starting to cry. He looked so sad, embarrassed, and frightened. Clearly, my outburst earlier had made my poor kid feel as if he'd lost his last ally!

"I hugged him then, and so did Paul. Now we both understand that Tim feels just as frustrated and helpless as we do. It's obvious we need special help."

The Counselor Replies

Martin B. Scharf, Ph.D., is director of the Center for Research in Sleep Disorders, in Cincinnati, and the author of Waking Up Dry: How to End Bedwetting Forever *(Writer's Digest Books).*

"When the Springers called the center, I asked them to come in with Tim and to bring a record of his most recent physical exam.

" 'Do you really think you can help?' Paul wondered aloud when the Springers arrived at my office.

" 'Yes,' I said. 'But first I need to know more about Tim.'

"Emily told me that she and Paul had tried everything from making sure Tim didn't drink anything after he'd eaten supper to getting him up to go to the bathroom before they went to bed but that he still wet his bed most nights.

" 'But not *every* night!' Tim protested.

" 'You know, Tim,' I said, 'I used to wet, too, when I was your age.' Tim looked shocked. 'It's true,' I went on. 'My room used to smell, and I fought with my parents, and my brother used to tease me.'

"Tim laughed and looked very relieved. But then he turned serious. 'I just *hate* it,' he said with feeling.

"I replied, 'I'm sure you do.' And then I asked him, 'Why do you think you wet your bed, Tim?'

"Tim sighed. 'I don't know,' he said. 'All I know is I can't help it. And I really am trying hard.'

" 'I'm sure you are,' I said sincerely. Then I asked if he knew what it meant to inherit something. He said yes. 'Do you know what a bladder is?' I asked. 'Yes,' he said. 'Mom told me. It's the little balloon inside that holds the . . . you know, pee.'

" 'Well, your dad mentioned to me on the phone that he sometimes used to wet his bed. Maybe he had a small bladder as a child, and then when he got bigger, so did his bladder. Maybe it's the same with you.' I then explained that three out of four bed wetters have a parent who had the same problem.

"Tim was amazed to hear about his dad. 'You mean I never told you I used to wet?' Paul asked, looking surprised, too. 'Well, I did!' he said. 'And I was so ashamed of it that I wanted to make sure you wouldn't go through all the misery and isolation that I experienced as a kid.

" 'That's why I've been pushing you so hard to get over it,' Paul went on. 'I felt that my parents never did enough to help me, and as a result, I didn't stop until I was eleven.'

"Tim looked at his father. 'Wow, poor you!' he said. 'I don't want to wait that long to stop wetting!'

" 'Okay, Tim,' I said. 'If we work real hard, I'm sure we can beat your dad.' Tim grinned—and so did his parents. 'But you'll have to do the work,' I added. 'I'll just be your coach.'

"While Tim thought that over, I went over some basic facts with Paul and Emily. I told them that bed-wetting—or nocturnal enuresis, as it's called—is common. Five to seven million children in the United States wet their bed with regularity. I said that 90 percent of them are 'primary' bed wetters (those who, like Tim, have never had a dry period of two months or longer).

"I told the Springers that although various medical and psychological factors can contribute to primary bed-wetting, the two most common causes are a too-small bladder capacity and what we call an 'irritable bladder,' which is one that feels full—and contracts—before actual fullness has been reached.

"Emily looked perplexed. 'Then you're saying this isn't a big *psychological* problem?'

"I said, 'Primary bed-wetting itself doesn't reflect a serious problem. We're only concerned when it impairs a child's psychological and social development.' I explained that since Tim was doing so well in the other areas of his life, we could concentrate on practical matters—teaching Tim how to increase his bladder capacity; to be more aware of signals from a full bladder; and to respond to bladder contractions by using his outer sphincter muscle to withhold urine.

" 'You can *teach* him those things?' Paul said skeptically.

" 'Yes,' I said, 'but the whole process is less like learning to ride a bike than it is like growing taller or gaining weight. Tim would outgrow this on his own someday, but we're giving nature a little push.'

"When I told Tim we'd have to measure his bladder, he looked very nervous until I explained how we'd do it. 'You won't mind this,' I assured him. On Saturday he was to drink a whole can of soda—and not to share even a sip with his brother. 'Then,' I said, 'you mustn't go to the bathroom, not until you're jumping from one foot to the other.'

" 'Then ask your mom for her favorite measuring cup—and use it!' Tim looked at his mother, and they both giggled. 'When you can make eight ounces of pee in the cup,' I went on, 'I'll give you a dollar.'

"The measuring would take place just on Saturdays, but every day after school, Tim was to try to delay urinating as long as possible. 'The point of that,' I explained to Tim, 'is to stretch your bladder to make it bigger. A bigger bladder takes longer to fill . . . even at night.'

" 'Then I'll be dry!' Tim said excitedly.

" 'Yes,' I said. 'But wait. We also have to teach you how to hold it in at night. We do that by making your muscles stronger.' I told Tim, 'Each time you urinate I want you to stop and start the flow ten times.'

"As we made the next appointment I gave Tim two of my special 'Sandman Team' T-shirts: one for him and one for Matthew. 'Tell your brother he can be your helper,' I said. 'That means he's not to let anyone tease you or to tease you himself.'

"Two weeks later Tim reported that he'd made the four-ounce mark on the measuring cup. 'That's a good start,' I said. Then I showed him something new; a small buzzer on a strap, to be attached to his pajama bottoms and used as a wetness alarm. 'See, this is a great toy,' I said, making the buzzer sound. 'And when you're not wetting anymore, you can use it on your bike or skateboard or make it a doorbell so nobody can come into your room without ringing it.'

"I said that Tim should wear the buzzer at night, and if he began to wet, it would go off. 'Then what?' he asked. 'Then,' I said, 'you *stop* urinating, turn off the alarm, and go down the hall to the bathroom. Then you'll change your sheets and pajamas yourself.'

"Tim looked stricken. 'Changing the sheets isn't punishment,' I explained. 'It's not a matter of being mean to you; it's asking you to take responsibility for your own actions.' In addition, I told Emily and Paul that they must not turn off the alarm. Tim was the only person allowed to be in charge of that.

"To help the whole process along, I suggested that the Springers initiate a star system, giving Tim a gold star for each dry night and a silver star for just a small wet spot. A certain number of stars could earn him a present.

"Two weeks later Tim came in beaming. He had earned several silver stars and even a few gold ones. But Paul or Emily had still been waking Tim to take him to the bathroom at eleven o'clock.

"Now I suggested that they do it less often, especially after Tim had a few dry nights in a row. The point, I explained, was to start pulling his parents out of the picture and to put more and more of the responsibility for dryness on Tim.

"At our next session, three weeks later, Tim was enormously pleased: He could now make eight ounces in the measuring cup. With great ceremony, I presented him with the dollar. 'Wow!' he said. It wasn't that he'd never had a dollar before, but this one was really special.

"After nine weeks of treatment, Tim was having longer and longer series of dry nights.

"Then I changed the routine: Now Tim could stop his bladder-stretching exercise and do the stream-interruption exercise just once a day. I also asked him to pick two days a week to sleep without the buzzer. Emily looked startled. 'At this point, even if he does wet, he'll stop very quickly,' I assured her.

"And he did. Tim experienced a milestone the next week: For the first time he got up in the night *on his own* and went to the bathroom.

" 'I've been dry for thirteen whole nights in a row,' Tim said proudly on the next visit—and displayed the new baseball mitt his stars had earned him. I said, 'I don't think you need to use that alarm any longer.' Tim laughed. 'I haven't used it in over a week,' he said happily. 'Just like you said, it's my doorbell now.'

"I told the Springers that Tim was clearly succeeding. I said I wanted to see them once more, in a month. I suggested that in the meantime, if Tim felt very, very tired on any night, he should ask his parents to help him out by waking him once before they go to bed.

"When the Springers returned the following month, Tim was eager to tell me his news: He had been dry with no accidents and had just had a sleep-over at Teddy's house. Then he showed me a picture of his dog wearing his Sandman Team T-shirt. 'I don't really need it anymore,' he told me proudly. I shook his hand and said, 'Tim, I agree with you 100 percent!'

"Tim's bed-wetting had cast a heavy cloud over his life, but thanks to a little of the right kind of 'coaching,' the whole problem turned into a positive experience. Tim not only found relief but also had the joy of knowing that it was neither his parents nor the doctor but he, himself, who had done the real work and deserved all the credit."

SOCIAL ADJUSTMENT

> *Greg, six, is so desperate for acceptance at school that he does anything the other children tell him to do. How can we get him to understand that he'll never make friends unless he shows more spunk?*

Tina's Story

"I was surprised when my 6-year-old, Greg, didn't make friends right off the bat this past fall, when he started first grade," said Tina Nicholson, 36. "He's bright, funny, and friendly, and I would have thought he'd be a real magnet for other kids.

"Two years earlier our neighbors' little girl, Zoe, had made the same switch—from a small private kindergarten to the local public school—but Zoe, who is not as outgoing as Greg, had fit in easily. That made it all the more puzzling when Greg apparently didn't have an easy transition.

" 'Give him time,' my husband, Art, said, not sharing my concern. 'Zoe's a girl! Boys don't start the social stuff so early. I know I didn't.'

"That made sense to me. But when Halloween came and Greg didn't even have one pal from school to go trick-or-treating with, I asked his teacher, Mrs. Carey, 'When *do* the boys start getting to-gether?'

" 'Oh, but they are!' she said. 'In fact, one mom just commented that her son's social life is more exciting than hers.'

373

"I felt awful. Why wasn't Greg being included? Wasn't he everything a six-year-old ought to be—including a good athlete? I asked Mrs. Carey if Greg seemed to be having any problems with the other children.

"Mrs. Carey hesitated. 'Well, nothing really *major,*' she said. 'But he certainly could do with a little more self-confidence.' Mrs. Carey described Greg as timid, jumpy, easily startled. She said he was overcautious and reluctant to speak up or voice an opinion.

" 'Unfortunately the other kids pick up on this insecurity and dump on him,' she went on. 'They let him play the superhero game they all like, but Greg is usually assigned the role of the baby brother—or the dog.

" 'If someone says to him, "You can't build your block house here next to mine. Take it down!" Greg obeys. I'm afraid he's easily chased away, and he doesn't tolerate teasing or being bossed around very well.'

"I was shocked. I told Mrs. Carey that Greg's pre-K and kindergarten teachers had never described him as anything but popular and full of fun.

" 'Oh, I believe you,' Mrs. Carey said. 'But I don't see it. Just yesterday at recess he came running to me—almost crying—just because another child had *roared* at him.'

"I thought, Poor Greg! He'd certainly gotten off on the wrong foot this year. But when I asked Art what he thought we should do to help, he still said, 'Nothing!' Art said, 'I was a shy kid, too, and I'm sure Greg will grow out of this if we just leave him alone for a while.'

"Could it be that simple?

" 'Definitely!' my sisters, who had eight kids between them, assured me. 'All kids go through funny stages.'

"I hoped they were right, but that hope crumbled the following week, when I got a call from Mrs. Carey—quite upset that Greg had been throwing spitballs at some of the girls in his class.

" 'What a rascal!' Art said. 'Not that I approve, mind you, but you have to admit it wasn't exactly a *meek* or *shy* thing to do.'

"But as it turned out, Art was wrong! Greg hadn't thought up that mischief—and never would have done it if several of the other boys hadn't ordered him to do it!

"We told Greg we were disappointed, and he cried.

" 'Okay,' Art said. 'It's over now. But you've got to start to think for yourself. I mean, why let other kids get you into trouble?'

"That talk must have made a strong impression on Greg because there were no more complaints from Mrs. Carey. Then one day Greg came home from school and proudly announced that he was in a club.

" 'That's great,' we told him. But our pleasure—and Greg's— didn't last very long. The so-called club did not even exist and had been nothing more than a ploy to get Greg to cough up his entire treasured collection of toy cars and trucks (the price of his 'joining').

"I was furious. I told Greg he had to get those cars back. But Art said, 'No, he got suckered; maybe he'll finally learn something.'

"My sister, Ann, listened sympathetically. 'Maybe it's just a little self-esteem problem,' she offered. 'I'll bet that if you just stress all his good points and hold off on criticizing Greg, you'll see a big improvement in no time.'

"I followed her suggestions to the letter. But in spite of all my compliments, Greg came home one afternoon looking really down and said he hated the green-and-blue-striped shirt he was wearing.

"I said, 'How come? You liked it when we bought it.'

" 'The other kids all said that it's really babyish,' he complained.

" 'It is not,' I argued. 'In fact, it's just like one of Dad's.'

"Greg shook his head. 'It doesn't have writing or pictures on it,' he said. 'I don't want them to call me a baby anymore. So won't you take me to the mall to get some new stuff, Mom—please?'

"It went against my grain to be so conformist, but I thought, If new clothes give Greg the confidence he needs, it's worth it.

" 'Mom, I look cool,' he said the next day. I watched him as he happily and proudly swaggered off to school in his new *Ghostbusters* sweatshirt and a *Batman* hat.

"But that afternoon he came home without his hat.

"No, he hadn't lost it: He'd given it away when a kid named Tyler said, 'I'll be your best friend if you let me have that hat.'

"I couldn't *believe* it. When Art came home, he said, 'Greg, I thought you learned from the club fiasco: You can't *buy* friendship, and you only hurt yourself trying. If you keep on giving your stuff away, the other kids will just keep on taking advantage of you.'

" 'I know,' Greg retorted, defensive and miserable. 'Even a baby knows that.'

" 'Hey, I'm sorry.' Art put his arm around him. 'I didn't mean to hurt your feelings. It's just that we love you and think you're great, and we wish you'd get it through your head that you don't have to give up your cars and your clothes and your own good sense just to try to make people like you.'

"Greg cried a little and then hugged us both. I thought, Maybe now he's finally gotten the message and things will start to change.

"And then, like a good omen, Greg received an invitation to Robbie Voight's birthday party. Granted, the entire class was invited, but at least it was a party—and an important 'first' for Greg.

"I dropped him off, present in hand, at the pizza place, and said, 'Have a super time!' But instead of finding a happy, smiling Greg when I went to pick him up, I found him sitting by himself, looking miserable.

" 'I'm sorry!' Mrs. Voight said, rushing over to hand me a party bag. 'Poor Greg hasn't had a very good time. When I was getting the sodas, the other children told him to put a lot of garlic and hot peppers on his pizza and then talked him into eating it. They really shouldn't have pulled that with a kid like Greg.'

"So even the other mothers were aware that Greg would do anything the kids told him to! I felt sad for Greg—and frightened. It's not just that he lacks friends *now*, which is bad enough. But I think about his adolescence and wonder what trouble he'll get into then if he can't even 'just say no' at the age of six!

"I've decided to call the guidance counselor at school on Monday. I don't think that this problem is unimportant or that it is about to go away by itself."

The Counselor Replies

Psychologist Robert L. Selman, Ph.D., is professor of psychiatry and education at Harvard University. Selman is a coauthor of Making a Friend in Youth: Developmental Theory and Pair Therapy *(University of Chicago Press).*

"The Nicholsons couldn't figure out why Greg had changed so much or why he was so submissive and ingratiating with the other children in his class. They feared that Mrs. Gleason, the school guidance counselor, would find that Greg had a serious personality problem—perhaps one they themselves had caused.

"But Mrs. Gleason was reassuring. 'You're a good family, and Greg's a fine boy; he's just extremely shy,' she said. And with that she suggested that the Nicholsons get in touch with me concerning the Pair Therapy Project, which involved a special technique I developed ten years ago for children who were experiencing interpersonal difficulties.

" 'I don't know,' Art said when he and Tina first came to see me at my office at Harvard. 'I'm not really convinced that Greg needs psychotherapy. I think this is a stage that he will grow out of.'

"I told him that the Harvard project had more to do with learning new patterns of interacting with others than with undergoing therapy in the conventional sense. I said, 'The fact that Greg did fine in the calm, contained environment of his preschool, only to experience a kind of social paralysis in the much noisier and less nurturing hubbub of elementary school suggests to me that Greg is overwhelmed now for a different reason.'

"I said to the Nicholsons, 'I understand that Greg is easily startled, especially by loud noises. It sounds to me as though Greg is one of those children who is unusually sensitive and who becomes easily overloaded by too much external stimuli.'

"Tina looked startled, but I quickly explained that this is not unusual and that in fact, according to recent research, some 10 to 15 percent of the kids of this country behave similarly. The problem is that, as a result, these children 'freeze' and fail to develop appropriate social skills for their age group.

" 'Clearly Greg wants to establish friendships,' I said, 'but he doesn't know how to negotiate, which is why it often appears as though he has no will of his own.'

" 'It sounds pretty bad—and pretty permanent,' Art said unhappily. But I told him it was neither.

" 'Even though the problem may be temperamental or biological, it doesn't mean that he can't be treated and helped psychologically,' I said. 'Nor do we characterize this kind of problem as pathology;

rather, we regard it as a behavioral skill that needs to be developed. We take the approach that in order to learn social interaction, a child who hasn't yet learned it needs to practice, and the best environment we know of in which to accomplish that is a one-on-one situation.

" 'When Greg enters the project, I will work closely with him. I will be pairing him with a child of the opposite type, not a mean kid, but one who tends to be domineering.

" 'I will be sure to maintain a secure environment,' I assured the Nicholsons. 'The goal will be to move the children into some kind of balance and to help both of them replace their immature social strategies with more effective ones.

" 'We'll focus on cooperation,' I said. 'Greg will see what it's like to have more control, and the other child will learn how it feels to relax and let go a little.'

"Tina asked me how long the therapy would probably take. 'We'll meet regularly once a week for ten weeks, and if they like it—which most of the children do—we can keep going,' I said. 'The idea is not for these two children to become friends, though they might. Rather, the point is for the two of them to have fun together, and when a problem comes up, I will help both boys learn how to work it out appropriately.'

"The Nicholsons were eager to have Greg in the project. And so, three weeks later, I began to meet on a regular basis with Greg and his opposite type, a real eager beaver of a six-year-old named Darrell.

"In the first session I brought four choices of things to do: checkers, a selection of arts and crafts materials, plastic blocks, and some fantasy figures. I told the boys that there was only one rule in these play sessions, and that was that they had to agree on one activity and stay with it for the whole period.

" 'Blocks!' Darrell shouted, and, predictably, Greg didn't argue. The pattern of dominance was established, and I let it stay that way for the first two sessions.

"Then the third week I asked them, 'Are you two guys having any problems today?'

"They both said no. 'Oh,' I said. 'I notice Darrell's doing the activity choosing again. Greg, is that a problem for you?'

378

" 'No,' Greg said. 'I mean . . . well.' He looked at the floor. 'I don't like it when Darrell grabs or that he always gets to choose!'

"I asked, 'What can you guys do?'

" 'It's *his* fault,' Darrell said defensively. 'He never says anything or sticks up for himself!'

"I asked Greg, 'Why don't you?'

"Greg shrugged and kept his eyes on the floor. 'He wouldn't be my friend,' he said in a voice that was barely audible.

" 'Oh,' I said. 'You know, Greg, sometimes friends disagree. But just because you fight with someone doesn't mean you're not friends.' Both boys got that message immediately, and I could almost *see* it register, especially with Greg.

"Sure enough, in the next few sessions I saw real changes in both children: Darrell did much less impulsive grabbing and more verbalizing, though he still tended to order Greg around, as in 'Put your enemy guy there. No, not there, *there!*'

"Greg, meanwhile, was beginning to express his own needs and feelings. And little by little the two boys were able to share many decisions in their play.

"During the play sessions I continually mediated. For example, I'd comment, 'You said all that awfully fast, Darrell. Greg, is there something *you* want to say?'

"There was a happy breakthrough for both of the boys when Greg came up with the first of many ideas that Darrell really liked. 'Hey, that's totally awesome,' Darrell said, clearly impressed.

"Shortly after that session, the two boys began to crack jokes together, a significant and new shared experience for both of them.

"When the initial ten weeks were over, Darrell and Greg both wanted to continue through the summer and into the start of second grade. I was delighted that we would have the extra time, as these two boys with contrasting problems were clearly learning from each other and becoming more flexible.

"By this past October the picture had changed considerably, and the two boys felt comfortable about leaving the project. With his improved social skills, Greg was able to make friends with Hiro, a new boy at school who had just arrived from Japan.

"The Nicholsons talked so happily about the 'transformation' in their son that I had to remind them Greg had not turned into a different child, that he still was and always would be a cautious person who would probably prefer to be in small groups and quiet settings.

" 'What's important for Greg,' I said, 'is not that he has a million friends but that he's able to express himself better and to really connect with others.'

"Like Greg, many children reach school age without the social savvy we expect them to have. But thanks to the right kind of help, Greg is finding that he can do well in a social situation and even shine."

> *Our daughter, Betsy, complains that nobody likes her, but she's the one who's pushy, selfish, and annoying! Shouldn't a bright second grader know how other children want to be treated?*

Audrey's Story

"I had hoped that this year Betsy would stop being so defensive and start making friends," said Audrey Madden, 31. "But it hasn't happened. In fact, she's just as isolated as before, with no play dates and no valentines in her little paper mailbox, except for the one from her teacher.

"Betsy's always been a little on the spoiled, pushy side; I guess you could call it the only child syndrome. But that irritable and abrasive manner got worse—much worse—last year when she had so much trouble learning to read.

"Tutoring has helped; she's able to read now, though it's still slow and halting; but she evidently must still be feeling like a failure, because she acts like such a horrible prickly pear.

"As a result, she comes home from school and hangs all over me, wanting me to play with her because she has nobody else. I try to be giving, but it's never quite enough. And she pesters me incredibly until I finally lose my temper and *make* her go outside and find some kids to play with.

"Then she grudgingly goes out, but she doesn't play; she just gets into shouting matches with the other children on the block. Then she comes home, insisting that they're all just dumb nerds and troublemakers.

"This is what was happening—and why it seemed so perfect when the school's weekly bulletin announced that the Brownie Girl Scout leader was moving and a replacement was needed. Without hesitation, I called and volunteered myself. I remembered scouting from my own childhood, and I couldn't think of a better way for Betsy to 'find herself' in a social sense and to have some fun.

" 'Well, I hope it works,' my husband, Ian, said, patting my hand. Ian's a very friendly, gregarious person, and I know he's disappointed that Betsy isn't.

"Two weeks later, I was trained, uniformed, and ready to go. The six girls who showed up for the meeting seemed eager and excited as I told them about the trips and projects and fun I had planned for the troop. Betsy didn't say much, but she looked flushed and happy when we all joined hands to sing the good old Brownie Smile Song.

" 'I'm so glad you're the leader,' Betsy said on the way home, and I felt wonderful. At the next meeting, we were having a discussion on pet care when Betsy told a long and disjointed version of the time our big sheepdog got 'skunked' and we had to bathe him in tomato juice. Everyone laughed. Betsy beamed. But instead of giving someone else a chance, she sailed right into an even longer story—about the time our neighbor's cat had diarrhea.

" 'She just doesn't seem to know when to stop,' I told Ian that evening. 'Oh, she'll get the message sometime soon from the others,' he said. 'Kids always do.'

"I hoped so, but as the weeks went on, I wasn't sure. Betsy was loud and bossy. She seemed to feel that I was the queen of the troop . . . and that she was the princess. She interrupted, bragged, and hogged center stage—paying no attention to how restless and squirmy the other girls would get.

"Sometimes Betsy would blurt out really inappropriate remarks, like, 'Jill picks her nose and eats it,' or 'Tara's mom has little hairs growing on her chin.' Sometimes I didn't have the heart to do anything but lie and say, 'Oh, everything was fine,' when Ian asked me how the meeting had gone.

"I kept hoping that Betsy would finally feel secure enough to settle down, but she only got wilder. When we were working on our dance exercises (for one of the Brownie merit badges), Betsy kept shouting 'Oops!' and bumping into Michelle and Tara. Betsy seemed to think it was hilarious, but everyone else was seething! 'Why did you get so mad at me?' Betsy complained to me afterward.

"Even her style of showing affection to the other girls was bad. She was clingy with Celia and played—endlessly and annoyingly— what she called 'crinkle, crinkle' with Celia's Afro hairdo. Celia would try to get away, but Betsy always followed.

"In an equally annoying way, Betsy would grab Jill, the smallest girl in the troop, and lift her off the floor. 'Stop!' Jill would cry, but Betsy—pretending that Jill was her baby—kept it up . . . and kept me yelling, 'Cut it out or I'll punish you.'

"I'd made Betsy apologize, but it didn't make everything all right. I found myself feeling drained—and resentful. I'd longed to be a warm, loving mother, but Betsy was turning me into a full-time screamer. During the drive home after meetings, she'd angrily accuse me of picking on her all the time 'for no reason.'

"I'd say, 'You *know* all the things you did, and you'd better improve a lot by next week—or else!' Betsy would settle into sullen silence and sulk for the rest of the week. At home, she'd be more argumentative and demanding than ever.

" 'Mrs. Madden, when can we do something that's *fun?*' Michelle asked at one meeting, and I felt awful. It was true! In the past couple of months, I'd had to spend so much time dealing with Betsy that we hadn't done half the fun projects I'd planned—from writing and performing our own puppet show to making a large felt banner for the Memorial Day parade.

"In fact, I was surprised that one of our plans was actually coming to fruition: a party for some residents of a nearby nursing home. We'd learned two songs and a folk dance and we'd make punch and cookies.

" 'Look at how sweet and pretty they are!' and 'Aren't they *nice!*' the old people murmured on the day of the party. 'My mom's the leader, so I get to help!' Betsy cried, grabbing for the punch bowl that Tara and Jill were carrying in.

" 'Quit it!' Jill protested. Betsy pushed her—and when Jill pushed back, my glass punch bowl was smashed on the floor.

" 'It wasn't my fault, she's too shrimpy,' Betsy kept saying as I grimly moved the girls aside so I could clean up the mess.

"The performance was stiff and joyless. Betsy loudly whispered, 'You goofed,' when Celia, who was playing the piano, hit a wrong note. Afterward we served the cookies—and paper cups of water. We were thanked—politely—but nobody seemed sad to see us go.

"That night, I got two phone calls. Celia and both the Hayden twins, Michelle and Jill, were dropping out of the troop. Celia's mom mentioned a schedule conflict. But Geraldine Hayden told the truth: 'The girls just say it's not fun anymore.' 'Well, okay,' I told them. The school year and the Brownie troop were almost over anyway, to my relief.

"I hung up the phone, feeling embarrassed and angry. I'd taken on this project for *Betsy*—to help her feel accepted—but it hadn't worked. Betsy's reaction was typically defensive. 'Who cares?' she said. 'None of those creepoids liked me anyway.' But she's the one who's behaved so obnoxiously. Why won't she see how her behavior affects others?"

The Counselor Replies

Betty B. Osman, Ph.D., is a psychologist and faculty member in the graduate program at Sarah Lawrence College, in Bronxville, New York, and a psychologist for the Child and Adolescent Services in the Department of Psychiatry at White Plains Hospital Medical Center in New York. Osman is the author of No One to Play With: The Social Side of Learning Disabilities *and* Learning Disabilities: A Family Affair *(Warner Books).*

"The Maddens were clearly distressed as they told me how difficult, contrary, and selfish Betsy was, and how she seemed not to care about anyone else's feelings. 'It's almost as if she doesn't know any better,' Audrey sadly observed.

" 'Perhaps she doesn't,' I replied. 'It's not uncommon for children with learning disabilities to miss important signals. Betsy may not see what she's doing because she can't really see how her behavior strikes others ... until someone yells at her, and then she feels picked on. Just as Betsy has had trouble decoding the print on a page, she may also have trouble "reading" cues like body language, gestures and facial expressions.'

" 'I can't believe that,' Ian said, frowning.

" 'Well, look,' I went on, 'you've told me Betsy tends to talk too long or too loud, that she indulges in too much unwelcome touching and casually says things that are inappropriate and embarrassing to others. Most children learn to stop doing those things by the time they're seven or eight. But the fact that Betsy hasn't may suggest that she is unable to "read" the cues and signals most of us learn automatically . . . like a flicker of annoyance, a gesture of boredom—or a drawing back when feelings have been hurt.'

" 'Are you saying that all kids with learning disabilities have social adjustment problems?' Audrey asked. 'No,' I said, 'not at all. Just that *some* children's perceptual problems *do* extend beyond the classroom—with negative consequences. And the need for remedial help in this area often goes unrecognized, though it is just as important.'

"I said, 'Betsy sounds like a girl who wants very badly to be liked, but she tries too hard and in all the wrong ways, like bragging to impress, clinging to people she likes, or grabbing them. What's more, Betsy can't tell that her so-called jokes—like purposely bumping into people—are annoying. So she repeats them. And when she's rejected by the others or punished by you, she feels picked on and then wants to retaliate.'

"Ian looked discouraged. 'This is not the kind of child I expected,' he said. 'And really, I don't know what you mean about remedial help. Do you mean that you could *tutor* our daughter in decent behavior?'

" 'Yes, in a way,' I told him. 'Betsy can be taught a lot about how people feel and what they like and don't like. There are strategies we can use, and if we work together, we can certainly make some inroads.'

"The Maddens agreed, and I began to see Betsy once a week. Right from the start, it was clear that she enjoyed our sessions and having a 'friend' who would listen to her and not be critical. Mostly she talked about how everyone bothered her: friends were mean, and her parents picked on her.

"Little by little, we got into talking about people who are likable and what qualities make them likable, like how they listen without interrupting and try not to say things that might sound mean or embarrassing. Betsy said, 'I'd like to be that way.' I told her that I was sure she could learn to be, but in order to do so, we would need to do a lot of thinking and talking about how people feel and about why some behaviors are acceptable and some not.

"In addition to talking, Betsy and I would role-play many typical situations, both at school and at home, flaring up at each other and then trying alternative solutions, like trying to be more patient and cooperative or, for another example, telling someone, 'Your hair is pretty,' in words instead of fondling it when the person might not want you to touch her.

"I considered it a major triumph for Betsy when, two months after we'd begun working, she said, 'Do you mean just because Jill's small, she still might not like being picked up and hugged?'

"This was something she had never considered, and it was important because social deficits can occur on three levels: the first is not knowing how to act, the second is knowing but having needs that get in the way of self-control, and the third is knowing how to act *and* being able to control the undesirable impulses but just not knowing how your behavior comes across to others. The fact that Betsy was now so much more aware *and* in control of herself and now, for the first time, able to see another point of view, was truly heartening!

"I was also seeing Ian and Audrey on a regular but less frequent basis, so that they could be part of the important teamwork for Betsy. I suggested, for example, that they try not to reprimand Betsy very harshly—or even give her dirty looks—when they didn't like the way she was acting. 'That only reinforces what you don't like,' I said. By ignoring some of Betsy's superficial behaviors, her parents could give her an opportunity to internalize her newfound empathies, rather than always relying on parental signals.

"I also urged them not *always* to assume that every conflict was Betsy's fault; even when they *were* sure she was in the wrong, I said, it would be best to deal with her behavior privately.

"In addition, I suggested that the Maddens try to anticipate a problem *before* getting angry, that they try, for instance, not to say,

'Be good or else,' before Grandma arrives for a visit but to mention how much she likes pleases and thank-yous.

" 'What about all her mouthing off?' Audrey asked. 'Betsy can be so fresh, and even when I try not to get angry, I can't help it.' I told Audrey that I understood how trying it must be, but instead of letting herself get drawn in, I suggested that she try saying, 'Betsy, I know this is the only way you think you can tell me how angry you are, but maybe you could try a different way, and then I'll feel more like listening.'

"Within six months of starting treatment, there were many positive changes. As Betsy, who was now a third grader, began to apply her new insights to real-life situations more frequently, she felt very good: she was handling things better and she knew it.

"Audrey and Ian found her less argumentative at home, and less sullen. 'I don't hear her complaining all the time, and it's a joy!' Audrey reported.

"Betsy and I also spent time on bolstering her passing, but still less than dazzling, reading skills. As a result, Betsy moved into a higher reading group at school, adding further to her sense of self-worth.

" 'I think that for the first time in years I'm starting to see Betsy's positive aspects,' Ian admitted, 'like her boundless energy and enthusiasm, and a sweetness in her that I'd almost forgotten about.'

" 'I think we were both too angry and disappointed to see her as anything but a big problem with a kid attached,' Audrey agreed. 'But she does have strengths, including a good sense of humor, which is charming when it isn't at someone's expense.'

"In the eighth and final month of treatment, Betsy told me that she'd started to play games at recess; she had also given out *and* received a few valentine cards this year. And now, for the first time since kindergarten, she had been invited to a birthday party. 'That is really great,' I told her warmly and sincerely. And instead of saying, 'Naturally, *I'm* great,' Betsy smiled and said thank you.

"It's natural and human to react with annoyance, punishment, and even strong dislike when a child is always bothering others. But everyone felt better once the Maddens could see Betsy's lack of 'people sense' *not* as something to blame her for, but as something she needed them to help her overcome."

Kenny, seven, refuses to behave, and nothing, from reasoning to punishment, has any effect. Why would a boy with two loving parents act so defiantly? And what will it take to get him to change?

Nancy's Story

"I can't think of a time when Kenny wasn't a handful," said Nancy McLaren, 33. "Even as a toddler, if things weren't going exactly right, he was a holy terror!

"We didn't send him to preschool until he was four; we thought the extra time at home would help him settle down. When he did finally go, his teacher constantly complained that he was bossy and disruptive.

" 'Is that so unusual at four?' my husband, Jim, wondered.

" 'No,' the teacher replied. 'But Kenny does it much more than any of the others.' Naturally, I hoped he'd outgrow his aggressive *me-me-me* behavior. I tried to set limits at home, but Kenny only became more obstinate, ignoring what we asked him to do, and gleefully doing almost everything we begged him not to do.

"I tried to enforce the rules by sending him to his room when he wouldn't behave or taking away privileges, but the next day (or the next minute) he'd do something worse, and I'd end up yelling at him or spanking him. Then I felt terrible.

"One Saturday after a movie, Kenny and I were at the store. He'd just had candy at the movie, but he wanted more. I said no, but he kept on pleading. Then I found him crouched in another aisle, opening a box of chocolate-covered peanuts he'd taken. When I took it away, he started calling me names!

"I looked around the store, saw mothers with nice, well-behaved kids, and wondered enviously why being a parent seemed so easy for them and not for me.

"Jim has always been more patient than I. He says too much conflict isn't good, and he tries to defuse it. Once when Kenny had drawn all over some important papers on my desk, Jim said to him, 'That wasn't helpful. Will you promise to cooperate more in the future?'

"Kenny said yes, but he didn't improve at all. In fact, we can't even eat a civilized meal: He complains about the food, kicks his chair, uses his hands instead of a fork, and constantly interrupts when we speak.

"I used to wonder how he'd make it in the world without manners and respect for others. But my friend, Sarah, who has older kids, assured me that they only act this way with parents; that they somehow know what's expected on the outside.

"It was a reassuring thought, but it hasn't worked out that way with Kenny. We've already had several bad notes from his teacher: He's rough and starts fights, he scrawls four-letter words on the ground in the school yard, and he's constantly rude to his teacher, Mrs. Christoff.

"Jim said, 'I'll talk to him.' In the car on the way home from getting an Australia poster for Kenny's social studies project, Jim said, 'Ken, shape up. You're *too* big to be so naughty at school.'

" 'I'm *not* naughty!' Kenny protested. 'Mrs. Christoff *likes* to get me in trouble.' 'Then you need to be extra good. Right, Ken?' Jim said.

" 'Yup!' Kenny said; giggling, he reached forward, grabbed Jim's fishing hat off his head, and tossed it out the window. The traffic was heavy, and in a second, the hat was gone.

" 'You little monster!' said Jim, the soul of patience. He then pulled over and gave Kenny a spanking. Kenny cried.

" 'I'm sure not proud of myself,' Jim admitted that night. I felt bad, too. But the next day, Kenny was obedient, quiet—almost meek. And he worked hard on his project, a sheep ranch scene in a shoe box. It was a relief not having to spend the day saying, 'Stop it right now!'

"Maybe that explosion from a dad who 'never' loses his temper showed Kenny there were some limits. The next morning I drove Kenny to school. 'Hope your project is a hit,' I called as he went inside the building.

"That afternoon, I got a call from Mrs. Christoff. 'Kenny was out of control today,' she said. He couldn't stand waiting his turn, and as each child showed his project, Kenny was calling out, 'Hurry it up!'

"When Kenny cried, *'Bor-ing!'* in the middle of Marissa's presentation on India, Mrs. Christoff asked him to leave the room. Marissa snickered, at which point Kenny grabbed her Taj Mahal and smashed it before Mrs. Christoff could pull him away.

"I was shocked. Something *is* different about Kenny, and if he's to have any future—outside of jail—then we'd better make sure he gets professional help as soon as possible."

The Counselor Replies

Ronald J. Prinz, Ph.D., a child clinical psychologist and professor of psychology at the University of South Carolina, in Columbia, conducts research on treatments of childhood aggression in collaboration with Gloria E. Miller, Ph.D.

"The McLarens were in a lot of pain. 'But as bad as Kenny is,' Jim concluded, 'he's still lovable. When it's just him and me, he still tries to break the rules, but if I keep him in line and don't make a lot of demands on him, he's fine.'

"Nancy nodded. 'He can be a terrific kid,' she agreed. 'It's just that he's always *so intense* and unpredictable.'

"Nancy had tried disciplining Kenny by taking away privileges; but when he continued to defy her, she resorted to screaming and spanking.

"Jim had overlooked and excused a lot of Kenny's antics, but once or twice a year he got so fed up he snapped and spanked him—

after which Kenny was good for a couple of days and then went back to his old behavior. 'There must be a better way,' Nancy said.

" 'I think there is,' I agreed. 'I'd like to see Kenny, and then we'll talk about it.'

"When Kenny came in a few days later, I asked him why his parents had brought him to see me. 'Because I got in trouble at school,' he said. I asked him about it. 'Mrs. Christoff and those jerks at school don't like me, and I can't let them get away with it,' he explained vehemently.

" 'Get away with *what?*'

" 'They blame me for *everything.*'

" 'Do you want to change that?'

" 'Yes!' Kenny said.

" 'What about home?' I asked.

" 'I get in trouble there, too,' he said. 'My mom's always mad at me.'

"I said, 'You've taken a first step, Kenny. Admitting there's a problem is the way to start solving it.'

"I contacted Kenny's teacher, Mrs. Christoff, who described Kenny as the most difficult child she'd taught in years: angry, impulsive, unable to keep his hands to himself.

"I asked her to tell me some good things. 'He's bright and artistic, and he can be really sweet,' she said. But he often balked at finishing his work and wasted time arguing. Sometimes she would send him to the principal's office when he misbehaved; more often, she sent notes home so that his parents could deal with him.

"When I met with Jim and Nancy again and suggested treatment, Nancy said, 'We've really failed him.'

" 'It's normal to feel guilty when your child isn't functioning well,' I replied. 'But really it isn't useful. You're all caught up in a negative situation. Starting now, you're going to be part of the cure. I'm going to teach you to be effective with your child.'

"The McLarens looked bemused. I said, 'Think of it this way: When a child has a reading problem, we analyze it and devise an educational strategy to deal with it. But when a child engages in antisocial behavior, we tend to judge—when we *should* simply say that he hasn't learned appropriate social skills.'

" 'So we're going to teach Kenny new skills and help him get rid of his old behavior. We'll teach Kenny how to get along with other people.'

"But why didn't Kenny just learn this on his own, the way most children do?' Nancy wondered.

"I said, 'From all you tell me, you tried to teach him, but Kenny was intense and fussy and didn't catch on. You both tried strategies that didn't work—while Kenny kept on getting older.'

" 'Now,' I told them, 'you'll be giving Kenny an accelerated course in human behavior for several months. You'll have to be very persistent.' I explained that I would ask them to do exercises with Kenny and report back to me, and then we would analyze the results together.

"To begin, I urged Jim and Nancy to think and talk about Kenny's behavior in less emotional, more specific language. By pinpointing what Kenny actually *did* (and how often, for how long, and under what circumstances), they could see to what extent Kenny ignored them.

"I also asked them to note positive behavior, such as asking nicely for something, accepting adult authority, and accepting limits. I stressed that spanking doesn't solve anything and usually does more harm than good.

"Next, I taught the McLarens how to break the cycle of negative interaction. They could praise Kenny, describe to him in neutral terms what he was doing, or else ignore it. What they *couldn't* do was punish or criticize him.

"I said, 'This is just an exercise to help you enjoy Kenny when he isn't being reprimanded and to show you the connection between *your* actions and Kenny's responses.'

" 'Hold it,' Jim said. 'I thought you said this wasn't our fault.'

"I said, 'What's happened with Kenny has brought you *all* to a point where the negative dominates, and I'm trying to help you to break that cycle—to show you that you have more power than you thought.'

"I said, 'Kenny controls the environment now; the key to changing his behavior will be changing as much of that environment as you are able.'

"I emphasized the importance of ignoring all harmless but annoying behavior. One thing that feeds those behaviors is attention, which becomes a payoff. When a child gets attention from one adult, he'll try the same behavior with another.'

"After practicing a few times in my lab-playroom with a one-way mirror so that I could observe, coach, and make suggestions, the McLarens set aside time for practicing positive interaction at home every evening.

"Nancy began to see how Kenny goaded her into an angry response and how easily she allowed herself to be baited. She also discovered how much Kenny liked praise. She said, 'Somehow before it just got lost in the shuffle.'

"I said, 'Praise is a good way to show love.' I urged them to praise specific behaviors so that Kenny would know exactly what the praise was for, not to mix praise and criticism, which is confusing.

"I asked the McLarens to keep track of how often they criticized Kenny—without letting him know they *were* keeping track, and without trying to change his behavior. To their surprise, they found that they were correcting Kenny five times for every one time they praised him.

"The McLarens were distressed, but I pointed out, 'Criticizing doesn't make you bad parents. It shows that you're trying to teach Kenny. But commenting on what you *don't* like and ignoring what you do shows Kenny that he can get more attention for bad behavior than for good.'

"I urged the McLarens not to feel bad, just to see this as useful information. I said, 'For each time you criticize Kenny, find four other opportunities to tell him things you're pleased with.'

"Within a week, they began to notice changes. Kenny was still provocative, but working *not* to correct him helped Jim and Nancy feel better about themselves. And dinnertime was definitely more peaceful.

"Now we were ready to work on a new goal: getting Kenny to comply with a request. After a few weeks, I said, 'You must not make a request unless you plan to *require* him to carry it out: no begging, lecturing, or backing off. Make sure it's a reasonable request, one that Kenny understands and can do.'

"The plan was to praise Kenny for complying; but if he refused, he would have to take a time-out for four minutes. The same request would then be given again, and the time-out calmly repeated, until he complied.

"When we first practiced in the lab, it didn't go very well. Nancy became angry, and Jim was apologetic. I helped them see what they were doing, and they tried some role-playing without Kenny. Soon, Nancy learned not to react emotionally and began to change her thinking from 'I must be a bad mother' to 'He's not doing what he's supposed to because he hasn't mastered it yet.'

"Jim was learning to stop feeling guilty and to recognize that if Kenny didn't learn how to behave, he would be subject to rejection by others.

"Kenny's noncompliance got worse before it got better. I agreed that punishment, such as time-out, could be used appropriately— not as a vent for anger but rather as a teaching tool, and never without also rewarding the opposite behavior.

"Jim and Nancy helped each other avoid the old pitfalls of getting angry or caving in. Also, each time Kenny did what they asked, they would hug and praise him, gradually altering his desire to thwart them.

"Over their six-month course of treatment, I also helped the McLarens to become better listeners and to make Kenny more comfortable about expressing his feelings rather than acting them out.

"I told the McLarens to set up a report card for Kenny's social behavior that his teacher would send home each day. If Kenny did something good, he got a star—and his parents would praise and reward him. It was impossible to get a bad mark; only good marks were issued.

"For the first time, Kenny's parents felt that they had a positive means of spurring him on. He was even getting better grades, since he wasn't wasting so much energy defying the teacher and disrupting the class.

" 'His mouth still gets him in trouble,' Mrs. Christoff noted, 'and he still has a temper. But it's more typical behavior, and we accept him better.'

"The McLarens had been feeling helpless with Kenny. But their importance to their son was much greater than they realized. In the end, it was *their* caring and hard work that brought about the real changes, both in Kenny and in their family life."

SUBSTANCE ABUSE

Peter, fourteen, has changed from a good kid into a moody, defiant stranger. Is this what usually happens in adolescence, or do we have something else to worry about?

Alicia's Story

"The thought of Peter being anything but successful was hard to imagine," said Alicia Kagan, 34. "He had been such a leader in junior high: good in sports, head of the science club, and chairman of the food drive. Yet now that he was starting high school, he worried that he might not fit in or find friends.

"Then his long legs got him on the varsity track team, and we knew he'd be fine. 'Most freshmen would give their right arm to be on a varsity team,' my husband, Tom, said happily.

"But soon after the team's daily practices began, I started to wonder if the schedule was taking a toll on Peter. He seemed so tired and thin.

" 'It's demanding,' Tom agreed, putting an arm around Peter. 'But he can take it.' Tom didn't even feel it was a problem when Peter went to a team party and came home smelling like a brewery.

" 'All kids try drinking to be big shots,' Tom said. 'But aren't you glad he did it with his teammates and not with those long-haired jerks at the mall with their wine coolers?'

"Tom had a point, but why did Peter have to drink at all? My sister, Amy, had gone to drinking parties in high school, and later she developed a problem with Valium. The last thing I wanted was for Peter to get off on the wrong foot, but Tom just laughed and said, 'Don't compare Peter with a kook like *her!*'

"But was I overreacting? How would we know? Peter no longer brought his friends around. This year he was suddenly just gone. And when he was home, he seemed withdrawn.

" 'Not from me!' Tom insisted. 'Peter and I are always horsing around!' But was that true—or wishful thinking? One evening Peter was almost an hour late for dinner, so we started without him. 'Nice of you to join us,' Tom joked, holding up a chicken leg in a mock salute.

"Peter threw his books down and said something very rude.

" 'Peter!' Tom thundered, standing up. 'I demand an apology!' But Peter just swept some papers off a hall table and stomped out of the house.

"I said, 'You shouldn't have provoked him. . . .'

" 'It was a joke,' Tom said. 'Can't he even take a joke?' Moments later Peter was back. 'I'm sorry,' he said 'Can we just forget it?'

"Laughing with relief, I said, 'Yes!' And Tom said sheepishly, 'I guess he gets his temper from me.'

"One week later, while cleaning Peter's room, I found several failed quizzes in his trash basket. When he got home from school, I said, 'What's going on here?'

" 'You were snooping!' he said angrily. He claimed that the tests were only practice and didn't count. That didn't sound right, but I had to give him the benefit of the doubt. I think it's wrong to say to a child, 'I don't believe you.'

"But then, two weeks after I had confronted Peter about the quizzes, we learned that he *was* failing science—his best subject. 'Mrs. Horner's a jerk, and she hates me,' Peter said. 'Can't I drop the course?' I thought maybe he should. But Tom said, 'No way!' and told Peter, 'A kid of your caliber should be getting straight A's!'

"Peter wouldn't listen and barricaded himself in his room with his stereo way up. 'Okay!' Tom yelled through the door. 'But you just lost next week's allowance, and it's going to get worse if you don't buckle down in school.'

"Then in November Peter got an incomplete on a history report, and Tom grounded him. I thought that was harsh, and I hated always having to be the enforcer. One day Peter looked really miserable, and he said, 'Mom, I never get to see my friends.'

"So I let him go out, but I told him to be sure to get home before his father. When Tom asked me if Peter had studied, I said yes—and blushed. I felt guilty going behind Tom's back, but all I wanted was for Tom to stop yelling at Peter, and for Peter to cheer up and trust us again.

"On a morning talk show I heard someone say, 'Fourteen is the worst age, but, thank God, we all get through it.' I tried to feel encouraged, but I felt things were still going downhill. Tom and Peter were fighting over absolutely everything.

"But the worst came one evening, when Tom confronted Peter. 'Did you take some money from my desk?' he demanded. I intervened angrily and said, 'Tom, you know he wouldn't! You must have spent it yourself or misplaced it. It happens to me all the time.'

"Tom backed off and said, 'Maybe,' and apologized to Peter. But I couldn't forget the look of shock on Peter's face when Tom accused him.

"The next day I bought the new U2 tape and left it on Peter's bed. I had to let him know that one of his parents loved and trusted him 100 percent, no matter how sullen he could be and no matter what grades he got or how long his hair was.

"I was even starting to think, and not for the first time, that maybe we should go for counseling. If this was such a difficult, perplexing time for all of us, it had to be even worse for Peter, who was going through all the adolescent changes.

"But then Peter, who had just found the tape, said 'Thanks, Mom!' and gave me a big hug—the first I'd had from him in weeks. I felt that maybe we were finally seeing the light at the end of the tunnel.

"That incident was a week before my sister, Amy arrived for a visit. We hadn't seen her in a long time. Amy is my favorite sister and Peter's favorite aunt, but Tom was still quite judgmental about her addiction problems even though she had been off drugs for years.

"But dinner went well, and afterward Peter and Amy went out for a walk. 'Why does he talk to her and not us?' Tom grumbled.

"I said, 'Well, I'm glad that he's at least talking to *someone!*'

"When they came back, around ten o'clock, Amy said, 'You need to know what's going on with your son.'

"Tom responded, 'What in God's name are you talking about, Amy?'

"'I want Peter to tell you,' Amy said. Peter looked at her with pure hatred. Then, in a joking tone, he said, '*She* thinks I'm a drug addict.'

"'*What?*' Tom said.

"'Yes,' Amy said calmly. 'Peter told me that he's been smoking pot since the first week of school, and now he's using cocaine. Haven't you noticed your money missing? Tell them, Peter—how your Mom bought you a tape, but you still took money from her wallet that same night.'

"'And haven't you noticed his temper?' Amy went on. 'Your son was high that night he cursed you out, Tom. And lots of other times, too!'

"'Look here, Amy,' Tom said, 'just because *you're* a drug addict, don't accuse my son!' He glared at my sister. 'There were drugs when I was in college. Trying something doesn't mean anything serious. . . .'

"'Sure!' Amy agreed. 'But Peter is only *fourteen years old*. And besides, if anybody knows how to spot an addict, I do!'

"I can't believe this! Peter's never had problems. He doesn't live in some drug-infested slum. And we don't abuse any drugs in this house. There *must* be some mistake."

The Counselor Replies

Marion E. Breland, M.S.W., C.S.W., B.C.D., is director of Haverstraw Counseling Center and a therapist in private practice in Nyack, New York, where she specializes in the problems of people recovering from alcoholism and their families. She is a coauthor of Depression and Suicide in Youth: A Comprehensive Approach for Schools *(Rockland County Mental Health).*

"When the Kagans came in, Tom was angry. 'Our son has really disappointed us,' he said bitterly. But Alicia was still denying the problem. 'I don't see how it could happen to a happy, successful boy with two loving parents,' she insisted.

"I said, 'Many people think that it's only neglected or deviant kids—or children of addicts—who get involved with drugs, but this isn't so.'

"I explained that no child is exempt anymore, now that drugs are so easily available. 'But he's so young!' Alicia protested.

"I said, 'The first year of high school is a vulnerable time for any child. It's very tough to leave the security of middle school and suddenly find yourself at the bottom of a whole new pecking order.'

" 'But Peter's no ordinary kid,' Tom said. 'He was on a varsity team!'

" 'The team?' Peter jeered. 'Are you joking? All the guys on the team made fun of me! I felt like the biggest geek in the world.'

"Tom looked surprised—and then skeptical. 'Well, then why didn't you tell us?'

" 'You wouldn't have listened,' Peter retorted. 'You don't care *how* I feel. All you wanted was for me to be a big jock, so you could brag to your dumb friends.'

"Tom looked stricken. 'That's just not true,' he said softly. 'I was really proud of you!'

" 'Well, I can't understand why we didn't see it happening,' Alicia cut in.

"I said, 'Let's go over what you did see: a polite son who became increasingly withdrawn, unreliable, and belligerent. His relationships with you deteriorated, and his schoolwork fell off. And there were also things you *chose* not to see, like the money that was missing.'

" 'That evening when Peter was high, there was an opportunity to talk,' I went on. 'But from what you told me, you felt relieved when you didn't have to . . . and Peter was never made to feel responsible for his behavior.'

"Alicia's eyes filled with tears. 'I kept hoping it was just classic adolescent craziness,' she said. 'And even those few times when I'd thought of getting help, there was always an excuse not to pursue it.'

" 'Are you saying this is all our fault then?' Tom asked. 'And that we've failed as parents?'

"I said, 'It's clear to me that you're a good family and that you love your son. Your reaction was very natural. If you avoided seeing what was happening, it was only because you were afraid, not because you didn't care.'

"I explained that the first and most important task was for Peter to get off drugs—and *stay* off.

"Peter said, 'Okay, no problem!' in a cheerful way. But I explained that promises and good intentions alone would not work. In addition to regular therapy for Peter and his parents, I would require that Peter attend Alcoholics Anonymous meetings every day for at least three months—a program that really works for both narcotics abusers and alcoholics. And I wanted all the Kagans to attend a weekly substance-abuse education program sponsored by the county.

"The family agreed, but Tom seemed reluctant. 'Is all this necessary?' he wondered. 'I know Peter needs help, but it's not like he's really an *addict!*'

"I said, 'Any drug use is a big concern. Maybe Peter isn't lying in some gutter, like your stereotype of the addict. But he has been lying and stealing and failing at school. Don't you think that's enough?'

"Peter wiped away some tears. He said, 'I never meant it to get like this.' At first he had done it to feel good, he said—and it did. But then he was doing it more and more to make the good feelings better and the bad ones go away. And then it got harder and harder to do without.

"Did he know he needed help? Peter shrugged. 'Maybe I did,' he said sadly, 'but I couldn't ask my parents.'

" 'Why not, Peter?' Tom challenged. 'Didn't you think we loved you enough?'

" 'Dad, you're wrong,' Peter replied. 'I already felt like such a failure: I was ashamed of letting you down again.' Peter cried openly then, and his parents, looking shaken, tried to comfort him.

"But if that initial session had been a relief for Peter, the next few weeks were very hard. Without drugs, he felt uncomfortable and anxious. He was feeling strong cravings at school, but to his credit, he did not give in.

"Together we worked on techniques he could use to relax, to put his mind on other things, and to find good support. AA, of course,

402

was a great resource. Peter listened in the meetings and shared his own feelings and, as a result, felt less alone.

"As part of his recovery program, Peter also went to his teachers and said, 'I was using drugs, but I'm sorry, and I've stopped.' His teachers, without exception, were wonderful and offered him extra tutoring on their own time.

"However, Peter was still feeling tired and depressed a lot of the time, and this worried him. But I assured him that he'd start to feel better in a few weeks. And he did.

"In fact, he felt so good that I had to warn him that he was at the stage at which it's all too easy to relapse. 'This is when the omnipotent self says, Now I can handle it; I'll just be more careful this time,' I explained. 'But don't believe it! Just remember how bad it was, how rotten you felt about yourself when you were lying and stealing. And then just think, Do I really want to go through all that awful stuff again?'

"Meanwhile, Tom and Alicia were dealing with their own complex feelings, which included a lot of guilt for what had happened and also a great deal of anger at each other.

"Tom was blaming Alicia for lying and covering up, while Alicia felt that a lot of the problem had been Tom's fault for having been so harsh with Peter and forcing her into the middle as a buffer, protecting both of them from each other's disappointment.

"When Peter had become uncommunicative and hostile, Tom and Alicia had each tried in their own way to make things better: Alicia had been softhearted, while Tom—feeling hurt and rejected—withdrew his friendliness to Peter and instead became autocratic and controlling.

"I told them in a later therapy session, 'Maybe what you need to do is combine those two approaches: Tom could learn from Alicia that it's sometimes good just to listen instead of yelling and punishing. And Alicia could learn from Tom how to trust her own instincts when something seems really wrong and to become more assertive and take a stand, even if doing so makes Peter dislike her temporarily.

"The Kagans were happy for these insights. And I was glad when, just a few sessions later, Tom and Peter were able to talk frankly. At first there were a lot of accusations back and forth. But by the end of the session, both father and son realized how much they loved and needed love from each other . . . and how alike they were in having trouble admitting their weaknesses.

"Tom said, 'Peter, I assumed a lot of things about you, but from now on, I won't assume, I'll ask.' Peter said, 'Thanks, Dad!' and they hugged each other tightly.

"When summer was over and Peter was back in school as a sophomore and apparently doing well, Alicia and Tom had the difficult task of separating the normal issues of growing up from possible drug-abuse behavior.

"Alicia, for example, felt a sense of panic if Peter was acting moody or didn't want to tell her where he was going. Later she'd feel ashamed of having doubted him. I told her that this was perfectly normal; trust building takes time, and the family would have to accept that fact.

" 'But in the meantime,' I told the three of them, 'it will help if you can all be very honest and forthcoming with each other when it comes to expressing your feelings.'

"The Kagans continued to come in on an occasional basis through the spring, and by May—one year after they had started in therapy—things were much better. Peter was still drug-free and also participating in an antidrug peer-counseling program at his school.

"Peter still wants privacy, like any teenager, but his life is less of a secret now. He's started having friends over to the house again, and nobody feels the need to walk on eggshells the way they used to.

"With drug abuse so widespread and tolerated in this society, it can be hard for even very good kids to make the right decisions. What happened to the Kagans could have happened to any family. What makes them special is not that they experienced the problem but that they faced up to it and worked it through."

I was so happy when my husband, Roger, finally stopped drinking . . . but the tensions at home got worse than ever! Can we ever relax and be a "normal" family?

Alison's Story

"Roger hasn't touched a drop of alcohol in four months, so I should be ecstatic," said Alison Werner, 36, "But I'm not! I'm so disappointed at the way things are going, and the kids are nervous and upset. I thought our life at home would be perfect now, but it's anything but!

"Roger always had a drinking problem, but it took me years to see it. In college, *all* the guys drank a lot—it was part of fraternity life. After we were married, Roger justified his many vodka martinis as a way of relaxing from the pressures of his fast-paced job in advertising. 'It's harmless,' he told me, 'none of the other wives complain.' I loved Roger so much—I couldn't bear for him to see me as a nag. So I stopped talking about it.

"By the time our son, Tim, was six and Sally was two, Roger was regularly stopping off at a bar on the way home—to 'unwind.' He would forget he'd promised to come home to teach Tim to ride his new bike . . . so I would do it instead. On Sally's third birthday, he came home—looped—at ten o'clock. Sally had gone to bed in tears—even though I'd tried to comfort her with a fib about how 'Daddy must have gone to buy you a special present and just forgot the time.'

"It broke my heart that he had spent the evening out with drunks when his daughter needed him so badly. I prayed that he would see what he was doing—and stop.

"But then he got a series of promotions at work, which meant more money, but also a lot more pressure—and more drinking. By the time Tim was in fifth grade, Sally in first, and Pam, our youngest, was a toddler, Roger was usually coming home very late and *very* drunk.

"The rest of us did our best to cope, each in his or her own way. I saw to it that Roger never drove the kids anywhere when he'd been drinking. (Of course he insisted that he was in perfect control, so I had to come up with all kinds of excuses for doing the driving myself . . . like 'I'll take Tim to his soccer game. I have to stop off at the drugstore anyway. . . .')

"Tim took to diluting Roger's vodka . . . until he was caught and sent to his room. Another time, he put his bike lock on the liquor cabinet. Sally was dedicated to pretending that it wasn't happening. One day—one dreadful morning when Roger was drunk at breakfast, he stubbed his cigarette out in the oatmeal, and poor little Sally served herself some—and primly ate it as if nothing was wrong.

"Pam would simply hide behind her bed.

"We never did anything as a family. The kids didn't see him during the week, and on weekends, it was my job to keep them quiet and out of his hair so he wouldn't yell at them. I learned to be prepared for Roger's unpredictable moods: sometimes he would rage at me, other times ignore me, and still other times, he would start to make love—and then pass out. I also learned to raid Roger's wallet each Friday night, as it was the only way I could be sure of having money for the groceries, let alone replacing Tim's worn-out sneakers or getting Sally a down jacket. Roger earned good money, but if I didn't take it, it would be gone.

"Why did I put up with it all? I don't know. Having come from a broken home, I was convinced that our kids were better off as they were. The girls were sweethearts, and Tim, at thirteen, was so responsible and mature, I could always rely on him for help and advice. He was like an adult. I would hang in for their sake! Besides, as crazy as it sounds, I still loved Roger, and I had a sense that *if only* he'd quit drinking, our lives would be great.

"Four months ago, something happened, a near miss that could have been a tragedy: Roger was arrested for driving while intoxicated. He had come within *one inch* of hitting a girl on a bicycle. 'I'll never forget the look on her face,' Roger said. 'She thought I was going to kill her.'

"Shaken, my husband agreed to go into a 28-day drying-out program. 'Now,' I told the kids, 'you'll see what a loving man your daddy *really* is!' But that was three months ago, and we're still waiting for a sign of it.

"In one way it's just like before in that we don't see him! As soon as he gets home from work, he grabs a bite and then goes to his Alcoholics Anonymous meeting—every night. He wouldn't even skip his meeting on Pam's sixth birthday. So nothing's changed: he still would rather be out with drunks instead of home with us. When he saw I was upset, he exploded. He said, 'This is part of my recovery! If I'd had cancer, would you want me to skip my chemotherapy?' Of course I felt guilty.

"Besides, he felt that he *had* tried for togetherness—and flunked. The first Saturday he was home, he pulled out five circus tickets. He bought them as a surprise—$20 tickets—but when Tim said he didn't want to go, Roger turned purple and tore up Tim's ticket. The rest of us went, but none of us enjoyed it.

"Tim and Roger barely talk to each other! Roger has made a lot of rigid rules about how much TV on school nights and when Tim has to be home. I really can't say anything because Roger is, after all, the father. But I see Tim seething, and I feel bad.

"The girls are tense, too. Of course they were very shocked when Roger was arrested and went to the hospital. I didn't want them to hate their father, so I've spent a lot of time explaining about how alcoholism is a disease and how Daddy is *still* recovering, a day at a time. But Pam doesn't even want to go near him. Roger thinks I've turned her against him, which is so wrong.

"Sally, now nine, has become very clingy to Roger. She asks, 'Where's Dad?' if he leaves the room. She says, 'Mom! *Don't* be rude to my father' if she hears us arguing. Sometimes I really have to control my temper.

"I expected Roger to be much warmer to all of us, including me. I thought that once he was sober, he'd acknowledge how much I've put up with, how I've held this family together all these years. I'm not looking for a trophy, but he hasn't said one word of thanks or apology! He seems to think that he's the big hero because he stopped drinking.

"In fact, he just can't seem to stop talking about himself and his alcoholism. The other night, he was telling the kids—for the twentieth time—that they are at risk and must never drink. Pam started to cry. Roger just shook his head. 'What's the matter with the kids?' he wants to know.

"He finds fault with all of us. He even complains about how I'm handling our money. And I'm the one who's been doing it *all.* Considering the money he's wasted on booze, he's got a lot of nerve to question my signing Pam up for the ballet class!

"I thought we'd be so close once the booze was gone, but Roger seems angry and distant. I don't know when things will ever seem right. Sometimes, when he says he'll be home at ten and it gets to be eleven and he's still not home, I think, 'Oh, God, he's hitting the bars' and then he comes in—he's been having coffee with some of his AA friends—and I feel so guilty for not trusting.

"Yesterday, the local paper mentioned a therapist who works with recovering alcoholics and their families. If I don't lose my nerve, I will call on Monday. A part of me says, 'Things are so messed up now' and another part says, 'Roger's stopped drinking and that should be *enough!*' I don't know which part is right."

The Counselor Replies

Philip Diaz, M.S.W., Ph.D., author of Twelve Steps to Self-Parenting (Health Communications Inc.), *is a therapist and consultant specializing in parenting issues. Diaz was formerly Assistant Deputy for Prevention, Office of National Drug Control Policy, Executive Office of the President.*

"When Alison explained the problem, I told her that many families of alcoholics experience profound disappointment and bitterness when they see that simply *getting sober* fails to solve all their problems. I offered to see each member of the family, individually, to see what the specific problems were, and then to help Roger and Alison plan good strategies.

"Each one expressed a sense of deprivation and bewilderment. Roger was the first to come in. He said, 'I thought they'd be supportive, but nobody in the family gives a damn about me. Nobody outside of AA understands me. And why aren't the kids happier and nicer?' Alison also felt left out: 'He puts *his* needs and *his* friends in AA ahead of us,' she lamented. 'I still feel lonesome and unappreciated. I don't know him anymore.'

"The children described other stresses: Tim, at thirteen, primarily resented what he called his 'demotion' from man-of-the-house with many responsibilities to little kid with lots of arbitrary rules. 'My father tells me to study harder, but until a few months ago, he didn't even know or care what grade I was in,' Tim fumed. Sally, nine, was not so much angry as scared. She sensed her mother's quiet rage and thought, 'If I don't step in and protect my father, he will leave us or start drinking again.'

"Pam, at six, was very timid and had no intention of talking . . . until I brought out some puppets. Through them, she told me, 'I did something bad to make Daddy drink . . . now he might die ('He and Mommy say he's getting better only one day at a time') and 'Daddy says we're at risk, which means *I might catch it* so I have to stay away from him.'

"Altogether, it was clear that the Werner family was still very dominated by Roger's alcoholism. I told them that their goal would be to create a home life in which 'how I used to drink' or 'how I'm not drinking now' or 'why you kids mustn't drink' is *not* the chief topic of discussion. Instead, I told them, the focus should be on 'How was school?' 'What did you do today?' and eventually . . . 'I love you.'

"For starters, I suggested that they try to spend time together— not in a rigid or elaborately programmed way (like the circus-ticket fiasco) but to be together—casually and pleasantly for an early family supper and to be around just *in case* one of the children felt like going for a walk or playing cards. I explained that this would cut down on anxiety and build rapport.

"I said that there were times when it would be important and appropriate to talk about alcoholism with the children, but it would need to be done thoughtfully. Instead of burdening Pam with concepts that she was too young to understand, she should be reassured that 'Daddy is better now and that he is not contagious,' and also that *kids are never responsible for parents' drinking.* I assured Roger and Alison that they didn't need to panic about the risk of their children becoming alcoholics, that this was not an immediate danger, and that voicing concern at this point was doing more harm than good.

"Next, I gave Alison and Roger some specific strategies that would help to improve things. I had them begin couples therapy, once a week, in order to learn to start looking at each other with compassion: to talk and to listen to one another without blaming or stalking out.

"After just a couple of months, I was happy to see them developing some of the friendship and intimacy that had been missing, since most of their marriage had been spent with Roger drinking and Alison feeling victimized. But now they were starting to nurture each other in little ways, like hugging and smiling and offering to make a cup of tea.

"I also gave Alison and Roger individual tasks. For example, I told Roger that he would need to *balance* his recovery through AA—which was very important—with his family life, which was also very important. I told him that he must take responsibility for being home more, even if it meant going to his AA meeting at lunchtime a couple of days a week.

"It was also important for Roger to pay attention to his children and respect their feelings, instead of just issuing orders or ignoring them. I was pleased when he began talking with Tim . . . and understanding that Tim required some recognition of the past and how responsible he had been. 'I guess we could negotiate new rules, Tim,' he said, and his son responded with a warm and heartfelt, 'Thanks, Dad!' I was also glad to hear from both Alison and Roger that the girls—no longer fearful—were laughing and smiling more.

"I told Roger that he would need to be responsible—to his entire family—for the way he had neglected and disappointed them in the past. While he prided himself on never having hit his wife or children, he needed to know—and be willing to acknowledge—that his drinking had caused a lot of emotional pain. I told him, 'You don't have to say, "Hey, kids, remember all those birthdays I forgot?" but if it comes up in conversation, it's okay to say you are sorry.'

"I warned him that the girls might show some anger several months down the road, but that would not be ominous but, rather, a sign of progress—a sign that they feel safe enough to show it.

"Alison also had 'work' to do. For starters, she had to find other adults to get support from, instead of relying on Tim as she had in her desperation for companionship when Roger had been drinking. I urged her to join Al-Anon, an excellent self-help group for family members of alcoholics, and her only regret after joining was that she hadn't done it years earlier. 'It's a joy to be among friends who really understand because they've been there too,' she reported.

"When Alison told me that Roger was still 'bugging' her about money, I suggested that she sit down with him and try to agree on some budget guidelines instead of excluding him as she had (appropriately) done when he had been drinking. When she took my suggestion, she found, to her surprise, that Roger was willing to listen, cooperate, and compromise . . . all new skills, and all good for the marriage as well as the budget.

"It's now been six months since Roger became sober, and I've seen a real turnaround from that day Alison first phoned me. Roger attends his AA meetings conscientiously, but it's no longer at the exclusion of his wife and kids. He and Alison are closer than they've ever been. They have disagreements, like any married couple, but they've learned to talk them out.

"Tim—no longer needed as his mother's Rock of Gibraltar—has joined his school's soccer team—and he was very proud when his father was there to see him head in the winning goal in a recent game.

"Pam and Sally both have blossomed with new friends and activities, now that alcoholism no longer occupies center stage at home, spurring fears and fantasies.

"The Werners aren't problem-free, and probably they never will be; but they are a normal family at last, accepting the fact that normal *does not* mean perfect."

Helen, my wife, never used to drink a lot, but now she's become a real alcoholic. Is it my fault for not being a good enough husband? Or does the problem come from somewhere much deeper?

Dan's Story

"Having a big party for the people I worked with at the newspaper had been my idea," said Dan Simpson. "And it was for Helen's sake. She had just failed the bar exam for the third time, and she was down in the dumps.

"I thought a party might be just the distraction she needed. She really threw herself into all the preparations, designing invitations, arranging flowers, collecting unusual recipes, and choosing new outfits for our kids, Meg, six, and Jason, nine.

"But when the evening arrived, it was a disaster. Helen outdid herself with an incredible variety of hors d'oeuvres but miscalculated the number—and in minutes they were all gone.

"I offered to run to the deli for cold cuts and pretzels, but Helen said no, that would be too ordinary, and besides, dinner was almost ready. But in rushing her Spanish paella to the table, she wound up serving the chicken still pink inside; the shrimp, lobster tails, and clams half cooked; and the rice too hard to chew.

" 'Umm, how *delicious*,' my loyal assistant, Connie, lied, but Helen knew better. 'I blew it,' she said to me grimly in the kitchen.

" 'No way!' I said and gave her a kiss. But she pushed me away.

" 'Why do you always have to be so obnoxiously *nice?*' Helen cried. Draining her glass of wine, she went out to rejoin our guests. To my embarrassment, Helen began to deliver a monologue. I think she was trying to be Erma Bombeck, but it bombed. Her jokes—centering on living with a workaholic—sounded brittle and unfunny. My colleagues looked confused and embarrassed as they had their dessert and coffee. Then everyone stood up and began looking for their coats.

"The next day Helen slept until noon, and I let her. 'Oh, no!' she cried, sitting up and looking at the clock. 'Meg has gymnastics, and Jason was due at Jeremy's at ten o'clock. Why didn't you wake me?'

" 'No need,' I said reassuringly. I'd taken the kids where they needed to go and cleaned up from the party.

" 'That's the trouble,' Helen said. 'No need!' She put her head in her hands. 'I wouldn't even blame you for walking out on me after last night.'

" 'Don't say that,' I pleaded. 'You worked hard, and the party was fun!' Helen didn't answer. I said, 'Why don't you call up a friend and play tennis or come to the office and help me get some letters out?'

"But Helen spent the whole day in her nightgown and did nothing. 'Here,' I said that evening and handed her an item from the Sunday paper about an after-school program seeking volunteers. Helen stuck the clipping in a drawer.

"That night she was really upbeat at dinner. She laughed with the children and seemed happy. But then I noticed how much wine she was drinking. By dessert she was so looped she had to lie down.

"When I went in to her, she was crying. I said, 'Helen, don't give in to this. You have to fight it.'

"She said, 'You're right, Dan,' but when I got home the next evening, I found her just sitting with her glass of white wine. 'Did you call about the volunteer job?' I asked pointedly. Helen shrugged and took a sip of wine.

" 'I don't think *that's* going to solve anything,' I said softly. Helen said defensively, 'Maybe your mother was an alcoholic, but I'm not.' But when she stood up, she had to grab my arm to keep from falling.

" 'Don't give me that superior look,' she snapped. 'The heel of my shoe just got caught in the rug.' But she was too drunk to make dinner, so I ordered in a pizza.

" 'Is Mommy eating?' Meg asked.

" 'No,' I said. 'Mommy's taking a nap. She isn't feeling well.'

"Jason shook his head. 'Lately she's *always* not feeling well,' he said. For everyone's sake, if not just for Helen's, I had to do something.

"The next morning I took Helen in my arms. I said, 'Now hear this: You are beautiful and smart, and you have everything a woman could possibly want. Including me,' I joked.

"Helen looked suspicious. 'So what are you saying?' she asked.

" 'Just telling you to stop feeling sorry for yourself! You have so much to be proud of and to offer! Life is too short to sit around feeling miserable.'

"Helen said, 'You're right, Dan.' But she spent that day—and many others—moping around and refilling her wine glass. Then a couple of weeks ago she completely mortified Meg by arriving drunk at school for a class play. Helen apparently sat down in the first-grade classroom and actually lit a cigarette! Poor Meg tried to hide as the other children gawked and giggled. The teacher had to bring Helen a paper cup filled with water and ask her to douse it.

"An even scarier incident happened the week after, when Helen forgot to pick Jason up from his soccer practice. Unable to reach his mother, the poor kid had to phone my office and get me out of a meeting.

" 'My watch must have stopped,' Helen said when we came home. But she had obviously been drinking and had fallen asleep. I was thankful that Meg had spent the afternoon at her friend Mariko's house.

"I felt angry, but I also felt sorry for Helen: She looked so empty, so beaten down. What was going wrong? Was it me? Wasn't I loving and supportive enough?

" 'Helen,' I said, 'you know I'd do anything in the world for you. But it's *so* frustrating, trying to help when you won't even help yourself.'

" 'I'll try to be better,' she promised. And this time it sounded as if she really meant it. I thought, Thank God!

"But the following night I had to take a client out to dinner, and I didn't get home until eleven-thirty. I was surprised to see all the lights on, and there was Helen—slumped over the kitchen table, snoring.

" 'Dan?' Helen said, stirring. Then she reached up and tried to kiss me, but I shrank away, repulsed by the smell of liquor on her breath. I felt a wave of nausea.

" 'Get away from me,' I said coldly as she clutched at me. I wanted to hit her, smash her, anything to get her away from me.

"But I didn't touch her. I just left the room, feeling shaken. I had never come so close to hitting her before.

"I had to face the fact that I was married to an alcoholic—the last thing I'd ever expected. Somehow I feel that I'm the one responsible for this. I have to get her help before our whole family goes down the drain."

The Counselor Replies

Philip Diaz, M.S.W., Ph.D., author of Twelve Steps to Self-Parenting (Health Communications Inc.), *is a therapist and consultant specializing in parenting issues. Diaz was formerly Assistant Deputy for Prevention, Office of National Drug Control Policy, Executive Office of the President.*

"Dan and Helen Simpson came in together, with Helen looking sad and repentant while Dan did most of the talking.

" 'I'm afraid my wife is an alcoholic,' Dan said, and then he told me all that had been going on at home over the past three months. 'She needs to be in a hospital or to receive some very intensive treatment,' he concluded. 'We'll do what we have to, regardless of the cost.'

"I acknowledged Dan's concern and then asked if he would leave the room so I could talk to Helen.

" 'Helen, what do you think the problem is?' I asked when Dan had gone to sit in the waiting room.

" 'I don't know,' she said. 'Lately I've been feeling so worthless.' She stopped, but I urged her to go on.

" 'I wanted to be a lawyer,' she said, 'to keep up with Dan and make him proud of me. But then we had the kids, and it ended up taking six years and a lot of starting and stopping to make it

415

through law school. I finally graduated, but I still couldn't pass the bar exam. So it was all a waste. I felt so guilty because of the money and because Dan had been counting on me.

" 'I tried again and again, but when I found that I'd failed the bar for the third time, I thought, Now what? The kids hardly need me anymore. And I'm no help to Dan—I sure proved that when the party bombed. And I feel even worse when I can't cheer myself up.'

"I said, 'Isn't that appropriate when life seems so difficult?'

"Helen looked surprised. 'Nobody's said that before,' she said. 'Dan has no patience with my moping. In fact,' she said, laughing bitterly, 'he's always trying to cheer me up.'

" 'What would you rather he do?' I asked her.

" 'Just listen,' she said very quickly. 'And not give me solutions. Dan keeps trying to cheer me up and make everything fine, until I feel like screaming at him. Then I feel guilty. How can I scream at him when he's so good to me?'

"As Helen went on with her story I got the sense that her drinking was situational rather than chronic. In effect, she was not so much addicted to alcohol as she was using (and abusing) it in an attempt to 'medicate' her feelings of inadequacy.

"Helen asked if that still meant she really was an alcoholic.

"I said, 'Not necessarily. The best way to find out would be for you not to drink or use any mood-altering drugs at all for the next three months, while I work with you to help sort out some of your feelings.'

" 'In the meantime,' I went on, 'it would be good for you to attend Alcoholics Anonymous meetings twice a week. You can see if you identify with the speakers, and even if you don't, you can learn what the danger signals of alcohol addiction are.'

"Helen agreed. We called Dan back in, and Helen left the room so that Dan and I could talk privately.

"Dan initially seemed very concerned about Helen's well-being. When I asked him how *he* was doing, he looked surprised. 'Until the night I almost slugged her, I thought I was managing well,' he said. 'But now it's just more than I can cope with. I can't handle having to care for another alcoholic.'

" 'Another?' I asked Dan.

" 'My mother was an alcoholic!' he replied. 'I had to take care of her. In fact, I spent my whole life taking care of her until she died.'

" 'I swore I'd never go through that again,' Dan continued. 'Helen hardly drank at all, and that was one of the things that attracted me to her. But the other night, when I came home late and she was so drunk . . . and she started this kissing, coming on to me sexually . . . something snapped.'

"Dan looked pained. 'I guess it brought back all those childhood memories of my mother getting drunk and crawling into my bed and hugging me because she was lonely and my father wasn't home,' he said.

"I said, 'That must have been hard.'

" 'It was!' Dan agreed. 'But for years I thought I'd put it all behind me. I figured, after all, I'm an adult, and you can't spend your life crying over things that happened 30 years ago.'

" 'I understand your wish to be rid of those memories and feelings,' I said. 'But growing up in an alcoholic home has a profound impact we don't automatically escape just because we're grown.'

" 'In fact,' I went on, 'children who have the kind of childhood you describe can turn into adults who hide from their feelings by compulsively achieving—or taking care of others. It sounds as if that's what you've done, with yourself *and* with Helen.'

"Dan was silent, reflecting. 'Maybe so,' he said at last. 'But the fact remains that my wife *is* an alcoholic.'

"I said, 'I don't know if she is or isn't. That's part of what she and I will work on to find out. She may just have been abusing alcohol on a short-term basis, which is different from chronic alcoholism and doesn't necessarily lead to it, either.'

" 'But in any case,' I said, 'she's not the only one who needs help. You've both suffered significant setbacks in your lives, and it seems to me that you both have been busy avoiding some important issues. It's time now for the two of you to allow yourselves to feel the pain without looking for any quick-fix solutions.'

" 'Helen especially has to do some work and some searching. Let her do it at her own pace. Pushing her won't resolve things any sooner.'

"I assured Dan that he was not responsible for Helen's drinking problem. I told him, 'You didn't cause it, and you can't cure it.'

" 'You mean I can't help?'

" 'Oh, yes,' I said. I explained to Dan that Helen needed him to listen to her when she was sad, not to give her a pep talk, simply to listen.

"Dan said, 'That's hard for me!'

"I said, 'That's because you've never learned to listen to yourself.'

"In the weeks that followed I met with Dan and Helen, usually separately but sometimes together. As Dan learned to back off and stop pressuring Helen to 'snap out of' her depression, she became free to emerge from her feelings of failure and helplessness and to become less passive.

"Within a month of starting treatment, she began exploring some career possibilities and had applied for a job as assistant admissions director at a local college for continuing education. 'I think I can really relate to women my age who are searching to find themselves,' she explained.

"Helen experienced very few problems in giving up drinking. 'Does this mean she's really not an alcoholic then?' Dan wondered.

"I said, 'Some therapists claim that anyone who abuses alcohol is an alcoholic, but I think that some people go through periods of heavy drinking and then stop. Apparently Helen came to realize—largely through attending AA—that she had abused alcohol at one time but wasn't dependent on it. Once she realized that, she was able to stop using alcohol as a crutch and start facing her problems.'

"Dan decided to try some Al-Anon meetings for adult children of alcoholics. Shy at first, he just sat and listened—and found that many others had similar backgrounds and problems. As he began to share his experiences he discovered what he described as 'a whole new world of feelings—vulnerability, compassion, and forgiveness.'

"Dan learned to talk with Helen about his painful childhood, and that in turn made Helen feel more needed and valued by him. Even Jason and Meg benefited as they saw their mom 'all there' and their dad more relaxed than they had ever seen him.

"A drinking problem in a family is always very distressing. But because Dan and Helen sought help early, they changed what could have been an ominous period of their lives into an opportunity to find more fulfillment than they'd ever hoped for."

VIOLENCE
AND
CRIME

*Jeremy, ten, was coping so well—
first with the divorce and then
our move to the city. But now—
suddenly—he seems distraught.
What's up—and why can't
he tell me?*

Robin's Story

"I was very anxious and hopeful that the move would work out," said Robin Weaver, 33. "I had been offered a fantastic job promotion, and I couldn't wait! But it did mean that my son, Jeremy, ten, and I would have to move to the city. That in itself was not a problem so much as the fact that I was getting pressure from my ex-husband, Bradley (*and* his live-in girlfriend, Lucy) to go, and leave Jeremy with them.

" 'Dad says the city's really yucky and dangerous,' Jeremy reported after his customary midweek dinner at his father's house. 'That's your dad's opinion,' I said, 'I happen to think it'll be great.' I told him that we would be living in a very nice, safe neighborhood and that he'd be going—by school bus—to a top-rated grade school.

"What's more, the school had an extended-day program that was right up Jeremy's alley—with computers and sports, all the things he liked. 'This way,' I told him, 'you'll only be a latchkey kid for fifteen minutes before I get home.'

" 'Okay?' I asked. 'Sure,' he said, getting the vanilla fudge ice cream from the freezer. That was Jeremy: a really resilient, non-brooding child.

"Still, I wanted to make this move as comfortable and easy as possible for him. We moved two weeks before the start of school, and I invited some of his old friends to the city to spend a couple of days. I let Jeremy decorate his new room exactly as he wanted to so it would feel like home. I took him around to show him all the interesting things the city had to offer, and finally, I gave him a new wallet with all the emergency phone numbers he could need.

"And then I held my breath—and hoped! On that first day of school, I'm sure I must have had more butterflies than he did. Would he like it? Would he get on the right bus to go home?

"But everything seemed fine. He told me that there was a kid in his class named Ed who was funny. And the teacher, Miss Corcoran, knew a lot about science. And, oh, yes, computer club was totally awesome.

"Hooray for Jeremy—and me, I thought! How happy I was that I'd had the nerve to make this move.

"By Thanksgiving, I felt even surer. Brad was still calling Jeremy every day and saying, 'Are you sure you're okay?' But Jeremy was more than okay, he was terrific! Oh, once in a while, he seemed to miss his old school, or he'd complain that some kid in the class was a 'real dork.' But his report cards were glowing on the academic *and* the social side.

"What a pleasure it was to show good reports to Brad. Jeremy was seeing his father every other weekend and once each week for dinner, and he loved those visits. But he always seemed happy to come home again—to our apartment.

"At least that was what I thought—until the evening I came home from work and found him lying on his bed, shivering. 'I have a stomachache,' he groaned, looking strangely guilty.

"Later, I brought him some chicken soup. 'Mom,' he said. 'I just wish we were in the old house. I wish we could have just stayed where we were.'

"I said, 'I guess your dad's been working on you again.' But Jeremy defended him angrily. 'Stop it,' he shouted. 'Just stop saying that, okay?'

"The next day, Jeremy said he had a headache, so I let him stay home from school, which meant I had to stay home, too. I thought he might tell me what was bothering him, but he was grumpy, withdrawn, and uncommunicative, so I let him be. That evening, he felt well enough to go out when Brad came to take him to dinner. Afterward, Brad took me aside and asked, 'What the hell's going on?'

"I said, 'Look, have a heart. This transition takes time.' But Brad had that mean, determined look on his face, and I thought, 'Here we go again: the struggle continues.'

"The following day, Jeremy went back to school, but when I got home that evening, he was still moody and complained of a stomachache. He was grouchy the next morning. I tried not to panic.

"That noon, I got a call from Jeremy's teacher: 'Why didn't you respond to my note, Mrs. Weaver?' she asked. Note? What note? Jeremy was always so responsible that way.

"Well, apparently not this time! Jeremy had done no homework in three days and claimed he didn't know where his books were. 'He told me he did it in school,' I said. '*And* if he's going to continue to skip his after-school activities,' she continued, 'he will also need a note from home.'

"That night, I confronted Jeremy about the missing books and homework. He shrugged. And the note? 'I lost it.' And the after-school activities? 'I felt like coming home.'

" 'I don't want you here alone for that long,' I said. 'If you don't want to stay at school, I'll have to get a sitter.'

" 'I'm not a baby,' Jeremy shouted. 'Why don't you just stop bugging me? It's all your fault that we're here.'

" 'Jeremy,' I said. 'I don't understand all this. Tell me what's happened.' Suddenly he looked close to tears. 'I lost my wallet,' he said and looked at the floor.

"Was *that* why he was acting so peculiar—getting the whole world in an uproar? I'd been under pressure, and I just exploded. 'Well, darn it, that's *your* carelessness,' I told him. 'You can't seem to hold on to anything lately! And you had your father and me so worried. I think you ought to pay to replace that wallet yourself.' Then I calmed down and said, 'Jeremy, honestly, I'm trying to understand. All this losing stuff—and lying. It just isn't like you.'

"But Jeremy had no answer. I was sorry I'd lost my temper. I knew something was wrong, but I didn't know what it was, and

Jeremy would not tell me.

"Brad won't approve, but if Jeremy needs counseling, I want him to have *whatever* help he needs."

The Counselor Replies

Ann S. Kliman, M.A., is director of the Situational Crisis Service at the Center for Preventive Psychiatry in White Plains, New York. Kliman is also the author of Crisis: Psychological First Aid for Recovery and Growth, *Second Edition (Jason Aronson).*

"I asked the Weavers to come in together, but without Jeremy, so that I could get some background information.

" 'It's just that he's always coped so well before—with everything, even the divorce,' Robin said.

"I said, 'Children work very hard not to make their parents anxious. Maybe this time, he's overloaded.'

" 'I'm not sure we need a professional opinion! I knew the city would be bad for him,' Bradley said.

" 'We don't really know what it is yet,' I replied. 'But I think he must be experiencing some loyalty conflicts. So I'm very glad you can work together, despite your differences.'

"I told the Weavers that since Jeremy had been such a well-functioning child in the past, the recent change in his behavior *could* be a delayed reaction to the move or to the earlier divorce, or both. 'Or,' I said, 'it could be that, *plus* something we don't know about. It could even be *just* something we don't know about.'

"Clearly, I needed to talk to Jeremy, but Bradley was hesitant. 'I don't want my son to feel that we think he's crazy or anything,' Bradley said.

"I said, 'Why not just acknowledge his stomachaches and his unhappiness, and tell him that I'm here for kids to come and talk to about anything that bothers them?'

"When Jeremy did come in, he seemed bright and pleasant, but reserved. In my office, without his parents, he was nervous and wanted to know what I was going to do.

" 'We can just sit and talk, or play,' I told him. With that, he picked up a G.I. Joe doll and said, 'I used to play with these. But now I'm really into computers.'

"I said, 'Yes, your parents told me . . . and they also said you enjoyed your computer club so much, but not lately.'

" 'It got boring!'

" 'That must be disappointing for you,' I said.

" 'Yes,' he answered emotionally. And then he started to tell me how he hated school, missed his old friends, and wished that he could magically turn back the clock.

"I said, 'You have every reason to find changes very hard, Jeremy. Everyone does . . . but gee, you've done *so well!*'

"Suddenly Jeremy looked upset. 'I didn't mean to lose them,' he said softly and clutched his stomach.

" 'Lose what?' I asked.

" 'My wallet! My wallet and all my schoolbooks.'

"I said, 'I'm sure you didn't mean to. In fact, maybe you not only didn't mean to lose your things, maybe you didn't really lose them.'

"Jeremy stared at me. 'How did you *know?*' he asked.

" 'I didn't know,' I replied, 'but this didn't make sense to me, and I wondered if something happened and you're scared to tell your parents.'

"Jeremy was quiet, but he didn't say no. 'If you have a scary secret, you can tell me,' I said. 'And I won't tell anyone unless you say I can.'

" 'Well, this kid came up to me and took my stuff,' he said. 'And I let him—like a dork. I should have run after him and punched him, like my dad would have done. *But no,* I acted like a big baby! Afterward, I thought if I forget it and keep quiet, I'll feel better. But I can't stop thinking about it.'

" 'Jeremy,' I said, 'I don't think anyone, not even grown-ups, can keep scary secrets alone. In fact, we can't let go of the fear *until* we can share it with someone who understands. Will you tell me how it happened?'

"Haltingly, Jeremy told me how he was walking from the bus to his apartment house as it was getting dark, when a teenager came up and punched him in the stomach really hard and took his wallet and all his books. The guy said, 'I have a knife, and I'll cut you if you tell.'

" 'I don't want anyone to know what a . . . baby I am!'

" 'Oh, Jeremy, you're not!' I said. 'It's awful to be robbed and made fun of . . . I bet anybody, even your dad, would feel the same way if *he* were mugged, especially by someone bigger who had a weapon. You were smart not to fight back.'

" 'Jeremy, *you* did nothing wrong. You were the one who was hurt, not the one who committed a crime. Nobody who is victimized needs to feel ashamed. Truly, it's the mugger who should be ashamed. You feel ashamed, so instead of being angry at the mugger, you're mad at yourself, and you don't deserve that! Grown-ups understand this. Don't you think your parents would?'

" 'No!' he answered. 'They'd be disappointed in me.'

"I said, 'Jeremy, I think you're wrong. But let's find out, okay? I'll be here to help you tell them.'

"Jeremy agreed, and I've rarely seen a child more astonished by the response he did get from *both* parents, who were warm and constructive in praising his good judgment.

"Urging him to share the secret further, they took him to report the incident to the police, and Jeremy felt a wave of relief to be actively coping instead of helplessly suffering. 'This is the right kind of fighting back,' Robin told him. She also suggested reporting it at school. And while Jeremy was hesitant at first, he agreed that it might help other kids to be safer.

"To Jeremy's surprise, nobody ridiculed him. His teacher and his classmates were full of empathy. They talked about how you can't have perfect safety ever, no matter where you are and no matter how careful, but how there are things you can do to lower the risks, such as not dawdling and daydreaming in the street, going places with a buddy or in a group when it's dark, crossing the street or going into a store if you feel that someone might harm you.

"In addition, it was decided that the after-school bus would begin taking children right to their doors, and this made all the parents feel better.

" 'Jeremy, you helped everyone by coming forward, and you may have helped to avert an even worse incident,' Miss Corcoran told him.

"Bradley, who had been so concerned and worried about Jeremy's safety before the mugging, was heartened by the responsiveness of the police and the school. 'I see that you're really in a good place here after all, Jeremy,' he admitted.

"My involvement with the Weavers consisted of just a few sessions and a follow-up phone call with Robin, who reported 'one happy kid and one relieved mother.' This very brief therapy turned his frightening, upsetting experience into an ultimately positive one: Jeremy learned that he could trust his parents to support him and stand by him—always.

"Often, parents are reluctant to seek professional help for a troubled child because they don't want to embark on months of treatment. But sometimes (when the problem is not a deep one) a great deal can be accomplished in a session or two, especially when parents are alert and concerned enough to recognize a cryptic cry for help."

Our daughter, Jenny, twelve, isn't talking about the rape, and my husband, Stan, thinks that means she's okay. But how can we tell if Jenny is dealing with her terror or sweeping it under the rug?

Claudia's Story

"Stan says I should stop dwelling on what happened and let Jenny forget it," said Claudia Watson, 36. "But how can I, when I see her crying and hiding from her friends? Now she's started having bad dreams every night.

"Stan says it would be strange if she *didn't* have a few symptoms after all that she's been through, and I have to agree. But does that mean there's nothing to worry about?

"It happened just a week ago Saturday. Jenny had been sledding in the park, but instead of coming home when she was supposed to, she wanted to go down the giant hill one more time . . . and one more . . . until all of a sudden it was almost dark and she was alone.

"She picked up her sled and started running for home. Just then a policeman in a plain, brown car stopped beside her and said, 'You shouldn't be in the park this late. I'll drive you home.'

"Grateful and trusting, Jenny got in the car. But that policeman didn't take her home; he took her deeper into the park—where he threatened her with a knife, raped her, and then dumped her out of the car and drove off.

"We'd phoned her friends; my husband, Stan, had gone out looking; and finally, at seven, we'd called the police, who found her wandering, dazed and shivering. Her face was swollen, and there was blood all over her legs.

" 'Oh, my God,' Stan cried when he saw her in the emergency room. 'I'll kill whoever did this!' We had to wait while a doctor examined her, treated her injuries, and took all the necessary physical evidence.

"Then the police arrived and started firing questions at her. Jenny seemed more and more confused and upset as they pressed her for details. 'I don't remember,' she whimpered.

"But they kept on asking, relentlessly, until Jenny burst into tears and couldn't stop crying. Stan and I looked at each other. 'That's enough,' Stan said firmly. 'You're only making things worse for my daughter.'

"He was right! Obviously Jenny couldn't give enough of a description to help them—so why put her through that painful questioning?

"Stan and I agreed: We would keep what had happened very private for Jenny's sake. In fact, we'd keep it a secret. That way she wouldn't ever be embarrassed or hassled. 'The less that's said, the quicker she'll be able to put the whole thing behind her,' Stan said.

"The next day we all stayed quietly at home together. Jenny was clingy and tearful. 'It's all over now, and you're safe,' we told her.

"On Monday she didn't want to go to school, so I stayed home with her. But she didn't want to talk. She just watched TV game shows nonstop.

" 'So what—as long as she's happy again,' Stan said with a shrug, minimizing my concern. 'See that?' he said the next morning, when Jenny went off to school. 'She's a lot more resilient than you think she is.'

"But that evening Jenny was irritable—ready to start crying over the slightest thing. I found her hard to reach and utterly impossible to comfort.

"Later Stan said, 'Claudia, why do you keep rubbing her nose in it?'

" 'What?'

" 'You keep bringing it up! It was no wonder she left the table during dinner. Can't you see she doesn't want to talk about it? Look,' he went on, '*you* like to talk when you're upset, and that's fine—for you. But Jenny's private, like me, and you ought to respect that.'

" 'All right, fine,' I agreed. I'd try anything if it would help. And so, for the next few days, I tried to do it his way. I was affectionate with Jenny but at the same time careful to give her 'space' and make sure I made no reference to the rape.

"It wasn't easy! I could see how she was suffering—but how could I help her without mentioning the problem and (according to Stan) reopening the wound? Jenny refused an invitation to a slumber party for next month, and she wouldn't even come to the phone when her friends called. She said, 'I just want to be alone, okay?' So I didn't push.

"When Stan's cousin in London sent us a picture of her baby, Jenny took one look and said, '*I'm* not having any babies—ever! I'm never getting married.' I wanted to explain to Jenny that getting married, making love, and having babies aren't anything like that horrible attack she'd experienced in the park.

"But to keep the peace, I just said, 'Okay, but you may decide differently someday.' Stan noticed my restraint and smiled approvingly.

"That night I heard Jenny crying in her sleep. 'Let her be,' Stan insisted. 'She's getting it out of her system.' But *was* she? Would she ever be able to forget? Would we?

"The following Saturday morning I was delivering cookies for the school's bake sale when I ran into Jenny's teacher, Mrs. Price.

" 'I'm awfully glad to see you,' she said. 'I've been meaning to call.' She held my hand. 'I just wanted to make sure that Jenny is getting all the help she needs.'

" 'Help?' I said, surprised. 'Do you mean her math?'

" 'No, no, no,' she said quickly, smiling and then looking deeply serious. 'I was talking about . . . the rape.'

" 'Oh, but you're wrong. I mean, who told you?' I was confused. I'd only told two people, our very closest friends, and they had been *sworn* to secrecy.

" 'Actually, I've heard it from several different parents,' Mrs. Price said. 'It's the kind of secret that really can't be kept; people are too frightened when there's a rapist out there. Still, I'm mainly concerned about Jenny. Have you found a really good therapist for her?'

" 'We're not doing that,' I said. 'Jenny doesn't want to talk about it.'

" 'Well, I'm not an expert,' Mrs. Price replied gently. 'But the way Jenny's acting at school—very tense and furtive and avoiding her friends—suggests to me that she's suffering a lot of shame and guilt for what happened to her. And that's not fair to Jenny; she doesn't deserve it!'

"All the way home I wondered: *Was* counseling the answer? That first night at the hospital they'd suggested a therapist, but Jenny refused, and Stan backed her, saying, 'Let's not undermine her ability to heal herself.'

"Now it was clear that she could use some help. But would she talk to a stranger? That night, when we discussed therapy, Stan resisted the idea.

" 'She doesn't have to go if she doesn't want to,' Stan said.

"But the next day he agreed to go—just the two of us, though, not Jenny. Stan doesn't believe in counseling, but in his heart he knows that we have to do something."

The Counselor Replies

Ann S. Kliman, M.A., is director of the Situational Crisis Service at the Center for Preventive Psychiatry in White Plains, New York. She is also the author of Crisis: Psychological First Aid for Recovery and Growth, *Second Edition (Jason Aronson).*

"The Watsons told me their story, and then Stan said, 'I guess we might need some help,' but he wanted me to agree that talking about the rape would be counterproductive for Jenny.

"He said, 'We don't want to risk making her feel even worse.'

"I said, 'I understand your wish that Jenny could forget the attack and never have to talk about it. But we know from hostages and violent-crime victims that the only way to get over a traumatic experience is to talk and talk and talk about it and then talk about it some more, until the terror goes away.'

"Stan said, 'But Jenny doesn't *want* to talk.'

"Claudia agreed; 'I've tried to draw her out, but whenever I try, she gets so upset that she leaves the room.'

"I said, 'Maybe it's not that she doesn't want to talk but that she can't, at least not until she knows that the adults have the courage to hear what she must eventually say.'

"When the Watsons brought Jenny in to see me two days later, she appeared to be so deeply engrossed in a ski magazine that she barely even looked up at me.

"I said, 'I think I understand what you're going through, and I'm very, *very* angry at the rapist.' Jenny put the magazine down.

" 'Well, I don't need to be here, because I'm not crazy,' she said.

" 'Of course you're not crazy!' I agreed. 'But I'm glad you're here, because when something very scary happens, it interferes with our life when we're awake as well as when we're asleep, and we really have to talk to someone about it so we don't keep dreaming about it.'

"Jenny nodded. 'I have had some really gross dreams,' she admitted.

"We talked a little more, and then we set up some appointments, not only for Jenny, the primary victim, but also for her parents. At first Stan insisted that he didn't need any counseling, but I explained that parents, too, are profoundly affected by a child's rape and that they deserve an opportunity to work out their own feelings of guilt and anger and their sense of having been violated and damaged by the attack.

"Opening up wasn't easy for Stan. And even Claudia, who was more accustomed to talking about feelings, said that she felt 'selfish' spending time and money working on her own distress when Jenny was the one who really needed help.

"But it was only a few sessions before the Watsons both felt better and discovered that acknowledging and mastering their own feelings helped them to be a better and more responsive support system for Jenny.

"Jenny, a sensitive and thoughtful young person, had indeed been struggling, as her teacher suspected—not only with fear but also with enormous self-blame.

" 'I guess I asked for it,' Jenny said. I asked, 'Why?' Because, she explained, she was there (and hadn't left when the other kids did); because she willingly got in the car; and most of all because 'I was so scared I just went limp. I didn't even try to fight.'

"I said, 'Jenny, it was not inappropriate for you to be in the park, and even if you did stay a little late, that is absolutely *not* the same as *asking* to be raped.'

" 'Even getting in the car was understandable! After all, he had a policeman's uniform on. And as for not fighting, Jenny, that wasn't cowardly; that was very smart!'

" '*Smart?*' Jenny stared at me.

" 'Of course,' I said. 'The rape was terrible enough, but he had a knife! And whether you knew this or only sensed it, rapists often get more aggressive when a victim resists. Jenny, I'm really proud of you, because even in your terror you still had the good judgment not to fight.'

"Jenny said, 'I never thought of it that way.'

"I had been seeing the Watsons for almost three weeks when all their well-meant secrecy suddenly backfired—right in Jenny's face.

"It was in homeroom, just as the kids were straggling back from gym. There on the blackboard someone had written JENNY IS A SLUT. There was a lot of whispering. Mortified, Jenny tried to leave the room, but the teacher, Mrs. Price, motioned for her to sit down.

"Then Mrs. Price faced the class. 'I won't ask who did this,' she said and went on to talk about how when people are scared, they get very mean because they don't want anyone to know they're scared.

" 'Still,' she said, 'fear is *no* excuse for being cruel.'

"Mrs. Price explained that Jenny had been the victim of a rape, which made her no more of a slut than a child who'd been robbed or mugged or hit by a car.

"She said, 'There was nothing Jenny did to ask for what happened to her, and there's nothing any child could do to deserve such a horrendous assault. If you need to call names, do it to the rapist, because he—not Jenny—is the one who did something bad.'

" 'I'm sure your parents all told you not to talk about this,' Mrs. Price went on. 'But now that it's out in the open, it would be very nice to let Jenny know that you're still her friends.'

"At that point a lot of the kids did go out of their way to be

433

friendly, and Jenny began to feel less freaky. By the end of the week, she had decided to go to the slumber party after all.

"At this time, just as Jenny's nightmares were gradually fading away, Stan was starting to have trouble sleeping. Compulsively, he kept thinking of revenge. He said, 'I just want to go out and destroy that guy! I owe that to Jenny!'

"I told Stan that his feelings were legitimate but that if he allowed himself to go out of control and be violent, then he would be acting like the rapist, and it would give Jenny the message that *no* man was safe.

"Instead I urged the Watsons to let Jenny cooperate with the police. Claudia wondered, 'What good is it if Jenny can't describe the man or even his car?' And in fact, after a day of looking at mug shots, she came up with nothing.

"But then a police artist worked with Jenny, and three weeks later, thanks to the picture, they came up with a suspect and made an arrest.

"When they arrested him some 350 miles away, they found Jenny's underpants in the trunk of his car. In addition, it turned out, the man had raped several other children—all of whom (with the exception of Jenny) had been slashed when they'd tried to resist. And each time the man had been posing as a clergyman, a doctor, or a policeman—all people children have been taught to trust.

"When the trial came up, Jenny testified, along with some of the other young victims. She was understandably nervous, but the judge was respectful. The whole trial ended up as less of an ordeal for Jenny than a vindication. By testifying, Jenny gained a sense of strength, pride, and safety. The rapist was convicted and sentenced to a long prison term.

"Jenny had very much recovered by then. In a follow-up session I explained to her parents that there might be times ahead, in Jenny's adolescence, when it would be very appropriate and helpful to continue (as they had already begun) to stress to their daughter the difference between adult lovemaking and the violent and vicious sexual experience she had had.

"In addition, I suggested that as Jenny started pressing for more freedom and independence, as all young people do, the Watsons would need to set reasonable limits. But at the same time they would need to be careful not to overprotect her (which could make her feel like a victim again). And I urged Stan and Claudia to be aware that Jenny might well need some additional therapy along the way and that I would be there if needed.

"Sometimes, even with all reasonable precautions, terrible things can happen to children, things that are truly unspeakable. But as the Watsons discovered, nothing is so terrible that we can't overcome it, as long as we can talk about it and there's someone there to listen."

INDEX

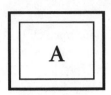

A

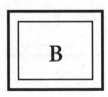

B

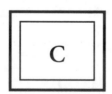

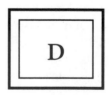

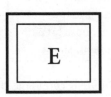

E

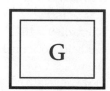

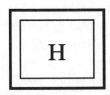
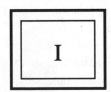
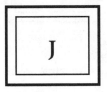
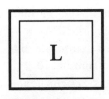

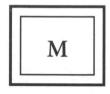

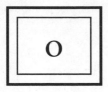

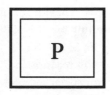

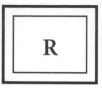

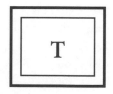

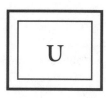

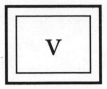

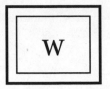